'I am of Vandemonian descent. Here is a book, clearly and lucidly written, which enhances my understanding of aspects of my family history while also adding another layer to my consciousness of Australian history.'

MARTIN FLANAGAN

'One of Australia's finest historians, this is McCalman at her very best. In Vandemonians she gives voice to the everyday convict throng, tracing the larger forces that shaped their personal lives and impacted their legacies. Through a meticulous analysis of cradle-to-grave data, this book illuminates the contradictions that shadow colonial history. It also provides salutary historical lessons for the ways in which contemporary carceral practice deals with the fractured lives of the vulnerable and the traumatised.'

PROFESSOR ANDREW J MAY

This is number two hundred and one in the
second numbered series of the
Miegunyah Volumes
made possible by the
Miegunyah Fund
established by bequests
under the wills of
Sir Russell and Lady Grimwade.

'Miegunyah' was Russell Grimwade's home
from 1911 to 1955
and Mab Grimwade's home
from 1911 to 1973.

VANDEMONIANS

THE REPRESSED HISTORY OF COLONIAL VICTORIA

JANET McCALMAN

THE MIEGUNYAH PRESS
An imprint of Melbourne University Publishing Limited
Level 1, 715 Swanston Street, Carlton, Victoria 3053, Australia
mup-contact@unimelb.edu.au
www.mup.com.au

First published 2021
Text © Janet McCalman, 2021
Design and typography © Melbourne University Publishing Limited, 2021

This book is copyright. Apart from any use permitted under the *Copyright Act 1968* and subsequent amendments, no part may be reproduced, stored in a retrieval system or transmitted by any means or process whatsoever without the prior written permission of the publishers.

Every attempt has been made to locate the copyright holders for material quoted in this book. Any person or organisation that may have been overlooked or misattributed may contact the publisher.

Cover and text design by Pfisterer + Freeman
Typeset in Freight Text 11.5/16pt by Cannon Typesetting
Printed in China

 A catalogue record for this book is available from the National Library of Australia

9780522877533 (paperback)
9780522877540 (ebook)

Contents

Introduction: Buzzwinker 1

1. PLEAS IN MITIGATION 15
2. PRISONERS: UNDER THE PAPER PANOPTICON 39
3. CUT FREE 64
4. TOPSY-TURVY 91
5. ROMEO LANE 113
6. DIGGERS 136
7. THE ROAD TO KYNETON 164
8. MOTHERS AND FATHERS AND THEIR CHILDREN 185
9. SECRETS AND LIES 212
10. FINAL VERDICT 236

Appendix A: Founders and Survivors Ships Project Data 253
Appendix B: Biographies 263
Acknowledgements 311
Bibliography 313
Notes 324
Index 331

In memory of Cecile Trioli
and Jenny Wells.

INTRODUCTION

Buzzwinker

—'Me name's Miles; Ellen Miles,' remarked an old woman at the City Court yesterday.
—'And you are charged with vagrancy,' stated Sergeant Eason. 'Can you show the Bench that you have means of support?'
—'How can I support myself when I'm continually in gaol and not a shilling coming into the house? What is it at all? What are us old people to do? There is no institution in the country,' replied Mrs Miles.
—Sergeant Eason: 'But the country has been keeping you for years.'
—Mrs Miles: 'What! The country supporting me. Why, I'm supporting the country. I've scattered my money over the colony for the last fifty years. To tell the truth, I've spent thousands and thousands of pounds.'
Accused, who was found sitting on the hospital steps in Little Lonsdale street, late at night, with a bandage over her eye nearly as large as a pillow, was sentenced to three months, as was also a companion named Bridget Jones.[1]

It was October 1896. Ellen Miles, which was her birth name, was almost seventy years old and she had indeed been scattering her money across the Colony of Victoria for fifty years. She would live for another twenty, still in and out of gaol and benevolent asylums, until she was too frail to escape the Ballarat institution where she would die. It was fitting, as it had been the Ballarat diggers who years before had dubbed her the 'Buzzwinker', an elaboration of the cant for 'pickpocket'. Later, a locomotive from the Phoenix Foundry that moved with a 'pronounced waddle' was named after her.[2] She was a child of the 1830s and lived until World War I. How aware she ever was of the Great World outside her tiny one of back lanes, brothels and bars, we have no idea, but she was one of those who spanned the history of Victoria from the discovery of gold to Gallipoli. Her underlife threaded through all the turning points; she waddled around the tent settlement of Canvas Town, Melbourne's city and suburbs, country towns, and for one mad adventure even Adelaide, her copious skirts concealing her latest stolen goods. Wherever there was a lurk to exploit and a lark to celebrate, Ellen was there.

Her first appearance in the press had been in September 1839: Ellen Miles, aged eleven, charged at the Guildhall with passing a counterfeit half-crown to a shopkeeper in Russell Street, Bloomsbury, London. Mr Field, an inspector at the Mint, said that this child was 'one of three sisters, all notorious utterers'. Ellen had already been in custody thirty times and sported three aliases. Her mother was dead. Her father claimed he could not control her and that it might be an act of mercy to transport her.[3] As predicted, her second appearance at the Old Bailey in October resulted in transportation. Her sister Ruth, when before the Old Bailey herself a few months later, gave the game away: their father, Moses Miles, a costermonger, wanted all his girls transported so as to be relieved of their support, and it was he who gave them the counterfeit coins to pass.[4] They had been in and out of St Pancras Workhouse since 1833, and Ellen had graduated at the age of ten after fourteen months in the Children's Ward on her own. It was there that she may have learned to read and write, and it was there, among the toughest, roughest females in London, that she learned to survive. Both sisters were fierce, voluble and violent, and they followed each other to Van Diemen's Land: Ellen transported for seven years in the *Gilbert Henderson* in 1839, Ruth five months later aboard the *Navarino*, with a sentence of fifteen.

The Miles sisters were actors in a great historical drama: the transportation across the seas to punishment by exile of around 73 000 men, women and children to Van Diemen's Land between 1803 and 1853.[5] They were expected to provide labour for the new colony, to improve themselves through industry, obedience and training, and to contribute to building a productive British society in the Antipodes. If they could control their tongues, suppress their rage and hurt, and do their work, they could survive and, one day, have freedom. A few could return home; others could achieve a stake in the country and establish a colonial lineage. The majority would do neither.

European Australia had a 'wretched beginning': a society where convicts provided the forced labour for affluent colonists to grab the land from its Indigenous owners and supplant both human beings and their 60 000-year-old culture with new animals, plants, technologies, diseases and, of course, humans.[6] The convicts, however, were not intended to be slaves. As British subjects, they had rights even under sentence: to earn money and save it; to the presumption of innocence and a trial before a magistrate or a jury for colonial offences; and, above all, to the chance of redemption. On freedom from servitude they could become subjects in their own country with all the same rights and privileges according to their social rank. Some men would vote for the first time in Victoria in 1857, and women from 1902—Ellen Miles, as Ellen Watkins, was enrolled at the Salvation Army

Women's Shelter, 273 Exhibition Street, Melbourne, in 1903. A few secured an old age pension when they lived beyond 1902 in Victoria; they could own property, start businesses and stand for public office. Those who came earliest to New South Wales and Van Diemen's Land were the most fortunate in the land grab, and the successful farmers established vast lineages that now include past prime ministers and many other distinguished Australians. But their numbers were small compared with the convicts who came later and entered a more competitive economy where the best land was long gone.

Land was the glint in the eye of almost every free and non-free immigrant to Australia. It was the prize in a global quest across the New World and beyond.[7] Land made life possible for Aboriginal people and for Europeans. Losing land meant losing life. If the colonisers were to live, the traditional owners had to starve. Land gave you food, rents or equity; with land you could borrow, invest, expand. Landless, you depended on your wits or on patronage or charity. You had only your labour to sell, and if there was no market for it, there was nothing. Entitlements to land in England had traditionally also included access to local commons where you could graze your animals and grow food. But since the early eighteenth century, the rural poor had been losing their rights to the commons through enclosures, and in the Highlands of Scotland, through rank seizure of land for grazing and expulsion of the crofters. Everywhere—in North America and South America, in Ireland, Scotland and rural England—colonisers were privileging the raising of cattle and sheep for meat and textiles over subsistence agriculture for the local population. Ireland and Scotland became the beef and wool producers for England.[8] This massive dispossession of rural people from their traditional entitlement to the use of land drove them to towns and cities where new forms of energy from fossil fuel and new technologies created new work in hideous conditions, displacing artisanal skills.

Where there was muck, there was money, and the productive heart of Britain became a black country.

Urban property was a proxy for the life-giving role of land: it gave you shelter, equity and status. It provided a base for business and family growth. Its value was increased by scarcity and inflation. Colonisers who took advantage of early settlements to purchase urban land could make a fortune in speculation and development. The smart investor who purchased land in the right places, at the right time, could sit back and watch the money grow without lifting a finger in real work. Those who arrived in the new colonies with capital could become rich, and most hoped, indeed initially expected, to one day become very rich. And for early nineteenth-century people, the greatest ambition was to become a person who did not need to work: a gentleman or gentlewoman. Even ex-convicts died with 'gentleman' on their death certificates because in old age they lived off rents or capital.

The other essential ingredient of survival was a 'character': the recognition by your peers and those ranked above you, either in writing or 'by repute', of you as a person to be trusted and capable. The traditional social structure of ranks and privileges persisted, and in a new society everyone was hoping to be recognised as a somebody with the connections that entitled them to entry to 'society'. Without connections, you could not be 'placed', recognised as a person worth knowing and to be trusted. New colonists had to build a social network immediately if they were to find mutual support, work or business opportunities. Everyone was trading on their alleged past and connections; everyone was claiming to be better connected than they really were; everyone clutched at every kinsman, however remote; at every fellow county or town man, however distant and previously unknown. New arrivals had to belong at once to some group if they were to survive, let alone thrive.

The most valuable social network was a family or, in the absence of a family, with a household—a secure place in someone else's household as a servant or apprentice or friend. English families had long been largely nuclear, while the Irish and Highland Scots still had extended families that embraced multiple generations and adult siblings. The other peculiarity of northern Europeans was that people tended to marry later, once they had the means to establish their own household. This acted as a brake on family size, but it also meant that many adults never married and were left without family support in old age. The Church had provided refuge for those without families, but after the dissolution of the monasteries by Henry VIII in the mid-sixteenth century, care for the 'friendless' had to be secularised with the 1601 Poor Law. This was the first welfare state, funded by a tax and operated from the local parish. Even at the end of the nineteenth century, just enough of the old parish Poor Law survived in some rural districts for elderly people to travel hundreds of miles to receive relief.[9]

However, by the time Ellen Miles was born, the Old Poor Law was collapsing under a surge in population, especially in towns and cities. In 1834, the New Poor Law abolished the giving of outdoor relief in urban areas, so that people without families or supporting households only had the streets or the workhouse. Not only did Ellen not have a home, neither did she possess tradeable skills; she could not cook properly, sew, make beer or keep house. All she had were the foraging skills of the urban destitute: thieving, pilfering, importuning, dealing, violence, intimidation, selling sex, and she would be imprisoned during her long life for all of these offences. Neither would she marry a man capable of supporting her—fellow ex-convict Thomas Watkins likewise knew only street dealing and crime.

Most convicts were destitute when they went into the penal system, and only a few had amassed some savings from paid work or dealing while under sentence by the time they were freed. A small minority possessed property back home, but they might not be free to return under the conditions of their release from servitude. They would have to begin anew. But most of all, they had no character. They had crossed a fatal Rubicon into an alien moral universe of the untrusted and the feared. One euphemism for being an ex-convict, or Vandemonian, was coming from 'the other side', and this applied as much to those who came from Sydney as to those who came over Bass Strait. As they tried to make their way in the colony, their past was to be their greatest burden. All they had were colonial remnants of the settlement they had acquired at birth from their native parish: the right to be relieved of destitution with food, shelter, nursing or education. And in the penal colonies, the convict system itself continued the responsibilities of the parish in caring for the infirm aged and educating children without capable parents. In the free colonies of Victoria and South Australia, a voluntary version of the parish welfare system developed, with benevolent asylums for the destitute, blind and deaf; orphanages and industrial schools for those without protectors; and charity hospitals for the sick poor. So yes, the colony did support Ellen Miles for most of her life, and her regular sojourns in gaol meant a wash, clean clothes, medical care, a dry bed and regular food, until finally she entered the care of the Ballarat Benevolent Asylum. It no doubt helped her live beyond her allotted three score years and ten.

But Ellen was not typical, however much she conformed to the feared stereotype of 'Vandemonian pollution'. Her mark on colonial Victoria died with her, and her story is only one of many among the Vandemonians. We don't know how many crossed Bass Strait to lose themselves in Victoria: the official records suggest 30 000, many of whom returned to Tasmania after a dabble at the diggings. Others think it was many more and could have been at least half of those who were transported to Van Diemen's Land, especially those who arrived after 1840. Others came after the gold rush, following their children. Certainly many crossed Bass Strait illegally or in ships whose records have been lost. The Vandemonian contribution to the European settling of Victoria, as James Boyce has shown, is significant.[10] Neither is it confined to the crime outbreak of the early gold rush that so terrified the respectable colonists and gold diggers. Most of the Vandemonian story is a secret history that people were anxious to put behind them as fast as they could. Most probably died without their neighbours nor even their children knowing about their convict past.

Many questions remain. Who were the Vandemonians and why did they offend in the first place? Were they so very different from their peers who arrived free in the Australian colonies? Did their penal servitude scar them for life, or did they benefit from being transplanted into a better climate with copious mutton and fresh air? Were their children taller, stronger and better behaved, or did they continue to be marked by their parents' pasts? Was Australia a gulag and Van Diemen's Land haunted by Gothic horrors? Or was it more benign and banal? Were the Vandemonians different as parents from those who arrived free, or did they pass on intergenerational toxic stress? What can we learn about the impact of stress and insults on the outcomes of their lives in mortality and fertility? Above all, did they make a distinctive contribution to the character and culture of the Australian people: was there a convict stain and for how long was it visible? It's time, therefore, to follow them outside the confines of the convict system and its records and to understand them within the contexts of their full lives in the wider world.

But how do we reconstruct the history of people who remain mute in the historical record? We see the convicts largely through the lens of the convict archive and through the eyes of their social superiors. As with so much social history, we are forced to write mostly about 'representations'—that is, articulate people's ideas about mute people—so that much of our history of those known as 'the common people' is in fact the history of their superiors' mental worlds, because those are the sources most readily available. Very few of those transported to Australia could tell their own story for posterity and the records, however detailed, are records made by the authorities about them. Only in press reports of court proceedings do we hear them occasionally speaking in their own defence or as witnesses.

Ellen Miles' voice is preserved for posterity in just three court reports, all in the more mellowed period of her criminal career. Yet she has left a detailed trace of her time under sentence and her peregrinations after. We have sightings of her around Melbourne, Geelong, Ballarat, Kyneton and Beechworth. Hers was a public life, lived in sight of the world. Rarely in her long life did she have a home outside gaol: she slept where she found shelter in corners of cottages, huts, shanties, outhouses, stables, public houses (pubs), parks, in gutters and lanes, and on the banks of the Yarra; she ate where she could and drank whenever she could afford it. She paid for her food and drink by theft and pilfering and selling her body. Her sex life, both personal and transactional, was rarely private and often conducted in parks and back lanes. She would rarely have used a privy but relieved herself in the street. She bathed mostly in gaol. Her clothes, probably stolen, lasted until, reduced to rags, they fell off her. When she was arrested in Melbourne's Little Lonsdale Street, she had that bandage the size of a pillow over one eye and in time she lost the eye completely. She sought invisibility from the law by changing her name, story and religion at whim. She never admitted she was a transported convict but claimed she had accompanied her long-deceased mother on the *Gilbert Henderson*. She generated criminal records under the names Buzzwinker, Ellen Watkins, Ellen Miles, Ann Myles, Ann Watkins, Ellen Burns, Ellen Grimes, Ellen Johnson and Bridget Brady, born in Ireland. She did, at one stage, even claim Spanish birth.

But these are only scraps of information, brief sightings, and the scaffolding of Ellen Miles' life is provided by institutional records from the workhouse, the penal system of Van Diemen's Land and the criminal records of the Colony of Victoria. While we have her death, but not her birth or a baptism, her 'moral career', to use the term of the sociologist Erving Goffman, was steadily recorded in the press from the age of eleven until eighty-six.[11] We have, therefore, many more fragments and sightings of Ellen Miles than we do of most of the common people. Yet Ellen was uncommon, a lifelong criminal offender and public nuisance. How do we tell the story of the quiet ones, the well behaved, the compliant? Can we write histories of people like the convicts by extracting from the archives only the rich stories full of incident and punishment when in fact that applied only to a minority of them? Ellen Miles cannot speak for convict women transported to Van Diemen's Land, only for her subset of unruly, unceasing offenders.

We historians, however, have some tricks up our sleeves. The technique of prosopography involves group biographies collated from diverse sources and sightings. When systematically collected within a frame of a 'defined universe', these can create a new picture of the past and liberate the mute in the historical record. This defined universe might be a period of the Roman Empire, or an aristocracy in a given epoch, or all the deputies elected to the French National Convention in 1792–93. In this story, we have a population created by the shared experience of convict transportation across the seas to Terra Australis by an imperial government that was highly skilled in the practices of recording people to make them visible. The imperative to make people perceptible had been one of the characteristics of enlightened despotism, from the centralising French state to the Kingdom of

Prussia and, most notably, in the Kingdom of Sweden. Family names became more common and helped to render people visible to the state.[12] For the British, this was needed to administer their Poor Law and, more importantly, to manage their military, naval and commercial operations. Record keeping was commercial as well as carceral for the deployment of forced labour—slaves and transported convicts—who provided the energy for conquest and exploitation. Sugar cultivation and processing required human muscle, as did the holding and cultivation of new lands that were unattractive to free labourers. Slaves could be forced to work where malaria and yellow fever deterred the free. And while the people of Africa built the massive wealth of Bristol and Liverpool that would finance the first industrial nation, the transportation of convicts offered the additional benefits of ridding the streets and gaols and workhouses of undesirables, working new lands, and giving flawed British subjects the opportunity, as Alan Atkinson puts it, of being free subjects again in a land of their own.[13]

The penal colonies of Australia began as open prisons where convicts were assigned as servants of all kinds who could work on their own account in their spare time—such as in Sydney, building their own place on The Rocks. Punishment and confinement were for their secondary offences, not their original crimes. The administration of the penal system of Van Diemen's Land attained a level of detail and comprehensiveness that has earned it the term the 'paper panopticon'—a bureaucratic record that saw everyone and everything. The whole island was managed, with a wide range of institutional arrangements of discipline and labour control, by the pen. The convicts, in an age without photography and finger printing, had to be minutely described so that they could be identified. Thus, the men, women and children in the Tasmanian convict records are arguably the most carefully described and recorded ordinary people of the nineteenth-century world. Under sentence, every infraction against convict discipline was recorded, tried and punished. Every assigned employer was noted and comments made. Each week, police magistrates all over the colony fed back to the clerks in the Convict Department (who were themselves convicts) every appearance of a convict before their bench and the outcome of the hearing. Thus, we can glimpse indications of character and personality, of weaknesses and strengths, as we read against the grain of their gaolers and masters.

Once convicts left the system, unless they became notorious reoffenders or outstanding social successes, we lose sight of their individuality. But now, with the genealogical tools available in the online world, and the digitisation of newspapers and public records, we can recover many more scraps of ordinary lives. If we frame those biographies with vital registrations and baptisms, we have the demographic contours of lives that begin to tell us a great deal about that population and those individuals. Historical demography gives us tools and insights that enable us to establish the wider historical context of our actors. Length of life, even when causes of death are unrecorded or unhelpful, tells us at a population level about the slings and arrows of outrageous fortune and the lucky breaks that can change a destiny. It remains the best measure we have in the population sciences of the cumulative effects of deprivation and insults, of advantage and opportunity.[14] We can see something of private behaviour in marriage, child-bearing and parenthood from the demographic analysis of family formation. And when we analyse prosopographies within a demographic framework and add variables that generally are missing from more conventional sources, we begin to see new factors, causes, significances and outcomes. We can be more precise about the social and economic geography of different phases of these people's lives; we can overlay large historical events and changes that may or may not have affected them. We can reconstruct the contours of these remote and mute lives, and in doing so, establish more clearly the significance of individual stories within the broader context of their times and places. We can even grasp the measure of some of their male descendants in the service records of the First Australian Imperial Force (AIF). By discovering their characteristics within a crowd, we more clearly appreciate their individuality.

This book draws on such a study, using its findings as the foundation for a more conventional social history of a people who were not meant to be part of colonial Victoria: they were not wanted in their own time, and Victorians, like South Australians, have ever since denied that Australia's history of penal servitude played a significant part in their history. The demographic prosopographies help us make sense of the trajectories of individual lives: were they typical or atypical, representative of what, driven by which particular factors, creating what effects? The study has been a collaboration between university scholars and genealogists, inspired by similar studies first in France, and later in Cambridge, Sweden, Quebec and, of course, the great Mormon genealogies of Utah.[15] This book is based on what we came to call 'the Ships Project', a subset of the database 'Founders and Survivors: Convict Life Courses in Historical Context' (1803–1930), led by the University of Tasmania (see Appendix A). The Ships Project at the University of Melbourne, including its partnership with the Female Convict Research Centre, was conducted by trained volunteers who researched the lives of each convict on a ship—people with a shared historical experience of a voyage. Online resources were used to discover their lives before sentencing, to record and code their experiences and conduct under sentence, and to trace their lives after the sentence to a recorded death. The histories of the families they were born into and the families they may have formed, either before or after sentencing, were expanded by any other sightings in newspapers or government records such as wills, probates, inquests and lunatic and criminal records. Thus, drawing on interactions with the state and fleeting sightings, we can begin to see them as people and as a population. And it is with that new knowledge that we can begin to understand better the impact of convict transportation on the making of Australia.

CHAPTER 1

Pleas in Mitigation

Spirited poachers, political prisoners and ever picturesque intelligent villains were but a small leaven in a lump that was wretched, listless and forlorn.

WK HANCOCK, *AUSTRALIA* (1930), p. 38

Were the convicts born bad or made bad? Before World War II confined eugenics to the scientific shame corner, many believed they were born bad: moral refuse disgorged from the prisons and workhouses of the Mother Country; flawed British stock; a stain to be forever removed to a faraway colony. And when the Victorian gold rush lured both ex-convicts and escapees from Van Diemen's Land in the early 1850s, the respectable of Port Phillip were outraged: 'Vandemonian Pollution'. Indeed, it had taken the gold finds to dampen fears of moral contamination and open up the Australian colonies to mass immigration. Even today, the last gasp of the Barmy Army fighting from the stands for the honour of the Marylebone Cricket Club is that Australians are convicts.

Australians, however, resisted. They did so first with a pact of mutual silence, especially in Tasmania where the one epithet you could not fling was being of convict stock.[1] Then came a new narrative of victimhood, accepted keenly by descendants: the theft of trivial items such as handkerchiefs or spoons, oblivious of their value in the underground market. Even more, it was theft to feed their starving family, a claim which the records sometimes support. Certainly, these people were not 'bad': they were 'young larrikins', 'naughty boys, and girls', political rebels, starving workers.

Yet some who were transported could be 'bad': Ellen Miles slashed her best friend's throat in an argument, and her preferred method of robbing other women was to invite them in for a drink, then bash them. Paul Duff (*Isabella Watson*, 1842), an illiterate Irish giant, was transported for malicious assault and became a 'lucky miner' in Ballarat, throwing his money around in public houses and brothels where his £50 bills were invariably stolen. He was described as both violent and stupid, and in 1866 he raped a ten-year-old girl, for which he received only two years' hard labour because the rape of a child under the age of twelve was a 'minor crime'. Soon after release, he was drunk and fighting again, until he was killed with a blow from a bottle. His killer was found not guilty, and the people of Ballarat felt safer.[2] Numerous convict women prostituted their own daughters, as probably their mothers had done to them. Some convict families were blighted by domestic violence and alcoholism. Above all, few of the convicts sent to Van Diemen's Land, with the exception of the Irish, were first offenders, although no-one had records approaching Ellen's thirty 'previous' by the age of eleven. Those who were political rebels behaved differently and often did well in their new lives after sentencing. Many young men were little more than juvenile delinquents who in time grew out of their offending and managed to stay straight. At the other extreme, for women and girls who found themselves destitute and homeless, their criminality and disorderliness were the means to survival. These were the unfortunate. But there was a core of seriously violent or dishonest people, or perhaps seriously damaged people, and to understand how all of these—good, bad and indifferent—found their way into a court of law to be transported, we need to look at their early lives and the places that shaped them.

DISRUPTION

The convicts' world was in the throes of deep economic and social change. The oldest among them were born at the beginning of what is known as the 'modern rise in population' from 1760, and the last of them were to die at the beginning of the Great Depression of the 1930s.[3] Most of those who found themselves in Van Diemen's Land were born on either side of the Napoleonic Wars and were children and adolescents from the 1810s to the 1840s—the crisis of the industrial revolution. The end of the Napoleonic Wars in 1815 thrust thousands into unemployment, from officers to men, triggering a crime wave that outpaced the rise in population and peaked in 1842.[4] Crime rates rose and fell in concert with economic cycles and political unrest.

England and Scotland were urbanising at a frenetic pace. Ireland's population, despite a famine in 1815, was growing on the diet of the potato and a surge in early marriage. Everywhere, as the world became more complex, mobile and unsettled, the poor, from the countryside to the industrial villages to the towns and cities, lost the entitlements and lurks that had enabled them to survive. In 1814, the Statute of Artificers was repealed in England, robbing young males of protection as apprentices and thrusting them into a marginal existence in their early years of adulthood.[5] As the agrarian revolution enclosed the common pastures and gardens, the rural poor lost their access to land to grow their own food and graze their own animals. The law criminalised the hunting of game in the forests, alienating the common people from what had been their major source of meat since the beginning of time. Clearances drove the crofters from their plots and into the slums of Glasgow or the frigid wastes of Canada. The rural poor were turned into day labourers, dependent on seasonal wages, and apart from the support of the parish poor relief, were newly exposed to hunger and destitution. Women were excluded from farm work and therefore from gleaning the leftovers of crops for food. Nowhere was rural poverty worse than in the southern and eastern counties of England, the Scottish Highlands and in Ireland. The rural poor all over Europe had never ceased to be hunter-gatherers, harvesting fungi, berries and game—a foraging economy that made the difference between life and death. And while young men had always gone 'on tramp' to see the world and improve their skills, young women had also ventured afar in the hope of a better position and a husband. Now, whole families were on the move to places with new factories and mines, to bigger towns and cities. And as the population shifted and exploded, the traditional structures of social support came under strain.

If people did not have the access to land to feed themselves, nor the obligations, trades or enterprises to earn money, they depended on charity. It was a spiritual obligation of Christians to provide for the sick and the poor. People of means carried coins with them to give to beggars, especially when visiting towns and cities. London had a vast army of beggars, nearly all of them women with dependent children, and pedestrians expected to be forever handing out alms.[6] While the Church accepted this obligation through its institutions, after the Reformation and the dissolution of monasteries, this became secularised in many Protestant countries through the local parish. In 1601 the Elizabethan Poor Law had established the first welfare state, where the parish, funded by a tax or poor rate, was obliged to care for those without a family to support them: the destitute poor, the aged, the sick and the orphaned. Even bastard children born within the parish bounds were entitled to be a charge upon the parish for the rest of their lives, and the parish was obliged as a 'civic parent' to pay for their education and apprenticeship. This would be incorporated into the penal system that was built in the Australian colonies, especially in Van Diemen's Land, and into early conceptions of the 'protection' of Aboriginal people.[7]

By the end of the seventeenth century, English people had a statutory right to be relieved of poverty, and every man, woman and child had a lifelong entitlement, or settlement, from their natal parish. The idle poor, however, could be consigned to a house of industry, where they picked hemp or performed other heavy and unpleasant work. The convicted were sent to a house of correction. The seventeenth century was very hard in Europe, bitterly cold and savaged by bubonic plague epidemics that seemed to come every thirty years. But the English survived relatively well, despite a destructive civil war and plague in the 1660s, and the early transformations of the industrial revolution are now ascribed to the quality of England's artisans—trained by apprenticeships, educated by village schools, and fed, in times of scarcity, by the parish. This was in fact a golden age of economic growth, underpinned by social welfare and investment in human capital.[8]

But the parish relief system worked only in a small, relatively immobile society, and it restricted workers from moving to find work. As the growing cities and towns pressed against their medieval walls and institutions, the numbers of the destitute, underfed and barely clothed overwhelmed parish resources. The most visible signs were the women and children of the streets, begging, selling anything portable and their own bodies. The crisis came from families that were fractured by death, desertion or illegitimacy. If you had no family to support and protect you, there was only the parish, and if the parish was failing in the cities, or you were far from your native place, survival was perilous. The 1834 New Poor Law brought larger grim workhouses to England, where poverty was criminalised. Ireland did not have workhouses until 1838 and no outdoor relief until the Great Famine, or Great Hunger—when the staple potato crop repeatedly failed—forced the hand of the authorities. Scotland's poor law was not passed until 1846.[9] Private charity, gleaning, pilfering and theft were the only means of survival when work or trade disappeared.

This murky world of the daily struggle for a bed, food and drink has been called an economy of makeshifts.[10] It formed a porous boundary between the legal and the sub-legal, where it was ever so easy to cross from salvage and pilfering into theft, from cultivating a supporting lover into prostitution, from servants' entitlements to leftovers to larceny as a servant. For street people and wanderers, every day brought a new challenge, to scrounge the funds or favours for food and shelter, and the currency of social transactions was alcohol even more than sex: 'Buy us a drink and we'll get a bed.'

The economy of makeshifts could easily blend into the economy of crime, especially for the desperate, the young and the impulsive. The convicts transported to Australia were not all schooled in crime by criminal families. Indeed, some came from apparently stable, respectable families, and some of the most colourful were consumed with a social ambition that exceeded their economic means. These were the imposters, the high-class thieves of jewels and precious objects, the perpetrators of fraud, forgery and embezzlement, mostly operating from the great cities, fluid in their identities, full of invented family histories and connections, charming, plausible and articulate. The newspapers reported their escapades with obvious glee, and many left their mark on the wider world, both in the Australian colonies and the various exotic places to which they fled. Some of the women among them were astonishingly adventurous and resourceful. Their capital was their wits and their looks. But some convicts did learn their trade from their parents, as did Ellen Miles. Some were in family businesses of animal theft for butchers or smuggling. Mothers and daughters often operated in pairs, with the daughters doing the nifty work on the streets or targeting customers, and the mothers doing the receiving and pawning. Brothers often worked crimes together, and young people, as everywhere, sought courage in gangs both small and large.

FRAGILE FAMILIES

On 23 November 1840, George Pickering (*Lord Goderich*, 1841), aged thirteen, and Daniel Backway (*Tortoise*, 1842), aged sixteen, were each sentenced at the Old Bailey to seven years' transportation for theft: George had stolen a pair of shoes after previous convictions for picking pockets, Daniel a coat. They were transported to Van Diemen's Land on different vessels, and George, because of his youth, was sent to the Point Puer juvenile reformatory at Port Arthur. There he was punished for assault. Daniel entered the adult convict system and his only offence was complaining on behalf of another prisoner. They each served their seven years and left Van Diemen's Land for Victoria in 1852. They married in the same year: George to another convict, Daniel to the daughter of a convict. George headed for the red-light district of gold-rush Melbourne and matured from an artful dodger into a colonial Bill Sikes, brutalising his wife and children and living off their earnings from prostitution. His descendants died out. Daniel went to the goldfields, learned to be a miner and was on the electoral roll in 1856, when Van Diemen's Land was renamed Tasmania. He reassembled his wife's extended family and they settled on a miner's right in the town of Maryborough that was still providing a family home for his descendants a century later. He had eleven children, six of whom survived to adulthood, establishing a lineage that flourishes to this day. Three of his grandsons served in World War I. George died, estranged from his only surviving daughter, in the Melbourne Benevolent Asylum at the age of fifty-seven from advancing paralysis, probably tertiary syphilis. Daniel's lungs were weak, and he died from pneumonia in his own home in a street full of his extended family, also at the age of fifty-seven.

What had been different about their early lives? George had an intact family: his father Thomas was a wine cooper but a poor provider, and the Pickerings, like the Miles family, were in and out of the workhouse. Coopers were notorious drunkards, scavenging the alcoholic residuum from their casks. George's older brother Thomas was transported for ten years just two months after George, also for picking pockets. And their father went to gaol for three months the following year for taking pegs and spites for his cooper's work. By the 1851 census, George's mother Jane was a widow but had had two more children. She was a costermonger, selling fruit, and lived in Stepney. She was still alive in 1861, living in a packed tenement in Whitechapel with an older son who was a porter and a daughter, a hawker like herself. George called himself an oysterman in Melbourne, but street trading and crime were all he knew. His brother was a rebellious convict who was twice reconvicted for burglary, finishing his second sentence at Port Arthur whereupon he disappeared.

If George Pickering was an artful dodger, Daniel Backway was an Oliver Twist. His father had been a Thames waterman, a member of an honourable guild, but his mother died when he was six and his father perished in the 1832 cholera epidemic. Daniel, aged eight, was sent to the Limehouse workhouse. After two years he was inveigled by a chimney sweep to become a climbing boy. In October 1834 he was in court—weeping, emaciated, ragged, filthy, covered in cuts and sores. He bore the marks of having been shackled and his master had thrust his nails into the boy's chest. The sweep and his de facto were convicted of 'gross cruelty' despite their whining protestations that they had been a 'mother and father to the boy' and had 'used him as tenderly as possible'.[11] The workhouse apprenticed him out again as a climbing boy but again he ran away from his master. It was that first 'crime' that compounded the theft of a coat in a gang of boys and had him transported. Somehow, he had learned to read and write, perhaps in the workhouse school—George never learned, despite the classes that would have been on his transport ship and at Point Puer.

What was distinctive about the men, women and children transported to Van Diemen's Land was that, like Daniel Backway, they disproportionately came from fractured families where one or both parents were dead or absent.[12] The economy of the familial household was damaged, and the emotional bonds of family strained by insecurity and loss. If there were criminal families who trained their children in lawbreaking, there were also criminal neighbourhoods that tempted adolescents with riotous behaviour and theft. But there were also children with 'respectable connections' like Daniel Backway, or the Bodycott brothers of Leicester who were transported a year apart in the early 1840s, trapped in a local economic crisis, their mother dead, their father ageing.

The Bodycotts' story takes us into the West Midlands, and the crisis of industrialisation. They were the two youngest in a family of framework knitters who made worsted stockings on machines, crowded into tiny houses in what was a collapsing cottage industry. Leicester had a great radical tradition of resistance to new machinery dating from the first Luddite riots in the early nineteenth century, and it was a centre of the working-class suffrage movement known as Chartism, being the home of the Chartist orator Thomas Cooper. The Bodycotts' parish of St Margaret's was overrun with new inhabitants and the parish relief system crashed. In 1847, 19 000 people sought support and a new workhouse had to be built. A Polish refugee depicted the parish in that year as a maze of 'miserable huts and pestiferous atmosphere', with 'its pale, thin dull-looking people, who seemed to be ready for eternity, yet are clinging to the streets'.[13] By the age of twenty-one, Thomas (*Duncan*, 1841) was destitute: convicted twice for vagrancy, he was transported for seven years for stealing the worsted yarn needed for knitting. His younger brother John, perhaps less adept at framework knitting with fingers covered with scars, was transported for ten years for housebreaking and taking sugar; his previous convictions were for the theft of cherries and bread. The brothers bore a 'bad character', but while Thomas had numerous minor offences under sentence, John had none. Thomas finished his sentence and immediately returned to Leicester, where he married and settled into a life as a framework knitter, dying at eighty-seven. John was so desperate to return to the family that he absconded, stowing away on a ship to get back to Leicester before the extirpation of his sentence. When his plea for a pardon in 1851 was refused, he disappeared.[14]

GROWING UP IN CRIME

The convicts transported to Van Diemen's Land came from all over the British Isles, from British colonies in the Caribbean and the Americas, and from Europe. Some were black. A tiny handful were former slaves who had fought for the British in the American wars. But most were British and Irish, with around half from rural communities. The Irish were the most rural, the Scots the most urban. They often found each other's speech incomprehensible—as did the clerks who recorded the convicts' reported birthplaces phonetically: one who was born in High Holborn, London, was recorded as being born in Oban, in the west of Scotland. Irish placenames were avoided altogether apart from those relating to major towns and counties. Those from the west and south spoke Irish as a first language and were routinely reported as illiterate. And if the Irish recorded the lowest English literacy, the Scots and the Londoners recorded the highest. But nationality tells us only so much. What distinguished these individuals from each other was the 'crime economy' into which they had been born.

'The crime economy' was the way in which people could profit from crime in a given community. Rural convicts were more likely to have stolen animals or food, or if on the coast, to have been smugglers. Londoners and others from more cosmopolitan communities with affluent citizens were more likely to steal from the person: picking pockets; 'bilking', which was when prostitutes stripped clients of their money while they were undressed and preferably unconscious from alcohol; highway robbery; stealing reams of cloth or pieces of clothing for resale. Stealing from the person required victims who had something valuable on their person, and it also depended on the ease with which stolen goods could be sold on or exchanged by pawnbrokers and fences. Prostitution and theft from the person flourished where there were large numbers of transient males in search of a drink and sex—in port cities, the capital and garrison towns. Burglary of valuables required houses with valuables in them. Theft of cloth and work materials depended on the manufacturing and retail trades of the area. Forgery and embezzlement needed businesses and trade, excise offices and moneylenders. Crimes of deception and imposition could be committed discreetly in large communities where people did not necessarily know much about their neighbours.

London was the capital for fencing valuable stolen goods, for commercial offences, for crimes of deception and imposition. But it was also the world's greatest city, a vast service economy that revolved around the London social season and the court, which drove demand for high-class clothing and household goods of all kinds, that then surged down to demand for the 'slop trades'. It housed the greatest market for personal service, from the liveried servants of the rich to the ragged orphan children despatched from the workhouses to cook and clean and mind the families of the poor and tradesmen. And with domestic service came the temptation to steal from masters and mistresses. London was a powerful magnet for immigrants from everywhere, the 'contagion of numbers' enticing those seeking work, fortune, even love. Poor Irish sisters would take their chances in London; country girls took servant positions only to be dismissed for a small dishonesty, or a mistake or a lack of skill or a flirtation with a male servant, and upon dismissal, deprived of their 'character' or reference, they became homeless and destitute and went 'on the town'.

London was unique, yet its rich past and character have come to speak for the rest of the nation in its criminal history. Other places were even more dangerous to children born into poverty. By contrast, convicts with rural childhoods would do best in their new homeland: living longer, marrying and raising families more successfully. Next to them came the London-born, who proved to be resilient, whereas those who migrated to London continued to reflect their places of birth. And after the Londoners came the rural Irish, including those whose late childhood and adolescence coincided with the Great Famine from 1845. But even they did better than the children born in smoky factory districts in Lancashire and the Midlands, where female mortality was high from overwork, tuberculosis, exhaustion and malnutrition, while males suffered from the collapse of their traditional crafts under the impact of new technology. More than one former convict in Victoria told his friends that he was a 'weaver' over half a century since he had worked as one.

But those who would die youngest, commit the most offences in the convict system, and have the most difficult lives, were the children of seaports: Liverpool, Bristol, Southampton, Portsmouth, Plymouth,

Edinburgh (Leith), Glasgow, Dublin, Belfast and Cork. These were liminal places, full of transients, grog shops, brothels and lost souls. A woman left without a reliable male breadwinner and with children to feed had to choose between starvation wages as a needlewoman or washerwoman and prostitution. Edinburgh, for instance, was notorious for its lack of respectable work for women and its 'swarms of prostitutes'. In Liverpool, women and girls lived in 'drunken savagery' near the docks. The public houses roared night after night with intoxicated people; violence was the currency of human relationships.[15] Glasgow at least had some industrial work for women in weaving at Paisley, but the city was the fastest growing in the British Isles, its vile slums bulging with dispossessed Highlanders and, after 1847, Irish famine refugees. Liverpool also was swamped with destitute Irish who could not afford even the so-called 'coffin ships' across the Atlantic, let alone an assisted passage to Australia. One hundred and fifty years later, both cities still bear the scars of the Irish famine in their demographics of inequality and health.

The most vulnerable in these vicious and desperate places were young females. As the notorious 'Walter' in his memoir *My Secret Life* testified ad nauseam, the daughters of the poor were fair sexual game.[16] The age of consent was twelve, a good three to four years before most girls reached puberty and began to become women. A child sent unaccompanied to bring a jug of beer from the public house could expect to be felt up, grabbed and even raped. Very few of the very poor reached middle adolescence with their virginity intact. Young virgins held high currency, however, among procurers and brothel madams as a believed cure for syphilis. Prostitutes sold their own daughters as soon as they were worth something. In crowded places with people sleeping together, incest and abuse were inevitable. Girls learned early to be tough, to brawl or use knives. They, and boys who had known only violence from their world, would grow up touchy, quick to take offence, suspicious, and never afraid to kick, punch and bash, even kill. Abuse—sexual, physical, emotional—was everyday. Abused children grew up to be abusive parents. Seaports would produce the most vulnerable convicts because they were the worst places for mothers, while the smoky industrial towns were lethal for young women's physical health.

London had filth, and stenches, and wild port taverns, and thousands upon thousands selling sex, from high-class courtesans to the 'lurkers' who solicited in the parks at night, too diseased to appear in daylight. Estimates of the number on the town were guesses, but they were still huge. Females on the town were 'public women' (like public houses), picking up men for a drink, a feed and then sex if they failed to get their customers intoxicated enough to rob without their noticing. They were almost homeless, sharing rooms with other girls in rough lodging houses, but often looking for a bed for the night that would be paid for by their client. As they aged, the most important part of the transaction was the drink: few avoided alcoholism, many succumbed to it at very early ages.

Mary Evans and her two partners in crime, Catherine Oakford and Lydia Miles (all *Royal Admiral*, 1842), operated from a 'low brothel' in London's decrepit Gray's Inn Lane, opposite the Georgian Verulam buildings of Gray's Inn.[17] On 4 November 1842, Thomas Longfoot had been 'cruising' around town when he was picked up by Lydia Miles, but he was so drunk that later he could not remember whether or with whom he went to bed. What he did know when he awoke the next morning was that he was sans trousers, coat, waistcoat and braces. Evans and Oakford were arrested while hailing a cab with his clothing hidden under their skirts. Both Catherine Oakford and Lydia Miles claimed to have been married but were fending for themselves. Nonetheless, their respective fathers petitioned the Crown for mercy. Mary Evans had no-one to speak for her except herself and she fiercely interjected throughout the trial. Lydia and Catherine, both with some form of family, at least married in Australia. Mary, who towered over her 'sisters', as convict women described their 'mates', did not. None of them would bear a child.

Just as the loss of parents pushed young women towards crime, so did desertions or deaths of male partners—husbands, lovers, protectors. Soldiers' women, even when legally married, were left with no material support when their men were posted away: the husband of Mary Holehouse (*Tory*, 1845) was away with the 48th regiment and she had been on the town in Newport for three years to support herself and her child. And Elizabeth Morgan (*America*, 1831) was widowed in Glamorgan just after giving birth. Both Welshwomen would decades later become notorious in Ballarat East. Young girls who fell pregnant followed their child's father, only to find themselves far from home, their child usually dead and their future desolate.

IN COUNTRY PLACES

If pickpockets and prostitutes were urban scavengers, so it had always been in rural society that the poor supplemented their food supplies illegally. Most meat consumed before the late nineteenth century was game that had to be killed or trapped. In the early nineteenth century, the great landowners began closing down on poaching with even harder restrictions than the notorious Black Act of 1723: indeed, the Night Poaching Act of 1828 and the Game Act of 1831 are still in force. Poaching had become less of a social crime, however, as organised gangs supplied the demands of urban gentlemen and innkeepers and victuallers.[18]

Samuel Phillips (*Mary*, 1830) was a young, illiterate rural labourer from Colby in Northamptonshire: the county of 'spires and squires', with its great houses and castles and forbidding forests taunting the poor in their cottages and huts. He was a poacher only of rabbits rather than more exotic game like pheasant, but he had twice been gaoled for breaking the game laws when he was finally transported in 1829 'for going around in the night to destroy rabbits' with two accomplices.[19] His sentence was fourteen years. His de-facto partner at the time, Sarah Patrick, had just given birth to their first child. Neither of them could read and write, but they would be miraculously reunited twenty-four years later. Samuel was to be a very lucky convict.

Peter Appleyard (*Norfolk*, 1835), of the brewing town of Tadcaster between Leeds and York, at twenty-five had a wife and three children to feed. When Thomas Powell found four of his ducks missing one morning, having locked them in his barn the previous night, he sent a constable to Appleyard's place. Appleyard had twice been fined for poaching and Thomas Powell's suspicions were vindicated. Seven years' transportation.[20] The Bones brothers of Buxted in Sussex (*Henry Porcher*, 1836)—Thomas the elder and daft, Benjamin younger and sharper—stole eleven fowls in 1834, and because their characters and connections were 'bad', they received seven years each. John Lawrence Mansfield Wagstaff (*Layton*, 1835) had been a bastard on the parish at the village of Great Gransden in Huntingdonshire. He had done time in the hulks—decommissioned ships used as prisons—for stealing apples, but this time he thieved timber from the local vicar: seven years' transportation, leaving behind a wife. His reputation was 'bad in every respect'.

The wives and children left behind became burdens upon the parish, but parish relief was scarcely sufficient to allay the growing immiseration of the landless. The New Poor Law abolished outdoor relief in cities and towns, forcing the separation of families and requiring mindless labour picking oakum (separating tar from a ship's rope fibres) or breaking stones in return for shelter and rations. In many rural areas, the old parish relief continued and would do so for another sixty years, even if the resources were scant. Some parishes, however, raised the funds to pay for convicts' families to join them in Van Diemen's Land, which was especially so with the Swing Rioters.

The Swing Riots of 1830 were the last great eruption of agrarian political protest in British history. The Speenhamland System (1793-1815) had operated as a form of universal basic income during the crisis of the French revolutionary and Napoleonic wars, and had successfully depressed wages, indirectly subsidising the farmers rather than the labourers. With peace came a further collapse in prices, rural rents and wages, and a surfeit of labour. Enclosures had been increasing since the 1801 Enclosure Act, and although food production grew with agricultural consolidation and new methods of farming and animal husbandry, this did nothing for the landless labourers who no longer had the security of annual hirings and were reduced to casual, often day wages. Then came the threshing machines and the shires erupted. Mobs of otherwise respectable rural people sent letters from a fictional Captain Swing demanding better wages, lower church tithes and no machines, and when their demands of the parsons, large farmers, magistrates and Poor Law guardians were denied, they retaliated by night, smashing threshing machines, attacking tithe barns and workhouses, and setting fires. The government was pitiless: in 1831, almost 2000 people were sent to trial, and 252 of them were sentenced to death. The general public were outraged, however, and finally only nineteen were executed; a further 644 were imprisoned and 481 transported to Van Diemen's Land.[21] With them came James Kimber from Wiltshire, Richard Venville from Gloucestershire and Elizabeth Studham, the only female rioter, all of whom would eventually make a life in Victoria. Poor Farewell Whitaker from Norfolk, who left behind a wife and six children, became so distressed in his first year in Van Diemen's Land that he was rejected by his assigned master, 'being it is believed insane'. He came to Victoria in 1837 and was to die in Brunswick in 1857 from 'colonial fever' or typhoid, tended by a new wife, Euphemia.

If the rural shires were crushed by 1831, radicals' disappointment at the failure of the 1832 Reform Act to give workingmen suffrage saw the outbreak of political agitation in the industrial regions of the North and the Midlands. Chartism was a sophisticated mass movement with a national newspaper, Sunday schools and women's groups; its newspaper even advertised methods of birth control. It embodied the great debate of radical politics between moral force and physical force, or democratic suasion and political violence. It advanced a 'People's Charter' of political reform: manhood suffrage, no property qualification, annual parliaments, equal representation, payment of members of parliament, and a secret ballot. The author of the charter, William Lovett, had even canvassed including the vote for women in 1838, but feared that was a bridge too far. In 1843, Chartist riots brought a new contingent of political prisoners to Van Diemen's Land in the *John Renwick*. Among them were Edward Ellis, a collier from Staffordshire who demolished 'Squire Parker's house at the riots for increase of wages', and Thomas Banks, a fellow collier, who broke 'into a box in Parson Vale's house during a row'. Jeremiah McCormick, a Catholic weaver from Manchester with a wife and two children, also took advantage of the riots to steal 'bread from Mrs Daines of Ship Gate at the riots'. Edward Ellis and Thomas Banks were each on the Victorian electoral roll as holders of a miner's right in 1856: the first workingmen's vote in the world.

THE CELTS

The Irish came late to Van Diemen's Land. No convict ships arrived direct from Irish ports before 1840, when transportation to New

South Wales was ceasing. Before then, all Irish-born convicts had been convicted outside Ireland as migrants and fugitives in England and Scotland. Julia Smith per *Westmoreland* was one of many Irish girls who ended up in London; allegedly a widow by the age of twenty-one and born in County Mayo, she was living on the town, stealing from the person. Judith McCoy, born in Dublin and two years on the town in Liverpool, was transported in the *Atwick* in 1838 for stealing clothes and silver spoons. Elizabeth Disney, a native of the city of Cork, was married to a London cabinet-maker and the mother of five children. She blamed her thieving on drunkenness, and she was to continue drinking heavily while under sentence. With her on board the *Harmony* in 1828 were three young sons.

But these were migrants, people already dislocated. With ships coming direct from Ireland, a mixed bag of political, economic and 'criminal convicts' arrived in two significant waves: one before the start of the Great Famine in 1845, and another, rather different in character, from 1848, full of famine survivors. They were not predominantly political rebels, although there were more of these sprinkled in the Irish convict population than among the English or the Scots. And Irish political rebellion was essentially against the land laws rather than the wage or political system.

Daniel Cuddihy, along with two brothers named Seymour, was transported for 'assaulting a habitation' in County Tipperary in 1843. Daniel left behind his widowed mother and no siblings. With him in the *Duke of Richmond* was Michael McLoughlin, whose descendant, Garry McLoughlin, has unearthed his story.

On St Patrick's Day in 1843, two men visited Castlefleming Lodge in Queen's County, owned by Robert H Stubber, where they stole a gun, a powder horn and shot pouch, and allegedly 'threatened the inmates'. Four months later, on 17 July, Michael McLoughlin and Martin Kirwin were arrested, and despite no prior convictions and the hazy evidence of a fourteen-year-old boy, they were tried and sentenced to ten years' transportation. They embarked on the *Duke of Richmond* on 21 September, arriving in Hobart on 2 January 1844.

It seemed like a smooth operation of ridding Ireland of two potential troublemakers, except that McLoughlin vigorously protested his innocence. He was a farm labourer, just twenty-two years old, the youngest of six surviving children of the late Patrick McLoughlin and his wife Bridget, tenant farmers of Grangemore, Aghaboe. He could read and write and was described in his first appeal to the Governor of Ireland, which was signed by fifteen prominent local citizens, as a 'quiet, inoffensive, remarkably industrious young man'. But even though evidence was brought to doubt the young witness, and there had been sightings of Michael at a local racecourse, the appeal failed.

On 11 November 1844, while he was still working out his probation near Cygnet in Van Diemen's Land, his mother Bridget lodged an appeal of her own, addressed to Queen Victoria. Michael was innocent and she requested a reduction in his sentence, this time with the support not just of local gentry and clergy, but that of Robert Stubber himself, the victim of the crime, who vouched for the young man's good character in the neighbourhood. The queen was unmoved.

Bridget, now aged seventy-one, appealed for a third time in March 1845, again with Robert Stubber's support, pleading that she was an 'aged, infirm, broken hearted ... and distressed widow'. To no avail. The following year, the Great Famine erupted in Ireland, while Michael served out eight of his ten years in faraway Van Diemen's Land. He received an early conditional pardon, and he had been an exemplary convict, but he could not return home.[22]

Irish courts were quicker to transport than those in the rest of the British Isles, and many male Irish convicts had little or no previous form, unlike in England and particularly Scotland, where the courts preferred to transport those who were criminals by 'habit and repute'. But driving the flood of Irish convicts were unique economic conditions that were to be devastatingly exacerbated by the Great Famine. A shortage of ships for transporting convicts led to a hiatus that did not break until 1848. The *Blenheim* (1849) carried the first shipload of post-famine Irish men, and they were different: the surgeon on the *Blenheim* noted that the prisoners who had been held in the wretched Kilmainham Gaol in Dublin for more than two years were nonetheless in better health after prison rations than the soldiers who had enlisted for the ship's company and who had been living free amidst the famine. Gaol and the workhouse were safer than the outside world, and Van Diemen's Land was possible salvation. Some deliberately committed crimes in order to be transported and admitted as much in the dock. Sydney Keelen (*Earl Grey*, 1850) conspired with three other young girls to steal a cow after hopes of being accepted for an emigration scheme were dashed. The quartet had unblemished records but 'were transported by their own special and urgent request'.[23] A small number of older women took to arson.[24] A family called Keogh serially offended, reunited in Tasmania, bought a farm and prospered—a form of chain migration by transportation. But the underlying causes of Irish poverty and vulnerability to famine lay deeper.

Irish agriculture was low in productivity. Land tenure with long leases did not encourage innovation, and sub-tenants were left with tiny plots that provided a meagre subsistence from the potato. In the countryside, medium-sized farms were few and the sub-tenants huddled into typical Celtic clachans, or clusters of houses—without a church, public house, store, school or persons of quality to lead or advocate for them. Survival depended on blood relatives, the more the better. And beyond these sub-tenants was a shadowy army of landless, destitute people, mostly women and children. Before the famine, marriage rates were high, but de-facto relationships among the very poor were common too. Children of such casual unions were acutely vulnerable if their mother lost her man. Prostitution flourished in Ireland, particularly in seaports and towns with military barracks. Until the 1838 Poor Law Act, there was no outdoor relief and almost no indoor relief, and women without menfolk, living by casual labour, found themselves excluded from farmhouses lest their lack of morals corrupt the farmer's daughters—they lived in ditches and rough huts or with the farm animals. The 'Curragh Wrens' were camp followers who lived in hollows in the ground covered by furze.[25] Once the workhouses had more places, they lived rough in the summer and took themselves and their children to the workhouse for the winter.[26]

Irish convicts, more than any other national group sent to Van Diemen's Land, were most likely to have lost one or both parents: to come from families fractured by death, imprisonment, desertion or, particularly after the famine, emigration. Loss of family was catastrophic for the Irish poor, and women had become even more vulnerable since the other grave change in the Irish economy: the decline of the cottage industries, of wool and linen weaving in particular. Cottage industry provided both work for women and girls and a vital second income to cultivation.[27]

In 1842, Rose McQuade found herself widowed with a nine-year-old son in Lowertown in Fermanagh, a Protestant plantation town, scarcely friendly to lone, destitute Catholic women. She stole a cow and was transported in the *East London* (1843) with a ten-year sentence, taking her son William with her. Her crime doubtless saved his life, if not her own. Eight years later, the sisters Anne and Mary O'Brien (*Blackfriar*, 1851), born in County Clare but now wandering about in Kerry, also stole a cow and received ten and seven years' transportation, respectively. Their previous crimes had been for stealing turnips and a shirt, and their offending gave them a future they would not have had in Ireland.

Rose McQuade and Mary O'Brien's lives would intersect in the Victorian port town of Warrnambool and its hinterland, and perhaps they even touched on two Scottish women who also concluded their lives there. Rose Ann Smith (*Margaret*, 1843) was a member of a gang of girls in Edinburgh's Old Town, run by the mother of one of her co-offenders, Johan Patterson. She was twenty-five and her previous convictions were for drunkenness and breaking a window. She had been in a de-facto relationship for six years but had no surviving children; she did have five siblings but no parents. And unlike her Irish fellow convicts, she was literate. She would find security in another de-facto relationship in Warrnambool. Jane Robertson (*Rajah*, 1841) was born in Yorkshire, where she said her father was a schoolmaster. He had died from cholera and her mother had married a travelling showman. Jane had become a traveller herself, teamed with her cousin Nancye, living rough and stealing what they could around Inverness. She was illiterate, did not know her age, and was in a poor way psychologically. Her time in Warrnambool would end in 1861 when her husband, Henry Cavanagh (*Enchantress*, 1833), aged fifty, fatally slashed his throat in front of her while holding her hand. He had been unable to find work and had been reading a book on insanity. With their seven children, she took to the road again, and to the bottle.

Scottish convicts were different again from the Irish and the English. There were many more women among them, as the courts were keen to rid the cities of women of ill repute. They all had long criminal records, but they too were souls adrift in the world without families and households. When the family of William McIver (*William Jardine*, 1844) emigrated to America, he fell into housebreaking and serious theft. He was eighteen then and pimply, but his transportation to Australia would see him live to be ninety-three, outlived by only one of his six children. William Burnett (*Barossa*, 1844), just a year older, had lost both parents and had only a brother and a half-sister. Born in

Banff, he was housebreaking around Aberdeen when he received ten years in light of his previous offences. He was to father fifteen new Victorians. The Highlanders would prove to be more resilient and more fertile, the seaport offenders more fragile.

What was distinctive about convicts, what separated them from their peers who had avoided the punitive power of the state, was that in the background of their offending lay a family crisis of death or desertion, a failure of the household to support its members both materially and psychologically. Loss of one parent thrust the survivor into peril: of having to care for children while working as a father; of losing all entitlement to support as a mother in a world where women were meant to be supported by men—husbands, fathers, brothers, employers. And the failure of households was most acute in seaports full of transients and lacking respectable work for women needing to feed and house themselves and a family. The vulnerability was increased by the instability and insecurity of neighbourhoods. Destitution, alcohol and violence fed off each other and compounded the damage they inflicted on the young and the unprotected. These were the intimate push factors for offending amidst the larger pressures of a rapidly changing economy. The convict's plea in mitigation was one of misfortune, abandonment, abuse, neglect and destitution: human flotsam and jetsam caught in the massive transformation of the industrial and agricultural revolutions, the pursuit of empire and the insatiable hunger for land. And as they became prisoners and then colonisers themselves, they were pawns in a vast enterprise of conquest and possession. How well would they fare?

CHAPTER 2

Prisoners
Under the Paper
Panopticon

A few more words about convicts. It is not well to reside among them for many reasons. The constant sight of them lessens your self-respect; and you feel less regard, less veneration for mankind generally. Too many of them are, in habits, manners, in aspect and in intelligence, the commonest human animals; and strongly suggest to the sceptical the mere materiality of man. Creatures endowed liberally with a low kind of instinctive cunning, but woefully deficient, apparently, of any kindliness of disposition, any ennobling attribute of the soul. They seem, like the aborigines, imitative but unoriginative; the merest human blocks; as though they had been very recently fashioned by some Pygmalion, out of wood or stone. Of the earth, earthy—if they are allied to any kind of ethereality they give no evidence of it.

RICHARD HOWITT, *IMPRESSIONS OF AUSTRALIA FELIX* (1845), p. 326

Now they were captives—measured, described, watched, recorded and contained by a paper panopticon that saw all. They were being sent to an island prison where their management, unless they committed further offences, would be by observation and regulation. And when they did offend, the punishment would be harsh. Yet it was a cruel age, where children and animals were beaten to within an inch of their lives; where sailors and soldiers were flogged; where the poor were confined, isolated from their families, even subjected to solitary confinement; where people went hungry, children were stunted, workers were bullied and driven until they dropped at their looms. A society to prevent cruelty to animals would be founded fully half a century before one to prevent cruelty to children.

When Britain began sending convicts to Australia, it was still trading in slaves, but over the half-century of transportation to Van Diemen's Land, from 1803 to 1853, ideas and practices concerning penal servitude and rehabilitation would change. The gaolers wanted their charges to reform and contribute to the colonial economy. As for the paper panopticon, it not only kept watch on where the convicts were in the landscape and how they were behaving, it was also a form of accounting, a bookkeeping of the prisoner's moral career. The penal system in the Australian colonies was a moral economy where hard work, obedience, deference and good deeds would earn you a ticket-of-leave, perhaps a full and early pardon. Exceptional virtue and service might even erase the convict stain. And the convicts selected were, as much as possible, to be young and fit enough to make a new start. Unlike slavery, convicts retained some rights under the common law and the hope of freedom through moral reconstruction. This penal system was not uniquely brutal, and convict bodies remained the property of the governor, not their private masters.[1]

THE VOYAGE

'This day commences a new era in your existence,' announced the surgeon superintendent to the assembled convicts aboard the *Elphinstone* in 1836.[2] They were facing exile from kith and kin, probably for life. They would now be convict workers, building a new British society unimaginably far away. Some were distraught, some were resigned. But this new era in their existence also meant banishment to a new moral universe—what they would call 'the other side', where they had 'lost their character'. They had become, justly or unjustly, a moral subspecies. If women usually 'lost their character' from an extra-nuptial pregnancy that banished them from respectability, all convicts now inhabited a moral underworld that many, and their immediate descendants, would never escape. They were, in Richard Howitt's dreadful words, 'the merest human blocks'.

Not all dreaded their fate, however. By the 1830s, stories were circulating that the penal colony offered opportunity. Early convicts were able to get land, marry, raise families. A handful who had essential skills, such as forestry and milling, made money and were almost respectable. Over time, some families would plan their escape from starvation and misery with forced chain migration. Some were following siblings or spouses or children via transportation. Yet even if transportation was devoutly to be wished, they were still prisoners— still under the control of authority figures, forced to work, still subject to bullying and humiliation. They were people on the margin, and they were exiles, most never to see their families and friends again.

Yet some were to be surprised by their experience. On 21 October 1839, little Ellen Miles was taken down from the dock at the Old Bailey and conveyed to the National Penitentiary to await transportation. She was accustomed to confinement, having spent portions of her life since the age of seven in either the St Pancras Workhouse or in houses of correction. She had been taken into police custody fully thirty-one times, and she was already an old hand. A month later, with ninety-two other London prisoners, she was conveyed by coach to Woolwich to board the *Gilbert Henderson*. Joining her were forty-one individuals from Liverpool, twenty from Leith, and ten from Exeter, all jurisdictions serving seaports, while small numbers came from other prisons across England and Scotland, travelling by ship and coach to the docks. For once, Ellen was in luck. The surgeon superintendent, Sir John Hamett, who controlled the ship's company at sea, was most conscientious. He found his charges in reasonable health, except for those who had been in solitary confinement, and was determined to improve their physical and mental condition during the voyage. Only eight women refused to be examined and treated.

Ellen was not the only child convict on board, and a child she still was, no taller than a modern ten-year-old. There was Agnes Mosley from Glasgow, a little older than Ellen but the size of a nine-year-old. Ellen Leary, born in South London, was the right height for her age. However, Janet Dunn, also from Glasgow, at the age of twelve looked like a seven-year-old. All these children would one day make a life in Victoria. The young girls did not prove troublesome; only the old women did. The sea voyage was to be the adventure of a lifetime.

The convicts found themselves organised into messes (living quarters) of eight, usually chosen with women from their own area, and shipboard duties of serving food, cleaning and nursing were assigned. The most literate were made governesses, and each day, classes in reading and writing were held on deck. Ellen may have started to learn to read and write her name in the workhouse, but by the time she finished her sentence, she was literate enough to sign her marriage certificate with a good hand. Hand work, often quilting, was provided by the London Ladies' Missionary Society, as well as sewing kits and personal items for the women, most of whom possessed nothing that they could take with them.³ Improving tracts and small Bibles were essentials, for the most important purpose of literacy was to be able to read the Scriptures.

The worst part of the voyage was the start, through the terrible seas of the Bay of Biscay. Everyone was seasick and the surgeon superintendent was frantic in his efforts to keep the ship clean and ventilated. Women were more inclined to seasickness, and if pregnant or breastfeeding they lost condition rapidly, imperilling the lives of their children and themselves. The sickness was so severe that Sir John asked that the ship stop at Tenerife, one of the Canary Islands, to take fresh food on board to guard against scurvy in his weakened charges. He was particularly attentive to their diet, that it be varied and palatable. Once clear of the coasts of Europe, however, the voyage became a cruise. After cleaning their bedding, themselves and their clothes, the convicts spent all day on deck, sewing, studying or simply chatting, flirting with the sailors and guards, singing, reciting, and—as on all convict ships, whether transporting males or females—dancing to maintain their fitness and good spirits. Locked down at night, the women continued their singing and theatricals, a rich common people's culture of romance, satire and bawd. Women could not be flogged, only confined to a box for a number of hours. Neither were they shackled, unless out of control. The ultimate and dreaded punishment was head shaving. Only once did a woman offend to this extent, but her pleas for mercy were heard by Sir John, who cut off only a quarter of an inch, earning her undying gratitude for the rest of the voyage. A young midshipman aboard would many years later publish an account of this voyage, being enchanted with its orderly contentment. There was even some licence: a group of women from the north of England decided to carry out a customary 'tossing' of gentlemen in the air, seizing first on a pompous cabin passenger, but finally tossing the surgeon and the captain. When the

Gilbert Henderson reached Hobart, many wept bitterly and declared they wished they could spend all their sentence on board under the care of Sir John.[4]

After the disastrous voyage of the Second Fleet to Port Jackson in 1789, which involved conditions so poor that a quarter of the convicts did not survive the trip, the management of shipboard life had been handed over to the naval surgeons. Bonuses were paid to captains and surgeons who brought a cargo of prisoners safely to the colonies, so that mortality was lower on convict ships than on emigrant ships, and certainly nothing like the horrors of the slave ships were endured. By practising a strict regime of public health against miasmas—the cleaning of all surfaces daily, ventilation, and washing bedding, clothes and bodies regularly—they kept infectious disease at bay. They also did all they could to exclude from embarkation convicts who might be diseased, especially with consumption or eye afflictions that were highly contagious. Some always slipped through, but the deaths on board were remarkably few. It can be argued that the health transition occurred first at sea in the floating laboratories of convict ships.[5]

But this care and regularity had an interesting effect on behaviour. Many convicts embarked with a bad record from gaol or the hulks, only to disembark with a good record from the surgeon. Many of the surgeons were kindly, and for numerous convicts it must have been the first time an official treated them as human beings. And they responded. Rarely did a convict receive a bad report from the surgeon. Alexandrina Grant (*Tory*, 1845) did, being described as 'pert'. A few were compulsive thieves or dirty in their habits. But violent behaviour was more often the consequence of mental illness, and hysteria afflicted both men and women on leaving their homeland, especially if they had been in solitary confinement.[6] The surgeons were motivated to care for their charges, and it was appreciated. When a surgeon failed—was drunken, lazy or incompetent—the effects were dire, such as the fate that afflicted the Irish women on the *East London* in 1843, where the surgeon's refusal to take on fresh food led to a serious outbreak of scurvy and the deaths of nineteen women and twelve accompanying children.[7]

The surgeon on the *Claudine*, which arrived in 1821, wrote his surgeon's log as a daily diary, revealing the routines of ship life:

> 11th October
>
> At 6 AM the prisoners all on Deck with their Bedding—upper and prison decks cleaned. Breakfast, Dinner & Lime Juice served out at the usual hour. At 9 AM William Whitehorse received 2 Dozen Lashes for using threatening language to me—also Joseph Bolton a Boy received 2 Dozen lashes on his Backside for being dirty & concealing his clothes. Fires kept lighted on the prison deck during the day at 6 PM all the prisoners' beds sent below. From 6 to 8 PM all on Deck Dancing.[8]

THE INDENT

On a ship's arrival in Hobart came the taking of the indent: a detailed description and assessment of the human cargo about to be unloaded. Male convicts were stripped to the waist; females had to reveal their arms and upper chest. Heights, facial features, colouring, deformities, physical oddities, tattoos, even scars and moles, were all needed to be able to identify convicts throughout their servitude. The prisoners were asked about their offences and whether they admitted to them. Then their nearest relatives and their locations were noted. Records carried forward from prisons, hulks and on ships were added. If women had been reported to have been on the town, this was recorded along with the length of time—but that information was not forwarded as they later moved through the system, to improve their chances of rehabilitation.[9]

Great care was taken to assess the convicts' usefulness to the colonial economy: they were forced labour first, prisoners second. Industrial and city convicts rarely had skills that would be of use: weavers, stockingers, nailers, potters and costermongers were reassigned as labourers if they had little aptitude for anything more skilled; countrymen found themselves made ploughmen. For women, the colony needed servants, dressmakers and housekeepers, skills that few had the opportunity to acquire unless they had actually been in service and trained; by contrast, women's skills of luring men and picking their pockets were of little value. During the voyage, women were known to quickly reinvent themselves as maids, housekeepers and usefuls. Those assigned by the Convict Department to be nursemaids were generally the youngest and most ignorant. Those with some refinement were assigned as ladies' maids. Lucky were those convicts with good literacy, business, trade, artistic and professional skills: sinecures as convict clerks, schoolmasters, butlers, architects, dressmakers, milliners, jewellers and artists awaited them. 'Can cook,' a few women said, and likely were snapped up. Alexandrina Grant, with her self-aggrandising imagination, was later disciplined for 'misrepresenting her abilities' and was sentenced to two months' hard labour. Men with timber-working skills were treasured as the European invaders began to rape the forests, and a couple would eventually make money as timber merchants. Stonemasons, brickmakers, carpenters, ship builders, blacksmiths—all were needed in the new colony. Above all, those who were skilled horticulturalists were worth their weight in gold. Samuel Phillips, the poacher, became a champion ploughman.

To remain useful, all the convicts had to do was bite their tongues; touch their forelocks; speak only when spoken to; withstand insults and bullying; abstain from alcohol; remain celibate unless given permission to marry; acquiesce to the master's sexual advances; not fall pregnant; refrain from stealing food, however hungry, or clothing, however cold and drab; and work. Around half of them over the period of convict transportation succeeded, their conduct records blank or almost so. Somehow, they held on until their time was up.

THE CONDUCT RECORDS

Those blank or almost-empty conduct records have proven a problem for posterity. Compared with those who continued to break the rules and commit colonial crimes, there is nothing to say about these convicts' time under sentence. It is an *absence* that has obscured the story of those many convicts whose time under the paper panopticon was not a Gothic horror. On the other hand, for those who did rebel, every charge, from insolence to refusal to work, absconding, being absent without leave (usually overnight), drunkenness, being disorderly in public houses, sexual misconduct, theft, damaging government property, violence and murder, was a formal charge that had to be heard before a magistrate or a judge, although the balance of power was with the plaintiffs rather than the defendants. Convicts were still presumed innocent until proved guilty; serious offences beyond penal indiscipline could entail a trial by jury with defending counsel. As the emancipist population grew, juries were often more sympathetic to those still 'on the other side', and it was sometimes difficult to secure a guilty verdict. It is also likely that convict workers who were very valuable to their masters, especially at critical stages of the agrarian calendar, were indulged and their absences overnight or drunken sprees left unpunished.

The *Claudine* (1821) and the *Gilbert Henderson* (1840) arrived during the assignment period, when convicts were assigned as servants to settlers either in the rural areas or in the towns and villages. The nature of the convict's experience lay in the arbitrary hands of their masters: some were fair, others cruel. In the first two decades of the penal settlement, additional punishment generally took the form of restraint by irons and chains, including neck collars both with and without protruding spikes; the stocks; the treadmill; and, of course, flogging. Secondary punishment began to be institutionalised and industrialised from the early 1820s, with a penal station for men at Macquarie Harbour utilising an industrial system with forced labour not unlike the Caribbean slave industry.[10] The first female factories (houses of correction) were introduced on the advice of the English prison reformer Elizabeth Fry. By the 1830s, female convicts were being divided into crime classes, either regressing to more severe punishment or progressing to assignment as servants where they received board and lodging, but no pay. Their hard labour was at the washtubs, doing the laundry for the system and the town. Secondary punishments for men became more varied: the treadmill, hard labour while chained in a gang, and later, working in the mines on the Tasman Peninsula. Then Port Arthur was commenced as a state-of-the-art secondary punishment institution that incorporated a productive economy, a hospital and a madhouse.

Thomas Brooks was transported in the *William Miles* in 1828 for stealing eleven fowls near High Wycombe in Buckinghamshire. He had previously stolen geese and been imprisoned three times for poaching. He received a life sentence, aged twenty-three and already the father of two children. In early 1829 he wrote to his wife Ann:

> Launceston Van Diemen's Land January 4th
> Dear Wife—this comes with my kind love to you and my dear little children, hoping it will find you and them in good health as it leaves me at present. You must excuse my long silence,

as I wished to let you know how I was situated before I wrote. I am 124 miles from Hobart town with Mr Hobler, a farmer, and I am doing very well considering I am a prisoner, but I should do much better if you were here. I am allowed 12lbs of flour, 12 of meat, one of sugar, two ounces of tea and two ounces of soap per week. Our labour hours is from sunrise to sunset. We had a very prosperous voyage. We touched no where until we made this colony, which is improving yearly. It is a fine country but very mountainous. Meat is very cheap and sometimes bread, but wearing apparel is very dear indeed. Labour is paid for here three times as well as in England, and a man that is free may soon earn a competency to keep him comfortably in his old age; but drunkenness is a vice that prevents them, so they are obliged to work in their old age as well as when they are young.

THOMAS BROOKS, AT MR HOBLER'S, KILLAFADDY, NEAR VAN DIEMEN'S LAND.[11]

Letters home from convicts are rare, and this one achieved immediate fame on being reprinted in multiple British newspapers, before appearing again in August 1829 in the *Launceston Chronicle*. Convicts' letters home devoted much attention to the price of food and their rations: the single most important thing in poor people's lives. Thomas' rations were very generous, but he was a working convict and a tall man for his time. His optimistic account of Van Diemen's Land pleased the locals but would in time displease critics of transportation in that it was giving offenders too great a second chance. Indeed, the reality of his convict experience was a little different from that described in his letter.

In August 1829 Brooks was caught stealing oats from his master, the grazier and adventurer George Hobler. He was sentenced to two years in a penal settlement to work in chains on government projects.

Next, while working on the new Orphans' School, he was found in a public house and reprimanded. In May 1835 he was found working in the bush on his own account and was again sent to government works, this time as a charcoal burner in Oatlands. Then he was seen lurking around John Edwards' house under suspicious circumstances. In April 1836 he was given fifty lashes for working on the Sabbath, and another thirty-five in September for cutting timber for private use. He seemed to be building a life for himself and perhaps for a partner. He received a ticket-of-leave in 1837 and a conditional pardon in 1841 which confined him to the colony. His wife never joined him. It is impossible to distinguish his fate from the eleven other Thomas Brooks who were transported, including another on the *William Miles*.

For all its inconsistencies and arbitrariness, the assignment system provided necessary labour for a new colony, and under the influence of kindly masters and mistresses, achieved much of its aim of rehabilitation. It mobilised mass human labour at low cost to settlers when immigration could not. It slotted neatly into a traditional society of ranks and orders, where your most important social relationships were with your social betters, who might or might not confer the patronage that could help with employment after servitude, business opportunities and land. Some convicts were elevated into respectability by the support and kindness of their masters; others were brutalised by sadists and bullies or ruined by sexual predators. Fortunate women married their seducers, and a few were elevated into affluence if not real acceptance by society; most did not.

FROM PUNISHING THE BODY TO REFORMING THE MIND

By the 1830s, critical voices were being raised in Great Britain that the assignment system was either too arbitrary or too lax. Transportation, for those who could avoid harsh punishment, was too often a lucky break. Emancipists were apparently doing too well, as critics noticed only the fortunate few who had established thriving businesses or farms. The *Molesworth Report* of 1837 brought transportation to New South Wales to an end, leaving Van Diemen's Land with a darkening stain. In 1839, a probation system began as a new experiment in penal discipline, where convicts were divided into classes according to their crimes, so that the degenerate were separated from the mere delinquent. They were forced to progress from labour in gangs through stages of decreasing severity until they were eligible to hire themselves out on the labour market as a passholder; every infringement threw them back into the system. Convicts were more commonly confined together, giving rise, later critics lamented, to 'unnatural crimes', so that homophobia was added to the arsenal of the anti-transportation campaigners. Women were all confined until ready for service, and from 1844, after their numbers had exploded, they spent time being trained in domestic arts. Those who reoffended or who were unruly from the beginning moved through the female factory classes according to their behaviour—a subset, known as the 'flash mob', preferred the conviviality of the desperately overcrowded factories to the petty tyrannies and social isolation of domestic service.

The crowning achievement of the reformers was the model prison that incorporated the silent treatment: prisoners never heard footsteps as all footwear was muffled; they never heard the clatter of a plate and knife as they too were muffled; no-one spoke to them; they took exercise in silence and in chapel they were contained in upright open 'coffins' so as to block out their fellows and make them concentrate their gaze on the preacher. Both in Van Diemen's Land and in the reforming prisons in England like Millbank, the silent treatment, conceived by rationalist and Christian reformers to focus the sinner's unremitting attention on their flawed soul, drove people insane. Women were placed in underground cells with no light and only two buckets: one for water, one for their waste. They became disorientated in time and place: Margaret Owen (*Gilbert Henderson*, 1840), screamed in terror at the prospect of more time in solitary. (She racked up 302 days in the darkness.)[12] When the reckoning came, flogging seems not to have shortened the lives of men convicts, but solitary confinement, in proportion to the number of days endured, did for both men and women.[13]

But this was not the experience of most convicts, even during the harshest periods. If some resisted, others complied. In the search for convict resistance that has interested many historians and is now being studied as proto-industrial protest, it has been easy to underestimate the compliers. Contemporary descriptions of convicts by their free fellow colonists are relatively few, and landscape painters preferred to insert figures of Aboriginal people who were not there in the farming districts, instead of the working convicts who were.

Hugh Munro Hull had come to Van Diemen's Land as a baby in 1818 when his father was appointed assistant commissary general. His later memoirs of Tasmanian life are peopled with men and women of quality and almost bereft of convicts. His one memory of prisoners, other than a brief comment on miserable convict burials, was of a chain gang he encountered at Lovely Banks in 1838. He found it astonishing that 300 men, 'some of whom had been transported for the very worst of crimes', laboured obediently under just five overseers—'who are men removed very little from their own station in society'—along with a couple of superintendents and twelve soldiers. He remarked: 'The Convicts are each of them armed with a stone-hammer made of iron, pick axes, spades etc.—and if they had any spirit, would soon put a quietus on their Guards.'[14]

Godfrey Charles Mundy, a British Army officer, toured Van Diemen's Land in 1850. He found the male convicts

> a painful spectacle of a band of silent, soured and scowling ruffians—some harnessed to others pushing at, and another driving, a hand cart, with clanking chains, toiling and sweating in their thick and dirty woollens along the street—each marked with his number and the name of his station on the back of his cap.[15]

Mundy also reported the concerns of Hobart ladies who were forced to employ convicts as tutors and portraitists, one of whom had been transported for poisoning and who would stand by a window and play with a knife.[16] That was probably Thomas Griffiths Wainewright, who produced his finest portraits while a convict but who fascinated as well as terrified his genteel mistresses. Agnes Power, wife of the surveyor general, seemed to enjoy the brush with evil, as he did a celebrated portrait of her youngest daughter (which, on being conveyed to her sister-in-law in London, the countess of Blessington, fascinated Charles Dickens and Edward Bulwer-Lytton, with the cast of the artist's own devilry transposed onto an innocent visage). Writing to her eldest daughter in London of Wainewright's death, she confessed:

> He certainly was a wonderful man, full of talent and fuller still of wickedness. The last time I ever saw him he said that all he wished for was to go home and murder the person who had transported him—of course, I affected to think he was joking, but I am quite sure he was in earnest.[17]

On his visit to the female factory, Mundy was impressed by the silence of the women: 'As we passed down the ranks the poor creatures saluted us with a running fire of curtseys, and a dead silence was everywhere observed.' At the washtubs, he wrote, 'Squads of women were up to their ankles in suds—carrying out the cruel process of wringing—or displaying their thick ankles as they spread the linen over the drying lines.' Even the sympathetic Mundy could not resist calling attention to the stigmata of female commonness: thick ankles. But he was unnerved, even unmanned, by what he saw when he entered a darkened solitary cell:

> It looked like the den of a wolf, and I almost started back when from the extreme end of the floor I found a pair of bright, flashing eyes fixed on mine. It was a small, slight and quite young girl—very beautiful in feature and complexion—but it was the fierce beauty of the wild cat! I am a steady married man, of a certain age—but at no period of my life would I, for a trifle, have shared for half-an-hour the cell of that sleek little savage. When she purred loudest I should have been most afraid of her claws!

When the cell door slammed shut, he felt a stab of pity, but he had no more stomach for solitary cells that day.[18]

If the moralisers recoiled at the embodied evil of the convicts but seemed equally appalled by their subservience, even the latter could be deceiving. Some well-behaved convicts became very wild after sentence. An early severe punishment seems to have often terrified younger convicts into acceptance of their fate, so that many decided to endure and work towards freedom. The Point Puer institution for boys on the Tasman Peninsula, which operated from 1834 to 1848, predated Parkhurst on the Isle of Wight as a juvenile reformatory by four years. It had become evident that children were not immediately employable in the convict labour system, so the expense of transporting such young offenders was justified as child rescue.[19] Boys learned trades, particularly shoemaking, and some earned their living by this later, but while the vocational training was reasonable, the schooling appears to have been erratic. George Pickering, for one, still did not learn to read and write in the reformatory.[20] The convict system continued the practices of the Old Poor Law: children without parents were to be housed and educated for useful work, and the orphan schools accommodated the children who came with their parents on the convict ships or who were born while their mothers were under sentence. Death rates were high, food was often insufficient and discipline harsh. But some children survived and were given back to their parents on completing their sentence.

Dissatisfaction with limited domestic skills, in particular those of women who had come from urban communities and not been in service, resulted in the conversion of the *Anson*, which had brought 500 male convicts in 1844, into a hulk moored in the Derwent River that doubled as a domestic training school, where women spent their first six months. One of those who experienced the *Anson* was Jane Burrell, who arrived on the *Tory* in 1848, under fourteen years' sentence for receiving. She was forty-eight years old and the mother of at least eight children. She was also a countrywoman, from near Lynn in Norfolk, who knew how to defer to mistresses and masters, and she realised that she now had to hold her tongue:

Dear Husband and Children

I have once more taken the liberty to address you without examination as I dare say you are anxious to know how I am situated, but I can assure you never better had I you all with me. I should have wrote sooner if I could, but from the effects of the Sea, for I was ill all the time we was crossing the Ocean's from the 1st of May to the 6th of August I was very much reduced and as soon as I heard the call of Land ahead I was better and have

had my health well ever since. You would not think I had been
ill if you was to see me. We had a fine passage and a quick one for
many rough seas but no danger. We was twice washed out of our
beds in the Bay of Biscay and what would you think to that but
was not at all afraid. We had the Old Charter performed on the
Line—two sailors shaved with tar and covered with water and
in the evening the King of the Seas performed. It was hot I got
upon Deck but in a few minutes the Skin was taken off my nose
and Forehead. I could tell you a deal about the Sea but time will
not allow me. When we got to our journeys end we was sent on
board her Majesty's Ship the Anson ... hulk, where we had six
months probation to do. We was well treated. There are all sorts
of needle work to do. We had one hundred women in our Ward,
about thirty of them time servers. I had the work to manage and
finish and gave great satisfaction. We went to school one day
in the week to write and sum. We had exercise twice a day one
hour each time. We had six hundred on board, some of all sorts.
I could not write at all when we anchored. The rules and regulations excellent. We have a Sunday Service in the morning and
prayers in the evening, prayers morning and evening the week
throughout. We were not under the silent act. I can assure you
I have seen some scores of fights—4 and 5 in a morning before
breakfast. We were not allowed to use any irriative language to
the Officers, nor they to use any to us, but I have done with all
I hope. The day we were landed we had some fun boats with
Ladys and Gentlemen from all parts for English Women to
see which should get there first. We were all in classes Cooks,
House Maids, Dairy maids not much wanted, farm servants are
very scarce. I should like to have gone up the country but our
Minister wished me to stay in Town. I have taken a Cooks place
for the present. Our hire is six months at the end of 6 months

I shall go up the Country as wages are very high there. You are not allowed to ask less than nine Pounds Government wages as much more as you please. If I had Hannah here she would get paid nine to twelve pounds, Elizabeth nine, Harriett from twelve to eighteen pounds. Good servants are prized like gold and a talented woman may get almost any money. We keep two cows—both are fine beasts but women neither milk nor churn. Our Lady very much liked my way of making butter and has had some sent in cakes for presents that her friends might see it. They do not make butter as we do—they make it in lumps ... It is a very fine country. I admire it. I cannot think I am so far from England for everything is so much like here as with you everything very cheap, wine and spirits very cheap. I get London Porter but that I give to the Gardener, as you know I never could drink it. Let S, A, and Elizabeth have my hightops? As if I come home I shall have some if keep my health.[21]

Jane Burrell never did go home, but as a skilled needlewoman she was able to earn her keep until old age forced her into a charitable institution.

THE ROUGH AND THE RESPECTABLE

Convicts were not homogeneous. They came from a society that was beginning to place a new premium on 'character', a portable social capital that enabled the bearer to be trusted in employment and respected in civil life. The traditional society of rank and privilege that flourished in stable communities both rural and urban, conferred 'trustworthiness' by patronage and bestowed 'character' on an employee. But the rapid population growth and geographic mobility that occurred from the late eighteenth century undermined those traditional connections. Mobile people needed mobile reputations—a character—increasingly in written form rather than simply word of mouth. Deprived of this, a poor man or woman had no hope of employment or commerce, hence the plight of the 'ruined' servant who was dismissed without a 'character', lost her 'home' and had no alternative but prostitution. Men also could lose their 'character' or written reference and find new work elusive. Deprived of cash and a roof over their head, the poor person's clothing deteriorated, becoming filthy and ragged, so that their appearance signalled to the world that they were destitute of both means and good reputation. The terror of many was losing their mother, lest they quickly descend into hunger and filth.

The rise of a culture of respectability and manly independence during the Victorian era signified a new, if limited, social mobility, more suited to an expanding economy and rapidly growing cities, and powered by the force of a respectable, trustworthy character. It could be accelerated by conspicuous membership of a church, and in the penal colonies, the Methodists were particularly welcoming. Attendance at workingmen's classes in mechanics' institutes educated generations of politicians and labour leaders. By the end of the nineteenth century, respectability came with regular employment; those still trapped in the irregular economy of casual work were doomed to remain rough. This became the great social divide of Victorian British societies: it was possible to be poor but honest, while only the aristocracy could get away with sin.

The rough culture of street dealing, lurks and petty thefts, drinking, fighting, swearing and illicit sex was the world of many convicts, but not all. The divide was not merely one of morality; it was also one of language, with the rough able to communicate secretly through 'flash cant'. Rough language, especially from female convict servants in front of children, caused much distress, repelling the young Charles Darwin when he toyed with the idea of emigration. Language, deportment, facial characteristics such as visible scars, clothing and cleanliness: all signalled to the world where you were placed on the moral spectrum. The world would read your character and place you by your appearance and speech. And the divide between the respectable and the rough existed even among the convict population. A son of a good family could have an adolescent outburst of delinquency, generally in company with fellow youths, but retain the stability to reform with maturity. Commonly, 'gentlemen' convicts had attempted to conceal financial embarrassment with forgery or embezzlement. With women, the Rubicon was more severe, generally an unmarried pregnancy that alienated them from respectability for life unless they married later. Those who had been on the town were the roughest, while young convicts from rural districts, especially in Ireland after the Great Famine, were generally the most respectable, and hence the most likely to marry early in their time under sentence and to become successful mothers. Men also varied in their attachment to 'rough culture'—many seem to have been able to cope with servitude with, at the minimum, dumb insolence, and at the maximum, deference and compliance. Of the *Claudine* men, 39 per cent received no punishment of any kind, and just 19 per cent suffered savage punishment of more than a hundred lashes. Some convicts appear to have pushed their captors' buttons from the beginning, and the escalating penal violence was embodied in a ferocious relationship between master and servant.

There were two young Samuels on the *Claudine*. Samuel Fletcher was a fourteen-year-old lad from Beeston, then a hamlet outside Nottingham. The convict clerk neglected to measure him and gleaned no information about his family. The other Samuel, Samuel Langham, was seventeen and the son of a stocking weaver from Leicester. They were both thieves: Fletcher had three previous convictions and a 'bad character'; Langham had one previous conviction for stealing cakes, for which he was whipped. Under the paper panopticon, Samuel Langham was a man with no history. Samuel Fletcher's, however, was copious: absconding five times and at large for almost twelve months; being reconvicted and sentenced to Port Arthur; and amassing 325 stripes. Finally free in 1840, he crossed to Port Phillip. In 1846 he was prosecuted for bolting from his hired service as a timber cutter for the pioneer Robert Simson of the Loddon region.[22] Just over a year later he died as he lived, thrown from a gig that was being 'driven furiously' in Flinders Lane, Melbourne.[23]

Samuel Langham, the convict with no history, served his seven years, married a free woman, set himself up as a timber merchant, joined the Methodist Church and, notwithstanding that, ran a public house in Launceston. In 1847, he too moved to Melbourne with his wife and children. He did well in business, but crippled by strokes and dementia, he was eventually confined to the Kew Lunatic Asylum—up until he died in 1872, he continued to recognise his family when they visited. His legacy was his family: his daughters married respectably; one son established a tannery in Castlemaine and was a celebrated sportsman; Frederick, the oldest and born before wedlock, was called to the Methodist ministry, became a leading missionary in Fiji, and revised the Fijian translation of the New Testament. Frederick was such a dominant political figure that he was dubbed 'the Cardinal'. His life was far removed from his father's transportation on the *Claudine*.[24]

Ships of arrival in Australia remained important throughout the nineteenth century. A convict's voyage was a key part of their colonial identity and essential for police tracing. But the journey was also a shared historical experience that created a cohort and often established relationships that endured long after. Shipmates' signatures can be found as witnesses of marriages in both Tasmania and Victoria, and crime and prostitution networks that had their origin in servitude were quickly formed after release. Convict ships were also time capsules that captured an historical population that shared an experience of life before sentencing. The early women's ships were few and small, but they carried a high proportion of women of the town as English workhouses sought to rid themselves of the most corrupting elements. The Scottish courts were also keen to transport women of ill repute to cleanse their cities. No ships sailed direct from Ireland until transportation was halted to New South Wales, so the Irish-born transported before the 1840s had been convicted elsewhere. Before the Great Famine, the Irish—apart from a larger number of essentially political offenders who, in line with the Tumultuous Risings Act (1831), were transported for 'assaulting a habitation' or, as Michael McLoughlin was charged, for stealing a weapon—were ordinary thieves, except that they were more rural and likely to have stolen food or animals. Those born in Dublin, Belfast and Cork were little different from their peers also born in seaports. A surplus of colonial labour and shortage of ships halted transportation between 1846 and 1848, and the last surge of transportation brought a very different Irish population of famine survivors.

By the end of the decade, the probation system was breaking down and these last convicts, once gold was discovered in Victoria, had to be induced to resist absconding by leniency. Severe punishment became very rare. Of the 288 Irishmen aboard the *Hyderabad* (1850), just 21 per cent were sentenced to solitary confinement, and merely four of them to more than fifty days during their sentence; just one was flogged. The 280 English and Scottish men on the *Aboukir* (1852) were more unruly: just under 40 per cent spent time in solitary, usually for less than ten days; none was flogged.

What mattered most to convicts, both male and female, young and old, was getting enough food and being clothed. Beyond that, money to buy or smuggle alcohol and tea and flashier clothes was worth risking punishment for. And there was sex: sex for relationships, perhaps a marriage under sentence that would ensure some independence from the system if not love, and sex for money. Convict marriage was encouraged as a reward for good behaviour and as a means of building the settlement. The most likely successful unions were those of young women who married early in their sentence and were assigned to their husband. Ellen Baldock (*Hector*, 1835) had been eight years on the town in Edinburgh and was sentenced to fourteen years for robbery from the person, but she married William Goodall (*Lady Harewood*, 1829) within twelve months of her arrival at Hobart and seems to have never looked back. Mary Bentley (*Atwick*, 1838) after a rough early life on the town and a fourteen-year sentence for highway robbery, likewise married wisely a year after arrival: William Peeler (*Woodford*, 1828). These were the unions most likely to produce large families and lineages. Pregnancy outside wedlock, however, was constituted as a crime that condemned the mother to confinement in a female factory and the almost certain death of her baby under institutional care.[25]

And finally, there was fun. Convicts were forbidden to drink alcohol, but of course most did, and a distinctive minority not only were punished severely for drunkenness, they persisted in their lust for the bottle and in being found in houses of ill fame. Prostitution remained a means of making money for women who needed to drink and wanted to bedeck themselves with ribbons. Some masters and mistresses were lenient and gave their convict servants the freedom to go out and enjoy themselves. Some provided decent clothes, although women convicts were rarely satisfied with their dress. But to have a good time, flash women soon discovered, was to stay in the female factory, where, as at night on board their ships, they were locked in and could sing, dance and be as lewd as they liked. They could dance naked and have sex with other women—women they loved and women they bullied. This was the flash mob who 'always had money, wear worked cap, silk handkerchiefs, earrings and other rings they are the greatest blackguards in the building. The other women were afraid of them. They led away the young girls by bad advice'.[26]

Ellen Miles had her first experience of solitary confinement two months after disembarkation. She continued to be insolent and to disobey orders, amassing a total of 134 days in solitary confinement over her eight years under sentence. In July 1841, aged fourteen, she was punished for being in the company of a Richard Nichols. In May 1842, six months was added to her sentence for absconding. Then in July, together with two notorious members of the flash mob, Mary Sheriff and Catherine Lowry, she was convicted of riot and breaking a table in the Launceston Female Factory. In August 1842, she and Mary Sheriff were convicted of gross insubordination: they earned three months' hard labour, two of them in solitary. After a month, Mary Sheriff could take no more. She had sharpened a dining knife into a weapon, and when the assistant surgeon, Dr Maddox, refused her plea that she was too sick to go back to solitary, she, along with Eliza Owens and Elizabeth Elmore, stabbed him. They were each sentenced to death but reprieved. Ellen must have been in the cells.

By the end of 1846 Ellen Miles was pregnant, and in July 1847 she received permission to marry Thomas Watkins (*Runnymeade*, 1840), a fellow cockney born in Deptford and transported for stealing from the person. In April 1847 she was free by servitude, and baby Thomas was born on 15 August. In March 1848 she married Thomas Watkins in the Wesleyan Church, and in July as a 'free lady' she was fined 5 shillings for 'making very bad use of her tongue in the public streets'.[27] Husband and wife were both free by the end of 1849. Now they had to make a life of their own.

CHAPTER 3

Cut Free

*I have never met with a more
lawless and infamous set.*

GEORGE AUGUSTUS ROBINSON, *JOURNALS OF
GA ROBINSON, 1840 AND 1841*, 15 MAY 1841

As soon as they left the protection of the convict system, the women began to die. Mary Kinnear, born in Dublin but convicted in Perth, Scotland, was transported on the *Margaret* in 1843. At the age of thirty-three, she had been five years on the town and the ship's surgeon noted that she was 'inclined to be insolent'. Under sentence, she was unruly, angry, drunken, and taking men to her bed. Cut free, she was homeless and unemployable. Syphilis ate at her body. At the coronial inquiry in May 1852, Thomas Harper testified:

> I have known her for six or seven years. She got her living by prostitution. The last time I saw her alive was on Friday evening last between nine and ten o'clock—she was in John Burns house lying in front of the fire—she was quite pale and her face was quite cold but she was sensible—I touched her face and she said 'Oh Tommy do not hurt me'—I left her and

did not see her again till the following morning when she was dead. She did not complain of anything when I saw her on the Friday evening—She appeared to be dying. She was covered with vermin and had an old coarse rug over her. It was Burns wife fetched me in to her—She was destitute—She used to sit on a stone at top of the court and creep into a hole under Burns house at night. Burns and his wife treated her as kindly as their circumstances permitted.[1]

Two of Ellen's shipmates, Margaret Anderson and Margaret Angus, were both dead from the complications of intemperance within three years of being cut free. Mary Lochrie, who had come as a diminutive 17-year-old on the *Margaret* in 1843, was dead by thirty-eight from phthisis, as was her shipmate Jane Perry on the Loddon goldfields at thirty-four. Two others died in childbirth. Mary Ann Wilson died from injuries while intoxicated, aged thirty-nine. Then there was Ellen Moriarty, who was found disembowelled on the Longford Racecourse in 1867, murdered while seeking safety in a group of fellow homeless travellers, living and working in order to drink.[2]

FINDING A LIVING AND A SAVIOUR

James Boyce has rewritten the history of Van Diemen's Land and early Port Phillip with an acute understanding of the pre-modern world.[3] If capital-intensive grazing and farming dominate the early economic history of south-eastern Australia, the material and social lives of the poor resembled much of the rural world before the completion of the enclosures, where the common people assumed an entitlement to the fruits of the forests and rivers, grew small subsistence crops, and might keep fowls, a cow, some goats and a pig, but rarely possess a horse and cart.[4] If they worked for wages, they were generally on day or short-term hire during a harvest. The fortunate had a more permanent relationship with a landowner that may have included accommodation, but the roaming poor shared food, drink and shelter with strangers. Their homes were huts on land to which they had no legal claim. (The 'hut culture' endures to this day in Tasmania.) The early penal colony had fared far better than Sydney Cove because of the initial abundance of native wildlife and the presence of hunting dogs.[5] Convicts who were assigned servants like Samuel Langham could live almost independent lives in the bush while under sentence, sometimes building small savings from selling timber, skins and meat. Under the probation system, ticket-of-leave men could similarly build or share a hut, selling their labour on the market. Wages were poor and unstable as the colonial economy boomed and went bust, but the land made subsistence and survival possible. The monied grabbed the best farmland and the military establishment were rewarded with generous land grants. Some emancipists were lucky in the early years and obtained viable farms, but by the early 1830s, the good land was all taken as the colony faced a major population increase from transportation. The last incursions into the wilderness, the colonisation of the forests, produced a world of rural poverty and isolation reminiscent of the Appalachians in North America, without the coal.[6] It is a legacy that still haunts the island.

To seek more secure employment entailed coming under the control of the Masters' and Servants' Act of 1856, under which you could be prosecuted, just like an assigned convict, for absence without leave, absconding or refusal of orders.[7] Independence came from self-employment using a skill or some capital, either brought to the colony and meticulously banked by the Convict Department or accumulated over time through paid work. It is very difficult to assess how many male convicts made a new life and a reliable income, but one measure is if they married and raised a family with a lineage. Perhaps no more than 20 per cent of all male convicts achieved that.[8] Even fewer were in the ranks of Samuel Crisp (*Earl St Vincent*, 1826), who built a sawmilling business that one day would merge with the timber firm Gunns, and whose descendants became judges and clergymen; or of George Ogilvie (*Barossa*, 1842), a blacksmith from Aberdeen who established a successful business, including decorative brass moulding in Hobart, and whose grandson would be premier of the state in the 1930s. With Ogilvie on the *Barossa* was the ancestor of another Tasmanian political and Methodist dynasty, the Goodlucks, descended from a family of five who survived into adulthood. These are the outliers. Many more were lost men living off the land than settled family heads.

Men could survive alone, with the company of mates, but women rarely could support themselves unless they were good domestic servants or skilled seamstresses or milliners. Widows of men of business such as shopkeepers, tradesmen or publicans commonly carried on the enterprise, and many thrived. But they needed capital, goodwill and property to do so. Most women had to find a man who could support them or go on the town. Sex ratios in Van Diemen's Land were so distorted that marriage technically was possible for all women other than the very old, the mad or the diseased. Indeed, most ex-convict women married, even if for a brief interval and only for convenience.[9] The most successful convict families tended to be those where the woman married within a few years of arriving in the penal colony, whereupon she was assigned to her husband as his 'servant' and could set about rearing a family. Early convicts were also more likely to obtain land, thus much of the convict-descended population derives from these first arrivals, and some family trees of these multigenerational 'super breeders' are now breathtaking. But they obscure the failure of the majority to establish a stake in the colony and produce an enduring lineage. In a patriarchal society, women needed both a male protector and a male breadwinner, and thus those who failed to secure such protection—choosing a husband unwisely, or unable to sustain a household through their own disturbed and drunken behaviour—were the most vulnerable members of society apart from Aboriginal Tasmanians. And so those who had accumulated psychological and biological damage in early life, who had been on the town or had become addicted to drink, were the ones to die first.

Elizabeth Morgan was a survivor, however. She was transported on the *America* in 1831 as a 32-year-old widow whose husband had died three months before, just after she had her first child, Margaret. She had been stealing to survive. It was not until eighteen months had elapsed after her arrival that she was found guilty of 'gross impropriety'. The next year she married another convict, William Naylor (*Surrey*, 1829), who had operated as a shoemaker in New Town and was thirteen years her junior. Within six months, she was reprimanded for 'disorderly conduct', most probably prostitution. Six months later, her husband was convicted of a 'most violent assault on his wife'.[10] The next year, their three-year-old son was burned to death after being left unsupervised in front of the hearth.[11] Family relations deteriorated further: in 1842, Margaret testified against her step-father in a case of the theft of three bushels of wheat, which saw him re-transported for seven years.[12] Meanwhile, Elizabeth, now known widely as 'Bet Naylor', had become one of the 'Wapping ladies', running prostitution around the noisome Hobart Rivulet—in 1845, a constable, Jonathan Hope, was dismissed for cohabiting with one of her daughters and soliciting young girls for Bet's business.[13] Bet Naylor was now notorious for her tongue and her courtroom theatrics. In May 1848, she staggered into court, half-intoxicated, accompanied by one of her girls, aged eight. She stared at the court defiantly: 'Gentlemen, you are taking a great view of me, but I am not so handsome as I was seventeen or eighteen years ago.' She was keeping a brothel called 'Cloudy Bay' in Baynton's Buildings, pleading that she had to support her daughters. Yet, as the chairman reminded the jury, her 'elderly daughter' had been an 'abandoned character' from an early age. The jury ignored her tears and she was sentenced to two years' imprisonment. The court committed to looking after the children.[14]

Ellen Baldock (*Hector*, 1835) and Mary Bentley (*Atwick*, 1838) were two Scottish women who had been on the town, yet both found good husbands quickly and quietened down as soon as they married. Both brides were pregnant, but the other thing they shared was a new religion. Methodism was the most successful religious movement on the frontier. All its theology was in its hymnbook and Methodists needed no church, not even an ordained pastor. Laymen could preach, and all that was needed otherwise was a violin, or a flute or an accordion. Above all, for those burdened with sin, Methodism offered a personal saviour and a life ever after bathed in His love.

> Breathe, O breathe thy loving Spirit
> into ev'ry troubled breast;
> let us all in thee inherit,
> let us find the promised rest:
> take away the love of sinning;
> Alpha and Omega be;
> End of faith, as its Beginning,
> set our hearts at liberty.[15]

Methodism also educated people. Class meetings trained the hesitant in opening their hearts to others and in speaking strongly. Attendees learned to organise and manage. Sunday schools would often educate children better than did formal schools. Social activities, sport and music provided a sense of community and connections. For many, their transformation was so complete that their descendants could have no inkling that they had arrived bond. John Woolf Walklate (*Marquis of Hastings*, 1842) died as a respected accountant and Wesleyan lay preacher in Launceston in 1893. His son became a prominent Methodist minister in Tasmania and Victoria, as did one of the sons of Samuel Crisp, the sawmiller, who became superintendent of the Wesley Central Mission in Melbourne. None of the other Protestant congregations was as welcoming as the Methodists, nor did any other church offer the laity such opportunities for leadership and personal growth. Methodism became the church of rural Tasmania, as it became the frontier church in Victoria.

Methodism brought sobriety, discipline and thrift. William Goodall received a conditional pardon in 1845 from his life sentence for horse stealing, and the following year had saved enough to procure a horse and wagon, providing carriage for passengers and their luggage between Evandale and Launceston. A year later his wife was free, and with their young children they were ready to cross Bass Strait to Port Phillip. They were to become Vandemonians.

AUSTRALIA FELIX

By the 1830s, Van Diemen's Land was too small for the ambitions of investors. The population was growing as the numbers of convicts and free settlers rose; and as more women arrived, more convict marriages were producing a new generation who might also want a farm. Across Bass Strait beckoned what Thomas Mitchell, the surveyor general of New South Wales, would call 'Australia Felix', an expansive, fertile, cultivated landscape of grains and tubers for people and grazing grounds for native animals. The white invaders did not see it that way, and it would take almost two centuries for historians to see explorers' descriptions of this land of bounty for what they really were. Instead, all they could see was food for their alien hooved animals and soil for exotic plants. Within a decade, the arrivals would despoil every open place and waterway that they and their animals touched.

What is now Victoria was rich in resources to support human life. It is now arguable that this was one of the most densely populated regions of Aboriginal Australia. Along the Murray River, food was so abundant that the Yorta Yorta had semi-permanent settlements, and the paleopathological evidence is closer to that of settled people living primarily from horticulture and fishing: that is, they suffered growth interruptions and periodic severe anaemia.[16] Since that work was undertaken by Stephen Webb, there has been a major advance in our understanding of the complexity of Aboriginal civilisation in south-eastern Australia: from the stone villages of the basaltic plains in the west, where the houses were not unlike the black houses of the Scottish Highlanders who violently displaced them; to the stunning aquaculture of eels through complex stone races and channels; to the extent of nardoo grain that was being ground into flour tens of thousands of years before the emergence of grain cultivation in the Fertile Crescent of the Middle East; to the expanses around what is now Melbourne, which were cultivated to produce staple carbohydrates. Building on the work of Harry Lourandos, Bill Gammage and others, Bruce Pascoe's *Dark Emu* may be the most transformative history of Victoria ever written, stimulating new interest in questions of Aboriginal economy and society prior to invasion.[17]

The original estimate of 15 000 for the Aboriginal population of Victoria was based on observation in the 1830s. We now know that this was already a remnant population, and that probably two visitations of smallpox—moving down the river systems and complex trading and communication routes in the late 1780s, and again in the late 1820s—would have likely cut the population each time by half, if the impacts were anything like those of smallpox and other Eurasian diseases in the Americas. Therefore, in 1770, when Captain James Cook mapped part of the east coast of the continent, 60 000 people is a reasonable demographic estimate. By 1901, after just two generations of European settlement, the population was down to 680. The colonisation of Victoria by diseases, humans, sheep, cattle, horses, dogs, and eventually roads, railways and the telegraph, must rate as perhaps the most rapid and devastating colonial dispossession of the nineteenth century.[18] Today, while around 48 000 people were able to claim Aboriginal ancestry in Victoria in the 2016 census, not one 'full blood' Victorian Aboriginal person is still alive. And as the European invasion advanced over water and land, at the sharp end, walking rather than astride horses, were convicts and ex-convicts. They were the infantry of the invasion—horseless men, known as 'crawlers'.[19]

The first incursions took place long before John Batman and John Pascoe Fawkner laid their claims to Melbourne or the Hentys to Portland. Whalers and sealers had been stopping along the coast since the late eighteenth century, the crews comprising some of the most lost and alienated men on earth. This was a world beyond civil society and nations. Escaped convicts and emancipists found refuge in this international brotherhood of homeless men, despite a government ban on convicts participating in whaling. The ships sought provisions, rest and women, and some set up temporary settlements at Portland Bay, Port Fairy, wherever, in fact, they could make landfall. Unknown numbers of absconders penetrated the coast of Gippsland, and if the Kurnai had been protected by the forest from contact with smallpox, they were not safe from the venereal diseases and tuberculosis carried by these new intruders. The hidden invaders were those slow-breeding infections that lingered in the original hosts without killing them, but which, on entering naive bodies never before exposed to them, were lethal. The women were either kidnapped and stolen or infected and left to bear no more children. These were the indirect 'killings', where women's fertility was damaged by disease, so that the most fundamental means of recovery from trauma and loss—building new families—became almost impossible. Aboriginal women were even more vulnerable than convict women: they had no entitlement to protection and respect; they were there for the taking. Thus, the first reports of explorers into far western Victoria would refer to Aboriginal women infected with syphilis: the germs were the first manifestation of the advancing frontier.[20] Aboriginal Victorians and their country were consumed by what Alfred Crosby has termed 'ecological imperialism'.[21]

THE ECONOMY OF VIOLENCE

The inland invasion was a tide of mobs of sheep, dogs and shepherds on foot. Within a decade, more than four million sheep trampled over the delicate soils, chewed the native plants to near extinction, and polluted and monopolised the waters, driving both people and native animals away. The speed of this incursion was extraordinary: within nine years, almost all of the land west of the Dividing Range along Major Thomas Mitchell's line, from the coast to the Murray River, was under squatting licences. Only the densest forests and the mountains remained intact.

The killings started with first contact. The first recorded massacre was at the Convincing Ground, near Portland, when whalers and Aboriginal people fought over a beached whale carcass; reports of deaths ranged from sixty to 200 people, including women and children. The massacre map of Victoria is thick with sites of murder: in the Western District, around Melbourne, along the Murray and in Gippsland.[22] When George Augustus Robinson began his first journey of discovery in January 1840, following Major Mitchell's line, he despaired that already around the Coliban River, Indigenous people had disappeared. Robinson noted that the country was fine: three squatters had already seized 280 miles (450 kilometres) of land between them, 'and they think it is a hardship if a native appears on their run, imagining that a £10 licence gives them a legal right to expel them'. He continued: 'I have not seen any natives since I have been out. What has become of them? ... Reports say they have been killed, and there are plains called Waterloo Plains where Goldwin's men shot them.'[23]

Robinson deplored the squatters' contempt for the blacks: 'Dr Kilgour like all new arrivals is an avowed enemy of the blacks ... He thinks the settlers will take the law into their own hands.' He noted that when a squatter reported that three convicts had absconded, taking two horses and a mare, the man declared it was no use chasing them: 'Thus these people sit down quietly with loss of £200 at least, in horses taken by convicts, when, if, through hunger, the original proprietors of the soil take 2 or 3 sheep they set up a hue and cry against them.' Loaded guns and pistols were in every hut, and their purpose had to be to destroy Aboriginal people. When Robinson did find remnant groups of people, they were desperately hungry and often stricken with syphilis.[24]

The squatters were men of means, often gentlemen, who lived in physical and moral squalor in the frontier. Far from the law and civilised society, they could drink, rape and kill, with many revelling in the freedom from all constraint. The only women there were either married and unavailable or native women. Robinson reported with disgust that sometimes native women offered sex as a transaction, but it was more often taken by force and transactions were never equal.²⁵ However, the squatters' mercenaries in the frontier war were convicts and emancipists. It has become customary to lay the blame for the savagery of the frontier at the feet of the semi-crazed, isolated shepherds and farm workers. Up-country, they outnumbered the men who had come free. Very few had wives or would ever have a wife. They were willing, after their years of hard labour in the Tasmanian bush, to take work that free immigrants were too frightened to take.²⁶ And they were cast by Robinson and everyone else as depraved and dangerous, the evil of colonisation projected onto the frontline troops: 'Shepherds are a bad class; lazy, impertinent and blasphemous', and 'there is no doubt as the greater part are emancipists, that when labour is cheap and men plentiful, and a better class introduced, that these old hands will turn to thieving, bushranging etc'.²⁷

Robinson reflected with horror on the fate of the people whom he was meant to defend:

> It is dreadful to reflect on the exposed and unexpected state of the original occupants of this soil. The past and present state of the Aborigines is one of annihilation or destruction. The chief class and by far the largest of the labouring men employed in the province have been convicts and for the 16 years I have been in these colonies I have never met with a more lawless and infamous set. They acknowledge no authority and if they will, set their employer at complete defiance.²⁸

But if these were the infantry, the officers who gave the orders and shot from astride their horses were the squatters and the overseers. As the frontier moved in the west along Major Mitchell's line, and fanned out from the ports at Melbourne and Geelong, in the east, Angus McMillan was leading overlanders from the north, bringing with them convict and ex-convict servants from the Sydney region, and killing over the next decade between 300 and 1000 Kurnai people. The Vandemonian invasion of Gippsland was more sporadic. Escaped convicts had been living in the bush, but whereas the ports at Port Fairy and Portland were established early, Gippsland's Port Albert was not opened until 1841. If the western ports and the growing port at Geelong were dealing in wool, Gippsland flourished as a provider of beef and mutton to Tasmania, especially as the island population grew in the 1840s. Much of this was illegal, involving the transportation of stolen cattle to Victoria where they were killed and preserved, to be returned in unidentifiable form whence they came.[29] Ex-convicts came to congregate in Port Albert, Tarraville and Rosedale, though some retreated even deeper into the bush.

The leading ports and settlements became Melbourne and Geelong. And in the latter, a village called Ashby (now Geelong West) became another haunt of the Vandemonians. Like the other early settlements, it was little more than a scattering of huts and tents, followed by small cottages, but that was sufficient to house drinking places and brothels. The immorality of the frontier and its violence extended to these places. When the victims were Aboriginal people, the great colonising project justified their destruction: policing was scant, and magistrates, according to Robinson, turned a blind eye to the violence. The frontier was an unregulated expression of toxic white masculinity that was barely kept in check by the restrictions on pastoral workers' access to alcohol while under contract. Once they had their cheque, then the binge drinking could begin, and Melbourne, Geelong and all the other small ports had the grog shanties, the pubs and the prostitutes. A chain of human exploitation linked frontier violence to sexual violence and exploitation in the places of recreation. Squatters had to wait until their workers had drunk their cheques before they could lure them back to their flocks. It was a pattern of rural work and urban bingeing that would last until World War II. And its biggest victims were the women, black and white, who lacked male protectors as either husbands, fathers or masters.[30] Penelope Edmonds has written of the desperate bands of destitute Aboriginal people on the fringes of the Melbourne settlement, begging food and drink, while the women were public sexual property, helpless before 'lawless villains'.[31]

The squatters may have been Port Phillip gentlemen, but behind the Melbourne Club lay the back lanes and theatre district of the city, where prostitution flourished, and where the Vandemonians, alongside free emigrants who had broken down or been deserted or widowed, drank their troubles away. This was the frontier sexual economy, fed by a chain of lonely, thirsty men up-country and by the growing tide of immigrants and seamen. It replicated the violence and abuse of the seaports that had bred and bruised so many of the Vandemonians.

INVISIBLE FOUNDING FATHERS AND MOTHERS

The Vandemonians, even when respectable, were meant to be invisible. Few of their names were entered into the foundational stories of Melbourne and Geelong, unless they were especially colourful. One such person was William 'Tulip' Wright (*Lady Harewood*, 1829), who had a short and turbulent career as Melbourne's chief constable after the dismissal of Henry Batman for corruption. Wright had been part of a gang of five in Lincolnshire who stole a gun and iron bars and arrived in the same ship as William Goodall. Known as 'Tulip' according to Michael Cannon, because of his red plush waistcoat and 'his big, bulbous, purply face', he made sufficient funds to buy the Deep Creek Inn at Bulla.[32] It was a fortuitous investment, ideally placed to capture the cash of gold-diggers making for Mount Alexander and Bendigo. He reportedly died 'in affluence' and was possessed of a 'genial disposition and a thorough English character'.[33]

At the first land sale in Port Phillip on 1 June 1836, George Scarborough and Gilbert Marshall each bought a town lot for £18. Scarborough sold his for £1050 on 23 October 1839, just before the colony suffered its first depression. Scarborough purchased 222 acres (90 hectares) at gold rush prices in 1854 at Mount Cottrell near Rockbank, and he also invested in land in Flemington that he leased out to market gardeners. Gilbert Marshall, meanwhile, ran the Black Boy Inn until 1846 and then began likewise to amass considerable and diverse property within and outside Melbourne: he had a farm on the Plenty River, property in Richmond, and he came to own much of the Collingwood Flat. Scarborough had crossed over to the Port Phillip settlement in November 1835 in charge of fifty pure Hereford cows for Dr Alexander Thomson. With him came his wife Mary Ann and their three children; their next child was to be the first white boy born in Melbourne and baptised at St James' Church. And by 1840, in addition to his land dealings, he had secured the valuable position of pound keeper to the settlement. Gilbert Marshall had arrived soon after Scarborough, in January 1836, with his wife and first child. Both men would raise good-sized families, share land investments, leave property to their children, and establish a lineage with descendants serving in the First AIF. Both men were also former convicts, as were their wives, and the lives of the two families would remain intertwined for the next fifty years.

George Scarborough, born in Kentish Town, London, had been a gentleman's servant and was convicted at the Old Bailey of passing counterfeit notes, arriving in Van Diemen's Land on *The Caledonian* in 1820. Under sentence he was punished severely only once, given twenty-five lashes for neglect of duty. In 1831, while holding a ticket-of-leave, he married Mary Ann Williams, also a Londoner, born in Soho, who seems to have lived with a Mr Gower, but she was now on the town. Aged seventeen, she had stolen bedding from her 'ready furnished room' in company with Sarah Waters. Both arrived on the *Harmony* in January 1829. (Sarah Waters proved the more rebellious of the two, and after absconding for a second time, she had her hair cut off and was placed in an iron collar for a month.)

Gilbert Marshall's convict career was grimmer: transported first to Sydney, he was re-transported to Port Macquarie for robbery, before reinventing himself in the southern colony as a constable. In January 1834 he married Janet Black (*Lady of the Lake*, 1829), an orphan from Glasgow who was so small that the bench thought she was ten. She was not reported to have been on the town, but she had been living by thieving and was by character and disposition 'bad'. Under sentence she was disobedient, insolent and profane: in 1831 she had a man in her bed; in 1833 she was found in a public house. A month after her marriage, she was convicted of running off with her husband's property and sentenced to a further six months at the washtubs. The first of nine children was born the next year and the family was off to Port Phillip. Three children were christened at St James', with John Pascoe Fawkner as their godfather.

By the 1850s, both families were relatively wealthy, at least in assets, and in September 1853 Gilbert Marshall drew up a complicated will that provided an annuity for Janet and carefully apportioned his land holdings and assets to provide for all his children—George Scarborough and Thomas Griffiths, a cabinet-maker from South Melbourne, were named as executors. At Christmas 1855, while the Marshalls were living at Plenty, an old Richmond friend, Mrs Catherine Austin, suffocated in a soft pillow in strange circumstances. Gilbert came down to Richmond for the wake and to collect rents from his many properties on the flat, now overrun with new gold-rush arrivals. He became so intoxicated that his friends thought it best if he slept it off in a tent, except that a candle was not snuffed, the tent took fire and Gilbert was 'burnt to a cinder'.[34] On hearing the news at

Plenty, Janet rushed to Richmond, only to be bitten by a centipede. She was not expected to recover according to the press, but she would defy the predictions.[35]

Janet Black, who had had such a terrible start in life, was left with eight children, the youngest just one year old. Perhaps she was already unstable and drinking heavily, hence the complicated will that provided for her while protecting the children. But she now disintegrated entirely. Within six years she was a vagrant alcoholic around Melbourne's louche districts, kept alive by Scarborough dutifully paying her portion of the annuity of £16 intended to support her and the four youngest children each month, which she promptly drank. In 1866, her youngest child Charles, who had been a baby when Gilbert Marshall perished, was arrested in Flemington for stealing about 30 pounds (14 kilograms) of fat from the city abattoirs. He had been 'nearly naked' and trying to sell the fat to Scarborough's wife. The court dismissed the charge of theft and called on Scarborough to appear before the court to answer for this neglect.[36] Charles, then aged eleven, subsequently disappeared from the historical record.

Also in 1866, Janet remarried, taking as her new husband a John Danley Harris, 'of somewhat bloated appearance', who took advantage of her increasing confusion and illiteracy and succeeded in having the Supreme Court appoint him receiver to her estate. This now consisted of an income of around £300 a year from the farm at Plenty and the renting of other property in Melbourne—each of Janet's eight surviving children would be entitled to £300 cash as soon as Charles was twenty-one. Janet was now meant to receive £200 a year, except that Harris took it all. He had been ordered by the courts to pay her 30 shillings a month, but by 1876 he had deserted her and evaded the police.[37] As it was, Janet was in and out of gaol. Soon after Harris began taking her money in 1867, already scantily dressed, she deliberately undressed herself at the Russell Street police barracks, refused to leave when ordered, and was taken into custody for vagrancy. The following year she was sent to the hulks for six months. She was becoming more confused and subject to fits. In February 1871 she threw herself onto the railway tracks at Hawthorn, adroitly moving to between the rails at the approach of a train. In 1880 she died alone in the Immigrants Home of epilepsy. Her sons, aside from Charles, continued to farm at Plenty.

George Scarborough remained involved with Gilbert Marshall's land into the 1870s. He remarried and carefully transferred the title of his acreage near Rockbank to his sons, leaving only cash in his will as a sufficiency for his second wife. At least four grandsons bearing his family name served in World War I, and he was remembered fondly by fellow pioneers as a member of John Batman's party.

In 1905, Victoria's oldest pioneer, Mrs Louisa Humphries, who had come to Van Diemen's Land in the first free emigrant ship, remembered:

> George Scarborough, quite a character, was the first pound keeper and the first pound was near the river bank between Swanston and Russell streets. We went to the first races held at Flemington in 1840 in Scarborough's bullock-dray. Coming home, Scarborough was three sheets in the wind, and we came down Batman's Hill through Collins-street at racing pace. Mrs Scarborough and I, who were sitting on the bottom of the dray, being nearly tipped out when the bullocks rounded into Elizabeth street.[38]

STRATEGIES FOR SUCCESS

The path to respectability, or at least invisibility, in Van Diemen's Land had often involved being appointed a constable or attaching oneself as a valued servant or overseer to a settler. Similarly, once in Victoria, close attachment to a master or patron built a new character. Loyalty was essential, a tradition of master and servant that was only a little better than the position of being an assigned convict. Yet it was customary, and the best path to a home and household for those without land.

Peter Appleyard, the Tadcaster father of three who stole four ducks, was able to obtain permission to remarry on the grounds of no contact from his wife or that she had died, and married a young free immigrant, Harriet Wheatley. Emancipists who married non-convicts often did better than those who chose fellow prisoners. In 1846, the couple moved to Alberton, Gippsland, where Peter rose to be the permanent overseer for a Scottish squatter, John Gellion.[39] The Gellion lineage did not survive beyond World War II, but the Appleyards became a vast extended family, just one branch alone providing six sons for the First AIF, with two making the supreme sacrifice. The Appleyards became farmers and leading sportsmen and continue to live in the region.

Making money on your own account was easiest for those with driving skills who could venture into carrying, which is how William Goodall made the funds to buy land at Merri, near Warrnambool; however, when he found it subject to flooding, he moved to a new farm he called 'Wanstead', at Allansford. He was a founding member of the Warrnambool Wesleyan church, and today, Goodall and Wanstead streets in the township commemorate him. One of his sons became a law clerk. Another, his namesake, William, learned an Aboriginal language through playing with local children, and at the age of twenty-three, after spending time as a schoolteacher, he was appointed the manager of the Aboriginal reserve at Framlingham. He would devote his life to Aboriginal Victorians, until the forced removal, against his entreaties, of people from the Corranderrk reserve to the one at Lake Tyers. At Framlingham he would be remembered for his encouragement of young men to seek work outside the station and for teaching them football and cricket. As the manager of Corranderrk, his administration was more troubled.[40] But over his long public service, the convict's son repaired a little of the terrible hurt inflicted on Aboriginal people.

The Goodalls were not the only ex-convicts to commit themselves to the Aboriginal people. John Hinkins (*Earl St Vincent*, 1826) was a literate young Londoner, seemingly in a complicated relationship with a woman who kept a house of ill fame (or so he alleged). When she failed to keep him as she had promised, he stole two watches and pawned them; he was twenty-one. Under sentence he was difficult, absent from his place, thieving, dealing, receiving 100 lashes over three offences, and was confined to a chain gang. After two years of freedom, working as a shoemaker, he married a free immigrant, Jane Theobald, who bore two children, but she died after giving birth to their daughter in 1840. Hinkins was now a single father, and in 1842 he tried his luck at Port Albert as a shoemaker, with a local businessman lending him some cash to get started. However, he was cheated out of his hut and furnishings. He then went to Melbourne, where he found work managing a sheep run with 2000 animals at Gunbower, 12 miles (19 kilometres) from Mount Hope on the Lower Murray. His son stayed in Melbourne for schooling, while his young daughter went with him up-country, as he had had great difficulty in placing her in private care. On arrival at Gunbower, Hinkins and his daughter were greeted by a large group of Aboriginal people who had heard that a new master was arriving with a 'white pickaninny'. Little Jane, blonde and blue-eyed, helped create an apparent bond of affection between the ex-convict and 'the blacks'.[41]

Hinkins blossomed in the role of authoritative white master, missionary, and benevolent protector of the 'native race'. In his memoirs, published posthumously by his second wife in 1884, he found the dreaded Lower Murray blacks to be the 'best of friends' once they were treated well. Hinkins returned to Geelong after two years with a new mission: to help Aboriginal people, in particular orphaned—or believed to be orphaned—boys. He adopted two and educated them, although their adult lives were troubled. He also found a new career as a teacher after marrying the widow running the school attended by his daughter. He was now respectable and respected, finally settling in Moonee Ponds, where he founded the local school and built the post office in Mount Alexander Road, which provided a steady income and a public position for the rest of his life.[42] Along with Thomas Halfpenny (*Lady Harewood*, 1829), John Hinkins was one of only four Vandemonians out of 713 pioneers who featured in TF Chuck's photographic montage *The Explorers and Early Colonists of Victoria*, completed in 1872. A third was Samuel Marlow (*Sir Godfrey Webster*, 1823).

THE PUBLICAN NETWORK

It was the drink trade, brewing and owning a public house, as did Gilbert Marshall and Tulip Wright, that could quickly raise capital for investment in land. Samuel Marlow was a Londoner from The Boro (Southwark). He arrived early in Port Phillip with John Mills (*Andromeda*, 1827), who had been assigned to Henry Stallard, from whom he learned brewing. By 1836, Mills, a free man, had married sixteen-year-old Hannah Hale, whose family had emigrated from Gloucestershire, specifically a village near Mills' own native place. In 1837, John and Hannah, along with Samuel Marlow, arrived in Port Phillip on the *Enterprize*. Mills was already a wealthy man, though he only lived until 1841, leaving his young daughter Emma, born in 1838, a minor heiress—she would marry William à Beckett, the judge, and become the greatly loved grandmother of the Boyd family of artists and writers. Samuel Marlow likewise brewed beer and also made cordial and ran a hotel, living the rest of his life in inner Melbourne; he was a man born to the city. But Marlow had another talent as a self-trained architect, designing Tavistock House in Flinders Lane, the remnants of which survive under an Edwardian makeover. He too speculated in land, selling 283 acres (114 hectares) near Dandenong in 1864. However, by the time he died aged eighty-three in 1882, he was blind, his house in Goldie Lane was neglected, and his surviving daughter, who had married another former convict, was widowed.

The fourth pioneer with a portrait, William Sidebottom (*Medway*, 1825), was another link in this chain of Vandemonian ex-convict brewers. The second son of a respectable family named Langford, at the age of twenty-five he was convicted for life for highway robbery under his mother's maiden name of Sidebottom. After a convict career that included two floggings and four and a half years at Maria Island, he received a conditional pardon in 1836. He moved to Launceston where he came under the patronage of John Mills, following the brewer to Port Phillip; investing in land, including dubious deals with John Batman; opening public houses in central Melbourne and at Pentridge (Coburg); and setting up at the latter as a farmer. He also married the sister of John Mills' wife, following a common pattern of former convicts marrying within their own trusted circle. A month after his marriage in 1839, he was granted an absolute pardon, but rather than return to England, he persuaded his family to join him in Port Phillip and to take the name Sidebottom, so as not to undermine his new reputation. The Sidebottoms/Langfords became prominent settlers in the Mickleham district and leading members of the Methodist Church. William died in 1849 having built a platform of land and wealth that elevated his brothers and their descendants into prosperity.

Of course, in the history of convict founders, such success stories are the tip of the iceberg. Success, as ever, depended on luck, connections and a means of raising cash to buy cheap land that would appreciate quickly in value. Carting and beer were the easiest pathways to quick cash, and intermarriage and careful cultivation of Vandemonian connections who remained sober and capable were essential. Beautiful expirees or the children of expirees could marry out of obscurity and poverty. But of all the convict groups, the Jews were probably the most successful simply because of their powerful community connections that provided both social and financial support.[43]

THE DEMONISATION OF THE VANDEMONIANS

Free immigrants soon overwhelmed the Vandemonians in Port Phillip. Ten thousand arrived in 1841, almost doubling the population, and just in time for a sudden depression. Work was so scarce that the government provided jobs for 350 married men, building dams and roads, while families crowded into huts and cottages in noisome alleys. In 1846, the respectable inhabitants of the western junction of Lonsdale and Elizabeth streets in Melbourne (then, as now, prone to flooding), 'loudly complained of a rookery of disorderly houses in the rear of their premises, in which, night after night, the most outrageous orgies are perpetrated'.[44] Further east along Lonsdale Street, a huge hole of filth consumed the road, and a red-light district centred on Little Bourke Street was full of tenants whose 'squalid and wretched appearance show they are little given to honest industry'. Pools of stagnant water enriched with human, animal and vegetable waste were to be seen at nearly every door.[45] It had taken just a decade for the new settlement of Melbourne to develop backstreet slums.

By 1846, Port Phillip had 23 531 residents, with more than half of them living in Melbourne. New immigrants were reluctant to live in the bush, but many Vandemonians, even those born in big cities, had become excellent bushmen and were willing to do so. The bush also offered a refuge from discrimination, especially if an ex-convict could attach himself to a master as patron. In the towns, the fresh immigrants had little tolerance of current or past felons: the appeal of Port Phillip was its reputed freedom from the taint of convictism. But as the colonial economy recovered, labour shortages, especially up-country, forced the squatters to organise immigration schemes from Van Diemen's Land: bringing single men and married couples to Geelong and Portland for employment in the Western District, and paying shepherds £25 or £35 a year.

These Vandemonian migrants were more visible, often because they came as married couples who were initially more stable, or as unmarried, unsettled men who gravitated to Melbourne or Geelong where they got into trouble for drunkenness or crime. Many among the immigrants under the Geelong and Portland Bay Emigration Scheme were the children of convicts, like young William Pretty (*Surrey*, 1829), who started as a tinsmith in Melbourne but whose life collapsed under his increasing alcoholism and violence. A few in the scheme were married couples, such as William and Martha Guise. Martha Bellamy (*Sovereign*, 1827), a seventeen-year-old prostitute in Soho, London, had caused the surgeon on her ship much trouble because of her sexual misconduct on the deck. She remained rebellious as an assigned convict, until she married William Guise (*Chapman*, 1824) and grew her family of eight children. The Guises arrived in Geelong in 1846 with four young children and by 1851 they had become lodging housekeepers in Yarra Street, Ashby—where they would appear in court again, but this time as witnesses rather than in the dock. William then found security in Melbourne as the watchman at the flagstaff used for signalling between the town and the port of Melbourne, a sinecure that enabled the purchase of a cottage in Station Street, Carlton. The Guises had put their pasts behind them and established a lineage, even though at William's death only three adult children were still alive.

William Wildman (*Clyde*, 1830) was sufficiently literate to be employed as a clerk in the Convict Department, but he kept on thieving and was reconvicted, serving fifteen years instead of his original seven. As soon as he was cut free, in 1845, he came to Geelong under the emigration scheme. In 1848 he was arrested in Sydney on a charge of forgery with two others: the cheque in question was for £72, and a witness had been told that 'Wildman was a very clever fellow and could do anything, and that he [Wildman's accomplice, Williams] and Wildman made a very good thing of it at Melbourne by drawing cheques'. Wildman was sentenced to ten years' transportation, but by March 1851 he had a ticket-of-leave for Moreton Bay, only to abscond and continue to forge cheques until he was recaptured and recharged that December. By May 1856, he was reported to be one of the 'most expert forgers the old country has produced'. He was indicted in Melbourne again for forgery with the Vandemonian Francis Huxley. Huxley, like William Pretty, had been transported as the child of a convict, in this case as one of Ann Huxley's five children, in the *Edward* in 1834—the Huxleys were to produce three generations of offenders in Melbourne, remaining active until the 1930s.

Some could not wait until they received their conditional pardon. Nancye Robertson (*Rajah*, 1841), who had been convicted with her cousin Jane Robertson (Cavanagh) as young homeless travellers around Inverness, had a turbulent time under sentence and was determined to escape with her husband to Port Phillip in 1847. They conceived the cunning plan of hiding her in a box in the hold of the *Shamrock*, except that hay was placed over it, blocking the airholes.

Her corpse rapidly decomposed from the heat of the engine, so that when the smell alerted the crew to investigate, they found her with her eyes popping and her tongue protruding and she had to be buried at sea. Her young husband sobbed on discovering what had happened.

The tide of Vandemonians began to cause alarm—one estimate was of at least 3000 in the years 1845 to 1846. While government men had been welcome up-country, this was not the case in the towns. Vandemonians were attractive employees in that they could be paid less than free immigrants, but a number of firms, it was reported, had found this to be a false economy when their ungrateful, underpaid Vandemonian staff took off with the stock or the cash.[46] There had always been anxiety about any contamination of Port Phillip and South Australia by convicts, but their labour was necessary. By the late 1840s, as their numbers were increasing, the so-called 'Pentonville Exiles', men on tickets-of-leave from England, were being imported: they were young, possibly incorrigible, and therefore had been dubbed 'Pentonvillains' to pair with the demonised 'Vandemonians'. But there was another demographic: convict women were becoming widowed or being deserted, and the older convicts were breaking down in health and drifting to the towns to beg and find a bed and some light employment.

The Argus deplored the case of a feeble and destitute old man lying in the streets, too weak to work: 'who is supposed to have been shipped at Van Diemen's Land with a view to getting rid of them at the future cost of Port Phillip'. At least the authorities were kinder than *The Argus*: the mayor procured a cab to convey the helpless man to gaol, and a Dr Cussen promised to provide eight days of care.[47] In the same issue, *The Argus* reported on a dying recent arrival from Van Diemen's Land who was incoherent from lunacy. In November, the paper began to report on the origins of people appearing before the Criminal Sessions. Among the horse stealers was the convict author Owen

Suffolk and a certain Margaret Richmond nee Richards (*Hindostan*, 1839): of the seventeen cases, five were Pentonvillains, seven were from Van Diemen's Land, and six had arrived free, including the only one charged with murder.[48] *The Argus* had a new owner and editor, Edward Wilson, a radical and a fierce opponent of convict transportation, so Van Diemen's Land now became the 'Dust hole'. Wilson pushed a theme of 'Vandemonian Pollution' blamed on the island's governor, Sir William Denison, who was ridding the place of 'the worst part of her population by driving them over to this Province'.[49]

'Vandemonian Pollution' fed a deeper fear of depraved people, a human subspecies whose internal moral squalor 'fret channels down their cheeks'. Homophobia, ignited by the *Molesworth Report*, compounded the horror.[50] Richard Howitt could find them in a crowd, writing in 1845 of the peculiarities of Australian life: 'you see many people not to be mistaken; hard-face, grim-visaged dry-countenanced workmen—and women too—whom at a glance you recognize to have been convicts. Even among the richer folk there are some, not disguised by dress or wealth.'[51]

By the end of 1850, around 4000 convicts and ex-convicts had joined the 60 000-strong population of Port Phillip, of whom 23 143 were in Melbourne and 8000 in Geelong. There were more than 300 000 head of cattle, almost six million sheep, and room for merely 5000 traditional owners of the land. Then, on 6 February 1851, the bush exploded into the most extensive fire in Victoria's history. 'Black Thursday' would be first in the series of 'black days' that have savaged the state's flora and fauna and destroyed homes and lives ever since. The people who had curated the landscape with cultural burning and extended horticulture were now dead or on the run. The legacy of European colonisation would now be a land beset by unstoppable fires.

CHAPTER 4

Topsy-turvy

One of the greatest wonders of the present day is the number of formerly poor men who are now daily drawing large sums of money from the local banks in exchange for gold and cheques for gold. A person of some experience who has come down from goldfields declares it as his opinion that generally speaking the Vandemonian expirees are the most fortunate of the diggers, a very large proportion of them having managed to secure their fair share of the 'nuggets'.

GEELONG ADVERTISER, 12 DECEMBER 1851, p. 2

Gold changed everything.[1] Suddenly, the distant and tainted British colony was offering instant riches. Dennis O'Reilly sang that you 'could pick up lumps of gold' while 'gold dust lay all around the streets and miners' rights were free'.[2] And at Mount Alexander in the early weeks, they did exactly that, picking nuggets out of the earth. The luckiest diggers were those who were first on the scene—shepherds and bush labourers, farmers and graziers, local trades and businesses. After the first discoveries at Clunes and Anderson's Creek, Buninyong, Ballarat and Bendigo followed with spectacular finds. Poor men and women, with no property or capital to their name, might now get fabulously rich. It was intoxicating. Men abandoned their masters, their families and their businesses. They were either 'anxious pilgrims' or small tradesmen 'who cannot dig' but who were 'compelled from stagnation of trade to follow their runaway customers'.[3] Hundreds a week were leaving Melbourne; from Geelong one day in September, 'thirteen pedestrians' were observed in company, 'dressed up in new tin dishes, tin plates, tin pots, tin pannikins, which reflecting the sun's rays, gave them the appearance of huge animated brilliants'. Meanwhile, a gentleman on horseback, with a crowbar as a horsewhip, was hurrying about the town offering 'good old hands 12 shillings a day and their grub to go gold digging for him'.[4]

While gold had been discovered in Victoria in 1849, and its value confirmed by the Vandemonian jeweller Charles Brentani (*Aurora*, 1835), fear of Californian-style disorder prompted the government to suppress the news.[5] This time, it could not be concealed. The Australian colonies had been fascinated and horrified by the Californian goldfields, and some adventurers, like James Esmond, who would make the first discovery at Clunes, had set off across the Pacific, staying long enough to develop an eye for auriferous country. The early findings were staggering and utterly irresistible. It was going to be even bigger than California, and everyone wanted to join the rush. In the first week of August 1851, GH Wathen found fifty men at work at Clunes, as well as a woman who had set up a laundry within an enclosure of green boughs to service the diggers 'with great profit to herself'. There were settlers, servants from the bush, artisans from the towns. However,

> A volley of rank Vandemonian slang thickly interlarded with oaths issuing from groups here and there, showed that 'old hands' and 'Pentonvillains' were not wanting—the elements

of vice and crime which (thanks to the paternal policy of the Colonial Office) are so largely diffused through the land, were already at work in this infant community.[6]

By late 1851, 7000 people had arrived by sea from other colonies and over 20 000 were scrambling over the Castlemaine diggings. There was scant water, the flies were terrible, food supplies were uncertain, and there were no police to speak of. Sanitation was unspeakable and 'colonial fever', or typhoid and dysentery, began to cut through the diggers. Still, in 1852, a further 14 000 people would arrive from New South Wales, 15 000 from South Australia and Western Australia, 1000 from New Zealand, and, most alarmingly of all, 19 000 just from Van Diemen's Land. And these were just the recorded arrivals. Many unrecorded thousands came overland or via secret, private voyages across Bass Strait, leaving no trace of their arrival.

Thomas Watkins and Mrs Watkins set sail for Port Phillip aboard the *Pilot* on 6 January 1852 and Ellen was in court for theft by March: Thomas the elder may have gone to the diggings; young Thomas had disappeared from the historical record.[7] In February 1853, it seemed that the flash mob had joined her, as she was one of three 'gaily dressed women' who were gaoled for being 'inmates of a house of ill-repute in Flinders Lane, and being associates of thieves and vagabonds'. They were now 'well-known to the police' and carrying considerable money, which the court ordered be directed towards their care in gaol.[8]

Catherine Murray (*Emma Eugenia*, 1843), a youthful graduate of the streets of Liverpool, also left for Melbourne in January 1852 with three male accomplices. She had a refined modus operandi, feigning both respectability and distress, that attracted sympathetic male attention until her team caught the victim off-guard and rifled his pockets. It was all downhill from there: there was the use of 'vile and disgusting language', and various assaults on other women and a boy, the last with a knife. In January 1859, Catherine was charged with abandoning her infant child, who died the following year. She herself died (as Catherine Thornton) in Yarra Bend Lunatic Asylum of phthisis in 1863.[9]

By 1853, the colonials were to be swamped by the arrivals from overseas: mostly from the British Isles, including Ireland, but there were significant groups of Germans, Italian-Swiss, French, Scandinavians and, of course, Americans. By the end of the decade, half a million newcomers had passed through the colony, with half of them destined to stay. Victoria was suddenly the place to be for the adventurous and the greedy, for the charlatan and the booster, for the family settler and the professional, for the tubercular and the thief. Historians then and since have celebrated the 'marvellous generation' of gold rush immigrants who went on to shape a distinctive culture, with institutions, habits and values that built a colonial liberalism. Gold and tuberculosis brought gifted young people who sought adventure, opportunity and quick riches, and those whose wretched lungs needed sunshine and clean air.

A young Irish doctor, Richard Tracy, frustrated by an overcrowded profession, tossed up between joining the army and heading to the colonies, chose the latter, and after arriving in a near-deserted Adelaide, set off himself for the Loddon goldfields—only to discover that he could do better as a physician. By 1856 he had found a partner in Dr John Maund, who had emigrated for his health, and they established the Melbourne Lying-In Hospital, now the Royal Women's Hospital, to care for the many women left pregnant and unprotected while their menfolk went to the diggings. Over time, other health refugees joined them as consultants. Both men were brilliant—Maund as a laboratory scientist, Tracy as a surgeon—but they were only two among an astonishingly talented professional class that suddenly appeared in Victoria. Tracy was among the founders of the colony's first professional medical society and its medical journal, and he was the first lecturer in obstetrics in Australasia's pioneering medical school at the new University of Melbourne. Another fine mind was Baron von Mueller, creator of Melbourne's Royal Botanic Gardens and a champion of Australian flora around the world; he too had a bad chest. Still another brilliant young immigrant was William Henry Archer, an actuary and keen member of the London Statistical Society, where he had come under the influence of the father of modern vital statistics, Dr William Farr. When Archer was invited to become the colony's statistician and its first registrar of births, deaths and marriages, he found himself able to implement the full recommendations of the London Statistical Society, endowing Victoria with the best vital registration regime in the English-speaking world.

This was emblematic of the tidal wave of modernity that engulfed Victoria in the 1850s, embodied in a ready-made middle class built from an immigrant population that had paid its own way—this would not be replicated again in Australian history until the 2010s.[10] Even the poor Irish who came as assisted immigrants needed to have more means to pay for the accompaniments of the longer voyage to Australia. Melbourne became the most literate place in the British Empire. Many of the arrivals were talented men and women who were interested in changing the way politics was organised and how land was distributed. They were interested in changing the way politics was organised and how land was distributed. Charles Gavan Duffy was perhaps the most gifted politician to disembark, in 1856, making his mark quickly and giving his name to land Acts to feed the property hunger that drove both rich and poor. But while the hope of land was more than a spark in many an immigrant's eye, gold suddenly produced the cash to boost what had been a pastoral economy dependent on the seasons and distant sales of wool. Now there was a growing local market for meat and food, beer and spirits, boots and shoes, and there was cash to buy it with.

Historians from Karl Marx to Eric Hobsbawm to Geoffrey Blainey have argued that the Californian and Australian gold rushes marked the foundation of the 'global industrial economy'. In 1853, Australia bought 15 per cent of the total value of goods exported from Great Britain, and the massive increase in British exports to North America and Australia from 1846 to 1853 revived Britain's stagnating economy. As Blainey has noted, this 'sent a chain reaction of prosperity around much of the civilized world'. Gold created new money, new money created new wealth, and new wealth profoundly changed society.[11] Geoffrey Serle was to argue that the disordered morals of Victoria's golden age would reach their apogee in the disgraces of the land boom and the bank collapses by the end of the century.[12]

LUCKY DIGGERS

Not only were the vile Vandemonians in the midst of this brave new Britain, they were first to the gold. It would prove very difficult later for them to win recognition for their discoveries—indeed, at the time, it proved equally difficult for them to hold on to their new wealth. Almost forty years after the discovery of gold at Bendigo Creek in late 1851, no-one had made a claim and it was still contested. In 1890, one Henry Fencham petitioned the Victorian Parliament to hold a select committee of inquiry, and twelve others, either on their own or family members' behalf, made claims to the £1000 reward.[13] The squatters and gentlemen demanded their entitlements, although at the time they were relying on the work of their employees and wished to suppress the news so that their shearers did not run off, while they were trying to sell scabby sheep. Two women, wives of the Ravenswood overseer and the station cooper, Mrs Kennedy and Mrs Farrell, claimed they had panned for specimens after Mr Kennedy returned from Mount Alexander and told them that the gravel in the creek looked similar to what he'd seen on his trip. Today, they are generally credited with the discovery, the only women so honoured in the Victorian gold canon. Yet the 1890 inquiry seemed to find, without naming them, that it was a station hand—Christian Asquith (*Maria*, 1820), the hut keeper—and a pair of shepherds—James Graham (likely arrived on the *Sir Charles Forbes*, 1823) and Benjamin Bannister (*Aurora*, 1835)—who had told the ladies about the gold. The three ex-convicts all died as poor men, only Asquith leaving a family that survived to remember him and make the claim. Yet other evidence presented named an Aboriginal trooper, Johnson, from Sydney, as the finder.

The history of the Bendigo finds is thus an inverse hierarchy of social inferiority. The women remembered the bullying by the squatters, who considered gold found on their land to be theirs, and the fear of violence while in the family huts on their own until they were able to buy three licences. Even then, they had no cash and could only pay in gold, while remaining at the mercy of gold dealers to give them a fair price. What mattered was secrecy. 'Those were very queer times,' wrote William Edward Coleman to the committee of inquiry, 'and it was necessary about giving information to inquisitive strangers.'

Those who found gold then had to run the gauntlet of officials, dealers, bankers, landowners, fellow diggers and thieves to hold on to it and make away with their new wealth. Serle estimated that more men died at the diggings than made a fortune, although many made enough of a living to persist for years, dreaming of El Dorado.[14] How many lost their gold through fraud, theft and drunkenness, we will never know. Those who made some real money kept quiet and sober, and their success has been passed down through their families, not via the public record.

Samuel Phillips, the poacher from Corby in Northamptonshire, after a quiet time in Van Diemen's Land, travelled to Port Phillip at the end of April 1852. Twenty months later, he sailed for England aboard the SS *Great Britain*. On 30 March 1854, six weeks after he'd landed at Liverpool, there was a double service in the parish church at Colby, where Samuel married the Sarah Patrick whom he had left behind, twenty-four years before; the second service was to christen their first grandchild, the son of the daughter Sarah had been carrying when Samuel was transported. Neither of them had married during that quarter-century, and they were both still illiterate. But there was more. On 17 May 1855, Samuel paid £1038 (more than $200 000 in today's money) for 38 acres (15 hectares) of freehold woodland. As his descendant Jane Starsmore Duvall has noted:

> The land was situated in the Parish of Passenham, in Northamptonshire, about 40 miles [64 kilometres] from Weldon. It was part of the former Royal Forest of Whittlewood that had been disafforested by an Act of Parliament in 1853 that permitted the government to sell the land to raise funds. It was in an 'out of the way' location but was also immediately adjacent to Wakefield Lodge and Estate which, at that time, was the country residence of the Duke of Grafton.
>
> The choice of this property is interesting for several reasons: firstly, because it cost a large amount of money; secondly, because the purchase was made at an auction which was a common means of sale in VDL; thirdly, because creating the farm would require pioneer skills similar to those used in VDL; fourthly, because it had been part of a Royal Forest, like Rockingham Forest where Samuel was born; fifthly, because

it suggests a willingness to thumb his nose up to authority by choosing to be a Duke's next door (and probably unwelcome) neighbour; and lastly, because it shows a remarkable sense of purpose and prudence.[15]

The farm and the beautiful stone house that Samuel built are still in the family; the farm is worked to this day. The grandson christened on Samuel's return became a Conservative county councillor. Samuel Phillips had kept his pot of gold.

In 1888, Alexander Sutherland included a modest biography in his grand *Victoria and Its Metropolis* of a modest pioneer, James Kimber, who was celebrated as being a citizen who had fed the people with his market gardens, orchard and bacon curing. His was a story of hard work and good fortune. He had been working as a gardener in Richmond, and raising his young family, when news of the gold finds disrupted the colony and he joined the first rush. In fifteen months he made £1500. This he invested in 15 acres (6 hectares) in South Preston, worked it for fifteen years, then let it out on rental. He purchased undeveloped property in Richmond, including half an acre from Dr McCrae in Rotherwood Street, bordering Mulberry Street. There he built Mulberry Cottage, retiring from business around 1878. He invested wisely in both farming and urban land and endowed his four surviving children with a useful inheritance.[16] What Alexander Sutherland did not know, but which James Kimber apparently did not hide from his family, was that on 23 November 1830, as James Kimmer, he had gone to Totteridge farm, which dominated his village at Milton Lilbourne, near Pewsey in Wiltshire, and smashed Richard Litten's new threshing machine. Mobs of up to 500 were roaming the countryside, demanding higher wages and threatening arson and violence against farmers and parsons. Kimber was eighteen years old, and he focused on the machine that was destroying the livelihood of his family and neighbours. On 8 January 1831, along with twenty-three other Swing Rioters, he was sentenced to seven years' transportation to Van Diemen's Land aboard the *Eliza*.

The Swing Rioters had been warmly welcomed in the penal colony for their superior farming skills, and Kimber was assigned to the Van Diemen's Land Company in the north-west of the island. There, he did so well growing vegetables and fruit that the fractious manager, Edward Curr, used Kimber's one disciplinary lapse—being in the company of a female servant in his master's plantation—to prevent his being granted a ticket-of-leave; this female servant may well have been his future wife, a free emigrant from Ireland. In 1836, the Swing Rioters, with a small number of exceptions, were given full pardons in consideration of their superior conduct as useful prisoners and the outrage in England at their severe prosecution in the first place. Kimber began making a name for himself in Van Diemen's Land for his prize-winning cucumbers of around 23 inches (58 centimetres), and from 1838 he did well in Melbourne as a gardener, until the gold rush transformed his fortunes. He died a 'gentleman', aged eighty-seven, from asthenia after a tram accident. His estate went for probate at nearly £10,000 comprising land and mortgages, apparently well managed, yet he still signed with a cross.[17]

LIGHT-FINGERED GENTRY

James Kimber and Samuel Phillips were expirees who could 'pass': the convict taint was not visible in a ruined face and rough language. Those who were afflicted with what was called the 'Vandemonian cast' aroused instant suspicion. In the midst of all this delirious excitement there was a problem: the moral rottenness embodied in Australia's convict origins and the human beings who had survived them. They were a social pollutant. They threatened the bright new reputation of the golden colonies. Worse, their numbers were being inflated by the transportation of the Pentonville Exiles. The discovery of gold might bring to the Australian colonies the moral mayhem of California:

> Another [danger] is that when the mines are inundated with the refuse of the colony—the Pentonvillains of Victoria, the expirees of Van Diemen's Land—there should be acted in this colony those fearful scenes of rapine and murder which have made California a bye-word and a reproach.[18]

And by the end of 1851, that was believed to have happened. As eager gold seekers flocked into Victoria, Melbourne had just ten police in a population of 30 000:

> Our streets are scenes of drunkenness and riot and are traversed at the risk of being knocked down and trampled on by the horse of some furious and unskilful rider. Those robberies that were formerly attempted under cover of darkness, are now fearlessly perpetrated in open daylight, and numerous instances have occurred in the last two days in which bushmen have been surrounded, held and plundered, by the scamps who infest the various public houses. Yesterday two fellows entered a lodging in Queen-street, kept by a man named Wood, and robbed the inmates of £40. On Wednesday night, two respectable young men were stopped near the Catholic church at an early hour in the evening by a party of seven ruffians, who placed their hands over their mouths, and plundered them of £9. On the same evening, an unfortunate sailor was met near the burial ground by two fellows, who presented a pistol at him, and compelled him to deliver five ounces of gold and two

one-pound notes, and then nearly stunned him by a blow on the head with [the] butt end of their weapons, and by this time tomorrow we expect to hear of more than one deed of violence and perhaps bloodshed.[19]

On the roads to and from the diggings, especially through the Black Forest, bushrangers were holding up gold escorts and stripping diggers of their gold and personal possessions. The most daring and dashing was Captain Francis Melville, a Scot of various names transported as Edward/Francis Malvelle/McCallum/Melville on the *Minerva* in 1838. He came to Port Phillip in October 1851, posing as a gentleman, and within two months had decided that bushranging was more profitable. As self-proclaimed leader of the Mount Macedon gang, he attacked travellers in the Black Forest, then moved west into the Wimmera, holding up isolated station owners. He raided the Mackinnon family at Marida Yallock and, after ordering the daughters to entertain him, played the piano himself and sang for them. He left himself open to capture by celebrating recent hauls at Christy's Inn at Geelong, where his boasting and the £500 reward offered for his capture proved irresistible to a local woman. His most notorious days were in fact in captivity aboard the hulks in Port Phillip Bay: he attempted to bite off a sergeant's nose; he incited a mutiny. And, after a period of good behaviour where he was permitted to work in the Port Gellibrand quarry and ostensibly translate the Bible into an Aboriginal language, he in fact prepared a daring escape with eight others, including another Vandemonian bushranger, Harry Power (*Isabella*, 1842), who would later mentor the young Ned Kelly. The party captured a towboat, with a constable Owens as hostage. As the water police closed in on them, one of the fugitives smashed Owens' skull and leapt into the sea to his death. Melville was reported as saying when captured: 'I would sooner have died than suffer what I have been subjected to in these hulks the last four years.' The trials were a sensation and the culprits spared the death penalty on a legal nicety. Melville was transferred to the Melbourne Gaol, where he suffered outbursts of fury. Then, at dawn on 12 August 1857 a warder found him dead in his cell, strangled by a red-spotted scarf. It remains unknown whether it was by his own hand or that of another.[20]

A military detachment was brought in to guard the Treasury and the tent of the commissioner in charge of the goldfields, and troops were ordered to accompany the gold escorts. At night, the diggings rang out with the sounds of guns being fired into the air to warn would-be thieves that the tent owner was armed. As new rushes started, hordes of diggers were followed by grog sellers and prostitutes. Far from the gaze of the Melbourne authorities, the diggers believed they had no alternative but to take the law into their own hands.[21] They did so in Mount Alexander in February 1852, as a private letter republished in *Bell's Life in Sydney and Sporting Reviewer* the following month revealed:

> Numberless robberies are committed by bands of armed desperadoes, principally Vandemonians, who plunder openly in broad daylight; and no one dares stir from his tent at night. The honest portion of the diggers have been compelled, for want of police protection, to take the law into their own hands and adopt the Lynching code. They have made croppies of some, drowned others, and slung a lot up by the middle to limbs of trees. Last Monday they hung one outright for murdering his mate. This is a fearful state of things, but what is to be done![22]

The respectable saw the evil hand of Vandemonians everywhere. Even worse, they were becoming cocky and contemptuous of authority: one of the Melbourne city police saw a former 'flash man, dashing past him, well-dressed and well-mounted'. The constable recognised the 'gent' as a 'double-distilled vagabond' whom he had arrested for both theft and vagrancy. The 'gent' returned the stare and declared 'now he didn't care one damn for the rascally traps', and setting his spurs in his horse, was soon out of sight.[23] In early 1852, two 'recent importations from Van Diemen's Land' were charged with drawing a knife on a constable who had attempted to quell a fight between them in Bourke Street, when they said they were Vandemonians and were 'not to be bullied'.[24] Thus, it was not just the plunder and violence, it was the defiance of social norms, of proper authority, of the rights of the deserving privileged to remain deserving. Now, it was topsy-turvy. Poor men and women could also have gold—one used nuggets instead of bullets to fire his evening warning volley, it was said.

The defining trope of topsy-turvy, however, was popularised by the 'Digger's Wedding', published in Charles Dickens' *Household Words* and republished in the Australian newspapers in November 1853. This story started in a low lodging house in Little Bourke Street, where the 'nuggetter', with his pile of gold, seduced the 'impudent, vulgar, fat, flashy daughter' of the woman of the house. The bride 'would have been downright ugly but for a pair of great leering eyes of considerable brilliancy'. The marriage would be a sham, but for a glorious two weeks they would live like 'dookies and duchesses' while all of the man's old Vandemonian friends would share the joy: 'They ate, they drank, they smoked, they brawled—they made riot half the night and slept half the morning.' Then they drove around the town in carriages: the bride 'dressed in the most expensive satins and silks and flying ribbons; and the men in scarlet mining shirts, with short pipes in their mouths'. And when the money was finally spent, the bride returned to her mother's brothel and the miner to the diggings.[25]

Frances Perry, the witty and adventurous wife of the bishop of Melbourne, and co-founder with Richard Tracy and John Maund of the Lying-In Hospital, was a little more charitable on 2 September 1852:

After the mob, came a carriage and four dashing past, full of white veils and white satins. It is most amusing to see how completely the tables are turned. There is now a stand of some eighteen or twenty carriages in Collins Street; and these may be seen careering around all day long in parts of the town and suburbs, full of diggers, varied occasionally, as I have said with white veils. Fancy some of these inexpressibly awkward-looking, fat, firm, red-faced Irish girls from the unions, dressed out in the best satin, lace and flowers which Melbourne can produce![26]

The class anxiety was clear: these vulgar, common, ill-bred people did not know how to spend money with good taste and proper style, as immortalised in the watercolour 'The Diggers Wedding' by ST Gill in 1869. Here was all that was debauched, spendthrift, careless and, above all, undeserving. They were the 'cashed-up bogans' of the 1850s, and it simply wouldn't do.

Gold was the great disrupter that changed personal fortunes and economies, and therefore social relationships. It threatened the social order predicated on the privileged ownership of land.[27] It was an accelerant on the fires burning deep inside a society of resentments, exclusion and poverty. Implicit in lieutenant-governor Charles La Trobe's anxious dispatches to London was the fear of political disorder threatening property and propriety. Gold offered those trapped on the wrong side of the divide of respectability, and therefore without an entitlement to reward through work and success, sudden liberation from misery and humiliation. In an editorial of February 1852, *The Argus* thundered:

Lawlessness and utter confusion are fast thickening around, the felon prowls night and day for this prey; quiet, peaceable, industrious men are being rapidly driven to desperation and Judge Lynch rears his bloody head in the finest colony in the British Crown.[28]

Two days later, Thomas McCombie wrote from Stephen Street in Melbourne calling for better policing, especially at Forest Creek, and increased armed escorts for the gold through the Black Forest, as well as a post office. He too warned that if 'Judge Lynch' were permitted to take over, the colony's reputation would suffer immense damage.[29] A correspondent to *The Argus* went even further: 'Better a Judge Lynch than Turpinism.'[30]

But the dangers went beyond the diggings and the Black Forest. Lucky diggers wanted to celebrate. Nuggets and huge sums of cash were carried in the pockets of miners looking for alcohol and sex in Melbourne. The crime economy of the seaports that had educated so many young convicts in the arts of picking pockets, bilking and bashing, was supercharged with big rewards. If Ellen Miles could boast in her old age that she had spent 'thousands and thousands' on the colony in her time, these were the golden years when that was possible for common prostitutes and petty thieves.

Some Vandemonians were very deft operators. In January 1852, two successful diggers carrying 16 ounces (450 grams) of gold and £27 in notes shared a four-bed room at the Royal Oak Inn. In the other two beds were two Vandemonians who had only just landed the previous day. The diggers slept, but the Vandemonians remained 'wide awake', relieving their victims of their gold and notes without causing them to stir.[31] And there was the 'Vandemonian hug', which entailed being caught from behind with your arms pinned to your sides, while an accomplice relieved you of your money. There was little sympathy for the victims of bilking:

Margaret Robson, a bloated and disgusting specimen of fallen humanity, was charged at the City Court yesterday with robbing one Henry Hartman of £28 in a house of ill-fame in Lt Bourke Street. Hartman is one of those rude and navvy class of diggers who so frequently figure in such cases of depravity, having worked hard for a bit of gold on the diggings, and then foolishly and libidinously expose themselves to robbery on their return to town.[32]

At least Mr Hartman reported the theft to police. Gentlemen could generally be relied upon to be too embarrassed to do so.

Diggers were remarkably careless with their treasure. A digger known as 'Dr Thomas Hampton' took a room at a boarding house in Little Bourke Street East, by now Melbourne's red-light district, whose owner was known as 'Long Sam'. The digger converted his gold into 203 and a half sovereigns ($20 000 in today's money) and kept them safely until the next morning when he was going out early. Long Sam was still asleep, so the digger gave his sovereigns to Perry the cook, asking him to give it to the owner for safekeeping. Perry, naturally, was never seen again, nor was the money.[33] And on the first day of 1853, Mr Howard, a butcher in Little Bourke Street, was robbed of £400 from his premises, hardly the proceeds of recent meat sales in that district.[34]

But the most important currency of celebration, sex and crime was alcohol. Not only did too many who scraped a living out of Melbourne's meaner streets have a persistent thirst, but the alcohol they purchased, especially in the cheapest establishments, was lethal: higher in proof alcohol than permitted in Great Britain, and spruced up with various narcotics so that it could be watered down for sale without losing its potency. Drunkenness among the poor, therefore, could induce a level of violence and rage akin to modern methamphetamines.

Victorians preferred spirits to beer for serious drinking: brandy, rum, colonial whiskey. Champagne was for lavish celebration and high-class brothels, fine wines for the more refined. A man named Hobbs, newly arrived from Van Diemen's Land with his 'housekeeper' while his wife remained behind, was enticed by Luke Lindon (Luke Sindon, *Marquis of Hastings*, 1842) to take up lodgings with his family in Stephen (now Exhibition) Street. Lindon/Sindon kept the couple in a drunken stupor for two days with drugged ale and succeeded in extracting the £55 Hobbs had hidden under his pillow. Ann Sindon was later found with £42 18s 6d on her person, but the court was only able to convict her and her husband of vagrancy.[35]

The response of the authorities was not simply to police the crime wave, but to control public disorder with new laws regulating public houses, and against gambling and obscene language, against the sale of liquor, and against unauthorised mining on waste lands of the Crown. Prostitution remained legal but vagrancy was criminalised. Only consorting with prostitutes and profiting from them were offences: running or living in a 'disorderly house', living off earnings, associating with disorderly persons and vagabonds. Drunkenness was criminalised—and remained on the statute books until 2021 in Victoria (which had been among the last states in Australia to prosecute drunkenness), with often dire consequences for people who were ill as well as drunk, and who were confined to a local lock-up. All of these public order offences disciplined the rowdy behaviour of the very poor—the low life.[36] And their administration and prosecution would consume more time in the courts than any other offences and entrap many more Vandemonians for the rest of their moral careers than would felonies like robbery, robbery under arms, horse stealing, rape or murder.

For women in particular, their vulnerability when destitute would destroy them. Catherine Fleming (*Rajah*, 1841) was Irish-born, but her criminal career had developed on the streets of Liverpool. When transported at the age of twenty-two, she had already been on the town for nine years, since she was a child. No family was recorded in her indent. She was stunted and had been in prison for vagrancy nine times. Her crime was the seaport specialty of stealing from the person, this time the sum of £45 from a journeyman. Her ten years under sentence were tumultuous: absconding, drunkenness, indecent language, disorderly behaviour, and violence against another prisoner in an attempt to intimidate her. In July 1847 she was permitted to marry Thomas Bennett in Hobart, and she had her ticket-of-leave soon after. Now she could live with Bennett. Except that she couldn't. Soon it was reported to the Convict Department that, after a row when he threw her out of the house, she took a long knife and threatened murder.[37] Bennett left her and went to Melbourne, where he set up house with another. Once Fleming was cut free, she followed, but Bennett refused to take her in, so she took further to drink and 'other habits of dissipation'. In August 1856, in what was described as a 'scene of depravity', she was charged by Bennett with breaking his windows. She claimed he had deserted her; he counterclaimed that they had never been married; she responded by showing her marriage certificate. She was not convicted, but neither were her rights to support restored—the beginning of a long further career of prostitution, vagrancy, stealing from the person and drunkenness.[38]

George Pickering and Daniel Backway, who had been convicted on the same day at the Old Bailey, also made their way quickly to Victoria in 1852. Daniel made two exploratory trips, the first of which enabled him to claim a local vessel as his ship of arrival in Van Diemen's Land, thereby concealing his convict past. George also lied when he set sail in January 1852, claiming that Jane Eskitt/Escott/Hawkins

(*Garland Grove*, 1841) was his wife, when they in fact were to celebrate a September wedding in Scots' Church, Collins Street. Jane was from Glasgow, a first offender aged sixteen who had stolen money and drapery from her employer. She had few offences under sentence but was delivered of an illegitimate son, Samuel, who died in the Dynnyrne Nursery; she may well have had another child with George before they decamped. Even before they tied the knot, George was charged with a brutal assault on a female child named Hawkins.[39] His next assault was on Mary Harrold nee Lochrie (*Margaret*, 1843), from the streets of Glasgow, like his wife.[40] Two years after his wedding, he was in court for threatening to murder his wife and children, and this remained the pattern of the couple's domestic life until Jane disappeared and most of the children had died. When George was brought to court by the police, Jane always shrank from pressing charges.[41]

Protest meetings, an invigorated anti-transportation movement in both Sydney and Tasmania, and a hysterical press: all demanded the removal of the Vandemonian poison. It had not helped that the few constables present up to the discovery of gold had included expirees in their ranks, having been appointed officers while still under sentence: a pathway to redemption under the paper panopticon. The Melbourne police in particular preferred to go to the diggings—just two were on duty for the 1852 new year—which intensified the panic. A select committee led by a Peter Snodgrass discovered not merely a deficiency of numbers, but also rackets where constables were entitled to a portion of a fine imposed for an offence against public order: when drunkenness only imposed a fine of 5 shillings, obscene language was worth an enticing 30 shillings. The committee's report led to the formation in January 1853 of a colony-wide integrated police force for Melbourne, modelled on the London Metropolitan Police, and a largely mounted force for the goldfields and farming districts, modelled on the Royal Irish Constabulary. The officers were heavily armed.

But the question remained as to how serious the 'crime crisis' actually was.[42] Ross McMullin's analysis of court cases revealed an increase in crime as was to be expected with a gold rush, inadequate policing and rapid population growth.[43] The press took care to highlight the proportion of Vandemonians and Pentonvillains before the courts, yet a third to a half of the persons accused of felonies appeared to have arrived free—as did many of the women arrested for disorderly behaviour, having fallen foul of the desperate straits inflicted on unsupported women with no chance of respectable work. When the *Victorian Police Gazette* commenced in 1855, the immediate crisis was under control, but over the next forty years, fewer than 500 Vandemonian men could be identified among the discharged prisoners, and most of the relevant offences were against public order or involved petty thefts that secured the offender a warm, dry bed and a feed in gaol when they were homeless. The Tasmanian Founders and Survivors team have estimated from their knowledge of the departure records that perhaps 30 000 possible expirees and absconders crossed into Victoria. And looking at the criminal records, perhaps under 2000 men were to offend again, and over 200 of the women. Many more public order offences were recorded against ageing Vandemonians as they succumbed to the drink or sought a dry bed in a cell.[44]

Such 'facts' had no impact, however, on the moral panic of 'Vandemonaphobia', driven by a press that could see a winner for sales. If Vandemonians were 'all that was vile and disgraceful', they were also convenient scapegoats for a murderous frontier society that had been drink-sodden, violent and nasty for women and Indigenous people from the beginning.[45] Licentiousness could be projected onto those from 'the other side', and not only did transportation have to be stopped, but Golden Victoria itself must erect an immigration wall against the tide of corruption from across Bass Strait.[46] In the second half of 1852, a Convicts' Prevention Act was passed in the colony before being sent to London for final approval. As the gold seekers from overseas began to arrive from August 1852, one expiree on return to Tasmania reported: 'The place [Melbourne] is full of "Jemmys" [immigrants] and labour is dirt-cheap, but they'd sooner work there for five bob a day than come here for a pound. The down they've got on the Vandemonians is awful.'[47] But still they came, legislation or not, bribing police in Tasmania as absconders had already been doing, finding sympathetic ship's captains, concealing their convict pasts from the authorities.[48]

Among them, some time in 1853, came Daniel Backway, this time with his new young wife Mary Ann Moxham and her sister Elizabeth. They had come to settle. The sisters were daughters of a convict, Margaret Stevens, who had remarried John Moxham but was sliding into helpless alcoholism. Mary Ann was only seventeen and Daniel set out to reassemble the family, advertising in *The Argus* on 11 May 1854 for the brother John to write to his sisters, as they were very anxious to hear from him.[49] The London climbing boy was about to begin a working life as a skilled miner, to be followed by two generations of gold and coal miners in Victoria.

CHAPTER 5

Romeo Lane

Official appropriations of history, however ostensibly benevolent in intent and graced with accredited consultants, will always be chary of the actual mess and stink of the past, and as a consequence, they will always gravitate towards the condition of the theme park.

LUC SANTE, *THE OTHER PARIS* (2015), pp. 30–1

Today, Romeo Lane is a chic bar in Crossley Street, a short street that runs between Bourke and Little Bourke streets, nestling amidst what was the heart of the theatre district of gold-rush Melbourne. It commemorates a right-of-way first called Romeo Lane, which had a twin, further up the hill, known as Juliet Terrace. The waste ground between them was dubbed 'Bilking Square'. Juliet Terrace was eventually renamed Liverpool Street, just as Stephen Street was made respectable as Exhibition Street in 1880 to celebrate the International Exhibition. Since 1954, Pellegrini's Espresso Bar has graced the corner of the one-time Romeo Lane and Bourke Street.

In 1850, Mr Crossley was a butcher on the corner opposite that on which Pellegrini's now sits, and while his shop was presentable, he released the blood and guts from this butchery into Romeo Lane.[1]

There it mingled with vegetable and fish waste, along with the urine, vomitus and excreta of a community without adequate toilets and water. People dug cesspits, but with the city's solid clay base, the contents drained away slowly and the pits overflowed when it rained, thus 'with the slightest descent of rain upon the heaps of rubbish and putrefying matter which prevail in such abundance, the thoroughfares become literally impassable'.[2] Throughout the poorest parts of the city, a permanent sludge of human and animal waste spread under floorboards and across earthen floors. At the time Crossley was plying his trade, hundreds of homeless people, day workers and nocturnal visitors relieved themselves in rights-of-way and lanes, and they would do so for the rest of the century. (The first urinal for men was erected in Bourke Street in 1859, near Elizabeth Street, and the first underground toilets where women were accommodated in 1902.)

Melbourne soon resembled London, where rich and poor lived in adjacent streets and lanes, providing the rich with poor workers to exploit, and the poor with rich people to exploit, either honestly or dishonestly. While Melbourne's fine main streets filled with businesses, banks and houses, the poor crammed into the lanes and rights-of-way, living, raising children, working and dealing from tiny, filthy two-roomed cottages. Drinking places proliferated, both licensed and sly, and while some became 'dead houses' where the insensible could sleep off their consumption, others were places where prostitutes could take their clients, before making off with their wallets and watches.

James Reeves (*London*, 1844) and William Thomas (*Surrey*, 1842) robbed Thomas Edwards of £70 while he was 'conversing' with one of three women and four men in a house in Little Bourke Street on a Monday evening. He was seized by the throat and dragged into the yard by one of the men while another rifled his pockets. Nearly suffocating, he was unable to call for assistance until he left the house and found some police near a theatre, who went back with him and captured his assailants in the street—Reeves and Thomas had only £4 left on them, the remainder having been shared around.[3] Reeves and Thomas were both Londoners, as well as old hands. Londoners tended to gravitate to Melbourne, where they knew how to work an urban street economy, if not by crime then by dealing and street selling as costermongers.[4] They knew how to graft, pilfer and make do. George Pickering, once in the city, left it only to die in the Melbourne Benevolent Asylum in North Melbourne. He styled himself as an oysterman, which was in fact both selling oysters and acting as a bully for prostitutes—oyster bars were notorious as fronts for the sex trade. Another Londoner, and a 'villainous looking fellow', was William Dalton (*David Clarke*, 1841), who was sentenced to ten years' hard labour for highway robbery against Thomas Morris in a right-of-way off Little Bourke Street.

A non-Londoner, Benjamin Gosling (*Surrey*, 1833), started in the disorderly house business in 1848. In 1859, his wife Mary Ann was running a lodging house with 'dressed women' in Little Lonsdale Street when one girl ran off with wearing apparel in preparation for a voyage to Vancouver. Mary Ann was still only forty-two years old but unable to walk unaided into court because of paralysis.[5] When Mary Ann's health failed, the couple took to vegetable selling, and when that failed, Benjamin took to receiving. His last convictions were for indecent exposure.[6]

Melbourne's red-light district extended from Flinders Street to Lonsdale Street. Stephen Street and Lonsdale Street had the smartest establishments, while Romeo Lane, Juliet Terrace and Little Bourke Street had the meanest, until the Chinese built their community in Little Bourke Street and the sex trade moved to Little Lonsdale Street. In 1852, Joseph Rowe's American Circus set up on the corner of Stephen and Lonsdale streets, and soon, 'nearly all that was profligate and abandoned in the city of Melbourne was congregated in the purlieus of Rowe's Circus' and 'the most frightful enormities were everyday occurrences'. To loosen patrons' inhibitions, unlicensed boarding houses selling sly grog popped up on every corner and down every noisome lane. John Cray (*Isabella*, 1842), from Longacre in London, and his Welsh wife Mary Holehouse (*Tory*, 1845) were fined £30 in July 1853 for running a 'disreputable house' and charging 10 shillings for a bottle of porter.[7] In July 1855, after Rowe's circus had moved on, the police raided twenty local establishments, including eight in Little Bourke Street and six in Stephen Street: charges were sustained against nine, a number of them run by Vandemonians.[8] (The Crays had already gone to Ballarat to set up other establishments, including an oyster parlour.) In 1863, a new clean-up moved the brothels in Spring Street that were too close to the new Model School for comfort.[9]

The theatre district was concentrated in the north-eastern corner of the city grid. The Theatre Royal was lower down in Bourke Street, near Swanston Street, and after opening in 1855 with Richard Brinsley Sheridan's *School for Scandal*, it quickly sank to staging Lola Montez and her notorious spider dance, and its vestibule became a 'saddling paddock' for prostitutes to link up with their clients.[10] The entrepreneur George Coppin restored the theatre's reputation, but the cheaper and rougher establishments staging vaudeville and louche plays fed the brothels in the back lanes and in Lonsdale and Stephen streets. At the top of Bourke Street, for instance, the Excelsior Hotel incorporated a hall and staged vaudeville, boxing and wrestling. There was George Coppin's Haymarket Theatre; the Olympic on the corner of Stephen and Lonsdale streets (known as the Iron Pot); the Opera House, which became the Tivoli; and the Royal Colosseum. Most of them burned down at one time or another, only to rise again from the ashes.

As for markets, Paddy's Market opened in 1847 on the corner of Bourke and Stephen streets and was the city's premier fresh food market until the early 1870s, when its closure during the building of the handsome Eastern Market on that site drove the fresh food trade to the Queen Victoria Market. Markets were ideal settings for sub-legal trade: fencing or selling stolen goods, or hawking spoiled or damaged ones.

THE HARLOT'S PROGRESS

A rich honeypot awaited the Vandemonian flash mob and the Vandemonian wives of thieves, fences, bullies, bushrangers and thugs after they'd explored the opportunities around the diggings or rested in gaol. Once gold was discovered, a constant supply of cash and precious metal surged through Melbourne's drinking places, theatres and brothels. In September 1857, a 'lucky digger' from Smythe's Creek was relieved of £400 in £10 and £20 notes when 'his evil destiny prompted him to turn into Romeo Lane'.[11] This was the economy of gold and theft, with sex sold largely as a lure to being bilked. It provided income for both the prostitutes and their male family members or companions. Often, they worked in teams, the men overpowering the victims if they resisted, or robbing them with a Vandemonian hug. Likewise, prostitution could involve the assistance of another: as a decoy for a client's attention, to rifle pockets and clothes while clients were otherwise occupied or insensible, or to provide a community of gaiety, a drinking party, that could put a customer off his guard. Teamwork and networks were also necessary to obtain rooms for customers as well as places to sleep. Bush workers used brothels for somewhere to slumber and store their clothes while they drank their way through their pay cheques.

The grand brothels, such as Madame Brussel's and Mother Fraser's that would flourish in Lonsdale and Stephen streets, specialised in sexual services and glamour. There, champagne was the beverage of choice. But there was nothing glamorous about Romeo Lane and its surrounds. Respectable neighbours despaired as their environs and property values sank.

In March 1857, Dr John Singleton, physician to the poor and fallen, presented a report to the Melbourne City Court on 'Immorality in Melbourne'. He condemned the

> number of dissolute and miserable women that hang around the bars of public houses, or stalk abroad in the streets in open day, especially in the vicinity of the theatres, and with the most shameless effrontery—indecently attired, in general more or less intoxicated, often quarrelling with each other, and making use of the most obscene and revolting language.[12]

In 1859, a study using the methodology of Dr William Acton's *Prostitution, Considered in Its Moral, Social and Sanitary Aspects*, reported that around 500 women were known to the police as prostitutes in the city and suburbs, and of those, around 200 were just in the block enclosed within Spring, Russell, Latrobe and Bourke streets. (Singleton two years earlier had counted 257 in the quarter.) In those narrow streets and lanes, the 'most abandoned of their order' lived in 106 houses occupied as brothels, besides 'single apartments occupied by women who choose to live apart from the rest'. The report went further: of the 106,

> about thirty-five were frequented by low thieves; nine by professional burglars; six by sharpers; nine by fighting and fancy men; two by American coloured men; five by Jew dealers and

petty tradesmen; two by foreigners; six by cabmen exclusively; and twenty-two by bushmen, diggers, employees in business premises, and 'flash' men generally.[13]

High-class prostitution required beautiful girls, the younger the better. But by the time most Vandemonian women had survived their grim early lives and the penal system, they were beginning to lose their looks. Their assets remained their quick wits and nifty fingers, their street wisdom and their ruthlessness. Their customers were unlikely to be gentlemen unless they were sexual 'slummers' who liked 'rough trade'. Most of their clients were men of their own class who had saved wages while working up-country, or had struck it lucky at the diggings, or who were themselves thieves. Alcohol was the currency of the transaction, even more than the sex. Prostitutes would 'go out' to purchase a bottle of spirits or porter and often receive part of the inflated sly grog price. The police reported that the stench from their bodies when undressing was 'something awful', and that the air in their hovels so putrid that it could extinguish an investigator's candle.[14] If William Hogarth illustrated 'The Harlot's Progress' from nubile beauty to diseased old hag, the biographies of the Vandemonian women who worked the street told the same story.

Margaret Richardson, like Ellen Miles, came from Bloomsbury, London, and thieved with her sister Ann. According to the *London Evening Standard* of 16 November 1838, the two, aged fourteen and thirteen respectively, were convicted of stealing 9 yards (8 metres) of printed cotton. Both had previous convictions, and both had been in confinement as disorderly prostitutes. They were each very short, just 4 feet 9 inches (145 centimetres), and remained so for the rest of their lives, hence the possible underestimation of their ages. Sentenced to seven years' transportation for their own good, Ann reacted furiously by striking the gaoler with her umbrella, then whacked Margaret on the back because her sister was crying. Margaret travelled on the *Hindostan* with women who would remain her mates in Melbourne, Ann on the *Gilbert Henderson* with Ellen Miles. Margaret proved the more refractory convict, but both received permission to marry in 1842, whereupon Ann disappears from view. Margaret married Thomas Richmond, who had been born in the rough port of Southampton and arrived in the colony as a seventeen-year-old on the *Arab* in 1834. By the time they wed, he was free and she was still under sentence. They were both still illiterate. Margaret received her certificate of freedom in November 1845, and six weeks later the pair were on their way to Melbourne.

Margaret Richmond was quick to take to the streets and to men's pockets, committing her first offence in August 1846, already a 'young girl' of 'questionable reputation'. This was the beginning of a three-decade career as a woman of the town, repeatedly convicted for disorderly behaviour, obscene language, indecent behaviour, assault, and being drunk and disorderly. All that changed over the years was the crudity of the press descriptions of her deteriorating looks and a desperate increase in personal violence as her sexual capital decayed. Already in December 1847, after a quarrel in a house of ill fame in Little Bourke Street conducted by another Vandemonian, Julia Robinson (*Westmoreland*, 1846), she was described as 'one of the most desperate characters around town'.[15] By 1853, aged thirty-one, she was already a 'coarse looking woman'. In 1868 she was one of 'four repulsive-looking women of the town'.[16] By now she was known as 'the Bull Pup', and in 1871 *The Argus* commented after a ten-day clean-up of Romeo Lane that the 'cognomen was fully justified by her physiognomy':

> Though so ugly now, being a squat, brown-faced woman, about 4ft high, and nearly as broad, she was at one time the queen of the *demi-monde* of Canvas Town, in the primitive days of Melbourne,

and for a long time fascinated the hearts of lucky diggers whose gold she easily obtained and more easily squandered.[17]

She was one of between forty and fifty thieves, bullies and women of the town rounded up that day to be paraded through the City Court. We rarely hear Margaret Richmond's voice, but when charged with 'habitual profligacy' in 1857, she retorted that 'her character had been sworn away by the police and that she had been shamefully shown up in newspapers, so much so, that she was never believed in anything'.[18] All of which was true. In January 1857 she was found in the company of three other Vandemonian women, walking down the street, 'leading two mere children by the hand and singing obscene songs'. In her defence, her barrister argued that she was not a vagrant as he could prove her husband could support her. It was to no avail and she received three months' hard labour.[19] As to what had actually happened to Thomas Richmond, after a couple of early brushes with the law over drunkenness and fighting, this remains a mystery. Margaret Richmond's final appearance in the public record was for her inquest: she died in Melbourne Gaol in 1876, aged fifty-four—the press estimated her age on arrest at eighty.[20] The official cause was dysentery, but the doctor performing the post-mortem reported that she had been previously treated in the gaol hospital for 'paralysis' and 'diseases'. She died alone, tended only by the gaol hospital staff. The official record was twenty-eight times convicted over thirty years, in addition to fines and warnings, and acquittals when witnesses failed to appear.[21]

SISTERS AND MATES

Margaret Richmond had always stuck to her Vandemonian mates. The women clubbed together to pay each other's fines and to care for each other's children. Margaret liked to work in a team and she loved to drink in a group. In early January 1858, the police happened upon a party—a 'pretty lot'—of seven women, including Margaret Richmond, and five men, all 'old hands' in 'one of the lowest brothels in Little Bourke Street and the whole lot were supposed to be connected with the den'.[22] Two of them, Mary Lewis and Eliza White, were shipmates of Margaret on the *Hindostan*. Eliza White, or Eliza Clements, also often caught newspaper reporters' eyes for her flaming red hair and eloquence; she too was from Bloomsbury. Other shipmates living around the red-light district were Ann Perrin, from Aldersgate, and Ann Jones from St Giles. The two other *Hindostan* women of the town came from Edinburgh and Liverpool. Mary Perry, an older, Irish-born *Hindostan* transportee, at the age of forty-eight was described after a court appearance for stealing from the person as 'a repulsive-looking woman of the worst character'.[23]

As for Margaret Richmond's sister Ann and Ellen Miles on the *Gilbert Henderson*, many of their young shipmates ended up as women of the town in the environs of Romeo Lane. Tiny Agnes Mosley from Glasgow, after a time under sentence of misconduct, disobedience of orders and 'out after hours' totalling 183 days in solitary confinement, by 1844 had taken up serious prostitution. Free by servitude two years later, she was by 1848 'the celebrated Agnes Mosley' who was keeping a Hobart brothel. In 1851 she moved to Melbourne, married a Samuel Lewis and started a family as well as a business. In July 1856, as a resident of a right-of-way off Little Bourke Street, she was sent for trial after a coronial inquiry into the death of her baby found that the infant had been 'alive and well' on her lap while she was 'in a beastly state of intoxication', only to be found the next morning dead at her feet, with a bruise on its temple.[24] Agnes fled to Adelaide after the trial to continue running brothels. Ellen Leary, just twelve at transportation, and who earned 118 days in solitary under sentence, became Ellen Burgess, moved to Melbourne in 1849, and continued the drinking career she had commenced under sentence. And tiny Janet Dunn from Glasgow, after a blameless time under sentence, was found in a common brothel in 1845, ten months after she had married Archibald Boyle (later known as Archibald Bogle McKenzie). She bore him at least three children, but within four years of the birth of the second child in 1858, she was going in and out of court in Melbourne for vagrancy. Now in her thirties, she was still diminutive, reaching only 4 feet 4.5 inches (133 centimetres). Her face was scarred and she was missing a front tooth. She teamed up again with Ellen Miles, being twice convicted with Ellen as a 'disorderly'. After almost a decade on the streets, she was admitted in 1871 to Ararat Lunatic Asylum with mania and died there ten years later of 'disease of the brain'.[25]

Ellen Hanley, who came from Limerick on the *Greenlaw* in 1844 as an eighteen-year-old, suffered the disaster of her husband John Roberts (*Frances Charlotte*, 1837) being convicted of highway robbery just weeks after they arrived in Melbourne in 1850, and getting five years on the roads. He was a bolter, absconding from the roadworks in May 1851, then serving a fifteen-year sentence in Adelaide, from where he escaped again, until in Sydney he served five years on Cockatoo Island in Sydney Harbour.[26] Ellen, now Nellie Roberts, had to fend for herself. Within a year she had joined the regular queue of drunkards before the Melbourne police courts. In July 1857 she was described as one of 'three wretchedly-filthy-looking women' charged with robbery of a man, a ship's captain, of £113 in gold. Then there was an act of indecency in a lane with a John Powell, and in May 1859 she was charged as a keeper of 'an infamous house' in Little Bourke Street, along with Ellen Miles, Bridget Harris (per *Waverley*, and known as Biddy from Sligo, Ireland, even though she came from Antrim) and Mary Ann Stewart, an Irish orphan girl who had arrived on the *Pemberton*. It was the 'resort of thieves and prostitutes who infested the area'.[27]

MADAMS AND MOTHERS

By the late 1850s, the old hands who still had some command of their senses had moved on to running brothels. These ranged from the 'most wretched hovels' to the stylish, a number owned by those who had made money on the first flush of the diggings. Others were rented out by pawnbrokers who furnished the establishments with 'flashy articles' and then lent rooms to lone operators 'at usurious rates'.[28] From low to high brothels, male partners were often behind the scenes 'managing' the 'girls'. By 1860, Matthew Wood (*Moffatt*, 1842) and his wife Ann Felton (*Emma Eugenia*, 1846) were keeping a disorderly house in Little Bourke Street where Wood 'was accustomed to beat and ill-treat the women who supported him, in the event of bringing him no money'. Ann Wood knew the business well, having started in prostitution in Wolverhampton at the age of fourteen before being transported at the age of twenty-two. She handled the money and ordered the alcohol, which was sold-on at exorbitant prices.[29]

The young girls now came from the immigrant ships, from the broken families of older settlers, and of course the Vandemonians' own families, for amidst the filth, the disease, the rampant drunkenness and the violence, children were being raised. Some family histories reveal three or more generations of offending, transmitted down either the female or the male line. Elizabeth Fowler (*Navarino*, 1841) was born in Belfast, but by 1840 she was in London, her mother and sister in Liverpool. Aged sixteen, Elizabeth was a servant in the house of Richard Chadwick of St Martin's Lane. He came home on one day to find a drawer open and empty of a purse containing £45 and a box of jewellery; Elizabeth was also missing. The banknotes were traced to Liverpool, as was Elizabeth, who was staying with her mother. They were both indicted, but the mother was acquitted of receiving. It was Elizabeth's third offence, the first having been a theft from her uncle—the penalty was ten years' transportation—although she was not known to have been on the town. Under sentence, her offences were few until she was found in a disorderly house in November 1845.

After two false starts with other men, Elizabeth Fowler married Richard Howe in August 1847. A year earlier she had given birth to Minnie, having already had two babies who had died. In 1853 she had her certificate of freedom and Victoria beckoned. But the marriage was not going well. Richard had tried to make a living as a hackney cab driver in Melbourne before the family moved to Ballarat in 1857. There, he was charged with wife-beating, Elizabeth's face being 'one mass of bruises and cuts', but she decided not to proceed with the charges. Richard was immediately rearrested on suspicion of robbing the local Horse Bazaar Hotel. By August 1859 the Howes were back in Melbourne, where Richard was charged with neglecting to support his wife and child, but that did not proceed either because by now the prosecutrix, according to the police, bore a 'bad character'. Elizabeth was busy in the disorderly house business, while Minnie, aged thirteen, made the first of many court appearances, charged with vagrancy—she was still young enough to burst into tears and was sent home. Five months later, however, Minnie was convicted with Emma and Mary Harrold, the two daughters of Mary Lochrie (*Margaret*, 1843), of vagrancy, with Harrold also convicted of keeping a disorderly house. Elizabeth Howe blamed Mary Harrold for seducing her Minnie into prostitution while under the guise of caring for her, but six months later, Minnie was accusing her mother of forcing her into prostitution against her will.

By now, Elizabeth, just thirty-six years old, was described as a 'disreputable-looking hag' who in a 'whining tone begged to be released this time and she would not repeat the offence'. Yet she was keeping two older prostitutes in her house and Minnie had been earning for a year. Minnie was also becoming violent, assaulting other prostitutes and being beaten up herself. By September 1862, her mother was in gaol again and kindly neighbours offered to find Minnie work after she had been found in the house of ill fame of Mary Read, known as 'Mother Read'.[30] At some point Minnie had two children and kept herself by theft: in February 1869, as a 'young but not prepossessing woman', she was accused of robbing a man called Merrick of nuggets, jewellery and money to the value of £40—the pickings were still good. In 1876 she married a local thief, Alfred Hopkins. On 7 February 1880, Minnie dropped dead, aged thirty-four, in Victoria Street from a cardiac arrest—she had fatty degeneration of the heart, the wages of drink.[31] Her son Richard died at twenty from phthisis. As for her mother, Elizabeth's alcoholism was only getting worse. In December 1866 she had been found huddled in some stables with ten other derelicts, 'all most wretched degraded looking objects'.[32] Eventually she was accepted into the Melbourne Benevolent Asylum, where she died at the remarkable age of eighty-eight: like her daughter, of fatty degeneration of the heart.

As for Mary Lochrie (Mrs Harrold), she too died in the Melbourne Benevolent Asylum, but at the age of thirty-eight, from phthisis. She had been four years on the town in Glasgow from the age of thirteen. She was small, red-haired, able to read and write, and 'tidy, clean and quiet' during the voyage on the *Margaret* in 1843. Under sentence she went absent without leave, suffered six days' solitary confinement, and never offended again. Her good behaviour entitled her to marry after three years under sentence, and she began her family with John Harrold, a cooper. Her two girls, Emma and Mary, were born in Tasmania, and two sons, John and James, were born in Melbourne while Mary and her husband were running a disorderly house and drinking heavily. James died at three months of age of a lack of natural nourishment (he was not being breast-fed) and John at age six in the Children's Hospital. Assaults and claims for maintenance signalled the disintegration of the household: the two girls were now on the town and their father had deserted. Young Emma also died in her early thirties; her sister survived much longer, but with only three of her six children still living when she passed away.

THE TRADE IN CHILDREN

The Vandemonian flash mob not only networked within inner Melbourne and regional towns like Ballarat, Bendigo, Castlemaine and Geelong. They also maintained their connections with former 'mates' in Tasmania to procure young girls. Mr Hill, the City Visitor for the Police, told the Parliamentary Select Committee on the Bill for the Prevention of Contagious Diseases in 1878 of the women who went there 'well dressed and with plenty of money' and dazzled girls with tales of marvellous Melbourne. Once in that city, they would put them up for a time, make them drunk or drug them, and organise their ruin. Some had landed up in the Melbourne Hospital Lock Ward for syphilitics and told Mr Hill their story. Fresh young virgins were high currency, for it was widely believed that connection with a virgin could cure syphilis. The select committee worked hard to blame 'Chinamen' for this ravaging of virgins, but the police witnesses alluded to the difficulties Chinese men had in finding relationships with anyone other than the most desperate prostitutes, hence their believed higher infection rate.[33] (Of women giving birth in the Lying-In Hospital in the 1870s, the Tasmanian-born had the smallest, sickest babies, after the Victorian-born and the English; Irish and Scots mothers had the biggest and healthiest babies. The single women giving birth came from the inner city, in particular the eastern corner.[34])

On 29 January 1864, a Friday, Margaret Cosgrove (*Waverley*, 1847), now Blackford, enticed Elizabeth Fisher, aged under fourteen and the daughter of a neighbour in a right-of-way off Little Lonsdale Street, into her house. Inside, Elizabeth saw a Chinese man sitting by the fire. Margaret Blackwood shut the door, put her back against it, and refused to allow Elizabeth to leave. The man gave Margaret Blackford some money and she offered Elizabeth some of it. Elizabeth said her mother would beat her for taking it. Blackford then tried to lock Elizabeth in a store with the Chinese man, but in a scuffle, Elizabeth escaped. On the way, she was given 5 shillings and told not to let her mother know. She did, of course, and Margaret Blackford was sentenced to six months' gaol.

Margaret Blackford was an Irish famine convict, transported from King's County for stealing flour, but with a record of violence. She was probably just fifteen at the time; she had no father but had not yet been on the town. Like Mary Lochrie, she was a quiet convict who went absent once without leave, was sentenced to solitary and behaved herself thereafter. After three years she was able to marry James Blackford, a rough London shoemaker who had first been transported to Sydney, absconded and been re-transported to Van Diemen's Land. He bore the marks of flagellation on his back and the scars of irons on his ankles. By 1852 the pair were free to try their luck on the goldfields, taking their two surviving children with them. Little Mary Ann had died of 'teething'. At Fryer's Creek in 1855, their son James died aged two of 'brain fever that lasted'. Margaret and five-year-old Jane headed for Little Bourke Street. By 1858, Margaret was being arrested for drunkenness, while James, who had remained at Forest Creek, was now beginning a long career of convictions for larceny, stealing and shop breaking that lasted from 1857 to 1872. In October 1860, Margaret was arrested along with Ellen Miles and Margaret Richmond for 'being a nuisance to neighbours'. The vagrancy convictions mounted up, the last in 1864. In 1867, at the age of just thirty-five, she died somewhere off Little Bourke Street, from phthisis. Her only surviving child died three years later at nineteen of the same affliction.

In January 1857, William Drinkwater (*Surrey*, 1833), a 'coarse looking man of middle age', and his de facto Harriet Shurley (*Emma Eugenia*, 1844), now Adlam, had their house in Little Bourke Street raided by the police, who found two young girls sitting at a table while two Chinese customers drank porter. More children appeared, the youngest of them Harriet's, and more older women known to be prostitutes. Drinkwater was in bed and refused to get up. Finally, the two little girls admitted they had been in bed with the Chinese men. The police estimated that they were both no older than eleven; one had a sister who was also a prostitute. As for the money, the Drinkwaters took almost all of it. Harriet Adlam had secured one of the girls by consulting the registry of neglected children who were wards of the state. The girls were returned into care. The men were found not primarily responsible for decoying the children and received only a caution. Drinkwater and Adlam merely received two sureties of £100.[35]

VIOLENCE AND MADNESS

Family life in Romeo Lane was a re-creation of the toxic early childhoods that had marked many of the convicts, certainly those who died first. These were the most troubled and vulnerable transportees, especially if they were female, coming from the docks and East End of London, from Liverpool, Bristol, Southampton, Portsmouth, Dublin, Belfast, Edinburgh and Glasgow. Seaports were 'service centres' for transient or unattached males, and respectable work for women outside domestic service was scarce. For many, prostitution was their only option as de factos or husbands died, disappeared, went to gaol, or were unendurably brutal. Sailors and newly arrived immigrants were among the victims of bilking and bashing in Romeo Lane, but most of all they were the cashed-up gold diggers and the vast army of lonely bush and urban workers. The violence was aggravated by the adulterated, high-proof alcohol that was hiding in every sly grogger's cupboard, but it was also driven by mental illness and viciousness.

Joseph Woollen (*Lady Nugent*, 1836) was a Manchester-born boot clicker (employed to cut out material for the upper parts of boots and shoes) who had taken to picking pockets and fighting. Tall and strong, he specialised in preying on the weak, especially women. His first crime under sentence was cruelty to a pig. Once established in Melbourne with a new de facto, he ran an eating house in Stephen Street that also traded in sly grog and sex. The recipients of his beatings and kickings were prostitutes, a number of them fellow Vandemonians.

Mary Ann Pryke (*Sea Queen*, 1846) had grown up in a brothel run by her mother in Bury St Edmunds in Suffolk. Transported at seventeen for shoplifting, she had a 'riotous irritable temper'. She married early to Humphrey Short (*Augusta Jessie*, 1838), an alcoholic, so Mary Ann had to set up business. In June 1858, Joseph Woollen's de facto assaulted her—all the parties were living in Little Bourke Street and the Woollens had invaded Mary Ann Short's house and attacked her and her friend Harriet Adlam/Drinkwater while they allegedly played the card games cribbage and all fours. The prosecutrix, 'a smart looking young woman', appeared in the witness box with 'both her optics variegated with all the colours of the rainbow'. When cross-examined, Mary Ann denied she was known as 'Fighting Polly'; indeed, most people generally called her 'Pretty Polly'. However, her memory of the incident in question was now deserting her, even though the defence counsel, Dr Sewell, called a number of 'battered, jaded, careworn creatures, once the *belles* of Bourke Street, and some very unpleasant men'. The jury was unimpressed by all parties.[36] Mary Ann might have kept her looks, but in January 1865 she died in the Melbourne Hospital of syphilis, with caries of the skull. She left two boys still living who were already in trouble with the police.

Even if the children escaped family abuse, they were surrounded by violence and extreme behaviour. Winifred Fitzgerald (*Waverley*, 1842) was mad even before she was transported at the age of seventeen from Dublin. She had already been on the town for more than two years and was 'violent and incorrigible'. In Van Diemen's Land, after 'gross disorderly conduct', she was confined in the New Norfolk Lunatic Asylum for three years. But confinement enraged her: she attacked staff and patients with any weapon she could find; she grabbed hair and would not let go; she broke every pane of glass she could reach. Locked away in a cell, she even attempted to escape by displacing bricks; she broke through the lath and plaster in the ceiling and hid in the roof cavity. In June 1845 she gave birth and descended into psychosis, threatening to destroy her child and 'plaster her walls with its brains'. Yet when the child was removed, she cried bitterly. That October she tried to kill herself by opening a vein in her arm with a piece of glass. And in December she broke into the engine house, seized a crowbar and threatened violence.[37]

In 1849 Winifred Fitzgerald was free by servitude and three years later she married Joseph Johnson in Melbourne. The court appearances for drunkenness and disorderly and bizarre behaviour accumulated. Just before Christmas 1856, after being sentenced to 'two months', on entering the Western Gaol she stripped herself of all her clothes and began using language 'of a frightful description'. There was only one woman who could control her, another prisoner— 'a strong masculine individual'—and Winifred was locked into a cell by herself. The next morning, the cell was empty. Somehow, by working a 'night-time tub' against the bricks, she had broken through them (as she had in the New Norfolk Lunatic Asylum), got into the courtyard, climbed on the roof and scaled the walls of the gaol. She was caught the next day on her way to the diggings, and this time it was a sentence of twelve months.[38] Her mate Anne King (*Angelina*, 1844) looked after her children while she was in gaol. But Anne King had her peculiarities also, being found dressed in men's clothes and boxing with an elderly man in Little Lonsdale Street in April 1858; she was fined only 20 shillings in consideration of her caring responsibilities.[39] Winifred died in Beechworth Lunatic Asylum in 1880, aged fifty-five, of tuberculosis and disease of the brain.

ONLY THE DRINK MATTERS

As the Vandemonians aged, they became solitaries, street wanderers: scavenging, stealing small items, occasionally picking up a desperate customer. Their relationships—marriages, de-facto liaisons and 'mates'—fell apart as their minds and bodies disintegrated. Partners died, deserted or ended up in gaol. Daily, there were alcohol-fuelled domestic bashings and other cruelties. In December 1867, Ellen Miles was drinking with her 'mate de jour', Jane Taafe, behind a pawn shop in Russell Street. Suddenly, Ellen became 'jealous' over their beer, grabbed a carving knife and slashed Jane across the throat, leaving her for dead with a life-threatening wound.[40] The drink was all that mattered.

Mary Evans, who had spoken for herself when tried at the Old Bailey in 1842 with Catherine Oakford and Lydia Miles for bilking near Gray's Inn, was now Kate Gorman and boss of a house in Romeo Lane. A Harriet Webb, a prostitute, was insensible from drink in the house when Kate arrived home one day. Where was the bottle of rum she always brought home with her, she asked Fanny Porter, a neighbour. It was nowhere to be seen in the house.

> [T]hat drunken beast Webb must have got up and drunk it. She [Gorman] got up and went into the room where Webb was, and commenced beating her. I heard Webb's head striking against the floor. Gorman called her a drunken beast and said she would take the worth of rum out of her. I saw Gorman with her hand in the woman's hair, knocking her head against the washing stand. I said to her not to beat the woman. She said she could not keep her hands off her ... The deceased remained all day on the floor with convulsions. Gorman was sober when she beat the deceased. Deceased was taken to hospital that night.[41]

Fanny Porter's courage failed her when the murder trial commenced, and Mary Evans went unprosecuted because no-one dared give evidence against her.

For most, the alcohol had the final victory. Ellen Miles admitted that she could take the drink or leave it, and that this, combined with regular times in gaol where venereal disease could be treated, food was regular if plain, drink forbidden and washing required, helped keep her alive much longer than most of her mates.

In 1878, a sergeant Dalton told the Select Committee Upon a Bill for the Prevention of Contagious Diseases:

> The quiet prostitutes die away like rotten sheep—prostitutes that look fine and healthy, and you would think really the picture of health, that you could take a lease out on their life, die away like rotten sheep. Not so the rowdy ones; they are constantly in and out; they get three months and go in; and they come out again, and in a month, or two, or three, or six, they go in again, and they come out as fresh as a trout.[42]

The Romeo Lane men did somewhat better. William Drinkwater lived to the age of seventy-eight, dying in the Metropolitan Lunatic

Asylum from chronic disease of the brain, most probably tertiary syphilis, as did George Pickering in 1884, aged sixty, in the Melbourne Benevolent Asylum—his wife dead, his only child's whereabouts unknown—of advancing paralysis, possibly also tertiary syphilis. Joseph Woollen's diseased liver killed him at the age of forty-five.

With Eliza Clements, the wheel turned full circle. She had cut a dash in her youth, with flaming red hair and wielding a rich vocabulary in her tirades from the dock. She had been tried at the Old Bailey with a mysterious youth called variously John/Charles Chapman or Edward Edwards, who hailed from Bedford and may have been a gypsy. The court reporter called him a genius, and Eliza was only a little less impressive in her presentation: 'What am I here for, my lord? Am I to be sacrificed because I happen to be passing by the Mansion-house when the boy was at the bar? I was never afore a magistrate in my life until this blessed minute.' But that was not true, and she and the boy were sentenced to ten years.[43] In Melbourne in 1855, as 'Carotty Liz', 'a furious red-headed virago', she let out a stream of abuse in high tones in court, until she was sentenced to merely three months. 'Is that all? I think I have got off very easily,' she said, whereupon 'she was removed in a humour changed from the furious to the jolly.'[44] But within a few years, the convictions for drunkenness and obscene language had ceased to be colourful. Her appearance deteriorated. By 1875, she was a 'half-clad, unshod, and dissipated looking creature' who wandered the town and claimed she lived by washing in Collingwood. She was still alive in 1899, now homeless around North Melbourne, unable to care for herself. The Melbourne Benevolent Asylum refused to take her, so the police remanded her from week to week to give her somewhere to sleep, until, they hoped, the Bendigo Benevolent Asylum would oblige.[45]

Sixty years earlier, Eliza Clements' mother Charlotte had come to London to say goodbye before the *Hindostan* sailed. Just over a year later, the Chartist *Northern Star and Leeds General Advertiser* reported a recent case of begging that had come before alderman Kelly at the Guildhall. It was Charlotte Clements.

> 'Well, if I did beg, is it not better to beg than to steal? One or the other I must do, or I must starve. I have not a bit to eat ...' she cried and her voice rang out through the Court. 'Look at my body', said she, raising her arms, which were each thrust into an old stocking leg, and turning herself around in the dock, exhibiting her breast and her back, covered only with a piece of ragged linen—'no dress, no shoes, no anything'.
>
> 'Now tell me', said she with great vehemence, the tears streaming down her cheeks, 'what am I to do? I could sell little things, but they must be bought; and if I go and beg the money, I am seized and sent to prison'.[46]

She had no-one in the world now. Eliza was her only living child out of thirteen, she claimed. The court sent her to Bridewell Prison for a few days to be fed and clothed.[47] Like her daughter, only the gaols would care for her. Both died as unrecorded paupers.

By the time Eliza Clements was in her last days, crime and alcohol abuse in the colonies were beginning to recede. The 1890s depression helped, as did new scientific tests and regulations to control adulteration.[48] But also, a generation had passed, the last generation of the gin and spirits craze that had overwhelmed traditional drinking habits of ale and beer. As in France with absinthe, the impact over generations of toxic spirits on the poor was devastating: the French novelist Lucien Descaves wrote that the absinthe scourge 'within three generations can completely extinguish the lineage of an alcoholic'.[49]

CHAPTER 6

Diggers

What men! And what costumes! Huge burley fellows with broad battered straw or cabbage-tree hats, huge beards, loose blue shirts, and trowsers yellow with clay and earth, many of them showing that they had been already digging in Sydney where there is much gold, but not so abundant or so pure as in this colony. Almost every man had a gun or pistols in his belt, and a huge dog, half hound and half mastiff, led by a chain. Each had this bundle, containing his sacking to sleep upon, his blanket and such slight change of linen as these diggers carry. They had, besides, their spades and picks tied together; and thus they marched up the country, bearing with them all they wanted, and lying out under the trees.

WILLIAM HOWITT, LAND, LABOUR AND GOLD (1855), P. 15

William Howitt was impressed by the Vandemonians, packed on ships' decks like the Irish leaving Liverpool for America. As the diggers and the fortune seekers poured into the Colony of Victoria from 1852, they built a distinctive new society. Gold not only created wealth, it supported a modern community of skilled workers, small businesses and capital-intensive investment that challenged the pastoral economy and its power. By the 1860s, the goldfields' towns and hamlets accounted for more people than the city of Melbourne. These were the places to be for both the ambitious and the desperate.[1] But for every person who might make a good living, there were others who could only subsist in the goldfields, often hidden in the bush from the wider society, fossicking, trading by barter and gold dust, cutting timber, living from their gardens and animals. And through the surrounding farmland, nomad tribes of lone men were forming, picking up farm work, thieving, bartering, surviving. These were the mobile destitute.[2]

COLONIAL DEVASTATION

Melbourne has been characterised as one of the 'instant cities' of the nineteenth-century world, along with Chicago. Likewise, the central Victorian goldfields—always more heavily populated and enduring than those in other Australian colonies—became 'instant' provincial societies and townships within a decade. They suddenly transformed from bush and pastoral expanses into blighted, deforested landscapes, riddled with holes, abandoned shafts, toxic mullock heaps, dying trees and putrid horse corpses. Not a few Vandemonians, both men and women, perished in the darkness of the night from falling into water-filled holes while intoxicated. Samuel Sugden survived the wreck of the convict ship *George III* in 1835, but not the water-filled death traps of Ballarat in 1871. Margaret McHague (*Royal Admiral*, 1841), as Margaret Lees, was the local midwife at Break 'O Day, now Corindhap. One Mrs Thornton called her out on a Sunday afternoon in August 1874 to attend to her imminent delivery, except that the midwife was diverted by a bottle and was last heard singing and swearing in the pitch dark before she fell head-first into a 30-foot (9-metre) shaft.

It was three days before her de facto, another Vandemonian, Frederick Bird (*Waverley*, 1841), found her with her legs in the air.[3]

For the surviving Aboriginal Victorians, now reduced to around 3000 people, and with their numbers still falling, it was a second devastation, even more ecologically catastrophic than the invasion of sheep and horses along with the animals' owners and minders. Aboriginal people tried to live among the loss of country and economy: they found gold and helped others find gold, they traded, they joined the native police, they tracked the lost, they pilfered and plundered—often making clear that it was still their land and the white men and women should be paying them for it rather than insisting that Indigenous people work for their sustenance. As the army of diggers was overwhelmingly masculine, Aboriginal women suffered the consequences of their sexual hunger. Finally, there was the grog, bringing temporary bliss before enslavement. However hard they tried, the traditional owners could not break through and were to remain outsiders, recipients of occasional kindness and pity, as the white invaders realised that they were the last of their people in their own country.[4]

The original Aboriginal Protection Board was disbanded in 1859, and in the early 1860s the process of sequestering people on mission-run reserves began—at Coranderrk, Framlingham, Ebenezer and, in East Gippsland, at Lake Tyers and Ramahyuck.[5] Around half the survivors went on the reserves, primarily because they were sick or had young children. Some old people also wandered onto the reserves for care as they were dying. Those who remained outside colonial surveillance appear to have left few direct descendants, apart from women who were absorbed into European families to become family secrets. Today, among the 48 000 people who identified as Indigenous in Victoria in the 2016 Australian census, the Victorian-born are predominantly the descendants of those who went on the reserves rather than continuing to live free, and it would not be until World War I that

Aboriginal Victoria would begin to recover.⁶ It had been a devastating demographic, biological and technological onslaught.

By the 1880s, within half a century of settlement, the Colony of Victoria was a dense network of roads and towns—each a buggy ride apart—to be followed by trains and later the telegraph. The land had been parcelled into neat selections and the pastoral leases broken up. Only the wildest mountains were almost intact but slowly succumbing to the miner's pickaxe and the settler's axe. Across the goldfields, after the rushes subsided, small communities remained, finding new means of living mixed with fossicking. The colonial map testifies to what was the most rapid and devastating act of colonisation in the nineteenth-century world, leaving a landscape marked by settlement modelled on the rural patchwork of southern England.

A NEW ORDER

From the 1850s, the Vandemonians could lose themselves in the crowd of immigrants. On the diggings, no-one wore fine clothes because garments quickly became filthy with mud and clay. Beards and other hair went untrimmed, and bodies went unwashed when water was scarce. A gentleman only gave himself away when he opened his mouth. Many commented then, and have done so since, on the easy democracy of manners—or cheek of the lower orders—that people who were once crushed by demands of deference to their superiors and gaolers could now enjoy. They were beholden to no-one if they could make their way on the goldfields, especially if they were lucky diggers. But the eager immigrants, who swooned on William Howitt's ship when the Port Phillip pilot confirmed that there was indeed gold in the distant hills, soon found it was very hard work, with very uncomfortable living, not a little fear of bushrangers, and multiple accidents with broken axles, wheels, limbs and heads. Indeed, Howitt advised anyone who fancied trying their luck in Golden Victoria to 'first dig a coal pit; then work a month in a stone-quarry; next sink a well in the wettest place he could find, of at least fifty feet deep; and finally, clear out a space of sixteen feet square of a bog twenty feet deep'. For sustenance he must also live on 'heavy unleavened bread, on tea without milk, and on mutton or beef without vegetables, and as tough as India-rubber'.[7] (Howitt himself was already sixty years old when he undertook his goldfields adventure with his two sons, Alfred and Charlton, and suffered only a severe bout of dysentery.) The goldfields were not for the faint-hearted, and ex-convicts, hardened by forced labour and bush living, could thrive there.

Deeper leads and wetter ground required machinery for pumping water and circulating air. This machinery in turn needed capital investment and, in Ballarat particularly, close partnerships were formed between town businessmen—shopkeepers and tradesmen—and miners.[8] Over time, a tight-knit community formed, bonded by common investment and risk-taking, and later, as all over rural Victoria, by marriage.[9] For Vandemonians, work as miners in the leading goldfields was for the reliable and the skilled. Most earned their living by dealing: as tradesmen, shopkeepers and publicans. Blacksmiths and butchers were always in high demand, and stonemasons, brickmakers and carpenters were needed for the building of townships. Shoemakers made a constant living in a world of hard usage of footwear. Tinsmiths repaired mining equipment and domestic utensils. All of these trades were both settled and itinerant. Publicans, of course, could do very well unless they drank as deeply as their customers. Those who remained miners tended to come from the industrial parts of England and Scotland, but many who died with 'Miner' as the occupation on their death certificate had long ceased to search for gold but retained a miner's right as a legal identity if they held a home through one.[10] Of a sample of 382 Vandemonian men who died in the goldfields' towns and hamlets, just 16 per cent died with 'miner' on their death certificate.[11] Vandemonians had to earn their living in the 'service' economy.

Digging for gold was, of course, expensive, and the inflated cost of absolutely everything soon consumed nest eggs. If a digger did not strike it lucky quickly, then he faced crippling licence fees, bullying police and offensive gold commissioners struggling to control the diggers and the diggings. As soon as the easy finds were exhausted, gold mining required men to work in teams, to form partnerships of trust where labour and winnings were shared. All over the goldfields, miners formed collective working groups to erect complicated water races, build dams, dig deep shafts, carry water and protect each other. Mining required solidarity—few could survive the diggings alone— so most ventured as members of parties of friends, relatives, fellow countrymen or, indeed, fellow Vandemonians, any link that might guarantee trust in a tight situation or contain jealousies and greed.

On the Ballarat flats, the shafts were soon very deep and very wet. Up to twenty men were needed to work together to sink a wet shaft, and the Vandemonians who had the best chance of being absorbed into these partnerships were those who could prove their worth. Daniel Backway could. He was not a 'burley' Vandemonian, but as a former London chimney cleaner's climbing boy, he could descend into tight places; he was still short and athletic. But Daniel did not join the mining teams at Ballarat. Rather, he struck out on his own, pegging his first claim at Fryer's Creek, where he was sufficiently well known for his claim to be used as a marker for others.[12] Within two years, his now extended family had settled in Maryborough, living on the main lead with their own claim. Paul Duff, on the other hand, did stand out as a burly Vandemonian, being a giant for his era at 6 feet (1.8 metres) tall. As described earlier, he was a simple, violent man, covered in scars from a fighting life. He was soon recruited to join a team and struck it lucky as a shareholder in the Nelson lead, making him moderately wealthy by the end of the 1850s. And yet he would have no friends and remain the butt of ridicule and be muscle for hire in Ballarat. He died as he lived.

This interdependent economy that depended on trust and partnerships, sometimes between people who had not known each other before and had no common link or shared history, nourished a certain voluntary collectivism where people formed groups and organisations for mutual profit and support. The colonisers also drew on deep historical collectivist instincts rooted in English rural life, where they'd been sustained by the commons and Poor Law entitlements. But this was also a self-selected colonial frontier of immigrants who had paid their own way, or who had the private means to supplement the still expensive assisted immigrant voyage to Australia. They were often people who felt blocked in the old country: thwarted by a lack of capital, connections and land. They wanted to be masters of their own world and secure land or property to guarantee the survival in old age of themselves and their lineage. They believed in emancipation through character, what the British came to call 'manliness', where even the workingman could earn respect and a place in the nation: 'He was poor, but he was honest.' Political emancipation was essential, and the miners brought with them the ideals of the Chartists, of the 1848 revolutionaries in Europe, of the suppressed trade societies and unions, of the growing cooperatives and friendly societies, and of the land-reform movements.

In every town, they raised the funds to build mechanics' institutes where they could attend lectures, hold meetings, and borrow books and newspapers. They were bent on self-improvement and almost all were literate. But even the illiterate were hungry for print, and from groups of swagmen and drovers to miners and settlers, being read to from the newspapers and periodicals was a deep and necessary pleasure. Newspapers of all kinds—overseas, metropolitan and regional—mixed news and advertising with serialised fiction (Charles Dickens was the author most favoured), popular science and serious discussion. Joseph Jenkins, the Welsh swagman, became a learned man of his time by reading the press and the Bible.[13] All this, too, was a colonial version of an old tradition, where artisans in workrooms or drinkers in a village taproom had a reader provide news and political ideas from the press. The miners, as well as the convicts who arrived later, had been educated by the radical periodical and newspaper press, in particular the Chartist *Northern Star and Leeds General Advertiser*, which, at its peak, achieved the second-largest circulation in England. They came to Golden Victoria with firm ideas about how the world should work, and they wanted land and the vote.

The trigger for the almost-inevitable uprising was the requirement of a gold licence that cost 30 shillings a month, irrespective of whether a digger had found gold or not. Few could afford it, and it was resented as taxation without representation. Agitation began in Bendigo, reaching its climax in August 1853 when over 23 000 miners signed a petition to lieutenant-governor Charles La Trobe, protesting that the licence was an unfair tax. Chartists shaped the protest and 10 000 diggers massed to present the petition in person, while supporters sported red ribbons to demonstrate their solidarity. The so-called Red Ribbon Movement spread to other goldfields, but in Ballarat, under the Chartist JB Humffray, the Ballarat Reform League drew up its own demands, mirroring most of William Lovett's 'People's Charter'. The subsequent Eureka Rebellion of December 1854, led by Peter Lalor, incorporated the many Irish who were now working the Eureka lead, so that Irish nationalist and land-reform passions were added to the Chartist demands. The Eureka Rebellion was thus the culmination of a long accumulation of tensions on the goldfields and the confluence of different radical movements. But the reform movement in Victoria extended beyond the diggers. Indeed, as the rebellion was erupting, the colony's new constitution was on the seas headed for the Mother Country for approval, destined to bring extended suffrage to Australia's most progressive colonies.

Peter Lalor and his fellow rebels were charged with treason but acquitted. More importantly, the ensuing royal commission into the goldfields converted the miner's licence into a miner's right, where, for a modest annual payment, a man could have a mining claim to work, or a town residence right where he could build a home, run a cow and poultry, and grow fruit and vegetables—and have the right to vote. Daniel Backway's name is on the electoral roll of 1856 as a possessor of a miner's right: the workhouse orphan and convict had become a citizen. Weston Bate and Heather Holst have argued that the miner's right was to prove far more important than gold itself in giving poor miners and settlers a place to call home.[14] Not only were the rights astonishingly cheap, but they could be inherited by widows, daughters and sons. Some families in Castlemaine and Ballarat remained on them until the late twentieth century; Daniel Backway's descendants were still living on theirs in Hope Street, Maryborough, in 1954—a century of occupation. As a form of secure, social housing, it saved thousands from homelessness, enabling people with no capital to have a home and make a life in a community. It also saved the gold towns from oblivion as the easy gold ran out, and it ensured that regional industry had a workforce in affordable housing. And it saved women.

Lydia Ford (*Royal Admiral*, 1842) married another convict, Henry Barker (*Circassian*, 1833) at the age of nineteen, and they came to Port Phillip in 1848. He was a butcher who dabbled in mining investments, and in 1858 he became insolvent and deserted his wife and four children.[15] Five years later, he appeared at Lydia's home in Tress Street,

Ballarat East, broke down the door, and threatened to shoot her for taking everything from him, including, presumably, their home on a miner's right. The court was sympathetic. She explained that she supported herself and the children by taking in boarders. Lydia Ford lived to the age of eighty-four, still in her house in Tress Street. Later generations of deserted wives have not been so fortunate concerning state support for their shelter.

Added to social housing was the creation of commons.[16] In the 1860s, 618 000 acres (250 000 hectares) of Crown land were set aside as goldfields commons for mining, grazing and wood collection. This dramatically enhanced the life chances of the rural poor, providing an area they could keep stock, split wood and sell it, even prospect for gold. Many Vandemonians eked out a living as wood splitters and harvesters: the work required strength, skill and specific tools, but not a good character. People could hide in the forest, safe from the prying eyes of respectable society and the law. Official foresters who policed the forests were not appointed until the early 1880s.[17] The commons, however, provided a vital transition from the land seized by the Crown as public property to private use, and marked the beginning of forest conservation for the timber industry and recreational national parks. Maryborough's commons are still visible in its town layout, and rights to grazing have endured almost to the present day. Thus, traditional entitlements to the use of land for living were re-created in the goldfields, ensuring the viability of those communities long after the gold had dwindled.

RE-CREATING THE PARISH

The miners also understood that a viable society needed institutions for care. Accidents were constant and often lethal. Using voluntary subscriptions, hospitals were built in almost all of the sizeable mining communities: Ballarat, Bendigo, Castlemaine, Daylesford, Amherst, Inglewood, Beechworth, Stawell (Pleasant Creek), Ararat, Maldon, Dunolly, Kyneton, Kilmore, Clunes, Creswick and St Arnaud. Most were handsome buildings, and many survive today, even if repurposed. Along with them in the biggest centres—Ballarat, Bendigo, Castlemaine, Beechworth and Daylesford—were benevolent asylums, providing care for the destitute aged, the disabled and the chronically ill.[18] A number of these had lying-in wards attached, or industrial schools for neglected children and young offenders. It was a re-creation of the Old Poor Law, with voluntary contributions by registered subscribers, and with colonial government oversight. There was also provision for the insane: two asylums in Melbourne which were to be augmented by another two later, and regional asylums at Bendigo, Ballarat, Ararat and Beechworth, amounting to a ratio of beds per inhabitant that was only exceeded by post-famine Ireland, where consignment to a lunatic asylum of burdensome relatives was depressingly common.[19]

Schooling for children was erratic, with patchy national school and denominational school provision, until the Victorian *Education Act 1872* established a free, compulsory and secular system—although bush children, especially those whose parents were mobile and unstable, could miss out altogether, and church-run schools remained outside the state's control, setting up Victoria's distinctively inequitable education system for posterity. More important were the schools of mines, again in Ballarat, Bendigo and Castlemaine, that provided higher education for trades and engineers and a vital pathway of upward social mobility. This infrastructure supported a thriving, diversified industrial economy where regional cities were home to heavy engineering for mining and the construction of trains and armaments, as well as a robust network of woollen and knitting mills. Ballarat and Bendigo both boasted trades halls for their unions to meet and for worker education; even Castlemaine had a tiny wooden one. And it would be in Ballarat and later Creswick that modern mass trade unionism would begin, in the 1870s.[20]

Thus, this was a substantial and complex instant society on virgin mining soil in a new land, and whose townships were now set up for survival as provincial centres, with fine buildings, theatres, churches and cathedrals, all created within a generation of the first major gold discoveries. But this was for the insiders. This was for the people of good character. The Vandemonian who joined had to be able to pass muster—in appearance, deportment and language. He or she had to mount a convincing performance of decency and respectability, and those messages about character had to be conveyed immediately: not after careful explanations of youthful deprivation leading to crime, but in a gaze and a manner that evoked trust. Ex-convicts who married free people could either conceal their past altogether from their new family or dissemble for the rest of their lives. Some lowered their ages to excise the seven 'unspeakable years' in their life story. Joining mainstream society also required self-confidence and the means to be included. If Daniel Backway with his miner's right was on the 1856 electoral roll, so was William Goodall as a landowner in Lava Street, Warrnambool, but they were exceptional. The process of civic incorporation, or assimilation into respectable society, was for those who made it a slow, careful process. Above all, every new day and every newcomer brought the risk of a voice declaring, ''Ere, I know you.' Colonial courts would be busy for the next thirty years adjudicating disputes where the injured party had been called 'a Vandemonian', 'a Derwent Duck', 'an old lag', or even worse, 'a two-times old lag'.[21]

GUILTY BY ASSOCIATION

Late on 17 October 1854, a Scottish miner by the name of James Scobie was already drunk when he banged on the doors and windows of the Eureka Hotel in Ballarat East, which was closed, demanding more drink. He then broke a window, and the publican's wife, Catherine Bentley, tried to fight him off with an umbrella. Scobie insulted her. Catherine's husband, James Francis Bentley (*Blundell*, 1844), was enraged, and despite being lame he, together with his barman John Farrell (*Forfarshire*, 1843) and a Henry Hance, chased Scobie before knocking him down and giving him a beating. Scobie died, perhaps from hitting his head on the ground rather than the actual beating. The three aggressors were arrested but acquitted, and outraged miners then set fire to Bentley's hotel.

James Francis Bentley was ambiguous. He had no scars, was tallish, with regular features and a high forehead, and was educated and well-spoken, with the complexion of a man who worked indoors. He could still pass for the gentleman he had been before his conviction for forgery in Manchester in 1842. He had been a merchant from Canada who had fallen on hard times after six weeks in England and cut corners. He pleaded guilty and was transported to Norfolk Island on a ten-year sentence, where he survived the regime and the mutiny of 1846, being shipped to Van Diemen's Land to have his probation period cut short by a year. Once a ticket-of-leave man, he earned his living working as a commercial clerk in Hobart. Conditionally pardoned for good behaviour by 1851, he quickly established businesses as a confectioner, moved to Victoria, and by 1853 had the means to build the impressive Eureka Hotel.

In Ballarat he had a new wife, despite having left one behind in Canada. Catherine Sherwin was also reinventing herself, having arrived in Victoria in 1848 with her sister as Catherine and Mary

Sheeran, aged eighteen and sixteen respectively, aboard the *Lady Kennaway*, the first shipment to Port Phillip of Irish famine orphans under the scheme masterminded by Henry, the third Earl Grey. Many in the colony questioned the suitability of Irish orphans for domestic service in respectable homes.[22] There were stories that some had become prostitutes. But the Sheeran sisters were both literate, and when they each found an English husband, albeit both ex-convicts, they anglicised their names and their religion. They had come from the town of Ballymote in County Sligo, where, according to Catherine's death certificate, her father was a civil servant. The most probable civil service in that town was the notorious Sligo Gaol, and Catherine's extended family were living in Gaol Street in the 1901 census.

The burning of the Eureka Hotel was a key part of the complex story of the Eureka Rebellion. An *Argus* report from October 1854 reveals a significant subplot:

> It is necessary to mention that Bentley's hotel had acquired a very bad name throughout the diggings, numerous robberies having occurred in it since its establishment; and complaints were general that although a favorite resort of thieves and Vandemonians, the establishment seemed to be under the protection of some of the Camp authorities as no notice was taken of its well-known irregularities. This explanation will in some measure account for the spirit evinced in its destruction.[23]

The 'Vandemonian' associations were critical. Vandemonians were the 'undeserving', the inherently dangerous, the evil lurking in the shadows. Yet the Eureka Hotel was no typical goldfields establishment: it was large and its owners were seen to have 'airs'. Worst of all, they were believed to be in the pockets of corrupt authority. Bentley and his co-offenders were rearrested and charged with murder.

The result was a conviction for manslaughter, an imprisonment Bentley underwent without a blemish, but he was persecuted for the rest of his life. As he tried to re-establish businesses around Victoria, he was pursued through the courts for debts; a refreshment tent was burned down in Kingarra; he was abused as he went about his business; he found himself blocked from obtaining a new hotel licence; and he wrote an eloquent letter to the *Bendigo Advertiser* protesting at being called 'an old convict' by the judiciary and the 'associate of the worst characters'. He concealed his transportation and blamed the vilification on his claim for £30 000 compensation against the government.[24] In October 1867, a man called Trahern accused Bentley of stealing £2 in the Coach and Horses Hotel, Fitzroy, but he was too inebriated to appear in court. In February 1871, by now a pickle-maker living in Little Bourke Street, Bentley was picked up in the Parliament Yard in a half-sensible condition, having swallowed a phial of laudanum. His stomach was pumped at Melbourne Hospital and he survived. Next time he tried, on 10 April 1873, in Carlton, he succeeded.[25]

This is not to defend Bentley but to understand the climate of distrust and fear that Vandemonians faced in gold-rush Victoria. James Bentley's misfortunes were among many such outrages—arson, beatings, shootings—meted out by Judge Lynch on outcasts. The Vandemonians were unwanted, the flies that spoiled the honeypot.

THE RUSHES

A rush had to be seen to be believed. In a few weeks, thousands of men overwhelmed the ground, stripping it of vegetation, erecting tents and shacks, and establishing essential services such as supplies and alcohol. Alcohol had been banned on the diggings in the first two years of the gold rush, but that did not stop its flow. Coffee tents, stores and lodgings became fronts for sly grog, and it was here that the Vandemonians, both male and female, had the nerve and the wits to go into business. They knew 'how to work the oracle' and avoid arrest.[26] If women were few on the diggings, a disproportionate number of them in the first years were Vandemonians, mostly as wives and de factos rather than as sole operators in the sly grog and sex trades.

Each rush was also followed by a colourful tail of camp followers, bringing illegal but necessary services to these instant communities: 'nowhere is the want of police protection more severely felt than at some of these newly peopled gold-fields', thundered *The Argus* from the safety of Melbourne.

> At Back Creek, for example, it is computed that upwards of 30 000 people are congregated, and upon the skirts of this immense industrial army hang some hundreds of thieves, cheats, loafers and scoundrels of all descriptions—men who will take by force what they cannot appropriate by fraud, and who will not scruple to achieve their ends by violence, or to conceal the evidence of their guilt by murder, if necessary. There is no security of life or property, and if the ruffian elements of the Back Creek population were capable of combining, they would be capable of establishing a reign of terror for a time. As it is, some of the atrocities perpetrated are of such a daring and flagritious character as to demonstrate the miserable weakness of the local authorities and the fearless hardihood of the Vandemonian desperadoes who have flocked to this new goldfield.[27]

Of course, increasingly by the end of the 1850s, the rogues and abandoned women were less likely to have been convicts as free immigrants swelled the ranks of the failed, the alcoholic and the sly. Indeed, the events cited in this *Argus* editorial implicated as many free immigrants as ex-convicts. This did not diminish the Vandemonaphobia, however, reinforcing the barriers to the moral and economic assimilation of emancipists. Even when they were not the actual perpetrators, their influence was blamed for the criminal behaviour of the arrived-free. *The Age* was prepared to acknowledge that the desperate housing conditions on arrival for steerage passengers—'tents, shanties and wigwams often filled with both sexes'—did not help, nor did the ubiquity of strong drink and immoral women. Nonetheless, the evil from the penal colony pervaded the lower orders and the courts, when in comparison to the poverty of the Old World, this booming New World gave people no excuse for prostitution and crime, insisted *The Age*. Women were fewer in number in the colony and there was plenty of respectable domestic service work, so there was no rationale for prostitution other than 'demoralising influences of quite another character than poverty [and] are the occasion of the flagrant immorality in Melbourne and at the gold-fields'.[28]

The Havelock rush, near Maryborough, began in late 1857 and reached its peak within months. Around 2 a.m. on 1 February 1858, four men burst into the Gumtree restaurant in the main street kept by a foreigner called Lopez. They demanded a bottle of brandy. Lopez refused them, so they dragged him outside. One of them fired a shot, hitting Lopez, whereupon his servant man came to his defence, and Lopez then grabbed a large knife and stabbed his assailant a number of times before dropping dead. The local constable arrived, but the assailant shot again and killed the policeman. The diggers now closed in on the murderer, seized him and took him to the lock-up, while other diggers and police found the other three men hiding in some of the surrounding restaurants. Then the crowd of furious diggers rioted, demanding the right to deal their own justice to the murderer, 'an old man who gave the name of Joseph Brooks'.

Brooks was in fact Daniel Cooper (*Red Rover*, 1831), who'd been born in Huddersfield around 1811. He had already served two years on the roads in Victoria for being 'armed with felonious intent'. Now he lay

> on his bed dangerously wounded, exposed to the threats and menaces of angry miners. It is computed that nearly five thousand men were admitted throughout the day, but ten or twenty at a time, to gaze upon the helpless ruffian. Through every window eyes were glaring at him, imprecations and abuse were showered on his head, whilst at intervals there arose from the hoarse murmurs of the crowd the ominous cries of 'Bring him out', 'Let us kill him', 'Give him to us', etc.[29]

Although rumours spread that the mob had succeeded in lynching Brooks, in fact he died of his wounds within a day. He was only forty-seven but had been aged by the lash and the chain gang. The three who were seized on the night of the murders were acquitted but later sentenced severely for theft: at least one was a fellow Vandemonian.[30] When they fronted the bench, they each touched their forelocks—the habits of deference to authority were deep.

ESMOND STREET

As in the city, around the goldfields the plight of women bereft of reputation and reliable male protectors was acute and prostitution their best option for survival. Male brothel keepers were common, but the most remembered in Ballarat were Ellen Miles, now known as 'Buzzwinker', and Bet Naylor (formerly Elizabeth Morgan). Each set up shop in Esmond (now York) Street, which straddled Main Street, flooded regularly, and was surrounded by stinking holes and mullock heaps. By 1861 a string of tents and shanties had been erected here by brothel keepers and sly-grog sellers, ready to serve the patrons of the hotels, theatres, dancing halls and skittle parlours. It was later alleged that Ballarat had a thousand hotels in the gold-rush years, providing a bed, food, sex and oblivion to the swarms of young men on the diggings. Striking, strong and foul-mouthed hostesses such as Maria Hartridge, known as the 'Great Eastern', or Nelly Gleeson, 'a splendid specimen of muscular femininity', lured the gullible and ejected the insensible. Margaret Bentley (nee Ford, per *Elizabeth and Henry*, 1847) was described as 'an Arcadian amazon, nearly six feet high'—she was 5 feet 6 inches (167 centimetres)—and was known as the 'Bell Topper'.[31] Spirits rather than ale was the beverage of choice and a Main Street specialty was 'The Knocker', made to the following recipe:

Half pint methylated spirits
Half cupful of cayenne pepper
Half a teaspoonful of Indian opium
2 gallons of water
2 gallons of Jamaica rum
Use hot water. Stir well. Allow to stand for twenty-four hours.[32]

Violence, drunkenness and lewd behaviour appalled the respectable who lived and worked nearby. Two 'notorious prostitutes' stripped to the waist and fought 'like two pugilists' near Canadian Gully in April 1860, egged on by a mob until the weaker of the two collapsed: 'Black eyes, bruises and blood, with no stint of filthy epithets were the lot of each of the miserable wretches.'[33] In March the following year, thirty persons, both European and Chinese, petitioned the Eastern Council to 'disperse the women of ill-fame' who had their residences in Esmond Street. On Sabbath nights especially, the 'disgraceful scenes enacted and the vile language used by the habitués and occupiers of the brothels' made it 'unsafe and disgusting' to pass through.[34] Weston Bate argued that anxiety over alcohol, and the daily struggle against human beings out of control while under the influence, exceeded concerns over the cost of gold licences and the policing of the diggings.[35]

The most theatrical Esmond Street Vandemonian was Bet Naylor, who had come a long way from being a mere 'Wapping Lady' in Hobart. She was even memorialised in 1867 in a bawdy chapbook titled *Bet Naylor's Conversion*, priced at a sixpence.[36] The Eastern Police Court saw her often, usually as an accessory or witness, and always vocal. Her most endearing characteristic was her consideration for her countrymen, for whom she provided sex in Welsh.[37] She invested astutely in property. She continued to prostitute her own daughters but made over her eight houses in Esmond Street to her younger daughter Louisa in 1866 without paying the transfer fee: running disorderly houses could be very profitable, but it seems that these were all obtained via irregular means. Louisa died impoverished in 1883, aged just thirty-nine, from an abscess on the liver. Bet lived into her eighties.[38]

John and Mary Cray were now in the sex business in Arcade (now Larter) Street, Ballarat. In 1853 the Crays had been in Melbourne and in trouble for running 'a very disreputable house in Little Bourke Street', and so they moved on to Ballarat. Six of Mary's fourteen children survived to adulthood, and all the daughters married steady men and produced surviving families and sons for the First AIF. The only son fared less well, getting a short gaol sentence for being idle and disorderly, as did his first wife, and their children were fostered out—but the kids survived and one also served in the AIF. Mining and miner's rights provided an economic floor for this next generation. John and Mary Cray never progressed beyond running brothels, but the children did remarkably well, considering the never-ending violence and drunkenness that the court records document.

John Cray was born in the London district of Limehouse and was transported at twenty for picking pockets, leaving behind only his mother. Mary Holehouse nee Morgan was Welsh, born in the port city of Newport, and had no surviving relatives apart from a brother. She had married a soldier who had either been posted elsewhere or deserted her—soldiers' wives received no financial support and were prominent in the multitude of prostitutes in urban areas at the time, especially London and port cities. She had been on the town, a public prostitute since the age of twenty-one. Aged twenty-three in 1845, she had an illegitimate child who came with her on the *Tory* to Van Diemen's Land, though the only record of that little girl was that she was on the sick list on the ship—presumably she died, because Mary was to name another daughter Mary in 1860. Mary Cray was to be convicted and imprisoned only once again, in 1875 in Ballarat, along with her husband, for being an occupier of a house frequented by vagrants.

In 1857 the Crays made the first of their many court appearances, charged with assault and robbery, and John subsequently found himself involved in repeated cases of violence, even a shooting: except that the accusers generally got cold feet by the time of the trial. By 1858, when he was calling himself a cook and running a brothel behind a small oyster shop, he began his regular appearances for assaulting his wife. In April 1861 the court heard that Cray, still only in his early forties but described as 'an elderly looking person with a singular cast of countenance', became 'so mad with drink' that Mary Cray had to ask 'the girls'—that is, her daughters and the prostitutes—to leave for their own safety.[39] Like victims of domestic violence still, in 1862 Mary declined to prosecute when John was charged with thrashing her.[40] Many such incidents later, in October 1864, she brought him to court again: 'he called her every vile name under the sun', and had recently raised a knife at her but fortunately 'stuck it in the table'. She was afraid for her life, 'especially as he was almost always drunk, and when in that state, extremely violent'. John Cray found it all very amusing and claimed that his back was 'black and blue with blows from the rolling pin, with which the prosecutrix had belaboured him'. He was bound over to keep the peace.

But Mary Cray could not protect her children from the outside world. In 1866, her daughter Mary, aged six, was raped by a 'mere lad' of twenty who came from a good family. For this unfortunate lapse he received eighteen months' gaol. It was noted that Mary had already lost her hymen, which diminished her rapist's culpability.[41] Similarly, in 1858, when seven-year-old Agnes Hayes, also the child of a Ballarat prostitute and a Vandemonian father, was raped, there was no prosecution for lack of reliable adult witnesses. By twelve, Agnes had been convicted of vagrancy and of being a drunken and disorderly person. In 1864 she was sent to a reformatory for four years but absconded. Three years later she was described as a 'young ruin'. She died at Sago Hill aged thirty-three.[42]

Mary Cray the younger did better. She lost an illegitimate baby at sixteen but married a miner and had a surviving family with AIF descendants. And it was Mary who provided a home for her mother, who passed away at sixty-six from 'general decay and debility'. John Cray died in the Ballarat Hospital, painfully, from a strangulated hernia at the age of sixty-nine.[43]

CHARCOAL GULLY

Bendigo was made of sterner moral stuff than Ballarat, ruled as it was by the police magistrate Lachlan McLachlan, or 'Bendigo Mac'.

Having spent time in Hobart and blessed with an excellent memory, he believed he could identify Vandemonians by sight and was determined to run them out of town.[44] Bendigo would later have its own red-light district, a small area in Bernal (now Chapel) Street, but it could not compete with Ballarat for sin. Likewise, Castlemaine and the other goldfields soon developed rough edges, with clusters of tents and crude huts, often close to Chinese camps, where the alcoholic and the desperate clung to life. But once mining became more industrial, the old rushes and leads were left with a population of fossickers and failures, lacking the skills, the strength and the health to obtain regular work. These were the poor men's diggings, where miners could garner just enough 'colour' to buy provisions at the local store and drinks at the pubs. Petty theft, pilfering, dealing, sly-grog selling and living off neighbours and friends enabled people to get by. Many lived simply to drink.

Charcoal Gully, part of Kangaroo Flat, became such a refuge. And as the successful moved on, its denizens appeared more often in the courts, as exemplified in the following piece from a late-1870 edition of the *Bendigo Advertiser*, creatively titled 'The Scissors Grinder Gives His Wife the Cut':

> An Australian, Mrs. Partington, appeared in the Sandhurst Police Court yesterday in the person of Mrs. Eliza Rogers [Schofield, *Asia*, 1847], who charged her husband, Thomas Rogers [*Lord Petre*, 1843], with having deserted her. The court have not [been] amused so much for a long time, she was a person of rather diminutive size, but a never ceasing tongue, and an indomitable spirit, who had left the town of her nationality, Hull, in Yorkshire, for her country's good many years ago, and she joined herself to Thomas Rogers, in Tasmania, where he kept Johnny Fawkner's lodge. The old lady had seen many ups

and downs, apparently, as her face of truly Vandemonian cast was scarred, and the bridge of her nose had suffered severely, to its utter collapse in an encounter with her husband, she said. In '53 they sought their fortunes in Tipperary Gully, and since then had many places seen, Mr. Rogers practising as a scissor-grinder and razor sharpener. About eighteen months ago they were wandering in Amherst, when the unfaithful Thomas deserted Eliza and her 'pretty boy', while the affectionate mother was buying the dear infant some grapes. Inconsolable for his loss, she wandered through many places, until at last she found him in Charcoal Gully living with another woman, who laid a prior claim to him, and she brought the action to recover her own dear Tom who, by the bye, great as was the stir made about him, would never pass even for a respectable Silenus. We must endeavour to give a slight idea of how the old woman spoke and behaved. When the Police Magistrate was too fast she would say in an admonishing soothing tone that sent every one into roars 'Stop, listen. She didn't come before the Bench to tell a lie. She gave herself to the Government because her husband had forsaken her.' 'Hold on, sir,' she cried to Mr. M'Lachlan, when he was supposing certain circumstances from a chain of evidence, 'I worked hard and industrious in Tipperary Gully. My husband does scissors-making and anything in the cutlery way. We went out on the street knife grinding. We have a pretty boy, sir.' The 'innocent abroad' was here called up and certainly looked as if he knew more than was good for him. His beauty was only discoverable by his mother. 'It's my grinding machine the vagabond ran away with, your worship. I haven't seen him since he left me at Amherst, until I found him residing with a woman in Charcoal Gully. The woman's ... married him afore me. You said so, didn't you?' she continued to the other woman, who was sitting in triumph on the other side. 'I did not' she retorted. 'You did: God forgive the pair of you', this pathetically. 'I was married in Blanket Flat your worship; the watch-house keeper there got my lines.' Here Mr. M'Lachlan admonished her 'to be quiet for a little'. 'Yes, your worship, I'll hold my nose.' He asked her how she spent her time ... 'I work some time, and then I play.' 'How?' 'That is, I take a little drink, sir.' 'Oh, ho! my good woman, you do.' 'Look here, sir,' this in a scream, as she was afraid she had made a bad impression. Mr. M'Cormick gave her a trial. 'My child was born with a caul, sir. I have it about me.' Some weak idiot in court, suggested most of our companies were ushered into the world with a similar appendance, which the shareholders would much sooner not have about them. 'Were you convicted, my good woman.' 'Oh! many a time. He (pointing to Thomas, the delinquent opposite) never was convicted; (ironically) oh, no! I can't tell you how many times I've been convicted, all through a vagabone. Go on, sir; I'll answer you. I've been in Melbourne, Ballarat, and other gaols. I was in the Ballarat gaol when they shaved my head (here she exposed a bald peri cranium). He wants Government to keep me.' The husband was scarcely less diverting. He said the woman robbed him of everything. 'He had once been very rich,' and was respected everywhere and by everyone, though only a scissors grinder. He was willing to support her. She had left him. Here the indomitable Eliza, on the other side of the court, raised her voice out of the wilderness of policemen, 'No fear my boy, no fear cockey.' The other woman, knife-grinding Thomas said, was an angel who had saved him; said he, 'If I left £5000 with her (meaning unhappy Eliza) it would be gone in five minutes.' 'Yes,' promptly responded Eliza, 'in the bank,' whereupon the laugh was turned against Thomas. Mr. M'Lachlan, to get rid of the pair, asked if she would go and live with her husband. She replied she would if he would put away the other dear charmer, but she decidedly objected to a co-partnership in the Adonis of Charcoal Gully. The magistrate told them to depart and live with each other. Off the three set out of court, but the two lovers were too fast for Eliza, and she returned in a second saying, 'They're gone!' Receiving no sympathy, she trotted off after them, and tried for some time to keep pace with the cutter, Apollo, and his Daphne, but her old feet failed, and the last we saw of her was surrounded by a sympathising crowd—her husband and his inamorata mounting a cab in the distance—left lamenting that the faithless Thomas had 'bilked' her.[45]

These were dangerous places for women. Mary Ann Axford (*Atwick*, 1838) died from being bashed on the head during a drunken spree by her de facto at Charcoal Gully in 1868.[46] Sarah Bickley (*Asia*, 1847) turned the tables, however, when in 1857 she stabbed her husband William Thompson (*Lord Petre*, 1843) cleanly in the breast in Muckleford. They were said to have lived 'very uncomfortably' and the court was impressed with her respectable dress and well-behaved little boy who stood in the dock with her. It was only manslaughter, the jury decided. Twenty-two years later she married another ex-convict in Castlemaine; her son also remained in Castlemaine, married and had a family. Her great-grandson enlisted in the First AIF from Castlemaine. They had settled as a family.

Jesse Pearce (*Tortoise*, 1842) was running a brothel in Charcoal Gully around the same time as Mary Ann Axford was bashed to death, using a prostitute and two little girls to bring in the customers.[47] He died in 1877, aged just fifty-six, from tertiary syphilis. But most poignant of all was the end of Anne Ward (*Mexborough*, 1841) who, after a riotous time on the goldfields, was abandoned by her husband

William Broom (*Atlas*, 1833). She had syphilis and tuberculosis and lived with her youngest child Mary, aged ten, in a hut at Back Creek. Men were known to come and go, though it was clear that the mother was dying. Locals were too afraid to enter the hut, but Mrs Catherine Finnane could not bear to see the child suffer and brought her soup. The child usually hid in the dark at the back of the hut, barricading the door against intruders. But it was to Mrs Finnane that the little girl went one morning to say that she could not rouse her mother. It was a 'wretched death'. When Mary was admitted as a ward of the state, it was obvious that Mrs Finnane had helped her wash, but she was half-nude.[48]

Most Vandemonians in the goldfields had better deaths, ostensibly because they died in the care of the institutions the miners had built: the benevolent asylums and goldfields hospitals. In the Ships Project goldfields sample, ninety-six people died in Ballarat or its surrounds: just eighteen at a named private address, thirty-four in the Benevolent Asylum and twenty-three in the hospital; twenty-one of the deaths were unspecified. Significantly, of the men, forty-one had not married in Australia—almost half of them, including twenty-nine of the thirty-four in the benevolent asylum. The system, like the Old Poor Law, looked after those without a family, giving them a dry bed, some soup, and perhaps a stimulant to smooth their dying brow.

Yet at least twenty-eight of the eighty-three men and thirteen of the women who passed away in Ballarat had a home to die in. And those who died in a house, even if it was on a miner's right, were more likely to have a trade: butcher, bricklayer, pastry cook, blacksmith, and of course miner. Indeed, despite court appearances for drunkenness for fighting, just five of the eighty-three men and one of the thirteen women had criminal records in the central Victorian prison system. In other words, despite the Vandemonaphobia, the majority were not recidivists, and most offences were against public order and involved alcohol.

There were successful marriages, and perhaps few of their neighbours later guessed that they had once been convicts. Ann Ramage (*Mellish*, 1830) and James Murfitt (*Thames*, 1829) were both under eighteen when they were transported, but they were permitted to marry early by the penal administration and Ann bore five of their eleven children while still under sentence. James became a bricklayer in Ballarat, dying at the age of seventy-nine from stomach cancer. Ann lived to be eighty-nine, dying at the family home at 50 Pleasant Street. Their descendants served in the AIF.

Margaret Cullen was a victim of the Irish famine, transported on the *Lord Auckland* in 1849 for killing sheep. She was then eighteen but still only 4 feet 10 inches (147 centimetres)—her growing years had spanned the Great Hunger. She lost a baby while under sentence but married an English convict, William Starr (*Marquis of Hastings*, 1849), a weaver from Norwich. They had one more daughter, who also died. They lived a long life at 305 Brougham Street, Soldiers Hill, and William's death certificate in 1903 rewrote his personal history so as to erase the convict taint: his marriage was shifted from Hobart to Ballarat East, and his time in Van Diemen's Land was transposed to New South Wales.[49] In 1903, Margaret was a voter and still working as a nurse, a common occupation for older former convicts. She inserted a heartfelt poem in tribute to her life partner in the *Ballarat Courier* in 1916 and died four years later aged ninety. Margaret and William share a grave.

CHAPTER 7

The Road to Kyneton

The rushes to Mount Alexander and Bendigo caused an enormous traffic to pass through Kyneton. It became a halfway house to the diggings. Hundreds of teams and drays and horsemen passed through here in a day, or halted for a spell. Hundreds on foot 'humped their bluey.' Cute traders saw there was much money to be made in supplying the wants of the ardent gold seeker en route to the mines and the returning lucky digger ... The Robert Burns Hotel was the largest house in early Kyneton ... At times, every nook and cranny would be crowded with returning diggers knocking down their dust and nuggets ... Every stair had its occupant, every stair was charged for a bed ... Dr Kelly narrated how, called out one night to a patient at a Kyneton hotel, he found the proprietor crooning a Gaelic song and washing his hands in a large toilet basin filled with the gold dust he had taken over his bar that day.

JOHN STANLEY JAMES (THE VAGABOND),
THE LEADER (16 SEPTEMBER 1893)[1]

Early on 16 September 1862, James Hamilton, a farmer from Redesdale, set off for Kyneton, the leading town of the Macedon Ranges north of Melbourne. Around 6 a.m. near the Black Hill, he came across the body of an elderly man with the marks of a cartwheel across his hips and blood around his groin. He recognised the deceased but did not know his name. About 100 yards (91 metres) further down the road he found a dray with a dead bullock, the bow still around its neck but not fastened to the pole. Later that day, at the inquest held in the Black Hill Hotel in Kyneton, a cursory post-mortem examination reported that the cause of death was a ruptured testicle, supervening on old age and intemperance.

Lewis Hughes, a carrier living at Langley, north of Kyneton, did know the victim and that his name was Edward Ing. Hughes was unlikely to know, of course, that Ing had been born in Uxbridge and transported for seven years in 1835 aboard the *Augusta Jessie*. He had left behind a wife and three children and passed a quiet time under sentence. Ing had been a tiny man, just 4 feet 11 inches (150 centimetres) and 'very hollow in the chest', who had worked as a shepherd and labourer. He had never remarried in the colony. But 15 September had been a convivial day, Ing meeting up with Lewis Hughes and asking him to take his swag on the bullock dray to his own camp, as they lived on the same road. When the happy pair left Kyneton at 3 p.m., neither was sober. They went on to drink a further three glasses of brandy at Banks's, about 3 miles (4.8 kilometres) from Kyneton, and had even more drinks at the Black Hill Hotel, where the landlord and Hughes had to assist Ing onto the dray. At least they left before dark, with Hughes driving the bullocks and Ing sound asleep with his swag. Hughes' memory of what followed was confused by alcohol. Suddenly one of the bullocks fell and the others took off towards home. He cooeed for assistance but no-one came, so he went after the bullocks, completely forgetting about Ing asleep on the dray.

Only this morning had he heard that his drinking companion was dead. He had no idea what had happened. The jury was lenient, finding it to be an accident.[2]

By the year of Edward Ing's death, Kyneton was a magnet for travellers and settlers. Founded early, it was surrounded by good land, with thick forests beyond. With a courthouse, local government, a mechanics' institute, fine churches that included a large Congregational place of worship, denominational schools and a handsome hospital, it prospered as a civic and economic hub, hosting up to six flour mills that processed the grain being grown in the district. Kyneton was a vital stopping place on the journey to the goldfields and further north, and its two-storey bluestone hospital was a place to die for those on the track or living on the margin. It had no auriferous ground of its own and therefore no miner's rights, but nearby Malmsbury, Blackwood and Blue Mountain (Trentham) had short rushes, while towns like Gisborne and Kilmore flourished as farming towns. If a man or a family wanted to settle, they had to acquire land to farm, build a hut or house, or pay rent, so the gap between the settlers and the travellers was wide. Kyneton was a place to settle as well as a place on the road to elsewhere.

LIFE AND DEATH IN THE BUSH

The coming of the railway was transformative economically in the long term and quite dramatic in the short term. In July 1861 there were 500 navvies,[3] most of them Irish, building the railway from Melbourne to the port at Echuca. They were on the stretch from Kyneton to Woodend when they heard that their wages were being reduced by a third to 5 shillings a day. They promptly marched down the line to Kyneton, smashing every piece of machinery and rolling stock on their way. They bore flags and banners and announced 'Monster meetings'—it was Eureka and the Chartists all over again. Police were brought in by train from Melbourne, and the protesters tried to stop the train. Then the 'quality' took to their horses as the 'Malmsbury Volunteers' to quell the revolution. Up came troopers mounted perhaps on thoroughbreds, led by captain Standish, the police chief commissioner. But Mr Lavender, the Kyneton police magistrate, prevented the police arresting the leaders: he was much criticised for not protecting property and life with more firmness.

Supporters of the strikers marched from Castlemaine, Harcourt and Woodend and around 600 met in the cutting outside Kyneton; the Castlemaine men carried a flag with the Harp of Erin for Ireland. But the meeting lacked clear leadership and the contractors were implacable. The banks in Kyneton had sent their gold to Melbourne and the shops were boarded up. The final meeting ended in the removal of the Union Jack from Kyneton's Albion Hotel, and the attendees dispersed in the bar.[4] Kyneton's revolution was over. The following year, the people of the hamlet of Navigators, near Warrenheip, petitioned to have their township's name changed to something with less 'undeserved odium'.[5] They were refused.

We can trace thirty-six Vandemonians to a death in or near Kyneton, and the circumstances of their decease provide a small window into these largely unrecorded and unremarkable lives—they also represent a cross-section of the fate of Vandemonians in regional Victoria. They comprised thirty men and just six women. Twenty-five left no surviving family in the colonies, and twelve of the men never partnered or married. If these were survivors, few became founders.

In the agricultural districts, travellers—what the writer Anthony Trollope called the 'nomad tribes'[6]—were everywhere. Carrying swags or camping in tents or rough huts, rarely able to afford a horse, they roved the bush looking for work, rations and alcohol. These were the unsettled, those without a permanent home. And if they did have some farming land, they were often forced to seek seasonal work shearing, harvesting, digging and sowing, to keep up their payments and feed their families.

John White (*Ratcliffe*, 1848) had a home at South Preston on Plenty Road, near Melbourne, but one Saturday in July 1869 he was returning by foot from Wangaratta. Around 8 miles (13 kilometres) from Kilmore, he pitched his canvas over some saplings, and to survive the cold night in the forest he left a log burning a few yards from his tent. But the wind changed and he awoke to find his clothing, blankets and tent on fire. He had £5 hidden in his blanket, and in his desperation to rescue the money he burned his hands severely. He didn't know what to do, so he remained by the fire until noon on the Sunday, and after wandering around a bit, spent all that night in the bush. On the Monday he somehow walked to Romsey police station, where the constable summoned a doctor and White was eventually taken to Kyneton Hospital. Dr William Langford lost all hope for the man once his clothes were removed: not only his hands but his belly and his side had deep burns that had completely destroyed the subcutaneous tissue. John White died the next day, 'without friends', far from home. All that the hospital knew about him was that he was forty-four years old, had been in the colony eleven years, and had been born in Birmingham.[7] There was no mention of a wife or children.

Most people like John White did not have families, or if they had partnered, those relationships were finished either by premature death or unhappiness. The bush enabled homeless people to survive until their bodies failed them. There was always a riverbank or a forest clearing or a tolerant homestead where a traveller could set up for a day or so. Some farmers had huts for casual workers, but the supply of labour generally exceeded the demand, and the wages were pitiful, usually supplemented by rations. As Banjo Paterson wrote:

> Ten pounds of beef, ten pounds of flour, some sugar and some tea,
> That's all they give a hungry man until the seventh day,
> You got to be mighty sparing, or you go with a hungry gut,
> That's one of the great misfortunes in the old bark hut.[8]

Not long before he died in the Kyneton Hospital in 1864, Patrick Mooney (*John Renwick*, 1845) commenced a desultory court case where he sued a local farmer, Mr Finch, for £6, 18 shillings and sixpence in unpaid wages, alleging he had been engaged for 12 shillings a week for fencing and grubbing out stumps. He had known the Finches for ten or eleven years, he said, and was 'very intimate' with them, going to work for them for rations when he was out of work: he had 'always made a home of the place'. But Mr Finch, while willing to provide a place to sleep and some tucker, was unwilling to pay for Mooney's labour as he was an old man and not able-bodied.[9] The case was dismissed, and the Kyneton Hospital, unable to secure Mooney a bed in a benevolent asylum, nursed him until he died of old age seven months later.

In death, Patrick Mooney's personal history underwent some embellishment, no doubt generated by his own stories. He was a Waterloo veteran, his death certificate recorded. And it seems he was, but his twenty-one years in the 28th Regiment was somehow extended to thirty-three years as a soldier in government service in the *Kyneton Observer* report.[10] Perhaps if his seven-year sentence for robbery during the Chartist riots in Manchester in 1842 were counted, his government service might be extended, but at fifty years of age, with no literacy or skills, and a wife and young child to support in Ancoats, Manchester, reputedly the world's first industrial suburb, he took advantage of the Chartist disorder to steal. He was an obedient convict, but by 1857 he had begun to appear in Kyneton Court for being drunk and disorderly. He never remarried and just worked for rations and alcohol.

For the men on the track, alcohol and conversation filled the empty hours and dulled the pain from damaged backs and legs. The daily architecture of their lives was set by drinking. Drunken fights and feuds provided excitement. Setting fire to mean farmers' haystacks was sweet revenge. Lone females, especially young girls in the bush, offered the chance of forced sex—the cases of sexual molestation of women and children that reached the courts were but the tip of an ugly iceberg of female vulnerability in sparsely settled areas.[11] Vandemonians were numerous among this roving population. While couples often hung on in the poor man's diggings, few women were able to survive a wandering existence. And it was in the agricultural districts that the surfeit of older males leading a solitary life was most apparent.

Twelve of the Kyneton Vandemonian deaths were of men who had never married, and half of those were Irish men who had arrived late as famine convicts. Most worked on farms, drank too much, and died lonely deaths in the hospital, though some were remembered by the local newspaper. James Banigan had been transported at sixteen aboard the *Equestrian* in 1845 from Edinburgh, and after weeks of heavy drinking, he hanged himself in his employer's shop in Gisborne at the age of sixty. James Starr, who came on the *Hyderabad* in 1849 from Ireland, had tried to farm a small acreage but went bankrupt in 1871. He then worked for a Mrs Murphy for many years, was 'well-known at Trentham', and died of liver disease aged seventy-six. Of the twelve, only one made a public name for himself: Luke Gilligan (*Marion*, 1844), who as the colourful 'Thomas Turnip' cut a dash stealing horses in the 1850s. He committed petty offences all around the gold districts and in Melbourne. But he had clearly lost his touch when, in February 1868, while camped on a bend of the Campaspe River near Runnymede, 'two ruffians' seized him in a Vandemonian hug and broke two ribs.[12] By 1887 he was losing his mind, and he died in 1890 at the Kyneton Hospital of 'general debility, want and exposure'.[13] He was sixty-three.

The bush and the itinerant life were also a refuge from the constraints of society: many tried to lead invisible lives to preserve their freedom. They lived by scavenging and bartering their labour. They took animals when they needed them for food or transport. If they had families, they often did not register births or deaths, and many marriages were de facto. They did not bother about schooling for their children. This was not simply the desire of expirees to evade the surveillance of the law but drew on the deep traditions of people who had maintained their freedom from the state by hiding in the forests or marshes or wastelands of Great Britain and Ireland.[14]

WOMEN'S FATES

Drink and loneliness compounded the violence that was an everyday part of male-dominated frontier societies around the world.[15] But some of the Vandemonians brought the violence within them. The bush was no place for a single woman, unless she had adult sons and a small stable community around her, and some who had made an unwise choice of partner paid with their lives.

When William Kendrick (*Persian*, 1830) died suddenly in 1869 from an aneurysm of the aorta, aggravated by intemperance at the Piper's Creek Hotel where he worked and boarded, the 'widower' on his death certificate concealed the suspicious death of his wife, Mary Ryan (Ellen Bannon, *Garland Grove*, 1842) fourteen years before. Ellen Bannon and her mother and sisters were operators from the Liverpool slums, much scarred. A jury had found that Ellen had died from excessive inflammation of the pericardium, accelerated by blows from her husband. Yet the witness statements on the violence from both her mother, who had been transported with her, and from the police, in addition to the coroner calling for a warrant on the charge of 'Wilful Murder', were insufficient and he went free.

The post-mortem examination found Ellen Bannon's stomach empty and her body wasted—the same finding as for Rhoda Wells (*Royal Admiral*, 1842) at her post-mortem in 1863. Rhoda was a stunted East Ender from Stepney. It was not difficult for her de facto Charles Forrester (*Coromandel*, 1838) to wrench her head from side to side and snap all the ligaments. She lay in agony on the ground all day in sight of Forrester, who was lying on a bed. Her offence? She had objected to Forrester establishing a ménage à trois with a widow, Mrs Winch, who lived nearby: they were part of an enclave of Vandemonians and rough people living at Mount Macedon, stripping the forest of timber for the diggings. Forrester also escaped prosecution, living another twenty-three years in Macedon, growing a few fruit trees, threatening people with firearms, and declaring his admiration for the Kelly Gang.[16]

A third woman who came to a grim end was Ellen McAnally (*Mexborough*, 1841), a shipmate of the wretched Anne Ward who died in a hut at Back Creek. In 1860, she travelled with her husband John Barfoot and three young children to visit his sister in Kyneton. Ellen drank day and night, brandy complemented by beer, until she died by asphyxiation when her head fell into a bucket of water on the family dray; she was just twenty-eight.

The Barfoots' hosts in Kyneton were James Hockey (*Sir Charles Forbes*, 1830) and Ann Barfoot, who seems to have followed her brother to Van Diemen's Land when he was transported from Sydney. Hockey had a strong personality and fingers in many pies. The couple had seven children and had come to Portland Bay in 1847. Hockey set up as a butcher in Melbourne, where he and Ann socialised among the Little Bourke Street Vandemonians. In 1850 he was a splitter at Macedon when his wife tried to run off with another man—Hockey was another violent husband—and by 1860 the two were living apart in Kyneton, where he called himself a farmer. He was speculating in land, having perhaps made money on the goldfields. But his daughters and his wife were associated with a 'low house' in Baynton Street run by a Mrs Clarke, and the police were taking a keen interest in everything James did. By December 1860, they had got him on a charge of vagrancy; that is, associating with convicted thieves such as the bushrangers and fellow Vandemonians Samuel Cherry (*Candahar*, 1842) and Benjamin Long (*Equestrian*, 1845). One witness testified that Hockey's house was a nursery of crime in the district and that every prisoner leaving Pentridge knew to call in there.[17]

James Hockey was sentenced to twelve months on the roads and never returned to Kyneton. But the following year, three young gentlemen, sons of the Kyneton 'quality', broke into the Baynton Street house and threatened his daughter Elizabeth with sexual assault. The bench faced a quandary: it was to be regretted that young men who were 'respectably connected' should be in court for an offence that normally would attract a two-year sentence. However, 'the house did not bear a good character', notwithstanding that the victim did. The compromise was a fine of £10.[18] Some of Hockey's children later lived remotely in Blackwood as splitters and joined the Blackwood Settlement set up during the 1890s depression, part of the dispersed collections of forest families. Baynton Street could not be more respectable today.

The three other Vandemonian women—Catherine Salmon (*Mellish*, 1830), Judith Murtagh (*East London*, 1843) and Sophia Leaver (*Tory*, 1845), who married a free man—seem to have stayed with their husbands. Sophia Leaver was widowed early and died at forty-three from cirrhosis of the liver. Catherine Salmon and her de facto

John Beatson (*Neptune*, 1838) had only two children, but from those two they were to have twenty grandchildren and a lineage. Judith Murtagh was transported at the age of forty for having murdered her newborn illegitimate child. With Richard Lloyd (*Sir Robert Peel*, 1844) she had no more children, but it seems the pair did enjoy a married life where they talked to each other and knew each other's histories, if we are to judge by Judith's death certificate. Richard survived his wife only by a year.

Death certificates tell us much about how families talked—or rather didn't talk—about the past. When children provided the evidence for the registration of a death, they often had only the vaguest idea of their mother's maiden names and their parents' places of birth, let alone of their grandparents' names and occupations. Were they simply not interested, or was this a family who either did not talk or preferred secrets and lies? Surviving spouses and children were often at pains to conceal the deceased's association with Van Diemen's Land. If the person had happened to marry there, that created a problem that was resolved by shortening the time in the colony to less than a minimum sentence of seven years (as though they had just popped by Hobart to fall in love and marry), or the marriage was relocated to South Australia: that fresh, convict-free colony was frequently invoked on death certificates to supply a gloss of respectability. Richard Lloyd omitted altogether from his wife's certificate that she had been in Tasmania, let alone that they had married there. And the witness for his own death the following year knew even less. Richard and Judith had erased their pasts from the public record and attained freedom from stigma by silence.[19]

Marriages between convicts were risky when the parties were vulnerable to heavy drinking and fighting. Alfred Watkins (*Hindostan*, 1839) walked away from his life in Little Bourke Street while his wife, Margaret Pickering (*Tasmania*, 1844), worked in a brothel.

Watkins was a nasty drunk who was once interrupted by a detective Lett while bashing his wife near the water tank by St Peter's Church, at Eastern Hill. On learning the pair were married, the policeman was 'prepared to let them fight it out, in accordance with general usage', until Watkins struck him violently in the face and three others turned up to put the boot in.[20] Watkins, now a single man again, worked as a plasterer in Kyneton.

A number of men whose wives died or disappeared, repartnered with free women and stayed with them; others joined the tribes of single men in the bush. The wife of Joseph Luck (*Moffatt*, 1834) died in Tasmania in 1850 and two years later he left for Port Phillip. After a conviction for larceny in 1857, he settled in Kyneton and ran a shop in the High Street. In 1878, as 'an old Kyneton identity', 'better known as "old Joe Luck"', he died in his shop of phthisis.[21] His past was unknown. Isaac Neville (*Red Rover*, 1831) was a Kyneton blacksmith who, after his first marriage failed, remarried a free woman, perhaps bigamously, in Melbourne in 1846. His three daughters went on to build a lineage with grandsons in the First AIF, including one killed in action. Isaac was on the electoral roll in 1856 as a freeholder, so he had a home and a smithy after a brief stint as a publican in Harcourt. He seemed to have been a braggart, dining out on his past: the *Police Gazette* described him in 1870 as 'fond of drink, and of talking about Van Diemen's Land and his property at Malmsbury'. At the time he was being sought on suspicion of passing valueless cheques.[22]

SETTLING IN TOWN

There were marriages to spouses who came free where the steadiness of the non-convict parents protected the children. George Sefton, a Presbyterian from County Antrim who stole a pig with his brother, arrived in the *Orator* in 1843. He was literate, very tall for his era and able to plough. His time under sentence was uneventful and he had his free certificate by 1850. He struggled to find his feet in Melbourne, though, and was sentenced to three months on the roads for larceny in 1853. By 1855 he had married a young fellow Presbyterian from Donegal whose family had fled first to Glasgow. But he was soon struggling again, abandoning his family in Williamstown and was subsequently arrested for deserting them. Eleven months later he was charged with horse-stealing but not convicted.

The move of the whole family to Kyneton created new opportunities. In 1856 George was on the electoral roll, but he still battled to provide for his family, his little store at Snodgrass Gully eventually going bankrupt. He took in lodgers and stole cattle, specialising in singling out a beast and butchering it quickly for sale. He also speculated in land. He was surrounded by extended family: his unmarried brother Edward, who had been transported with him but kept out of trouble, becoming a keen competitive ploughman around Tylden; his wife's family; and his five children, four of whom survived to adulthood. Family ties provided social and financial capital, with loans flowing, although not always harmoniously, between the generations. Catherine, however, had taken to the drink, so home life remained turbulent.[23] George was only sixty when he died in hospital from chronic Bright's disease, his youngest, Martha, just twelve at the time. His wife Catherine, despite the drink, lived to be eighty-seven in Melbourne. The four Sefton children and their spouses all became pioneers in the Wimmera around Pyramid Hill, having followed uncle Edward who died there in 1891.[24] Such extended family joint enterprises were common among the Scots and Irish, who used emotional and material capital to survive hard times.

Two English convicts, John Light (*Eden*, 1836) and Robert Metcalf (*Moffat*, 1834), became Kyneton tradesmen and settled in the town.

John Light was a seventeen-year-old stable boy from Bristol, transported for life for the theft of three watches. He took time to settle in Van Diemen's Land, twice being flogged and sentenced to the treadmill. But, like many who made a new life in Victoria, he came to the colony before the gold rush, marrying Emma Goddard in Scots' Church, Melbourne, in June 1851. They moved to Kyneton soon after and went on to have fourteen children, ten of whom survived their father. John Light had a job for life as a miller in Rannard's flour mill (later the Butter Factory) and lived in a crowded cottage in Piper Street that he occupied by licence. His only misdemeanour was a failure to send one of his sons to school. The children remained in Kyneton, one as a maltster, the others as labourers. But by 1873 John was having accidents at work and the community expressed concern at the fate of his many children. He too died of Bright's disease at the age of seventy in 1889. His grandson Edwin died of war wounds in France in August 1918.

As a nineteen-year-old in Hull, Yorkshire, Robert Metcalf had stabbed his master in the side during an altercation and been transported for manslaughter, as a shipmate of Joseph Luck on the *Moffatt* in 1834. Apart from insolence and some absences from one master, he never offended again. On the Kyneton electoral roll by 1856, he established himself as a shoemaker in Baynton Street, one of the first businesses in the town. He had married a free immigrant in Van Diemen's Land and they'd brought six children to Victoria. They were members of the Kyneton Methodist community, but misfortune with weapons continued to haunt the family. Robert's namesake son lost his wife to hydatids after she gave birth to their seventh child in 1886. The following year, Robert himself died after a freak accident with a shotgun that he had filled with sand to shoot a young magpie. Kyneton rallied to the plight of the seven orphaned children and ran a minstrel performance to raise funds.

The next tragedy was just as remarkable. Robert Metcalf's son George, aged thirty-four, was working at the Glenrowan quarries at the time of the siege involving the Kelly Gang. He was one of those imprisoned by Kelly in Jones' public house and was severely wounded in one eye. The question was by whom. The eye would not heal, and George needed specialist surgery to save his sight. He was a poor man and so claimed that the wound came from a ricocheting police bullet. Captain Standish, head of the police, agreed to pay his medical and accommodation costs for treatment at the Melbourne Eye and Ear Hospital under a Dr Gray. But the surgery failed and George died of infection after some months. Only now is it clear that the fatal shot was accidentally fired by Ned Kelly himself while cleaning a gun he had taken off the boss of the quarry.[25]

Robert Metcalf, the father, died in 1891 of angina. He had done more than survive, keeping clear of trouble, and raising his family—three of his children would produce twenty-one grandchildren for his Australian lineage. But when he died, his real estate was worth only £65 and his personal wealth just £5. His unmarried daughter received the house and most of the block in Baynton Street, while her married sister got the balance of the land. It was a modest accumulation.[26]

THE FARMERS

Finally, we come to the farmers in this rich agricultural district, the jewel in the crown of central Victoria. Just two of those thirty-six Vandemonians were farmers, and only one of those died a farmer: the problem was starting capital, farming knowledge and personal resources. Settling and establishing a lineage, for one thing, was difficult, requiring luck, steadiness, sobriety and hard work, and those who did so in Victoria were by far the exception rather than the rule. While we can find individuals like James Kimber or George Scarborough or William Goodall who were quick to take advantage of affordable land, few Vandemonians were to be so fortunate in Victoria, despite the push to 'unlock the lands' after the gold rush peaked. It was generally the second generation that established working farms that lasted: the transported generation were too old, too weak and sometimes too battered to be able to cope.

The first decades of small-scale selection farming were hard. Transport and capital were scarce, while roads were few and often impassable. Livestock could be moved by drovers to market, but growing and transporting perishables had to await the coming of trains to bring the Goulburn Valley or Gippsland within reach. Orchards and vegetable gardens supplied Melbourne from its nearby hills and riverbanks, but it took the example of the Chinese market gardeners to teach Europeans how to grow vegetables. Joseph Jenkins, the Welsh swagman, described a landscape of small farmers growing fruit and vegetables, and rearing pigs and poultry, dairy cows and sheep, but struggling against savage summers, recurrent drought and the waning fertility of the soil, which, to his way of thinking, the farmers did not know how to enrich and nourish. Their markets were nearby, however, in the goldfields, and labour was abundant as the nomad tribe of bush labourers tramped the countryside. Jenkins was a man of many skills and a prodigious work ethic who found work and saved money, only to lose it by lending it to fellow Welshmen whose farms were failing. As much as he loved living in the bush, as age and infirmity grew, he took up a miner's right and was delighted with the cottage he built—it would last him until his health completely failed and he returned to Wales.[27]

From their urban vantage points, colonial legislators did not understand this new land. Their perspectives were those of the Old Country and their aim was to establish a colonial yeomanry. They could not see that the land and the climate could not sustain small farms; that establishing European farming in a now-degraded Indigenous estate was hostile to its innate ecology and doomed to repeated disasters from drought, fire, flood, soil erosion and later salination. They saw the landscape as robust when it was fragile. They overestimated the fertility of the soils and depleted them of nutrients within a decade. Above all, they did not understand the seasons and the climate. Only now are European Australians, despite the many subsequent successes of Australian farming, appreciating the scale of the ecological tragedy inflicted by colonisation and later the fossil economy.

John McQuilton, in his historical geography of the so-called 'Kelly outbreak', noted how 'each ethnic group applied its own cultural values to the landscape'. The Chinese, for example, chose 20-acre (8-hectare) plots near riverbanks where they created market gardens, grew tobacco or ran dairy cattle. They knew how to fertilise the soil with human and animal waste, and how to manage water efficiently. And from there they could transport their wares to towns by horse and cart. The Irish and the Scots settled for around 100 acres (40 hectares), running horses and cattle or sheep respectively. English selectors preferred 150 acres (60 hectares) and expected to profit from growing grain, only to be forced back to mixed farming by repeated failures. The ones who selected the maximum of 640 acres (259 hectares) permitted under the selection Acts of the 1860s were either squatters or those who had already gained colonial farming experience. They had learned that the man with few acres could not survive.[28]

James Dowsett, who came on the *Henry Porcher* in 1836, was the only successful farmer among Kyneton's Vandemonians. By the time he died in 1865, his farm 'Pleasant Banks' amounted to 155 acres (63 hectares), and it was to generate £120 per annum rent for his widow, Ann Cann, and by 1868 accumulate £268 for his designated charities. James Dowsett had been a farm labourer in Essex in his early thirties, with a wife and son, when he fell foul of the law for stealing wheat. He had previous convictions for stealing corn and creating a 'row' and his 'character and connections' were considered 'bad'. Under sentence he behaved well and became a constable, achieving his conditional pardon in 1841. By 1842 he was in Port Phillip, and assuming that his wife back home was deceased or had deserted him, he married again, his new wife being Ann Cann. However successful he was, though, he had his moments. In 1862 he clashed with Patrick Mooney, the Waterloo veteran and Chartist rioter, by then 'a miserable looking old man with a contused countenance'. Mooney was charged with being drunk and disorderly and of knocking Dowsett senseless with a whip. Dowsett admitted that he was not sober either. 'Dowsett, a most loquacious old gentleman, after telling a story of a particular cock and bull character, wound up by expressing a strong desire that the accused should be discharged.' Mooney hobbled off, apparently very ill and declaring he had a rib broken in the affray.[29]

The story of Dowsett's will and its contestation in the courts reveals some of the private tragedies that transportation inflicted on marriages and the families left behind. James had no further children with Ann, but by the time of his death, he had been forced to call her Ann Cann, known as Mrs Dowsett. It seems that his domestic happiness was blown up by the arrival of his son Thomas from England. Hence James cut Thomas off with a shilling on account of 'his unkindness to me'. At the same time, he took great care to secure a home and income for his partner; to annul a mortgage he held for a neighbouring farmer, Richard Rogers, 'in thanks for his care for me during my illness'; and to provide £50 for his brother Daniel in Chelmsford, and, finally, two bequests: one for the education of impoverished children of the Independent faith in the local academy, and the other for the Kyneton Hospital. Thomas was enraged, attacking the tenant at the property, a Mr Fyfe, and contesting the will in court, though to no avail. James had achieved a great deal yet could still not read and write when he made his last will and testament. But he knew how to farm and he had enough land to make it work. These, too, were Kyneton's halcyon farming days before the soil was exhausted. The other local farmer, Michael McLoughlin, did not do so well, but unlike Dowsett he founded a lineage.

Irish immigrants and transportees were more interested in land in Australia than were the Irish in America, and in Victoria they were even more successful than in New South Wales in taking up farming.[30] They were countrymen with some farming skills. Most had not finished their sentence until the gold rush was over, and while land had been possible to find in Tasmania—albeit there were small but often unproductive farms, such as in the north-east—many still tried their luck in Victoria. In that colony, the land acquisitions came under the selection Acts, and the owners were inclined to marry later in life as they settled onto farms from the late 1860s. They would settle near Warrnambool and Koroit, Kilmore and Kyneton, specialising in growing potatoes or in dairying. Trentham (Blue Mountain) was especially suited to the potato. This came often after they'd made some money by carting. Irish workers were also valued as navvies for building roads and railways, and the most enterprising set themselves up as contractors.

Among those who made good was Michael McLoughlin (*Duke of Richmond*, 1844), a literate, hardworking and devout man who was possibly framed for the alleged theft of a firearm in Queen's County in 1841. He passed through penal servitude without further offending. He also knew how to court a wife, and married the daughter of free immigrants in Melbourne just a year after receiving his conditional pardon in 1852. His first wife bore three children before dying of scrofula in 1861, but within ten months he had found another, Mary Murphy, also a free Irish immigrant, and they went on to have another seven children.

In 1855 he purchased a modest 20 acres (8 hectares) at Lauriston using £1500 made from carting between Kyneton and the goldfields and on the Bendigo diggings. By 1868, with his oldest sons now able to work, he purchased another 80 acres (32 hectares) at Spring Hill. Now he had the typical Irish settler's farm of 100 acres (40 hectares), but the land was poor and the seasons erratic, and by December 1874 he could not afford his repayments nor any improvements:

> I trust that the Board will deal leniently with me and not carry out the forfeiture within the present year, as I am a very poor man and as before stated with a large family struggling to secure a home for them upon heavily timbered land and poor soil.[31]

McLoughlin gave up farming and made a home in Mitchell Street, Kyneton, where he died, aged seventy, in 1896. As for his lineage, he had failed to secure a stake in the land and his children faced a struggle to make a living as the economy collapsed into the 1890s depression. Two of his sons and a daughter went to the Western Australian goldfields in the 1890s, where one son, William, died in a mining accident, a month after his father had died. The daughter who went to Western Australia had married in St Patrick's Cathedral, Melbourne, and another daughter married a Kyneton constable, Arthur Albert Calwell, who rose to be a superintendent. The family were becoming established, and even though Michael passed on the names of his family in Ireland and their history, it seems likely that neither of his free-immigrant wives knew he had been a convict. Or if they did, they changed the story. The names of his mother and siblings were passed down the generations, but his widow told his grandson, Arthur Augustus Calwell, that Michael McLoughlin had jumped ship to get to the goldfields. That grandson was born two days after Michael died, and when he rose to be Australia's first Commonwealth minister for immigration, he asked some of his officers to check the shipping records to find out about his grandfather's arrival in Melbourne: they found nothing.

Arthur Calwell came within one seat of becoming prime minister in the 1961 federal election and served as a principled leader of the Labor Party during a time of savage factionalism. He was proud of his Irish heritage, which had shaped his politics, but he had assumed that his grandfather was a victim of the Great Hunger. That he was more a victim of Ireland's savage regime against Catholics may have been a greater source of pride.[32]

JUST PASSING BY

By the 1890s, the Vandemonian pioneers had passed on, and their descendants largely belonged to the rural working class and the marginalised, living in the forests and the old diggings. Sometimes they were just on the road. In November 1893, an old woman with a bandage over her eye was charged with being a vagrant in Kyneton. It was Ellen Miles, reportedly out of gaol since April after twelve months' imprisonment for vagrancy. The police were asked to find her a bed, so they locked her up and proceeded to look her up in the *Police Gazette*, only to find that she had been 'repeatedly convicted'. Ellen replied that she was on her way to Melbourne, where she had friends and means, but that she had been travelling hard. As for her repeated convictions, she commented: 'Oh, what's gone and past is gone and past.' The bench gave her six hours to get out of town, but she had the last word: 'Oh I'll run away if I fall down. God bless you gentlemen.'[33]

John Skinner Prout, *Untitled (Probation Station near Mount Dromedary)*, 1847, Grimwade Collection, University of Melbourne. A rare depiction of convicts in the landscape, wearing their bicolour 'magpie' uniforms.

Samuel Thomas Gill, *The Avengers*, (c. 1869), National Gallery of Victoria.

John Thomas Hinkins,
(*Earl St Vincent*, 1826).

Samuel Marlow,
(*Sir Godfrey Webster*, 1823).

William Sidebottom,
(*Medway*, 1825).

Thomas Halfpenny,
(*Lady Harewood*, 1829).

'Hail Victoria the Free', an anti-transportation and Vandemonian cartoon, Melbourne, 15 July 1851, ascribed to Charles Norton, State Library Victoria.

Let the orations vaunt their fame/from battlefields so gory; Victoria boasts a royal name,/(A triple nations glory)/

Her sons to raise fair freedom's flag/In Melbourne oft were meeting/And vowed that on her shores no lag/Should ever set his feet in./

By public voice alone she strives,/Eschewing dead wars rattle;/Those who should spend in jail their lives/Shall never tend her cattle—/

So Pentonville or Parkhurst Bay,/Or Vandemonian Pet,/Adieu your wished Victorian joy,/No living here you'll get./

Samuel Thomas Gill, *Digger's Wedding in Melbourne*, 1852–1853, State Library Victoria.

Samuel Thomas Gill, *Sunday Camp Meeting, Forest Creek*, 1852–1853, State Library Victoria.

Samuel Thomas Gill, *The King of Terrors and his Satellites*, 1850–1880, State Library NSW.

James Kimber (*Eliza*, 1831) in his garden at Mulberry Cottage, Rotherwood Street, Richmond.

Sarah Bickley (*Asia*, 1847) with her second husband, James Greenwood (*Recovery*, 1837).

George Pickering (*Lord Goderich*, 1841). Photographed unshaven and just off the street, and shorn. VPRS 515, nos. 7542, 2749. Public Record Office of Victoria.

Daniel Backway (*Tortoise*, 1842) and his family, Maryborough, c. 1865, public family tree, Ancestry, and with permission of Mark Backway.

Ellen Miles (*Gilbert Henderson*, 1840), after her arrest on the steps of the Melbourne Hospital and her prison record for that period of her career. Her eye had healed but she had lost it. VPRS 516 P2, vol. 9, p. 124, 1884, Public Record Office of Victoria. Above it is her conduct record from Van Diemen's Land, CON40/1/8 Page 25, Tasmanian Archives and Heritage Office.

CHAPTER 8

Mothers and Fathers and Their Children

Love and hunger, their aim is one, that life should cease not.

IVAN TURGENEV, 'THE TWO BROTHERS' (1878)

Settling meant finding a place to live, an income and perhaps a family. Indeed, we can measure the success or failure of Australia's convict pioneers by the basic milestones of establishing and maintaining a family, which then produces a lineage. Creating a lineage means more than simply reproduction. It necessitates a household that can nourish and protect children so that in their turn they can produce their own offspring. And that is a test of the society and the economy in which they live, as much as it is a test of the individual. Happy families flourish on security; unhappy families too often are economically precarious. Thus, while happy families, as Tolstoy said, are alike and in that sense unremarkable, unhappy families are troubled each in their own way, or at least they are more likely to leave traces in the historical record of their offences against society, their problems and their griefs. On the other hand, they are less likely to leave descendants, either because they never partnered to have children or because their children perished. They are the losers of history, which is written by the winners, the descendants of the founders who became survivors.

Forming a family is above all emotional work. The practicalities of preventing hunger are often hard but straightforward, but the demands of feeling and expressing love are often impossible for people whose early lives have been blighted by parental loss, homelessness, violence, neglect, alcohol abuse and deprivation. What distinguished Vandemonians from their peers back home who had not been transported by the courts across the seas was that the majority came from families fractured by premature death or the absence of one or both parents. These were childhoods where the household, as a material and emotional economy, had failed: childhoods of loss that some, like Daniel Backway, would work very hard in freedom to put behind them. As Jane Humphries has argued, many men were frail providers, handicapped by lack of skill, or physical stamina, or mental health, but if 'losing a mother at a very young age was a psychological blow, losing a father was economically catastrophic'.[1]

A minority of convicts had come from criminal families that had taught them the crafts of crime—such as Ellen Miles and George Pickering—and they were among those who proved quite incapable of sustaining loving relationships. Their adult behaviour suggests brutalising childhoods that instilled habits of aggression and deception that certainly enabled them to survive on the streets, but not in the home. A minority of Vandemonians displayed the hypervigilance and touchiness of the abused child. Alcohol aggravated dramatic mood swings, turning people into raging beasts. Overall, few had experienced love, security and trust, or if they had, it had been cut short by premature death. It was not a good recipe for becoming mothers and fathers themselves. They might love their children tenderly, but the injuries of the past too easily surfaced in sudden violence. Quick relief from pain, depression and fear lay in the bottle, and in the bottle too often lurked dangerous levels of alcohol and narcotics.

Trauma was passed from generation to generation. Children witnessed their parents' drunkenness, beatings, fighting, screaming, foul abuse, suicide and even murder. Convict women were three times more likely to be murdered than those who had arrived free.[2] Children lost parents through terrible accidents or childbirth or delirium tremens, and they were often present at those events. They were terrified by their parents' madness.

Remember Henry Cavanagh of Warrnambool who had become more and more depressed over the summer of 1861? He began reading a book about insanity and on 26 February slashed his throat in front of his wife, Jane Robertson: he 'gave one holloa and grinned and staggered on the bed'. Daughter Lydia, aged nine and illiterate, told the coroner:

> This morning I saw my mother go into the bedroom. I was then in the kitchen. My father was lying on the bed when my mother went in. I saw my father with a razor in his hand he jumped up and slammed the door. My mother opened the door and I saw my father shaking his head about and staggering. He was all over blood and shook a lot of blood on my mother. My father did not say anything when he cut his throat—he only screamed out. My mother and father did not quarrel last night nor this morning. They were both sober when they came home last night.[3]

Lydia then disappeared from the historical record. In later life, her older sister Martha joined their mother on the streets of Bendigo as alcoholic vagrants.

Ashton Woodhead (*Moffatt*, 1838) was morose, withdrawn, but 'very hasty in temper' with drink in him. He became paranoid: he believed that someone came to him at his remote splitter's camp near

Steiglitz to tell him that his wife had abandoned him and their eleven children and squandered all his money. His boss, Mr Bird, told the coronial inquiry that no-one had visited the camp who might have told him such a tale. Woodhead became 'remarkably quiet and silent' and talked only to himself in his hut, as though he was talking to his wife, or sang portions of hymns. Then one night he sank his sharp American axe into his own head. The youngest of his eleven children was just a baby. His wife Harriet had a brother in Steiglitz who was also a splitter, but she took her children to North Melbourne, settling near the putrid Moonee Ponds Creek and the tanneries where her sons would work. Tragedy continued to stalk the family: daughter Harriet overlay her newborn illegitimate baby in the Lying-In Hospital in October 1879 and was too distraught to give evidence. She died soon after, the hospital reported, of a 'broken heart'. Another baby in the family was overlain, and young Ashton, aged six, was killed in North Melbourne when he fell into the wheels of a lorry after swinging from its back. Of the three descendants who served in the First AIF, two were dead within five years of returning.[4]

Above all, children lived with their parents' drunkenness—with their obsessive quest for a drink before all other needs, and their consequent neglect. Children went hungry, dirty and unclothed because of their parents' alcoholic crazes. In 1858, four-year-old Margaret Holyoake was charged with stealing clothes from a draper. When the police went to her home, her mother Hannah Perry (*Rajah*, 1841) was drunk in bed and the bench found that the parents' 'neglect and bad character had been brought under the notice of the police'.[5] Hannah died in 1873 at the age of forty-nine, with her youngest child just eleven. Margaret, then twenty and working as a seamstress, witnessed the deaths of both her parents.

Open fires, pots and kettles of boiling water, combined with flowing skirts, meant that burns and scalds were a fact of life, but drunken parents elevated the risk. The mixture was deadly, and many never recovered from the trauma of a family member burning to death in their own home. It was not just the children who suffered. So too did neighbours, forced to listen to the oaths and screams, the fearful thuds. And it was neighbours who often went to the aid of children and women in danger, and then testified in the inquests and court cases, describing scenes of intimate violence in streets and lanes and gullies.

And so, while the majority of Vandemonians proved reasonably successful at finding enough work or criminal proceeds to feed themselves and secure some shelter, only a minority would succeed as mothers and fathers and rear children who themselves could function in society. One crude indication of this is whether they had descendants in the First AIF, and those service and repatriation records provide some measure of how well, or badly, the families were doing two or three generations later. These convict family histories open a window into intergenerational trauma, the transferring of violence and substance abuse down the generations, and the cost in human life of extreme poverty, marginalisation and neglect.

EXTENDED FAMILIES

A child needs more than parents. In the past, extended multigenerational families provided essential support, above all via grandmothers. New colonial societies, populated by young singles and couples, set about producing the second generation without the presence of the senior experienced women in the family who have been shown to reduce infant mortality.[6] Former convicts were even more bereft than immigrants, who often arrived in family groups of parents and children or of adult siblings. Many of the most successful Vandemonians benefited from marrying a free immigrant and joining their extended family, as did Michael McLoughlin in Kyneton. A minority of convicts were transported with family members, but many of those went their separate ways as though family feeling was absent: Margaret Richmond, Ellen Miles and George Pickering all had a sibling in the convict system but appear not to have established continuing bonds with them. Family members sometimes followed their convict to the colonies, especially during the gold rush. Some villages even paid for wives and children to travel to Van Diemen's Land and therefore not remain a burden on the parish.

The brother and sister of George Haynes (*Westmoreland*, 1841) left their native Liverpool and were already at Simpson's Diggings when George was reconvicted of a felony in 1855.[7] One of the most remarkable stories is of James Colreavy (*Navarino*, 1843), who was transported from County Longford for receiving stolen heifers. He already had a large family and brought two of his young sons with him. His wife Ann then emigrated to Sydney with the remaining four children. By the time he had finished his sentence, they were farming in Wellington, New South Wales, and became a respected and talented family.

The presence of extended family could make a great difference to an expiree's success after sentence. Sometimes children succeeded where parents could no longer cope. Elizabeth Disney brought three sons under the age of ten on the *Harmony* in 1828. They remained in the Queen's Orphanage until Elizabeth received her certificate of freedom in 1835. But under sentence she had a drinking problem, and after the family moved to Victoria, she died in the Vandemonian enclave in Geelong, in 1849. Her sons, however, were to prosper, with only one member of the extended family later struggling to survive and his children being made wards of the state. The rest settled mostly in Ballarat, were prominent Methodists and local tradesmen, and over time produced a father-and-son political combination: from a Labor member of the Legislative Assembly to a bastion of the Liberal Party and lord mayor of Melbourne who was knighted.

TO COLLINGWOOD

The first requirement for a settled family was the proximity of work and an affordable place to live. And it was in this respect that the suburbs of Melbourne, Bendigo, Ballarat and Geelong offered Vandemonians their best chances of work, a home, and a future for their children. Once the easy gold had been depleted, thousands had to find a way to earn a new living, and the Central Highlands goldfields lost their demographic dominance as people moved to Melbourne, regional cities or farming districts. During the 1860s and 1870s, as gold mining was becoming increasingly industrialised with a waged labour force, growth came from smaller-scale farming, town and infrastructure building, and house building, with its allied services. The physical splendour of Melbourne, which was to become 'Marvellous' in the 1880s, was in itself an economy, absorbing brickmakers and bricklayers, stonemasons, plasterers, painters, carpenters, cabinet-makers, cast-iron workers and blacksmiths, roofers, plumbers and later gasfitters. Even in the poorest parts of the towns, and in Melbourne itself, tents and rough huts were being replaced by miner's cottages with multiple rooms and a scullery, or by terraces of tiny houses, such as in Collingwood and the Richmond flats. Melbourne began to see the emergence of service manufacturing: furniture, meat processing, leather goods like boots and shoes, clothing, tobacco, and later food processing. These provided a living, though still often seasonal and precarious, and increasingly involving semi-skilled or unskilled work as technology led to women and juniors displacing skilled men over time. But it was work, and it was out of the weather.

Victoria led the way with factory legislation and minimum wages for some trades and piecework, though that did little for the thousands caught in irregular or seasonal work. It also did little for those who were ageing, injured, impaired, or distracted by mental torments. These were the men and women who found making a secure and stable household the most difficult. Yet for those who were fit, and who mastered a manufacturing process early, like being a clicker in the boot trade or a tailor in clothing, trade unions would organise them into a modern industrial working class by the 1890s.[8]

The character of Collingwood was different from Melbourne's city centre, or from North Melbourne where casual labour lived off the market and the docks. There was a living to be earned here, despite the trade cycles that followed the seasons.[9] But the first need for families was housing, and over the life cycle of these Vandemonians, it was in the suburbs that families with mothers and fathers were most numerous. And while ex-convicts were to be found in all the 'industrial suburbs', Collingwood was the Vandemonian heartland of suburban Melbourne. Fitzroy had been the city's first suburb, taking advantage of its elevation, and it was the Collingwood river flats that collected the filth and flooding that flowed down 'the slope' to pool in the clay soil. Its first industries utilised the Yarra River to wash away the noxious waste of tanning, boiling down, soap making and wool scouring. Six breweries came to belch their maltings over the rooftops, and boot and shoe factories both large and small rose in the narrow streets. It was here that land was cheapest, residential blocks the smallest and housing plentiful.[10] Collingwood bore the brunt of the gold-rush surge of immigrants: a tent could be pitched, then a one- or two-roomed hut erected. And soon it was here that a home could be purchased. Once building societies began to fill the streets with one-story terraces of typically three rooms and a scullery, most with frontages of merely 25 feet or less—the smallest was

8 feet (2.4 metres)—they were snapped up by owner-occupiers and investors building a nest egg for old age. The rate books of the time reveal a pattern of owning two or three houses, next door or close by, with the owners often living in one. The long-term result was a landlord class that, especially after the 1890s depression, had little cash to spend on maintenance.[11] Small blocks, poor drainage, inadequate foundations and jerry-building all made for a rapid descent into slums.

Still, for those with little, Collingwood was the place to establish a household. Even for Ellen Miles. In May 1863 she set up house in Raphael Street with Thomas Watkins, who may have been her real husband. One day late that month, when it was raining, a Mrs Riding passed the house and Ellen invited her inside for shelter and a glass of beer. Ellen attacked the woman, pulling off her wedding ring and snatching her shawl. She started beating Mrs Riding, striking her forehead against the ground and dragging her around the floor. Ellen paused only to ask Thomas whether she should kill her victim, but Thomas was too drunk to give his assent. The stolen articles were soon presented to Woolf Brash, a local pawnbroker. Ellen was sentenced to one month's gaol and Thomas was allowed to go free. There is no evidence of their living together ever again.[12]

Of the around sixty Ships Project convicts who can be traced to a death in Collingwood, nearly all of them passed away in their own home, and fully a third died with sufficient real or personal estates to go to probate.[13] A handful died rich, two of them in the 1850s probably leaving the profits of gold mining: Thomas Chuter (*Woodman*, 1826), a sawyer, left £800 to his widow in 1853;[14] and Henry Moxham (*Layton*, 1839), who had been a publican in Hobart and was working as a general dealer when some blood vessels burst, left his young wife £1200 to enable her to bring up their three surviving children, the youngest being just two months old (that baby would be in gaol before the age of twenty, as would Henry's grandson).[15] John Hipper (*Asia*, 1840), was an illiterate bricklayer from Norfolk who made money from horses, carting and cabs. He built houses and a livery stable, finishing with the Hotel Suffolk in a block on the flat bounded by Napoleon and Stanley streets. He married three times, once bigamously, and had no children. He made at least two trips to England and brought his mother out to spend her last days with him. When he died, his full estate was valued at £1796.[16] Another remarkable saver was Charles Frith (*William Jardine*, 1844), who became a leather cutter in Collingwood. In Yorkshire, his trade had been shoemaking and his crime was stealing sheepskins and wool. He left no real estate when he died but handed down an astonishing £1000 in personal wealth to his illiterate wife and her children from a previous marriage.[17]

Death and funeral notices in the newspapers also signalled respectability and integration into free society. Some lived long enough to die as esteemed early colonists. Thomas Halfpenny (*Lady Harewood*, 1829) came to Victoria in 1836, he claimed, and married twice in St Francis' Church in Melbourne. He had thirteen children, of whom only five were still alive when he died aged eighty-nine. He had been a government servant as the caretaker of Studley Park, and in 1892 *The Argus* made a successful fundraising appeal for the 'Old Colonist' who, at eighty-seven, was too frail to continue living by keeping lodgers. Thomas' son Philip, who had had a short larrikin career until he won a Royal Humane Society medal for bravery, became active in the Political Labor Council and for a term was elected to the Richmond City Council. By the family's third generation, his descendants were respected Richmond citizens, and two grandsons died in the war.[18] Of course, spouses, children and friends who completed death certificates either fudged or remained ignorant of their dear-departed's imprisonment in Van Diemen's Land. Ann McDonald (*Midlothian*, 1853) was recorded as spending merely ten months in the penal colony, just long enough to marry Adam Clements (*Mount Stewart*

Elphinstone, 1845). Clements was initially a greengrocer in Langridge Street, but by 1891 he was reduced to labouring in Reilly Street, a community being emptied out by the depression.[19]

Most of the estates included houses, however. Thomas Long (*Hyderabad*, 1849) was a famine convict from County Galway who had stolen barley, never married, and worked most of his life as a gardener at Nareeb Nareeb Station in the Western District. He invested his savings in two three-roomed cottages in Easey Street and retired to live in the same street for his declining years. At his death, he owed his landlady £25 for board and lodging, and his doctor £20. The balance of his estate was divided between the Melbourne Hospital and the Melbourne Benevolent Asylum.[20] Wills in fact give us an insight into people's relationships and connections. When Charlotte Kimpton (*Lloyds*, 1845) died in 1901, she had four cottages plus a shop and dwelling which she divided between the three children who were still living of the twelve she'd given birth to. Her husband, a general dealer, died eleven years later, leaving no real estate but £153 in personal property—the 1890s depression had wiped them out.[21] Most houses were valued at around £200, although a few were very small and worth even less. Edwin Gough (*Pestongee Bomangee*, 1847) left his son £292 and a four-room cottage on land 25 feet (7.6 metres) wide in Stafford Street that was worth £200 and could be let for 8 shillings a week in the early 1880s.[22]

If they had no heirs, some remembered the families left behind in their land of birth: William Chaplin (*Strathfieldsaye*, 1831), after leaving small legacies to friends and neighbours in gratitude for their kindness to him, bequeathed a property worth £400 to the siblings in England he had farewelled fifty-three years before.[23] Most workingmen earned less than £100 a year, so the amounts saved either to buy property or in savings in banks testify to discipline and determination. Only three of the Vandemonians died with unpaid mortgages, and as has been argued by RV Jackson, building societies do not feature in these workingmen's home purchases.[24] It is possible that some paid in cash or secured loans from local businessmen. John Bidgood (*Augusta Jessie*, 1835) had his tiny three-room house at 81 Sackville Street gifted to him by a certain Wilkins in consideration of his having 'very carefully attended to him in his last illness'. When the illiterate Bidgood died, it transpired that, although the title deed had been given to him, there had been no legal conveyance, but the court decided in favour of his equally illiterate widow, Mary Hill (*Navarino*, 1841).[25] The real estate value was £10.

THE BIOLOGY OF POVERTY

The Bidgoods had arrived in Port Phillip in 1852 with three children and went on to have another four. Yet the poverty of their circumstances cruelly claimed some of their offspring: two daughters died of tuberculosis and another of peritonitis after childbirth in the Lying-In Hospital, all before John himself died, while another son later died from tuberculosis, at the age of thirty-one. Premature death stalked nineteenth-century families, dispatching parents before their time as well as children. Death was in fact associated more with youth than with old age. People grieved just as much, but they knew that their children could easily die. A failure to thrive—recorded as marasmus, want of breastmilk, inanition—cut a swathe among new babies, especially the illegitimate. Of the babies born in Melbourne's Lying-In Hospital, the mortality rate for the illegitimate and the very poor was catastrophic, reaching almost 80 per cent in the affluent 1880s.[26]

The Lying-In Hospital took in poor women, mostly having their first child, and like the Irish lying-in hospitals, it did not discriminate against the unmarried. But nature did, with babies' birth weights and mortality determined by the extent of their mothers' poverty and helplessness. It was almost impossible for an unsupported mother—a woman with neither a parental home nor a husband to keep her—to keep her baby alive. Until manufactured artificial feeding began to appear in the 1890s, being hand-fed as a baby was a death sentence. The only chance of survival was wet-nursing, although even in wet-nursing there was a brutal hierarchy for determining whose babies deserved saving and whose babies should be sacrificed. Single mothers could not work and raise a child unless they found a domestic service position with an exceptionally tolerant mistress or master. Prostitutes banded together to mind their children, and rougher families incorporated the children of unwed sisters and daughters. But the majority of women who found themselves pregnant and alone were forced to put their child out to be nursed, while they sold their mother's milk to the better off. Some of those nurses were baby farmers: taking in babies and young children for pay was one of the few ways a married woman could earn a living. And if mothers ceased to pay or paid a lump sum, the sooner the baby 'faded away', the sooner another could take its place.

The scandalous infant mortality of the illegitimate and the destitute poor was not simply about gastrointestinal disease, even though that was associated with many deaths, from those apparently caused by 'teething' to those prompted by 'convulsions'. The underlying cause was that these were often unwanted babies, 'accidents', burdens on desperately poor people, and perhaps it 'were best if the poor little thing faded away'. This was ancient human practice—to not work hard to keep a baby alive if it had little or no future, if no-one really wanted it. It was a form of attenuated birth control and it continues in our time among the desperate poor around the world.[27]

Bess Ward (*Waverley*, 1842) as Elizabeth Wagstaff eked out a living for herself and her family through petty theft and prostitution around Campbell's Creek, near Castlemaine. In 1888, her youngest daughter, aged sixteen, gave birth while Bess was doing her housework. The mother and newborn were left on the floor, uncovered, quite possibly in the hope that the baby would soon die. When the baby didn't, Elizabeth fed her some farinaceous food, which promptly killed her.[28] When the family did try its best, its status as outcasts went against it. The inquest for Elizabeth's son William, who died from scarlatina in 1861 aged six, is a pitiful account of the eldest daughter's frantic attempts to get a doctor to come: neither local doctor bothered because 'the parents are such disreputable people that none of the neighbours will go near them'.[29] Women were hardened by poverty, the daily struggle to raise a family leaving them drained of feeling. And they were hardened by life: there was little future for bastard children. Elizabeth had birthed nine children, and three had died in childhood. Her three daughters gave birth to seven children out of wedlock. Elizabeth herself was fifteen when transported.

Yet the Wagstaff family proved to be survivors. The two oldest girls became prostitutes in the Chinese camp at Campbell's Creek as adolescents, and both eventually married Chinese men. The elder wed a successful and kindly publican who died soon after, but left her well provided for. The second was less fortunate, coming under the control of an opium dealer and brothel owner. However, the older sister moved them all to Ballarat where she ruled the two households strictly and brought up a successful extended family. The youngest daughter, who had the baby on the floor, also produced children who finally found secure jobs and served in the AIF. The surviving sons remained very poor but seem not to have become offenders.

If some of these families were big, for former convict women this was not the norm. Those who had large families to match the general pattern in colonial society were a minority. Ex-convicts and Victorian Aboriginal women paid a terrible price for their helplessness

against sexual exploitation, suffering severe secondary infertility—
the effect of their exposure to sexually transmitted diseases like
gonorrhoea and syphilis, sometimes since the womb and often since
childhood. Unattended birth injuries, and especially untreated
partial miscarriages, added to the burden of pelvic infection, pain
and consequent infertility. The lack of fertility in former convict
women caused a genetic bottleneck in Tasmania in the 1840s which
is still discernible. For Aboriginal Victorians, it prevented them from
rebuilding their families until the twentieth century.[30]

The poor attended each other in childbirth, and becoming a nurse
or midwife was common among older ex-convict women who had
acquired long experience. If doctors were ever summoned, let alone
if they attended, it was when the birth was going wrong. Midwives
also performed other services, like forcing open the cervix to induce
an abortion. They also could enable babies to pass away quietly. Ann
McNeil (*Tasmania*, 1845) as Ann Spong practised as a monthly nurse
and midwife from her home in Lonsdale Street, directly opposite the
Melbourne Hospital. In 1870 she was the subject of a double inquest
into a pair of neonatal deaths after two exhumations: the first where
she cared for a Mrs Foley's newborn by giving her castor oil and gin; the
second regarding her own grandchild. In the second case, despite her
expertise, she had failed to notice that her eighteen-year-old daughter
Sarah was with child, even though the girl's condition was obvious to
Sarah's brother. The baby died soon after, and the jury decided that the
death 'was occasioned by the gross neglect of its mother at its birth'.[31]

BURYING CHILDREN

Wherever Vandemonians settled and started families, the poorest
among them, like all poor families, lost a disproportionate number

of their children. Patrick Fitzgerald (*Isabella Watson*, 1842), after some early lapses in Van Diemen's Land, became a carrier, living in Park Street, Abbotsford: four of his seven children predeceased him. Charles Westcott (*Cressy*, 1843), a dealer, lost three of his four children, two of them in 1866. Mary Copping (*Rajah*, 1841) and Joseph Randall (*Susan*, 1843) lost nine of their twelve, and when Mary died, she was living with a surviving daughter in Robert Street, a lane—the family remained desperately poor into the next generation. Such constant loss could break parents. Caroline Burt (*Rajah*, 1841) bore six sons and a daughter but had only one boy survive childhood. In 1861, three of her boys died of diphtheria in a matter of weeks. She was dead herself within a year, aged thirty-seven.

These young colonials were ripe for infectious diseases that were still not endemic and for which herd immunity was only beginning. In 1859–60, diphtheria, measles and scarlatina joined diarrhoea and dysentery in cutting a swathe through the ranks of children everywhere, but especially in unsanitary places, which included rural gold communities like Daylesford and Inglewood. Daniel Backway in Maryborough lost two of his children to diphtheria, another to severe diarrhoea and marasmus, and a fourth to meningitis. But the sharpest loss must have been that of seven-year-old Daniel, who was playing in the family's mining shaft when he was buried in a fall of earth. The father could barely sign his witness statement.[32] In Collingwood alone in the second half of 1860, thirty-nine children died of measles, thirty of scarlet fever and 149 from 'all other diseases'; over the next six months, measles burned itself out and killed only one child, but seventy-seven died from scarlet fever, which could cause lifelong heart or kidney damage.[33] Scarlet fever and measles would return with a vengeance in the 1870s, but by then typhoid or 'colonial fever' was the defining killer of young and old. Ironically, it even killed James Blackburn (*Isabella*, 1833), Collingwood's most distinguished Vandemonian resident on 'the slope', who died just months after work had begun on the Yan Yean water supply he had designed for Melbourne.

DEADLY ENVIRONMENTS

The problem with Collingwood, everyone avowed, was defective drainage and flooding on the flat. Filth abounded: excrement of humans and animals, decomposing dead creatures, food remains, fish heads and entrails left by hawkers, all languishing in large pools of stagnant water after heavy rain. It was the miasmas that caused all the sickness, people believed, not the bacteria and viruses living in water and in the soil and on hands and faces, or in the contaminated and adulterated food and drink. Yet the atmospheric dangers came not so much from the detritus but from the bowels, throats, lungs and hands of sick people, and close contact and crowding intensified the dose of tuberculosis bacillus or coronavirus or enterovirus. People soon feared the night air as the bringer of disease, so even in the hottest weather, they kept windows closed, especially in the rooms of sick children. Despite the piped water service, pressure was low and often failed in heat waves.[34] Washing hands was difficult, and anyway no-one knew that it made a difference. Drinking water itself was contaminated, as was the milk from tubercular cows or from the filthy hands and churns of the dairy keepers. A century later, old people in Richmond would remember watching a dairyman in the 1910s milk his cow with fingers black with dirt.

What made it all that much more difficult was the crowding. The gold-rush generation of free immigrants had huge families that for the poor were crammed into two- or three-room houses. A bedroom would contain two beds with seven or eight sleeping top-to-tail. Only the kitchen provided a living space, so there was nowhere indoors for children to play or pass the time. Childhood, therefore, had to be lived out in public, not in private. In the city and suburbs, the children's world was the street, and in the industrial suburbs that street playground would endure until after World War II and the coming of the motor car. Of course, the streets weren't that safe. The five-year-old daughter of a Collingwood Vandemonian, Samuel Crowson (*Georgiana*, 1833), was raped, aged five, and because she could only answer 'Yes' or 'No', there was no conviction. In 1903, forty-six years later, she was taken in by the police from an abandoned house and described as the 'dirtiest vagrant they had ever arrested'; she was still living in Collingwood.[35]

In the country, children had much more room to play, but this meant they could also become lost or drown in creeks or fall into mineshafts or get raped by strangers. Benjamin Burman (*Mangles*, 1835) was a miner at Connell's Gully, Daylesford. On 30 January 1865, his fourteen-year-old son Arthur went with a friend to a nearby dam, dived into 6 feet (1.8 metres) of water and drowned. Two-and-a-half years later, Benjamin's youngest, Alfred, aged four, set off with William and Thomas Graham, aged six and four respectively, to look for goats. They were sighted by various people, looking confused, but when offered help they ran away. That night was bitterly cold. Despite a massive search from the next day, their remains were not found for three months, when a dog emerged from the Wombat Forest with a skull in its mouth. The children had been only a few hundred yards from safety.[36] Their tragedy, known locally as 'The Lost Children', was marked by an essay prize at the Daylesford school and is commemorated still in the town by a monument.

Bush children could run wild, especially if their parents were drunkards. When called to give evidence in court, some did not know how old they were and, to the horror of the respectable, knew nothing about God, the Bible and the law. In the city, it was generally easier to learn because of the density and interactions with other children and adults. But even there, some children remained illiterate and unaware. Of course, we are not to know how many suffered foetal alcohol syndrome or impaired cognitive development from violence and stress in the family. Certainly, those who came under the surveillance and control of the police and other authorities included a disproportionate number of children with learning difficulties and neurological disabilities.

The problem for poor children was that the colony failed to establish a universal education system on foundation. It was cruelled by the churches' insistence on maintaining control over schools: holding onto the flock was more important than widespread education. Not until the *Education Act 1872* was school compulsory and free, if not entirely secular. Even then, however, the children of the poor were still lackadaisical attenders, with only half the children in the industrial suburbs estimated to be regularly attending in the 1890s. In crammed stuffy classrooms, many never learned to read, besides which the outside world offered boys all sorts of lurks to make money, while their sisters were kept at home to help their mothers with the babies—or if the mother was dead or sick or drunk, to be a little mother. The daughters of the very poor would remain more vulnerable than their brothers to abuse, infectious disease and malnutrition, as the gendered distribution of food within the household robbed them of protein. Many were weak and anaemic, and were remembered to be so well into the twentieth century, and they were more likely to die in childhood or adolescence. Boys could escape a toxic household; girls could be trapped. It was girls who benefited most from their families moving into regular employment and therefore respectability.

If a family is to succeed in love, it needs to be embedded in a society that provides security, support and a safety net. It needs infrastructure like education and health care. It needs a community with laws that protect children against cruelty, exploitation as workers, and abuse of all kinds. And so in many ways, especially for those living on the margins, colonial society failed them. The age of consent for girls was initially from ten to twelve under English common law until it was raised to thirteen in 1875, and the sexual exploitation of children was rampant—in prostitution, within families because of incest, and in the outside world.

THE LOST GENERATION

A major incentive to leave school as early as possible was that work for juveniles was plentiful and the structures for apprenticeship weak. The gold-rush generation produced a tsunami of children that surged through the population structure until after World War I. The shortage of grandparents meant a shortage of mature wisdom. It was a young person's world. Sons of tradesmen became tradesmen, and everyone else did semi-skilled process work or unskilled work, and it was too easy for twelve- or thirteen-year-olds to get a job and then be trapped for life in low-wage casual employment. Victoria was more industrialised than any of the other colonies, but the work was still often seasonal and unskilled. This demographic surge and the neglect of education and apprenticeship contributed to Australia's excessive proportion of unskilled labourers, so that even in 1938, when the Depression was still being felt, there was a shortage of skilled workers. It would take World War II and the postwar reconstruction to train thousands in metal and other trades. Part of the problem of Australian poverty until that war was the excess of 'unemployables' with few skills and declining physical strength as they aged.

In the regional mining cities, however, the manufacturing industry offered work for wages for men and boys in engineering. Here, the goldfields led the metropolis in advanced engineering and education, with the schools of mines in Ballarat, Bendigo and Castlemaine offering the first opportunity for the sons and daughters of working-class families to acquire a higher education and professional qualifications. An example is the family of Thomas Wagstaffe (*John Renwick*, 1843), a literate potter from Hanley in Staffordshire who was convicted of demolishing a house in the Chartist riots of 1842. Thomas became a Bendigo gold miner, but as he was dying aged sixty-six from haemoptysis and phthisis in the Bendigo Benevolent Asylum, he described himself to the clerk as a potter, because that was his identity. One of his sons became the underground manager of the Eureka mine at Daylesford, until he was paralysed in an accident. A grandson became chief inspector of mines for Victoria, another the architect of the Victoria Racing Club, appearing in *Who's Who in Australia* in 1929. And it all started with the Bendigo School of Mines.

Such opportunities came much later in the metropolis and in agricultural Victoria. A great paradox of Victorian colonial history is that a colony that so led the world in democracy should work so hard from the beginning to erect class barriers through education. While New Zealand settlements typically established government secondary schools within a decade, from the beginning Victoria built fee-paying church schools. The first high school did not open for seventy years, the Working Men's College (now RMIT University) not until 1888, and then only with philanthropic help. Denominational and national schools catered fitfully to younger pupils, but it was the education that could advance students up the social scale that remained firmly dominated by the private sector until the 1960s. The new colonial Victorians were acutely sensitive to status differences and were protective of their castes, making integration and personal improvement all the more elusive for the working class, let alone the Vandemonians. By contrast, well into the twentieth century, the engine of upward social mobility remained in the regional schools of mines, with new high schools designed only to produce teachers and clerks. State scholarships were the sole mechanism for poor Protestants and Catholics alike to finish a full schooling.

LARRIKINS

And so the second generation was stuck. Barely literate, little skilled and often bored, they took to the streets, oblivious of the future, a free-living universe of youthful rebellion, anger and pleasure-seeking known by the early 1870s as 'larrikins'. The population 'kink' of the gold-rush baby boom flung thousands of young people out onto the streets to find fun, friendship and sometimes crime. By 1870, 42 per cent of the city's inhabitants were under fifteen years of age—in novelist Marcus Clarke's memorable words, they were a 'perspiring juvenile humanity'.[37] Their scorn was for the respectable and the church-going, the orderly and the moral, the representatives of law and order, and for all the people with nice clothes and nice lives.

The gangs had begun forming around inner-city Melbourne in the 1860s, with the children of Romeo Lane and Little Bourke Street lounging on corners, giving cheek, picking pockets and finding customers. By the early 1880s, one observer estimated there were 5000 of them to be found in the industrial suburbs of Collingwood, Fitzroy, Richmond, Carlton and North Melbourne. In July 1883, a mob of 500 larrikins, drawn from Collingwood and Emerald Hill, descended on Hotham (North Melbourne) to mock the Salvation Army. They formed themselves into a band called 'The Skeleton Army' and 'assembled with full force' outside the Temperance Hall in Queensberry Street, where divine service was in full voice. The police were called and the Skeleton soldiers were prevented from storming the Godly soldiers, so they retaliated by shouting and singing and using 'filthy language'. They were dispersed, but they returned an hour later armed with small bags of flour which they threw all over the policemen and others, leaving the doorman looking 'whiter than a miller'.[38]

The violence was not a laughing matter, though. It was ugly and desperate, and while police injuries were reported, larrikins' wounds were not. Many young people ran with the street for a while and then retreated to respectability, like Thomas Halfpenny's son Philip. A handful were to proceed to serious offending. Yet out of the sixty Collingwood households traced, only ten could be found to contain continuing older or young offenders. In Collingwood, the children of the Vandemonians blended into the urban working class, largely invisible among the workers in the boot, shoe and tobacco factories, and the clothing and textile workplaces. Where there was offending, there was nearly always alcohol and domestic violence, and so too sexual delinquency and premature death. This small clutch of troubled families continued to remain closely tied to the state: in prisons, in orphanages and industrial schools, in hospitals and benevolent asylums. Their lineages either died out completely or were sharply truncated by death in childhood and as young adults.

James Foy (*Surrey*, 1842) was a Londoner who had been a clerk in London, and a constable and telegraph man in Van Diemen's Land. In Melbourne, ill fortune beset his family, with three daughters dying in 1861. His wife then began to drink and go on the town. By 1865, the three remaining girls were wards of the state while their mother was in gaol. When James died, only two daughters remained: one who lived to be eighty-eight, the other who would be followed one day by grandsons but was dead herself by the age of twenty-nine. The two grandsons, who were in the First AIF, had good records, were tradesmen and members of the Church of Christ, and remained in Collingwood. They survived, but the attrition rate in this family was severe.

Francis Moran (*Oriental Queen*, 1853) and Mary Ann Ormisher (*Emma Eugenia*, 1851) had nine children, two of whom died as infants and another four who died as young adults. Four of the children were wards of the state while their parents were both in gaol, the youngest under medical treatment after 'leading an immoral life'. One son died after a fight with his brother, and the criminal lineage lasted three generations.

Margaret Byrne (*John William Dare*, 1852) had married in Ireland at age sixteen and given birth to four children by the time she was transported at age twenty-four, only to be single again. After marrying Thomas Wilkins (*Forfarshire*, 1843), she had another eleven babies, so fifteen in total. Five had died by the time she departed this life, afflicted with debility and premature old age at sixty-one. Four children became wards of the state, and a son, Thomas, went into the adult prison system for typical larrikin offences of damaging property and larceny. Thomas, whose head was covered with scars, was illiterate. He finally left gaol at the age of twenty-three. His three sisters, however, had been trained by their mother in a nasty specialty of big cities: intimidating and stealing from children. In 1879, Caroline, aged thirteen, along with

> Rebecca Oxley, and Henry Oxley—neglected children—[were] found by Constable Nolan in the street intoxicated and having part of a bottle of beer with them. A lady gave them a very bad character for drinking, smoking, and carrying on badly altogether. Isabella Cochran saw them fighting and smoking in the street. The girl Oxley was a nice little girl, but the other was a bad girl. Thomas Oxley, in employment at the Melbourne Gas Works, in receipt of £3 per week, has two children in the Industrial Schools, besides the two before the Court. Caroline Wilkins was sent to the Industrial Schools for three years.

The Oxleys were discharged. The Bench cautioned the father to make arrangements for having the children looked after. Mr Marsden said the man ought to be flogged, and he could hardly control his indignation.[39]

Young Elizabeth Wilkins, distraught at having been abandoned by the father of her two illegitimate children, took her own life with strychnine two years later. Three of the daughters served adult prison terms, and each of them was dead by the age of thirty. Only Thomas survived until 1934. His son, still living in Collingwood and also covered in scars by the age of twenty-one, enlisted in the AIF, but his service was cut short by valvular heart disease, and by the 1930s he was separated from his wife and unemployed. The family was still struggling eighty years and three generations after transportation.

Larrikins and larrikinesses aroused deep social anxieties, especially the sight of youthful female vice and criminality. The cases before the courts for the conviction of 'neglected' or 'wayward' children often featured wailing parents who declared they could no longer control their offspring, claiming they would not stay home but ran away to the freedom of the streets. Yet in some of these families, the children who were out of control and refused to go home were only the daughters. They were typically running away *from* something rather than *to* something.

Hugh Sumner (*Ratcliffe*, 1848) came from a rural family that had emigrated to the industrial north. At the time of sentencing his mother was dead and he remained illiterate, and his crimes were typical juvenile felonies, though under sentence he offended only twice. At twenty-one he married and, once free, came to Victoria where he was soon engaged in public life, 'signing' a petition to support a parliamentary candidate in 1858. He and his wife Catherine had thirteen children, of whom six predeceased him. In 1873 the family's fortunes went bad—there was sickness in the family and Richard, aged one, died. In January 1875, Hugh Sumner became insolvent, citing sickness and death in the family. He owed £20, 14 shillings and 8 pence, but only had assets of £3.[40] His four daughters—Ellen, Mary Ann, Ada and Alice—began to run wild in the streets with the larrikins, earning criminal records for offences against public order and decency; Alice, the youngest, was the wildest. But all four Sumner girls eventually settled and were recorded on their parents' death notices in *The Age* as married women. Only one Sumner son offended and that was for bigamy, so something or someone had driven the girls out of their home and its protection. The mother died of cirrhosis of the liver, but Hugh lived to the age of eighty-four, never appearing before the courts in Victoria. After many moves and midnight flits, the old couple, who registered to vote in the new federation in 1905, had had a settled life in old age.

INCONSPICUOUS LIVES

The majority of the Collingwood Vandemonians did not ever again appear in the local courts following their time under sentence in Van Diemen's Land. They merged into the local poor, buffeted by the downturns in the 1870s and by the terrible depression of the 1890s. By then, many houses were vacant as the urban poor were left to survive with only the reduced means of the Ladies' Benevolent Society and the churches to see them through. The second generation would try their luck in the Western Australian goldfields, some even in South Africa, but the Collingwood poor settled into a hand-to-mouth existence dependent on insecure work, seasonal cycles and sweated outwork. Employers were able to circumvent the *Factories and Shops Act* by keeping the number of workers under the statutory ten. Women and girls making collars and finishing for the sweaters laboured in their own crowded homes in fetid air and dim light, and the piece rates were so mean that they worked up to fourteen hours a day. Once households fell behind in the rent, they packed up their few possessions and moved on. The little houses, owned by almost-as-impoverished small landlords, then quickly deteriorated—the damp rose up their unproofed walls, the plaster crumbled, the floorboards broke. Rats, fleas, lice and bedbugs tormented the sleeping. Only the outbreak of World War I in 1914 broke the pattern, with the postwar status of being returned men and the meagre but real entitlements that became available. That said, most of the Vandemonian families were still in Collingwood on the eve of the Great War, and many were still there in the 1930s. Their first real chance to move up from society's lowest rung, almost a century after their forebears' release from servitude, would not come until World War II and postwar reconstruction.

These inner-suburban communities were intensely sociable. The great daily pleasure that cost nothing was conversation. The families and neighbours and shopkeepers and their customers were immersed in a world of talk—stories, boasts, lurks, gossip, a lot of politics. Above all, from 1892 the people of Collingwood had a proper football team, and if the geography of the flat had not succeeded in bonding them into a community, then the football provided an architecture to weekly life, a totally absorbing contest by 'our boys' with traditional rivals. In hard times, it would be the best thing happening in many people's lives.

As for the Vandemonians, in the suburbs of Melbourne they blended into the crowd. If a few were noted for their roughness and criminality, there were plenty of others in their gangs and haunts who had no Vandemonian heritage. In country towns, especially on the goldfields, the Vandemonians were more conspicuous, and their lineage was sometimes remembered in the lore of small-town life, but in Collingwood, they were now safe.

CHAPTER 9

Secrets and Lies

'A LADY SWINDLER', gasped the *Illustrated Australian News* in November 1867:

> A very clever series of depredations have recently been perpetrated by a lady swindler as she is termed by the victims. It appears that for a length of time the lady has been in the habit of visiting lodging houses and inquiring for apartments. Having satisfied herself of the respectability of the house, she proceeds to inquire into the character of the neighbourhood and having obtained the fullest information of the next door neighbour, she takes her leave of the lodging houses, stating that she has been recommended by the person she first visited. She describes herself as the wife of a squatter whose station is situated near Piggoreet, and that she requires the apartments for herself and [her] husband. Having agreed to take the lodgings she proceeds to pay a deposit, when, lo! on feeling in her pocket, she cries, 'I've lost my purse; they have stolen my purse,' and forthwith commences to lament and bemoan her loss, exclaiming, 'What shall I do; what will my husband say.' The landlady naturally takes compassion on her forlorn condition, and promptly offers her the loan of a few pounds to alleviate her distress until she has time to communicate with her husband. The offer is accepted after

many refusals, and the would-be lodger goes on her way rejoicing never to return again. Such are the facts as told in upwards of a dozen cases reported to the police, and there seems little doubt that the lady in each case is the same. The lady is always accompanied by a little boy, dressed in Highland costume, whose tears mingled with the sobs of his mother, are the secret of the facility with which she accomplishes her schemes.[1]

The lady swindler was Mrs Alexandrina Askew. Outside Melbourne she would suddenly appear from the bush and dematerialise back into it afterwards. Throughout all her cases, she insisted her husband was a wealthy squatter near Piggoreet with 30 000 sheep and 900 head of cattle. As she collected more funds, her clothes became more ladylike. Her final conquest in the suburb of Richmond in Melbourne involved the family of a coach-maker, one of whose buggies she fancied. They invited her to take sherry and conversation flowed: about the squatter husband, the home property. Mrs Askew took particular interest in the daughter of the family, who was feeling poorly and in need of country air, prompting her to invite the daughter to travel with her to Piggoreet and stay awhile to recover her health. Such a pity it was that the new friends should miss each other the next day at Spencer Street Station.[2]

Mrs Askew was to appear in courts in Geelong, Buninyong, Bacchus Marsh and Ballarat, each time able to evade conviction and long-term imprisonment because she had never actually asked for or demanded money or clothing—it was always freely offered to her. Only the Melbourne police were able to prosecute her under the *Vagrancy Act*. When a miner from Bulldog (later Illabarook) offered on behalf of Alexandrina's husband, in reality himself a poor miner at Bulldog, to pay back all the money she had 'borrowed', the judge said that was not sufficient and sentenced her to two weeks' gaol, in consideration of the five weeks spent on remand.[3]

Around 14 January 1868, Mrs Askew travelled from Melbourne to Ballarat after being discharged from gaol, obtaining a lift with the agent of a local politician: he described her as a 'short, stout woman with a baby in arms' whose husband had failed to collect her in Melbourne. She had been very communicative, explaining she was 'on business, on a lawsuit'. And she was a sister to a Mr Grant. She alighted by request near the settlement at Gordons, saying she wanted to go through the bush. She was still many miles across country from home.[4]

A week later, she was in Bacchus Marsh Court attending to the aforementioned lawsuit. This time she sat demurely with her counsel, Mr Gell, at the bar, not in the dock, nursing her youngest child. The case was brought by a fellow highlander, William McDonald, who complained that he had given her accommodation, and that she had regaled him with the account of her noble father who owned the Glenmoriston estate, her squatter husband who had 30 000 sheep, and her thriving shop in Ballarat. Furthermore, when she discovered in the morning that her purse was unaccountably empty of three cheques for £70, and a carriage and £3 were pressed upon her, she had promised her benefactor a cow, some Mountain Dew whiskey, and enough money to 'make him a gentleman'. Mrs Askew had a good barrister, who mocked William McDonald for his gullibility. The poor Highlander snapped back:

> I only took her to Mr Johnston's [for a buggy] because she was a Scotchwoman and represented herself as the daughter of a nobleman. She talked Gaelic to me and I to her. I have talked Gaelic to better than you Mr Gell.[5]

Who was Alexandrina Askew? And where did she really come from?

She arrived as Alexandrina Grant on the convict ship *Tory* in Hobart in 1845, along with thirty-eight other Scottish women among a shipload of 170 who were otherwise from England. She was eighteen, allegedly born in Inverness, and had been transported for 'falsehoods, fraud and wilful imposition' in obtaining clothes. Like all convicts transported by the Scottish courts, she had form: she'd already served sixty days for theft, and she reported that she had done six months for 'leaving my place'. She had been convicted in Aberdeen at the age of seventeen and had been on the town for two years. When she alighted in Hobart, she recited an imaginary family to the convict clerk: her father John, and her brothers William, James, Dennis, Alexander, John and Donald, plus her sister Elizabeth, all at her native place. But there is no sign of them in the census: in fact, there is no record of a Dennis Grant anywhere in Scotland before 1901.

Alexandrina's trial in Aberdeen in late September 1844 shed some light on her past. She was quite a sensation: 'a good-looking girl of rather genteel appearance' of about nineteen years of age. She was, said *The Aberdeen Journal*, 'well-known about Inverness, where she has, by her plausible manner and address and specious representations, contrived to take advantage of the anxiety which the public has to serve people of rank and importance, and obtain their patronage'. It was the same modus operandi as in her 1867 outbreak. The second charge, for instance, was that three months earlier, she had called at the shop in the High Street, Old Aberdeen, of a woman named M'Donald, and to

> this woman, the prisoner stated that she was the daughter of a General Cruickshank in the west country, and that she was residing in Mr Sutherland's cottage, betwixt the new and the old towns. She purchased some small articles, among which was a piece of ribbon and a napkin. She put the ribbon upon her bonnet in the shop; and when ready to go away, expressed her regret that she had forgot her purse. This, however, she said, would make

little difference, as she would call that night and pay the goods. Mrs M'Donald, although not absolutely suspicious of what kind of a customer she had to do with, was not altogether satisfied and would only allow her to take part of her purchases away. With these, the panel went off; and not appearing at the promised time, Mrs M'Donald took off in search of her, and, on the evening of the next day, found her in a house in the Gallowgate; but although she received a bonnet in token that the panel would pay her, she did not see her again until she was in custody.[6]

In prison, Alexandrina provided two separate identities and lineages, of Alexandrina Grant and of Jemima McKenzie, and offered that she had been twice convicted at Inverness under the latter name. The truth, however, was finally ascertained and her real family name was now thought to be Rose.

Her misfortunes began with her life because she was born in jail. Her father and mother were both, soon after her birth, banished, at separate times, to one of the penal colonies; and so circumstanced their poor offspring, having grown up without those on whom lay the duty of protecting and instructing her, has the more easily fallen into error. Having a fine person, agreeable manners, and uncommon ingenuity, she has made these her stock in trade, and her business, systematic fraud.[7]

On the voyage out, the perceptive ship's surgeon described Alexandrina as 'orderly but precious'. Under her seven-year sentence she was frequently absent without leave, meeting men at night, and consequently bore an illegitimate child in the Cascades Female Factory in 1849. She found no-one presumably good enough to marry her, and domestic service was not to her liking, so she spent most of her sentence in the female factories. She was twice dismissed for telling falsehoods and misrepresentation, and was forbidden to work in Hobart or Launceston. She did not make a good impression. Therefore, when she went to Port Phillip and quickly attracted a young new immigrant from Bermondsey in London, she lowered her age, excised her convict past, and reinvented herself to build the family, if not the social position, she craved.

Why is this story worth telling beyond its poignancy? It matters because Alexandrina Grant was a success among Scottish convict women transported to Van Diemen's Land. She lived into her ninth decade; was not a conspicuous drunkard; married a free man who stayed with her until his death; bore ten children, six of whom lived into middle life; and successfully delivered and reared the illegitimate child of her second daughter under the common fiction that it was her own. Moreover, two of her daughters, including the one who had a baby out of wedlock at sixteen, married good providers, even if one was an eccentric Swiss-Italian self-styled professor who dealt over the years variously in mesmerism, phrenology, homeopathy and marriage guidance. Some of her descendants continued to have problems differentiating fantasy from mundane reality, but despite periods of mental illness and fabulism, Alexandrina was apparently loved.[8] The final chapter of her life took place in Sydney, where she ran boarding houses at dubious addresses in Redfern, twice going bankrupt. Few of the 1636 Scottish women transported to Van Diemen's Land achieved anything like this ordinary triumph over poverty, stigma and marginalisation.

ASPIRATIONALS

Alexandrina, or Jemima or Alice, as she became in later life, illustrated in extreme personal form the pain of perceived inferiority and stigma:

the daily humiliations of being a nobody, without a family let alone a lineage. If her secrets and lies were spectacular, they were nonetheless reflective of the desperation of the socially thwarted and ignored. She felt she deserved to be a somebody, a woman of refinement, respected and deferred to—not an old lag, a former homeless woman of the town, a bastard child born in gaol to convict parents. She suffered a form of social dysphoria, born into the wrong social body. Alexandrina knew how to speak and deport herself like a lady, except that her secret was that she wasn't.

The terrible daily burden of the convict stain—of spoiled identity—meant that people had to lie and withhold secrets, even from their own partners and children. There were significant passages of their lives that could not be spoken of, stories that could not be recounted, memories that could not be shared. Always they had to calculate how best to obscure the missing seven or ten years of their servitude in their personal narrative. Many changed their name and then had to guard against dropping the wrong name, or place of birth, or work history, let alone criminal history. Many, it seems, succeeded admirably in concealing their convict past from their families, only to be found out later by assiduous genealogists.

Vandemonians were expected to re-enter society at the bottom of the human ladder and remain there. Over time they might be tolerated as amusing eccentrics, or shunned as people of untrustworthy character, but either way they could not rise and blend in with those who had been received. They had crossed over to 'the other side', and there they were doomed to remain. Yet some of them had genteel origins, if not aspirations. While women were more prone to elaborate deceptions and constructed identities—a practice that continues today with some nannies and wellness gurus—men also indulged in deception as magsmen (raconteurs) and tricksters. But among the convicts of Van Diemen's Land was a clutch of women whose crimes were yearnings for things above their station: for positions, husbands, lodgings, or finery or jewellery they could not pay for. They had the good fortune to be born good-looking and intelligent and so they could be plausible and ladylike. They were also especially vulnerable to seduction and abandonment, and the trigger for crime was often a betrayal or desertion by a lover.

Annette Meyers (*Emma Eugenia*, 1850), like many of the lady convicts, claimed French birth and aristocratic connections, but she was illegitimate. Her Coldstream Guard lover infected her with venereal disease, impregnated her, then dumped her when she refused to prostitute herself and give him her earnings. She killed him with a single shot to the back of the head in St James' Park. The court showed some clemency and she was sentenced to transportation for life. She ended her days a married woman in Park Place, off Park Street, South Yarra.

Lucy Taylor died in the Melbourne Gaol hospital of peritonitis in 1884 after she was found in a helpless condition sitting on a pavement. She was covered in vermin and her leg was hideously ulcerated. Born in Dublin, she had been transported as Lucilia De La Constantine (*Emma Eugenia*, 1846) after a career of theft and deception in Exeter, where she had been previously convicted as Alexina Flaurin. She had resided with a Mr Gosman for two years but had then had to fend for herself. It has been discovered that she used twenty different names during her forty-year public career, the plainest from her two marriages to a Mr Barker and a Mr Taylor. Her pretensions were always betrayed by her foul tongue and fondness for drink.

Mary Fennelly, born in Ireland, made a success of her new life, however. She came on the *Gilbert Henderson* in 1840 as a fifteen-year-old in company with Ellen Miles, Ellen Leary, Agnes Mosley and tiny Janet Dunn. Her original crime was a spectacular heist as a servant in Liverpool, whereupon she passed gold sovereigns and other coins to the value of over £100, plus clothing and jewellery, to her father, with both subsequently transported for ten years. Under sentence she offended four times. Forbidden to marry her lover, she bore a son in Evandale in 1844 to James Farrer, then married a Roger Parkinson in January 1846. They went to Port Phillip, where he disappeared and she became a housekeeper to a prominent early settler, Jesse Fairchild. Red-headed and intelligent, she won Jesse's heart, and in July 1849 they married at St James' Church, Melbourne. Mary's illegitimate son was adopted by Jesse as his own, and the Fairchilds became a formidable commercial couple. When Mary died aged eighty-five in 1907, the *Prahran Telegraph* told her remarkable story:

> On Saturday last, at the Esplanade Hotel, there passed away one of the oldest residents of St Kilda in Mrs. Mary Fairchild, relict of the late Mr. Jesse Fairchild, who himself was one of the earliest settlers in this State. The deceased lady's benevolence had for many years won her the esteem of the community, and her death, though not wholly unexpected—owing to her advanced age (85 years)—will be very generally regretted. Among her benefactions was a gift of £500 to the Old Colonists' Home, this sum to be devoted to the erection and endowment of a cottage, while £1000 was provided for the endowment to two more. As far back as 1840 Mr. Fairchild arrived in Victoria, and at once entered pastoral pursuits. He bought a station near Benalla, which he stocked with sheep, so disadvantageous as regarded values that he lost a considerable sum; in fact, all that he had. Being a man of spirit and perseverance, however, he was not daunted by this reverse, but came to Melbourne, where he obtained work at the fellmongery of Messrs. Jackson, Ray, and Co. After some years his push and business acumen asserted itself, and [with] certain changes taking place in the

business, he took over the whole concern. In this venture he was highly successful, being energetically and practically assisted by his wife. During the land boom fever of the eighties, however, Mr. Fairchild lost considerable money, and he himself frequently subsequently remarked that he might possibly have been disastrously reduced in circumstances but for the foresight and business tact of his helpmate. When Mr. Fairchild died his widow erected the imposing drinking fountain that still stands on the St Kilda Esplanade. The deceased lady only returned from England in November last, and had been residing at the Esplanade Hotel for some time past. An interesting record of travel is that she had been to England and the Continent no fewer than fourteen times. The remains were interred in the Boroondara Cemetery on Sunday, the funeral arrangements being most satisfactorily carried out by Mr. B. Matthews.[9]

The Fairchilds had lived in a beautiful terrace at 37 Dalgety Street, St Kilda, and on her death, Mary's estate was valued at £37 500: real estate of £10 000 and a personal estate of £27 500. Their biography was rewritten as a couple who had come to Port Phillip together in 1840, and her huge will endowed multiple extended family members in Australia and England as well as charitable bequests. The handsome drinking fountain she dedicated to her husband still stands on St Kilda's Esplanade.

Ellen Fraser (*Harmony*, 1829) was another convict who rose into respectability. She married Edward Butler (*Chapman*, 1827) after a de-facto relationship that produced a baby who did not survive. Butler became a successful farmer at Glenorchy, but when the couple's only surviving child, Jane Mary, married in Melbourne in 1857, they sold up and established a pawnbroker business in Victoria Parade. Jane Mary married well, to the Methodist Reverend James Walter Crisp, one of the many successful sons of Samuel Crisp (*Earl St Vincent*, 1826), who built a large timber business and died leaving twelve children, eighty grandchildren and eighteen great-grandchildren—the Crisps went from being a convict dynasty to a distinguished legal dynasty over several generations. Edward Butler died in 1867 and Ellen probably went to live with the Crisps as they moved around the Methodist circuits, including Warrnambool, where the Reverend Crisp became close to that other convict's son, William Goodall, the manager of the Framlingham Aboriginal reserve.[10] Jane Mary Crisp died at the age of fifty, with just three of her eight children surviving childhood. The reverend Crisp moved to the Melbourne circuits and spent time in North Melbourne, where his new wife Hope was so shocked by the misery of the slum children that the Crisps became active in child rescue. As a minister at the Wesley Church in the city, James helped build the City Mission, and in 1888, the Crisps were licensed by the state to rescue children from neglect and moral danger. This was the beginning of the work of the Methodist Church in Victoria on behalf of such children.[11] James Crisp's final parsonage was in Bell Street, Coburg, where he was the Methodist chaplain for Pentridge Prison.

It was in Coburg that Ellen Fraser, in her ninety-second year, died, still under James' care. When the reverend Crisp witnessed her death certificate, however, he appeared not to know the names of Ellen's parents, nor the fact that she had married in Van Diemen's Land, nor that his first wife was not only born there but had spent all her youth in the penal colony. As for Ellen, she had been seventy years in Victoria, he reported, making her a colonist before Batman and Fawkner.

The secrets and lies were rendered official for posterity by death certificates, especially if they were witnessed by family members. Mary Fairchild had had a son still living when she'd died—the one born during her de-facto relationship with James Farrer and who'd been adopted by Jesse Fairchild—but she too, it seems, had been in Victoria a long time, for sixty-three years, almost contemporaneously with Batman, and not in Tasmania for her son's birth.[12] Similarly for John Dudgeon (*Gilmore*, 1843), a horse-hair tradesman from Bermondsey who started as a tobacconist in Melbourne and built a very large business as a tobacco and snuff manufacturer, and whose probate in 1884, after he died from lung cancer, was valued at a massive £67 868. His death certificate was silent on his parents and omitted his ten years in Tasmania.[13]

Some did manage to successfully utilise their history rather than keeping it secret. The following appeared in Ireland under the loud headline 'HORRORS OF TRANSPORTATION BY A RETURNED FEMALE CONVICT':

> A lecture will be delivered in the Gallery of Art on Thursday and Friday evenings the 7th and 8th June by SYDNEY KEELEN on the 'Horrors of Transportation'. She was transported from Armagh in July 1849 and will give details of her whole life. Reserved Seats 1s Second Seats 6d. Doors open at 7.30pm Lecture commences at 8.00pm. Tickets to be had at Mr Henderson's Castle Place and at the door. Belfast 4th June 1860.[14]

The news made it all the way to Victoria, where, ten weeks later, the *Mount Alexander Mail* reported:

> Lecture by a Returned Convict—A young woman named Sidney Keelen, who was convicted at Armagh summer assizes, 1849, on a charge of stealing cattle, and transported for seven years, has just returned to Ireland, from Van Diemen's Land, and is at present delivering a course of lectures on her personal history

and the horrors of transportation, in various towns in Ulster. During the past week, she appeared in Castlebayney and Keady, and on Wednesday evening she addressed an audience in the Market House, Armagh. She was introduced by the Governor of Armagh Gaol. Miss Keelen speaks very fluently, though occasionally she betrays her imperfect education. She is about twenty-eight years of age, neatly attired, and seems perfectly at home before an audience. Her remarks show that she is an attentive observer, and desirous of doing something for her sex, especially warning them against whisky drinking, the bad effects of which she has seen so much of during her absence from Ireland.[15]

Sidney Keelen was one of the four young—and unlikely—female cattle thieves who had planned their escape from County Monaghan through forced rather than voluntary emigration in 1849. She was literate, a Protestant and intelligent. Her convict career was largely uneventful, but her relationships were confusing: she apparently married two men just eight months apart in 1852, a Thomas Jones and a John Naden. She left Tasmania with the latter, had one surviving child, and after John Naden died, she returned to Ireland and took up a career as a woman lecturer. At some stage she returned to Thomas Jones in Launceston, and on his death in 1872 he left her a handy £1040. She set up a business in Smith Street, Fitzroy, and in 1874 married James Maxwell, a draper of a good family. Over the next ten years she became a successful property developer in the 'rising suburb of Yarraville' until her decapitated corpse was found lying on the railway line near Ascot Vale Station. Her terrible death at age fifty-four was never explained, but she left Maxwell assets of over £5360.[16] Her death certificate was unashamed about her twenty-five years in Tasmania.

THE TAINT OF 'THE OLD DAYS'

Of course, those who broke through to respectability were rarely secure. Sometime, somewhere, someone might sidle up and whisper, 'You're from t'other side.' For John Moon Bryant (*Mangles*, 1835), this would be painfully public, but he brought it on himself.

A skilled wheelwright from Wiltshire of 'respectable connexions', and said to be industrious, John Moon Bryant stole some boards from his master. He then had to work hard as a convict as well. Once free he set up business in Hobart, only to go bankrupt in 1847, but a year later he was involved in business in Geelong. By 1854 he had made enough money as a storekeeper in Melbourne to build the magnificent bluestone Royal Terrace in Nicholson Street, Fitzroy, setting up himself and his family to live off rents, and moving into number 10, the last house in the block. For decades he was the largest property owner in Fitzroy and he eventually retired from business to concentrate on public life. But he was a disputatious character. His tenure on Fitzroy Council was cut short by a row with a Simeon Cohen over a deal over the mayoral election, and 'Vandemonian' associations were raised ever so obliquely by the local press. In 1872, when he was on the committee of the Melbourne Benevolent Asylum, he unwisely accused a popular collector, Mr Clegg, of minor embezzlement. In the course of Clegg's successful defence, allegations emerged that John Moon Bryant had been transported on the *Mangles*. Bryant sued for slander, engaged learned counsel, and constructed an elaborate backstory that had him come to Sydney as a free man who then lived for a time in Hobart, conducting a business. Clegg's witnesses swore that Bryant was remembered from a chain gang; Bryant's witnesses testified that they had known him only as a free man in Hobart. Childhood companions from England were also summoned. Bryant's neighbour from number 1 Royal Terrace, Dr William Crooke, who had also spent time in Hobart, swore that in a society where 'the separation between bond [was] broad and well maintained', Bryant 'was acknowledged and treated as a man who had come free to the colony'.[17] Nonetheless, Bryant was forced to resign from the Benevolent Asylum Committee. He counterattacked with allegations that his accusers had had their own appearances before the police courts, and with tears in his eyes, he submitted himself for a physical examination by Dr Crooke, who found no marks of flagellation on his back.[18] But that was the end of his public life.

Bryant died aged eighty-two in 1891. He was remembered as a devoted Wesleyan, as a benefactor of the Salvation Army in Fitzroy, and as an 'Old Colonist' who had come via Sydney in 1842 and a short stay in Hobart, where he did not care to remain. At probate in November 1891, his estate comprised no real estate—four houses in Royal Terrace having been transferred to his children—but £11 872 in shares in the Commercial Bank of Australia. Sixteen months later, the Commercial Bank closed its doors and, like so many, the family lost the lot. Only number 10 survived, and three unmarried siblings lived there for the remainder of their lives. The one married brother had his wedding clouded by his own investment failures and the collapse of the family fortunes, but his marriage survived and he had restored his social position by the early 1920s, with his daughters attending university.

A successful expiree could not afford to become too public. Accusations of Vandemonian origins were flung around the colonial hustings for instance to smear a genteel opponent of the radical Graham Berry who had been tainted simply by growing up in the penal colony. And John Pascoe Fawkner, who was the son of a convict, had to fight aspersions in the House. 'Old lag' remained an epithet that landed people in court for abusive language, though increasingly it was an accusation without foundation. The situation was made worse by how daily life, with survival often being hard, remained fractious: tensions ran high in dense neighbourhoods or small communities riven with personal feuds and blighted by neighbourly noise and drunkenness, and jealousies festered between hypervigilant associates. A Mrs Clarke accused her neighbour, Mr George Bryanton, of being 'a Vandemonian and an old lag' when he protested at her refusal to allow him to remove his goslings from her yard in Hawthorn. In Emerald Hill in 1872, a Mr Crofton accused his neighbours, Mrs Grant and her family, of being the illegitimate children of old lags; the older daughter was a 'whore'. This torrent of abuse was ignited simply by a fight between young sons of the two households.[19] And Mr Ferguson, an aspiring publican in South Yarra, had to submit a grovelling apology in court in 1869 when he accused his rival for the licence for the Botanical Hotel as having come from 'the other side'.[20]

In Tasmania over time, people seemed to agree to publicly forget it all, to not talk of 'the old days', so that by the twentieth century, most who were descendants of convicts were oblivious of their background. Alison Alexander makes the point that this meant that people refrained from casting convict aspersions in the pub, on the street or the sportsground, or in the school playground.[21] It was an astonishing act of group forgetting that depended on the reality that so many had a stake in shutting down the past. The Tasmanians who did not forget, of course, were the upper class, whose genealogical vigilance against marrying into ex-convict stock may have diminished their gene pool.[22]

In Victoria, Vandemonians in suburbs like Collingwood were able to blend anonymously into the community, but country towns have longer collective memories and more persistent class divisions in everyday life: a member of the Bendigo Family History Group reported that she was warned off playing with the children next door because they 'had been convicts'. Memories were reinforced when convict families married safely into other convict families, producing multi-family lineages with convict origins. But most reinvented the family story. Daniel Backway's descendants believed for generations that he had 'jumped ship' in the gold rush, as did Michael McLoughlin's. Death certificates that could not avoid including a Van Diemen's Land marriage often shortened the sojourn to just enough time for courtship and a wedding, well short of the telling seven- or ten-year sentence. William Goodall's certificate, witnessed by his son Thomas, a law clerk in Warrnambool, told the truth, however: eighteen years in the colony of Tasmania, where he was married aged twenty-five in Campbell Town, then thirty-eight years in Victoria.[23] Thomas even knew his grandmother's maiden name.

Those with a long history in Tasmania were more likely to be truthful, for it looked as if they were real (free) settlers, but many families simply did not know very much about their parents' pasts—people seem not to have talked about their own parents and their early days. This may or may not have been unusual generally, but the evidence is there in the death certificates that around a third of the roughly 208 000 people listed in the Victorian Pioneer Index who died over the age of twelve between 1836 and 1888 had their death registration witnessed by people who did not know their father's name or details of marriages or children: what they termed in the nineteenth century as 'died without friends'. When we take account of the high proportion of Vandemonian deaths in benevolent asylums and charity hospitals across Victoria—around 60 per cent of our Ships Project cohort deaths in Ballarat, and 40 per cent in Bendigo[24]—then the figure of those without friends becomes even higher, because these public institutions took great care on admission to obtain a full history of the new inmate. Only deaths in gaol and emergency admissions into hospitals or lunatic asylums were recorded without personal histories, generally because the patient was not well enough to give an account of themselves.[25] What this *absence* reveals is the toll of both immigration and transportation on the thousands of solitaries, mostly male, who failed to establish roots, links and a lineage in their new country. These are the forgotten colonisers, omitted from histories written by and about 'the winners' who had descendants.

FADING MEMORIES

As time passed, the convict stain faded. Crime rates fell in the last quarter of the nineteenth century, especially for homicide, and Tasmania in particular completed its transformation, according to John Braithwaite, from the high-crime frontier society of the 1830s and 1840s to the remarkably peaceable one of the 1890s.[26] Victoria reported an increase in crime in the 1880s, along with the burst of larrikinism previously described and the last great bandit outbreak personified by the Kelly Gang. But this new generation were the lost and frustrated offspring of the gold-rush generation, and most of their parents had not been convicts. The Vandemonians had found it more difficult to form families, especially enduring lineages. More importantly, the expirees across the colonies were dying. In the 1870s, a Sydney mathematics professor, MB Pell, calculated the mortality rates for New South Wales and concluded that the difference in mortality between England and Australia before 1866 was due to

> the habits and character of a certain class, of which a large proportion of the older inhabitants of the colony then consisted ... As this class has become gradually almost eliminated, the rates for higher ages, have gradually improved, more particularly for males of which the objectionable class mostly consisted.[27]

The Vandemonians faded from public sight, now appearing in court for offences against public order or for petty thefts or criminal damage designed to secure them a dry bed and a feed in gaol. They found places where they could beg, or rough areas where their chances of cadging food and drink from fellows were better. Not all wanted to go into the benevolent asylums, and some of the institutions were choosey about whom they admitted. Ellen Miles was discharged from gaol to various benevolent asylums fully eight times between 1904 and 1913, until she was too infirm to escape from the Ballarat Benevolent Asylum, where she died in 1916 at the age of eighty-nine. When the Vagabond visited the Melbourne Benevolent Asylum, the highlights were the 'old lags' to be found among the inmates, and a number of once violent, thieving and immoral men and women were able to end their days there.[28] Not that it was all that comfortable: the vast building was a fire risk, and with wobbly legs and shaky hands handling pipes, the inmates were banished from the wards during daylight hours. They hung around Errol and Victoria streets in North Melbourne, asking for a spare penny, killing time.

Within Melbourne, the network of institutions had a hierarchy of destitution and shame. The Immigrants' Home, founded by the most distinguished Vandemonian of them all, James Blackburn, was the closest to the English workhouses in its operations, with a casual ward. Those who died there were those abandoned by the world and their friends, people like Janet Black, the Glasgow orphan who married Gilbert Marshall, or William Trenwith (*Earl St Vincent*, 1826), a survivor of 447 lashes and the reprobate father of the rising union leader in Collingwood who would become a founder of the Victorian Socialist Party and a colonial and federal parliamentarian.[29] Jane Robertson (*Rajah*, 1841), as Jane Cavanagh, haunted the rough streets of Bendigo with her daughter, and by October 1899 the official count in town of her previous appearances before the bench was eighty-three.

Now, she declared, she wanted to get into the benevolent asylum, because of her rheumatics, claiming that she drank only to relieve them. But only the Immigrants' Home, by now partially removed to Royal Park, would admit her, and she died there two years later.[30] Fully half of the Vandemonians who died in South Melbourne and Emerald Hill died in the old Immigrants' Home. Likewise in North Melbourne (Hotham), most local Vandemonian deaths were in the Melbourne Benevolent Asylum at the commanding end of Victoria Street.

Finally, Vandemonians, like the poor, were the most likely to die in a hospital, as hospitals were for those without homes that were adequate for medical treatment, or who could not afford a doctor's private premises. Overwhelmingly, their Melbourne deaths were in the Melbourne Hospital—institutional deaths that testify to the failure of these Vandemonians to establish a home and a caring family network. Children quite often abandoned their alcoholic, unkempt parents to the authorities.

The amount of relief being offered by the asylums, both indoor and outdoor, was immense. In July 1884, the Bendigo institution distributed outdoor relief to no fewer than 1204 households, while 115 males, twenty-one females and sixty-one children were inmates in the wards.[31] Ballarat, meanwhile, operated what was essentially five institutions in one. These large provincial asylums and hospitals provided medical care, aged care, refuge for women and children at risk, orphanages, industrial schooling, and, with links, asylum for the mentally ill. The Castlemaine Benevolent Asylum was smaller and more select, however, and Joseph Jenkins, the Welsh swagman, regretted that he would have to pay to be admitted. It was haphazard, but for the time, the Victorian provision of care for the destitute aged and sick was the best of all the colonies—Tasmania and New South Wales transitioned their convict institutions into civil ones, retaining too much of the culture and crowded conditions of the penal era.

In a time of cruelty and neglect of the indigent and the delinquent, Victoria's voluntary hospital and benevolent asylum systems were a credit to the miners and immigrants who collected funds, sat on committees, oversaw governance and recommended people for care. The 1890s depression, however, devastated the resources of voluntary institutions, hospitals and charity organisations, as private philanthropy collapsed along with the banks.

In addition to all this, as time passed and the Vandemonians slipped from sight, memories softened. As the first colonists and gold-rush arrivals aged, they began to reminisce and to create legends. The horrors of the Vandemonian crime wave of the early 1850s could be remembered with some hindsight by 1864: the 'Vices so loathsome that it is an offence against decency to name them' and that were 'commonly practised in the Tasmanian gaols' were still deplored, but they were past.[32] By the late 1880s, Vandemonian outrages, especially bushranging, were now enthralling 'true crime', with the author cast as a doughty, principled pioneer/goldseeker/settler or 'ex-official'. Literary imaginations took flight, evoking 'gangs of Vandemonian marauders [that] held whole tracts of country': 'Bushranging with these "old hands" was a favourite pursuit, and brutality invariably accompanied their cowardly robberies. Diggers were found dead tied to trees, with some of their limbs cut off and stuffed in their mouths as gags.'[33] Needless to say, contemporary evidence to confirm such horrors remains elusive.

The Vandemonaphobia of the 1850s died with the alluvial rushes, one reason being that the Chinese replaced the Vandemonians as the despised 'others'. Larceny and receiving boomed and fell in Tasmania and Victoria from 1830 to 1914. They peaked in the former in the early gold rush as the authorities lost some control of the system, and crested in Victoria in the late 1850s, before both colonies recorded steep falls, with Tasmania becoming a most property-respecting community thereafter. Court appearances with verdicts of guilty, not guilty or 'other' for homicide by males also clearly show the periods of lawlessness and the increase in safety for both colonies, with Victoria completely outstripping Tasmania after the first gold-rush disorder.[34]

Data for offences against public order—drunkenness, obscene language, vagrancy, offensive behaviour—are more difficult to gather, emanating as they did from police courts all over the colony, but we do have arrests for drunkenness. What helped change behaviour was the gradual improvement in the safety of alcoholic beverages, as laboratory testing for adulteration by toxic substances or narcotics improved and regulations were imposed. The extreme, crazed violence that left so many men, women and children injured or dead tempered along with the fall in premature death from drink. But it was mostly the shortage of pennies—thanks to the 1890s depression—that reduced the arrests for drunkenness in Victoria, where they fell by almost 50 per cent during the crash. In 1877, one in twelve Victorian males aged nineteen or over was arrested for intoxication; by 1906 it was about one in twenty-four.[35] And with the rise in moderation and respectability, the terrible toll of alcohol on life and mind began to fall.

The mutation of stigma into legend was most pronounced with the public response to the Kelly Gang outbreak and the fate of Ned himself. The Kellys were the children of a convict, and Ned had been schooled in banditry by the Vandemonian Harry Power. Some of their associates and supporters were also from convict stock, but certainly a minority. There were plenty of others whose selections were too small for survival, who smarted at the condescension of the squatters, who made a bit on the side by duffing (stealing livestock) and horse stealing, and who hated the police. Among the Kelly supporters, the

McAuliffes (*Egyptian*, 1840) were Vandemonians, but old lags who became respectable could be enemies also.

Jeremiah McCormick had been transported on the *John Renwick* (1844) for his part in the Chartist riots in Lancashire. He had married Catherine Doherty (*Hope*, 1842) in Beechworth and set himself up as a hawker while grazing a few animals in Greta, near where the Kellys lived. In October 1870, McCormick accused Ned's friend Ben Gould of using a horse without permission, so Ben called in Ned to teach McCormick a lesson. Ned sent the childless Catherine a box containing two calf's testicles wrapped by an insulting note about her barrenness. McCormick protested and Ned knocked him down.[36] The fifteen-year-old Ned received three months' gaol, his first sentence. It was a nasty, embittered little world, locked away in the hills.

The Kelly story scarcely needs retelling, but the great petition calling for clemency and the thousands protesting in the streets suggested that villains had become entertainment rather than dangers, and that they could even be heroes or at least victims of police excess. Brian Lewis, growing up in a middle-class Methodist family in Kooyong Road just before World War I, could remember how all the boys admired Ned Kelly for his derring-do.[37]

Ellen Miles, in her final words for posterity, appeared in court in December 1902, charged under the name of Bridget Brady, born in Ireland and of the Catholic faith. She defended her good character and right to be respected:

Brady—My name is Ellen Watkins and I am a decent woman.
Sergeant Eason—Oh we know all about you, Bridget, you've been convicted of all sorts of offences—nine times larceny, six times soliciting.

This was too much for Ellen:

Brady—Soliciting is it? And I'm 82 (Laughter) [she had lost count and was seventy-five] 'Tis many a year since I was soliciting, I'm thinking (Laughter).
Sergeant Eason—Yes, the record goes back over thirty years.
Brady (contemptuously)—Thirty grandmothers (Laughter). Why it must be full sixty years ago man (Laughter).
Accused was sentenced to six months' imprisonment.[38]

If time healed, so did the secrets and lies. The evasions, the silences, the doctored death certificates were all ways of managing stigma and growing beyond it. The Vandemonians had served their time and there was no need to burden their descendants with their shame. When the next generation married 'out', there was likewise no obligation to pass on the unfortunate past of the family. If they did not bear 'the Vandemonian cast' and looked like everyone else, they could blend back into society as ordinary workers and mothers and fathers. The demons that disrupted that process were ones implanted in early life, and which they had brought with them to penal servitude.

CHAPTER 10

Final Verdict

On suburban railway stations—you may see them as you pass
There are signboards on the platforms saying, 'Wait here
  second class;'
And to me the whirr and thunder and the clucking of
  running gear
Seem to be for ever saying 'Second class wait here;—
'Wait here second class,
'Second class wait here.'
Seem to be for ever saying 'Second class wait here.'

HENRY LAWSON, *VERSES POPULAR AND HUMOROUS* (1900)

The charge levelled by posterity was whether the convicts had been born bad, or just made bad, or, indeed, were they bad at all? It was a blunt version of the question that has been asked by contemporaries, officials, historians and descendants ever since. When Charles Darwin came to Australia in the *Beagle* in 1836, his greatest interest was in 'the state of Society amongst the higher and the convict classes' and whether he should emigrate. In Sydney he found a rancorous, profligate community, devoted only to the pursuit of wealth.

He recoiled from the prospect of convicted persons looking after his children, cooking his meals and waiting at his table. Hobart was more agreeable than Sydney: there was more 'Society' and fewer upstart wealthy convicts, so that Van Diemen's Land was the lesser of two evils. He had no confidence that penal transportation achieved reform of the character.

Historians continue to wrestle with the character of the convicts, the significance of their contribution to the history of settler colonialism, the extent of their role in our economic development, and, indeed, such elusive phenomena as the Australian legend, our language, our self-image and our soul. Hancock, writing in 1930, had no doubt that Australia had a 'wretched beginning', having to build a new society from the detritus of the old. G Arnold Wood was the first to argue that the convicts were more sinned against than sinning, unfortunate victims of poverty and oppression vomited out by 'Old Corruption'. The historians' insights concentrated on Sydney and its particularities were assumed to apply to Van Diemen's Land until Lloyd Robson, himself a Tasmanian, conducted the first demographic history of the Van Diemen's Land story. He found the exceptions and the special convicts who left a personal mark on Australia, but he was more impressed with the prosaic venality of the majority. Similarly, AGL Shaw and Manning Clark were more than aware of the criminal pedigrees of those transported.[1]

Economic historians used convicts' heights as a retrospective measure of the biological standard of living during their growing years, and therefore of the impact of the industrial revolution on the poor.[2] They then recast the convicts as 'convict workers' who could be understood as otherwise ordinary working-class people who were unlucky to be caught at a time when theft and pilfering were daily necessities.[3] Reimagined in this way, convicts now assumed a new importance in the understanding of the early colonial economy, the contribution of forced labour, and as pawns in the global history of colonisation.⁴ Clare Anderson adapted Foucault's concept of the 'carceral archipelago' for a transnational project on forced labour and convict transportation that ranged from Portugal's first use of convict labour in North Africa in 1415 to the dissolution of Stalin's gulags in 1960.⁵ Slavery and forced labour have built the wealth of the dominant elites and nations since the emergence of complex, agricultural food production. They enabled energy in the form of human muscle to be harnessed for mass work at low cost. The bodies of African slaves supplied the 'industrial' energy to produce the sugar that built the fabulous wealth of European slave traders and merchants. That wealth, in turn, underwrote the industrial revolution when fossil fuel replaced human and animal energy, and the new economy colonised its own people in Scotland, Ireland and rural England and Wales. Forced labour and slavery transformed the distribution of peoples around the globe, and the original sin of human exploitation continues to poison politics, economics and private lives everywhere, including Australia. Convicts were not slaves: they had legal rights and entitlements that Aboriginal forced workers and islanders did not, but the colonisation of Australia was dependent on captive human workers.

The place of female convicts in the Australian narrative has been even more complicated, trapped in a double bind of gender and structural violence because they were women who had fallen. Stripped of their moral 'womanhood', they had no protection against the predations and violence of men, both their masters and their fellow convicts. If they alleged rape, even of their children, they were not believed and the perpetrators were not prosecuted—or at least, not appropriately punished. Mary Cray's daughter was only six when she was raped in Ballarat East, but her lack of a hymen was a mitigating factor in the light sentence of her well-dressed rapist. As Anne Summers famously wrote, in colonial Australia, women were either 'damned whores' or 'God's police'.[6] The loss of virtue was far more damaging for women than for men, and the stigma of impaired identity more crushing. Yet historians have recast women convicts as mothers rather than 'damned whores', and celebrated their place as the builders of families, some of them now with vast lineages.[7] As for the 'damned whores', they have been portrayed as practitioners of 'rough culture' that shocked their social betters, and their resistance to penal authority and respectable behaviour has been translated as feisty rebellion.[8]

Still others have looked more closely at the penal system itself: at the practices of discipline, the economics of convict labour and proto industry, and the interventions and opportunities for land grants and approved marriage as a means of reformation and colonial settlement.[9] All of this work, however, has derived largely from the rich archives of the penal system—in Van Diemen's Land, the paper panopticon. In other words, it is necessarily confined to a limited temporal lens of seven to eight years, more for some, which in the totality of a life may become less and less relevant with ageing.[10] Life before and after sentence is recorded largely by the continuing offenders or the notable individual success stories. Cradle-to-grave data that locates the convict experience in the context of the full life course, and within the discoverable family connections and geographic settings, is now possible. It can help us see the remarkable—the founders—or the mere survivors in historical context, and this book has been based on such a study.

Population studies, or demography as the study of birth, family formation and death, are powerful tools for understanding the past. And if we are to evaluate the effects of penal servitude, the best measure is length of life and manner of death. If we are to understand how well convict men and women did as fathers and mothers, we need to study family formation and relate that to life span. If we are to understand the effects of different life stages on an individual, we need to find out as much as we can about their lives with some knowledge of human development theory. Science in the form of social epidemiology; developmental psychology; the biology and psychology of trauma and attendant stress responses; the relationship between food, shelter, natural environment, disease, education and culture, social relationships, workplace conditions and dynamics; and finally politics and economic cycles, all can help us understand the course of a life: the nature of the stresses inflicted and the opportunities offered; the interventions of the state that helped and those that harmed. History is often said to be the queen of disciplines because almost everything lies within its compass. We can draw on all these disciplines to understand past times and persons: not with the scientific precision of controlled observational study in the present, but as insights into the dynamics of life and society. And the final measures of the sort of people who were transported to Van Diemen's Land between 1803 and 1853 are their length of life and their family formation. These measures are macro-measures; they blur individuals and exceptions, but if the population is large enough and the analysis statistically rigorous, they can provide the psychological, biological and social architecture of the lives of similar people. They cannot explain behaviour, events and outcomes at the individual level, but they can provide the context for assessing whether someone was typical or atypical.

Therefore, if we look at the convicts' probability of dying after they stepped down from the dock in the courtroom, having been sentenced to transportation across the seas, we find that men and women died at much the same rate as each other under sentence, but in the first decade after release, more women died as they struggled to support themselves in a world made for men. If we break that down into the annual probability of dying, by age and sex, younger men did worse under sentence, often from work accidents and drownings, and after sentence women did worse than men from the age of twenty-seven to fifty-five, but especially between thirty and thirty-eight years.[11] The telling life-span—survival—analysis, which plots how many survived to certain ages, compares male and female convicts with all Tasmanians and with men and women in England and Wales. This analysis necessarily begins when the subjects reach the age of twenty. Were it to be from birth, then the high infant and child mortality of the time would appear to further shorten adult lives.

Convicts did worse than a general population that included those who had come free or who were born in Tasmania, as well as emancipists, but the Tasmanian population, especially the males, did better than the general male population in England and Wales. Emancipated males in Tasmania did as well as their peers at home, which means that if we could break down the British figures by social class and region, the men transported to Van Diemen's Land lived longer than they would have had they remained in England or Wales. So we can discern a positive effect of transportation to a better climate with more food, especially meat, on health and longevity. Convicts under sentence did poorly, but so did emancipated women. In other words, transportation was good for men and compounded the risks for women.[12]

It needs to be remembered, however, that this was a select group of convicted men at least, chosen for their fitness to labour in the colonial economy. Both men and women were therefore hardy survivors of severe disease environments, individuals who had not succumbed to dysentery or childhood infections such as measles that could be aggravated by rickets; and if they had tuberculosis, to which almost all would have been exposed, that their disease was not apparent and active, or they would have been among the first to die under sentence. Again, since we have no data on causes of death under sentence apart from some accidents and executions, we can only surmise that tuberculosis might activate and kill them, especially if they were confined as secondary punishment. Many of the convicts would have carried asymptomatic or slow-burning infections that could flare or be passed on to others: typhoid, syphilis and, of course, tuberculosis.

The Ships Project commenced with many hypotheses as to which factors would affect convicts' life spans. Most of them proved to be wrong. The impact of height and literacy, for instance, was found to be insignificant, despite all the expectations regarding the bearing of higher biological and intellectual capital. Being short or illiterate was no bar to marriage for men, for one thing, nor to survival. The only effect found for height was an inverse relationship for tall men, who were more vulnerable to premature death, and various theories have been advanced to explain this: such as the fact that the taller convicts were more likely to have been in the army and were violent by nature as recalcitrant deserters. This needs further testing. It may also be that taller men were at greater risk working in dangerous conditions in the forests and mines, where their greater physical strength was exploited, but since the causes of death under sentence were only patchily recorded, that is difficult to investigate.

It was expected that the stresses and insults of convict discipline would affect life spans, but it was found that for men, surprisingly, flogging did not shorten their lives after sentence, nor did time in chains or at the treadmill. However, men's mortality rose in proportion for every day spent in solitary confinement. Thus, torment of the mind was more damaging than torment of the body in an age where physical punishment and exhausting labour were normal parts of life. This finding is important for an historical perspective on the effects of the unjust and harsh incarceration of refugees; prisoners of conscience; solitary punishment for all prisoners, particularly youthful offenders; and for victims of torture. Ironically, the humanitarian mission of the prison reformers to transfer punishment of the body to correction of the mind inflicted greater and more enduring pain.

But these were only some factors. Others were behavioural, in particular convictions for drunkenness while under sentence. It was forbidden for convicts to drink, but of course they did, and those who needed it most continued to offend and be punished. Convictions under sentence for drunkenness were highly related to premature death in female emancipists, as was having been on the town before sentence. In particular, the comparison between the general population and the mortality and risks suffered by convicts demonstrates the vulnerability of convict women who were alcoholic and/or had been on the town before transportation.[13] The women who did well were those who were either older, married or widowed when they arrived, and who had offended out of dire necessity; or they were young country girls who had not been forced into prostitution. If they married soon after sentence to a steady man, they had the biological window and the family support to have large families, and they typically did. These are the convict mothers who built the colonising population.

Family life was in fact at the heart of convicts' existential difficulties. The research did not show that they had largely come from criminal families, but rather that they were far more likely to have lost one or both parents, especially if they were Irish, both before and after the Great Famine. Fractured families or impaired households had driven them onto the streets and into gangs or partnerships in crime. Parental connections and training were the most common pathway to a working life: lose your parents and you lost your future. Desertion, death and parental frailty left children unsupported and unable to latch on to respectable associates or employment. It was harder to learn how to be an adult, a parent and a worker if you had no father or mother. In a remarkable analysis, Rebecca Kippen was able to estimate the probable risk of parental loss in England, Wales and Ireland, and compare that with the different classes of convicts in Van Diemen's Land.[14]

When it came to starting their own families in Australia, emancipists hit impediments. Men were restricted by the shortage of women and laboured under the stigma of convictism in finding a wife; many women went into marriage carrying crippling damage from childhood abuse, alcohol and sexually transmitted infections. Those who 'married out' often seem to have concealed their convict past, at least initially, such as Michael McLoughlin or Alexandrina Grant. Most emancipist women married, but they displayed a high incidence of acquired—or secondary—infertility from diseases, missed and incomplete abortions (miscarriages), postpartum infections, birth trauma and violence.[15] Marriage was good for men, adding—while controlling for other factors—1.4 years to their life expectancy, with each additional child adding 0.25 years; and survival to the third generation (that is, grandchildren) was associated with an increased life expectancy of 1.8 years. But this effect of family formation was not apparent for women until they became grandmothers, where the successful creation of a lineage to a third generation was associated with a 2.6-year increase in average life expectancy over the age of fifty.[16] What mattered was the capacity to raise healthy children who in turn could form their own families: a lineage.[17]

PARALLEL LIVES

This Vandemonian story ran in parallel with the colonisation of Aboriginal Victorian people, as Vandemonians were among the displacers and often in the front line of colonial physical and sexual violence. As the Aboriginal population catastrophically collapsed, until the survivors were corralled into reserves and missions by the 1870s, Indigenous people disappeared from sight for many colonial Victorians. However, on the reserves by the early 1880s, their numbers—and consequently their cost to the colonial government—were rising, principally through relationships with white men from outside the reserves. The *Half-Caste Act 1886* sought to resolve this growing burden on the Treasury by expelling all who were not 'fully Aboriginal' from the reserves, even if their mothers and other relatives remained living there. Families that had been fractured by violence, disease, dispossession and forced relocations of the colonial state, were fractured again. From the government's point of view, part-Aboriginal people were now legally white—except that no-one recognised their legal equality and entitlements to citizenship. As they famously said themselves, 'We were too black to be white and too white to be black.' They were still left barely educated, unemployed, homeless and marginalised. Doctors were still slow to attend to them and hospitals to admit them. And as child removal grew as an intervention, increasingly their children were in danger of being taken by the state. Many remained living near the reserves to maintain their relationships with their families. If they served in World War I, they somehow seemed to be bypassed by the entitlements that supported white veterans after the conflict. Some, like the Onus family of activists and artists, can be found on the electoral rolls after Federation, but they remained in limbo.[18] And from this perilous and unprotected position, their health as measured by the incidence of tuberculosis, high infant mortality and premature death of both men and women, failed to improve in concert with even the poorest whites. Thus, the infamous 'gap' widened in the first half of the twentieth century—a gap engineered by government policy.[19]

The population decline of Aboriginal Victorians was catastrophic, from a probable 60 000 people in 1788 to just over 600 recorded in 1900. Recovery was impeded not simply by early death and disease, but even more starkly by the impact of structural violence, this time racialised, on defenceless female bodies and minds, inflicted in hidden places in the bush. The rates of acquired infertility, from the same causes as for convict women, were just as severe and impaired the capacity of Aboriginal families to recover from the onslaught.[20] A few Aboriginal people survived in isolation in otherwise white families, often bearing a burden of 'shame' and terror of being 'outed' as Aboriginal, as Lynette Russell has so eloquently told us in her family history.[21] But the final recovery would be led by Aboriginal people themselves, exploding with the mass walk-off from the Cummeragunja mission in 1938. The Yorta Yorta people freed themselves from government control and camped on the flood plain at Mooroopna. They found seasonal work in fruit processing and picking, while being forced to live in squalor. They began to move to Melbourne, living around Fitzroy and mobilising under their own leaders such as pastor (later Sir) Doug Nicholls. They forced their way into the mainstream to become visible again. Finally, in the 1967 referendum, the nation began to see them.

RETHINKING THE CONVICT LEGACY

The most surprising finding of our project, however, was that when place of birth was coded for its crime economy, it remained one of the most persistent influences on life span and family formation. Analysed in combination with other risk factors as years of life expectancy lost, being born in a port city was the greatest early-life risk for men, followed by alcoholism and solitary confinement.

For women, being on the town, which was more common for those in port cities, and alcoholism plus refractory behaviour under sentence shortened lives.[22]

The persistence of toxic early-life effects and consequent behaviour such as heavy drinking, which easily provoked personal violence, is a familiar story in the modern scientific literature. Foetal alcohol spectrum syndrome, substance abuse during and after pregnancy, followed by exposure to toxic stress such as anger, depression, violence and neglect, are all now known to impair cognitive development, leaving children one to three years behind by the age of five.[23] The young people who pass through the courts today are commonly or functionally illiterate. One researcher has found that male adolescent detainees can suffer from speech disorders where their vocabularies are too restricted to enable them to understand and negotiate the world. Simply teaching them thirty new words, such as 'optimism', 'react', 'participation' and 'justice', was transformative.[24] Sexual abuse is too often the story behind young drug takers and sex workers, and teenage pregnancy, either followed by single motherhood or unwise partnering with a fragile male, can be a life sentence of poverty, abuse and marginalisation. We can see in these convict lives from two centuries ago the ugly face of our continuing neglect of the very poor, the unwell and the disabled.

Then, as now, when families failed, organised society or charity was all that stood between the destitute and starvation. Charity depended on the whim of the dispenser; support from the state, from 1674 in England, was a legal entitlement. During the lifetimes of most of the Vandemonians, however, the English Poor Law was reformed as a means of control of the urban mob, where poverty was criminalised. People with plenty feared that the poor were innately idle and insisted that these undeserving people, if they were to be relieved, had to be made to suffer. Workhouses under the new regime included solitary cells, and the cruel separation of family members—siblings, parents and children—continued well into the twentieth century. All of this experience and custom was transported inside the heads of the convicts as well as the expectations and ideas of free immigrants. And the penal system in Australia before the 1840s continued the traditional responsibilities of the Poor Law in attempts to teach reading and writing, trade skills, and to raise convict children.

Criminologists are now looking afresh at colonial transportation, at least during the assignment period, and seeing a more effective regime for prisoner rehabilitation than modern practices in anglophone countries, where young offenders in particular are taken out of society and away from relationships and work that could help them rebuild their lives.[25] And it could be argued that the Ships Project supports that finding. Those who continued to offend were a minority, both in Tasmania and Victoria, and much of that offending was in the form of drunkenness and offensive behaviour or trivial larcenies that were designed to secure a dry bed and a meal in a cell. Most of Ellen Miles' crimes beyond the age of fifty consisted of this form of self-provisioning, and her regular periods in gaol, with food, clean clothing and hospital care, surely contributed to her long life. The other factor that kept her going so long was that, while she liked to drink, she was never addicted. Her entire life was entwined with public institutions: the workhouse, prison and the Ballarat Benevolent Asylum, where she finally died. She may have complained that the colony should look after old people like herself, but the prosecutor was correct to reply that the colony had looked after her all her life.

So as visible and as interesting as Ellen Miles may be, she does not speak for the convict women who did make a family that survived, nor does George Pickering for the convict men who blended into the landscape and became invisible, at least outside Tasmania. There it was different, because everyone knew there were convicts while they were still alive, even though few have left any record of their interactions.

One of the few to do so was the poet Helen Power, daughter of the town clerk of Campbell Town and granddaughter of the Agnes Power who had been so thrilled by the wickedness of Thomas Griffiths Wainewright. Growing up in the 1870s and early 1880s, her Campbell Town was full of 'extraordinary identities'. She remembered their voices, the rich tapestry of accents and dialects, commenting that 'surely such a quaint collection was never seen in one small community before':

> The annals of the poor there were so very far from being short and simple; some of them, particularly, were long and lurid, as a good percentage of the old folk had been sent out in still earlier days for their country's good; and as they came from all parts of the old world, and had, like most people who have run against the law, some force of character, they stood out conspicuously from their unfamiliar environment.[26]

One old man, reputedly Joseph Barkley, had been a London costermonger, and still dressed in a 'velveteen coat, a bird's-eye red and white handkerchief round his neck, and a cap of some skin or fur. His fat, oily face was clean-shaven, and his hair, still thick and dark, was brushed into the most curious ear-locks on either side'. Jenny Byles, who raised 'hins', wore a skirt

> quite up to her knees, a pair of men's leather boots, a three-cornered worsted shawl, and a large straw hat, innocent of any trimmings. Her hair was drawn back in two peaks on either side of her forehead and was so thick with oil or grease that on warm

days, I have seen little runnels of blackish moisture making their way towards her jaws.[27]

One of the many old Irish women was straight out of the dramatist JM Synge: feeling ill, she told the Power family: 'it's destroyed I am, for whin I undresses mesilf at noight, sure the liver spans out and thin drops into the pit of me stomach.'[28]

These are the sounds and sights of the convict settlers of Australia that we miss. We hear their voices in court, but rarely in everyday life. Too much of the historical record, as in this book, is of their failures and faults when they came to public attention. Otherwise, aside from chuckling over colourful court reports in the newspaper, everyone pretended they were not there. John Glover, the Tasmanian painter, artfully arranged groups of Aboriginal people in his landscapes, almost as mute witnesses to their own dispossession, except that they really were not there. The people who were in the landscape every day—herding sheep, working in fields, serving households: the convicts—are never seen. One of the very few artworks to depict convicts is John Skinner Prout's 1844 painting of the Probation Station at Mount Dromedary.

In Victoria by the 1870s, the Vandemonians had begun to blend in and were soon forgotten, except for recollections of daring and dash in the gold rush. The broken old people on the streets, or in humpies and huts in the bush, were not assumed to have been transported. And forgotten is what they wanted to be. Henry Reynolds broke the spell with his essay on 'That Hated Stain', seeing a Tasmania where the enduring mark of convictism was timidity, withdrawal and deference to an assertive upper class that had policed its lineages.[29] Elsewhere, the Australian legend, the larrikin, disrespect for authority, political resistance, all are being sourced back to the convict founders. But outside Tasmania and even New South Wales, the sheer volume of both self-funded and assisted immigration from the 1840s swamped the emancipist population. And those who came to Victoria, including those who paid their way, brought radical ideas and sharpened understandings of class relations that swept aside the pre-industrial society of ranks and orders of the transportation era. Australia by 1900 was a very modern society in its values, its politics and its culture. It was highly urbanised. It would produce the most unionised army in World War I. It would be the first country in the world to elect a government of working-class men and to establish a court to set minimum wages. Yet Tasmania remained trapped in rural poverty, with a pastoral elite ensuring that everyone else knew their place.

The characteristics that historians are now claiming derive from the convict stain have more to do with class relationships, and the inculcation of shame and a feeling of inferiority that has always been the mental mark of being poor. And the convict stain that persisted was really the stain of intergenerational poverty. The descendants of convicts in the First AIF in Victoria were concentrated among the unskilled urban and rural poor. Some families were still struggling with family breakdown, mental illness and crime. Few had begun to climb the social ladder because the barriers were too great; it was too hard to find or make a pot of gold. Gold had been the great disrupter in the 1850s, but it ran out and there wasn't enough to go around. It would not be until after World War II, with the expansion of education, the achievement of full employment, and the investment of the state in industry and utilities, that the poorest of white Australians could find a secure job and at least get a government roof over their head. Australia was not the land of the 'fair go' for those born poor or troubled, let alone those, black or white, who suffered 'shame'.[30]

What matters most about the Vandemonians' story is not any Australian legend or 'hated stain', but the persistence of poverty over generations, of fragile families, of the silent pain of being a nobody.

It is about the life sentence dealt to the unprotected, abused and unloved. Once, Ellen Miles, the Buzzwinker, was a frightened little girl in the St Pancras Workhouse; and Margaret Richmond, the Bull Pup, was a weeping child in the dock at the Old Bailey being whacked by her older sister with an umbrella; and Daniel Backway was a sobbing, shaking boy in the Middlesex Sessions witness box, covered in sores and cuts and bruises, with the marks of having been shackled and of someone having thrust their nails into his chest.

APPENDIX A

Founders and Survivors Ships Project Data

Around 73 000 convicts were transported to Van Diemen's Land (now Tasmania) in the half-century from 1803 to 1853, and usable records have survived for around 68 000 of those people, with the best records dating from 1840. The data used in this book come from 126 ships that arrived between 1812 and 1853 and which produced a researched population of just under 25 000: 16 953 males and 7793 females. The Ships Project used convict voyages for easier linkage since colonial records continued to link convicts (and free settlers) to their ships of arrival.

The core transcriptions for this database commenced with the work of Deborah Oxley in the 1990s when she transcribed the indents for the probation period held in the United Kingdom. The Founders and Survivors: Australian Life Courses in Historical Context project, led by Hamish Maxwell-Stewart, then of the University of Tasmania, organised the digital imaging of the conduct records held in the Archives Office of Tasmania (AOT) and funded the transcription of the indents and conduct records of convicts in the assignment period. The transcription team was led by Alison Alexander. This provided an online dataset that collated all the various and varying mentions of a convict into readable text, and images from the AOT were linked. All of this created an ingenious platform for genealogists and researchers to collect data systematically.

The Ships Project, funded by a second grant from the Australian Research Council to the University of Melbourne, was conducted online by just over sixty volunteer genealogists, with a paid research team providing training, support and data validation. The data were entered on Google Docs spreadsheets, coding social, familial, economic and geographic factors, and counting as well as coding behaviour and punishment under sentence—insolence, refusal to work, violence, drunkenness, sexual offences, plus the total number of lashes and days spent in solitary confinement, hard labour or in chains. The researchers then traced life before and after sentence using online genealogical datasets, vital registrations in the United Kingdom and the Australian colonies, British and US censuses, colonial registers, and data sources such as police gazettes and the National Library of Australia's digitised archive of historical newspapers. Success in tracing convicts to a registered death varied over the time period of the sample, with the percentage traced ranging from 26 per cent to 72 per cent, with an average of 46 per cent. Logistic regression of convicts traced to death, excluding those who died within five years of arrival, showed that those who were more likely to be traced—that is, who remained visible—were:

1. English-born (compared with Irish- or Scottish-born)
2. village-born (compared with industrial urban, port city or London-born)
3. earlier arrivals
4. older at arrival
5. recorded with fewer offences under sentence.

There was a small bias towards those who came from rural areas, those who did not have Celtic names that are hard to trace, those who were less recalcitrant, and those who arrived early when land grants were available to enable settlement. Those who came from more urban communities and who were more 'street-wise' were more likely to assume new identities upon release. Moreover, the convict marriage approval system broke down towards the end of the transportation period, depriving researchers of valuable triangulating data for tracing.

REFEREED PUBLICATIONS

Journal Articles

Bradley, James, Rebecca Kippen, Hamish Maxwell-Stewart, Janet McCalman and Sandra Silcot, 'Research Note: "The Founders and Survivors Project"', *The History of the Family*, vol. 15, 2010, pp. 467–77.

Kippen, Rebecca, and Janet McCalman, 'Mortality under and after Sentence of Male Convicts Transported to Van Diemen's Land (Tasmania), 1840–1852', *The History of the Family*, vol. 20, no. 3, 2015, pp. 345–65.

——'Parental Loss in Young Convicts Transported to Van Diemen's Land (Tasmania), 1841–53', *The History of the Family*, vol. 23, no. 4, 2018, pp. 656–78. [See Figure A6 in this appendix.]

McCalman, Janet, and Len Smith, 'Family and Country: Accounting for Fractured Connections under Colonisation in Victoria, Australia', *Journal of Population Research*, vol. 33, 2016, pp. 51–65.

McCalman, Janet, and Rebecca Kippen, 'The Life-course Demography of Convict Transportation to Van Diemen's Land', *The History of the Family*, vol. 25, no. 3, 2020, pp. 432–54. [See figures A1–A5 in this appendix.]

Book Chapters

Kippen, Rebecca, and Janet McCalman, 'Crowdsourcing Convict Life Courses, or the Value of Volunteers in the Digital Age', in Koen Matthuis, Saskia Hin, Jan Kok and Hideko Matsuo (eds), *The Future of Historical Demography, Upside Down and Inside Out*, Acco Leuven, Den Haag, NL, 2016.

——'A Test of Character: A Case Study of Male Convicts Transported to Van Diemen's Land, 1826–1838', in K Inwood and P Baskerville (eds), *Lives in Transition*, McGill-Queens University Press, Montreal, 2015, pp. 19–42.

McCalman, Janet, and Rebecca Kippen, '"A Wise Provision of Nature for the Prevention of Too Many Children": Evidence from the Australian Colonies', in S Szreter (ed.), *The Hidden Affliction: Sexually Transmitted Infections and Infertility in History*, University of Rochester Press, New York, 2019, pp. 279–302. [See figures A7–A8 in this appendix.]

McCalman Janet, Len Smith, Sandra Silcot and Rebecca Kippen, 'Building a Life Course Dataset from Australian Convict Records—Founders and Survivors: Australian Life Courses in Historical Context, 1803-1920', in G Bloothooft, P Christen, CA Mandemakers and MP Schraagen (eds), *Population Reconstruction*, Springer, Heidelberg, 2015, pp. 285–98.

GRANTS

2007 ARC DP0771033 Discovery Grant, with Dr Hamish Maxwell-Stewart, Dr Rebecca Kippen, Mr Gavan McCarthy, A/Prof Ralph Shlomowitz, A/Prof Alison Venn, A/Prof David Meredith, A/Prof Shyamali Dharmage: 'Founders & Survivors: Australian Life Courses in Historical Context'.

2010 Institute for the Broadband Enabled Society: The Digital Panopticon.

2010 Australian National Data Service: Founders and Survivors' data management.

2011 ARC DP110102368: 'Land and Life: Aborigines, Convicts and Immigrants in Victoria, 1835–1985: An Interdisciplinary History'.

THE DATASET

McCalman, Janet, and Rebecca Kippen, 'Founders and Survivors: Life Course Ships Project', dataset of 25 000 convicts transported to Tasmania, 2017, figshare, https://doi.org/10.4225/03/59ed402437518

FIGURES

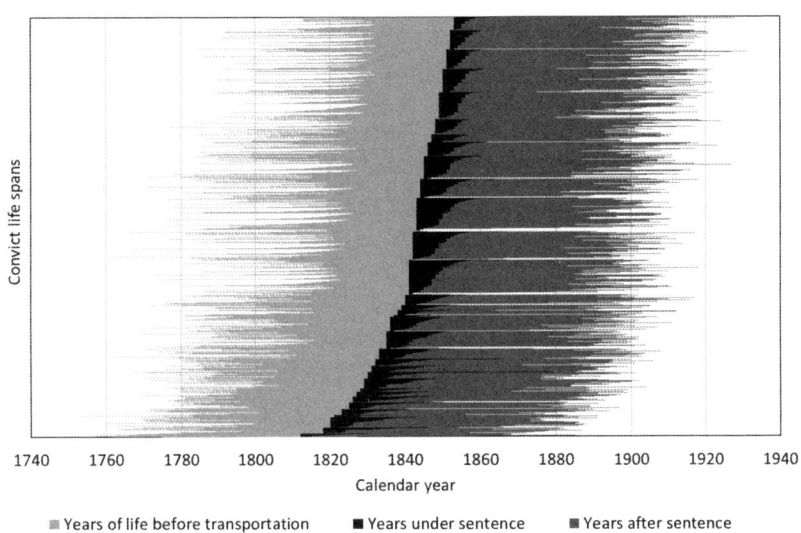

Figure A1 Years of life before transportation, under sentence, and after sentence, convicts in the Founders and Survivors Ships Project dataset

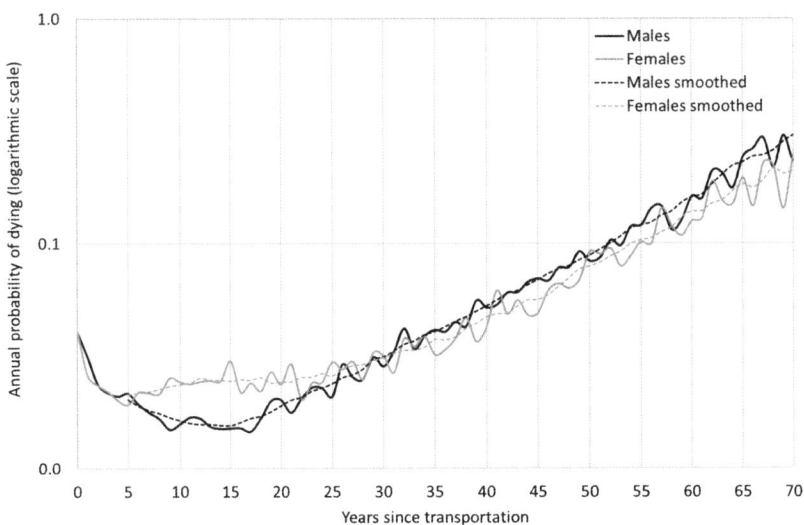

Figure A2 Annual probability of dying by years since transportation: male and female convicts

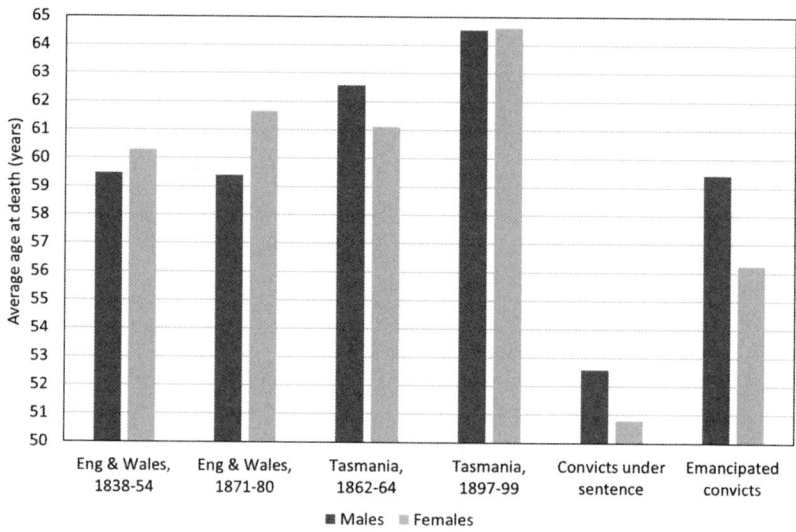

Figure A3 Average age at death for males and females given survival to age twenty years and based on age–sex-specific mortality rates: England and Wales, 1838–54; England and Wales, 1871–80; Tasmania, 1862–64; Tasmania, 1897–99; convicts under sentence; emancipated convicts

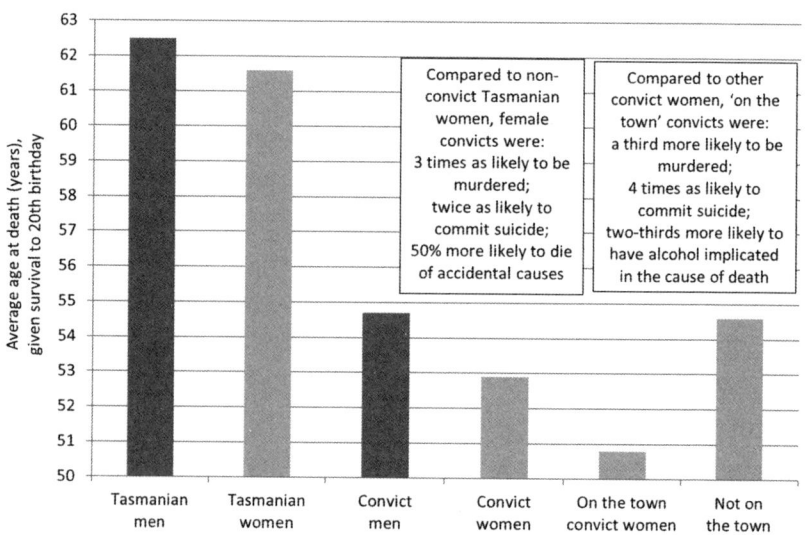

Figure A4 Average age to death given survival to twentieth birthday within Tasmania and among those who arrived bond

FOUNDERS AND SURVIVORS SHIPS PROJECT DATA

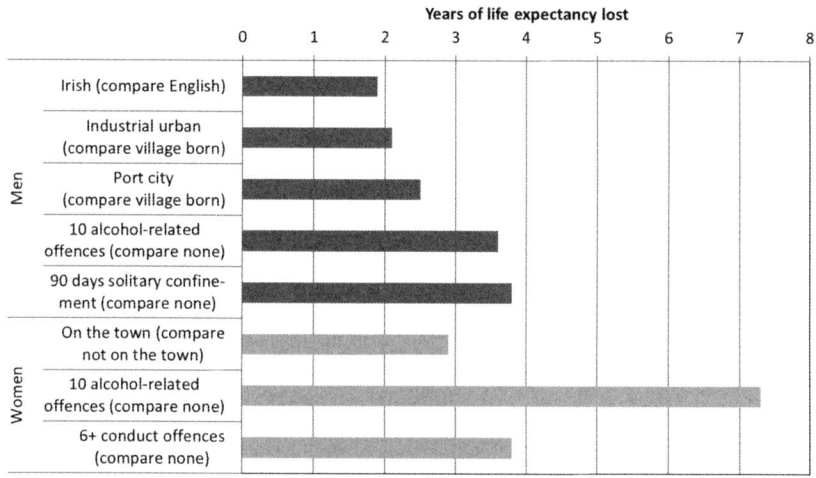

Figure A5 Years of life lost by selected risk factors: men and women

VANDEMONIANS

Parental Loss Sample and Analysis

Total ships researched: 126, in 1812–53; with 16 953 men and 7793 women: total 24 746 convicts.

This analysis: arrivals 1841 onwards, aged under twenty-five years—seventy-eight ships, 5586 men and 2836 women: total 8422 convicts.

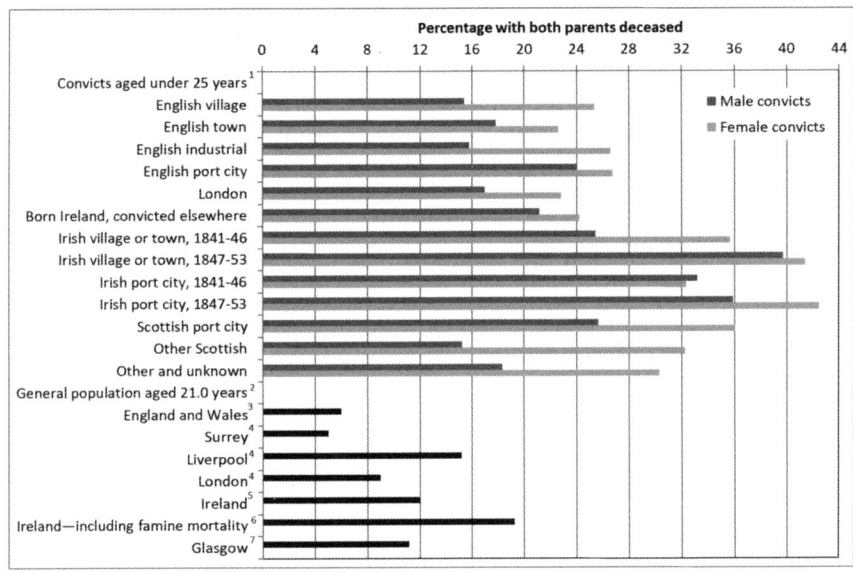

1. Convicts with 'Unknown' birth-family status are excluded from percentage calculations. Average age of convicts is 21 years.
2. Based on an assumed mother's average age at birth of exactly 30 years and a father's average age at conception of exactly 31.25 years, and the joint probability of mother and father dying before the child's 21st birthday (before exact ages 51 years and 53 years, respectively). Independence is assumed.
3. Survival probabilities drawn from 1841 England and Wales life tables (Human Mortality Database, 2015), with interpolation.
4. Survival probabilities drawn from 1841 life tables (Registrar General, 1843), with interpolation.
5. Survival probabilities drawn from 1821–41 life tables (Boyle and O'Grada, 1986), with interpolation.
6. Survival probabilities drawn from 1821–41 life tables for ages 31.25–48 years for males and ages 30–46 years for females, and famine life tables for ages 48–53 years for males and 46–51 years for females (Boyle and O'Grada, 1986), with interpolation.
7. Survival probabilities drawn from 1831 life tables calculated from Cleland (1836), with interpolation.

Figure A6 Population percentage with both parents deceased: sample of convicts aged under twenty-five years (average age twenty-one years) transported to Tasmania, 1841–53, by sex and place of birth; and general population aged twenty-one years of England and Wales, and Ireland, including famine mortality

FOUNDERS AND SURVIVORS SHIPS PROJECT DATA

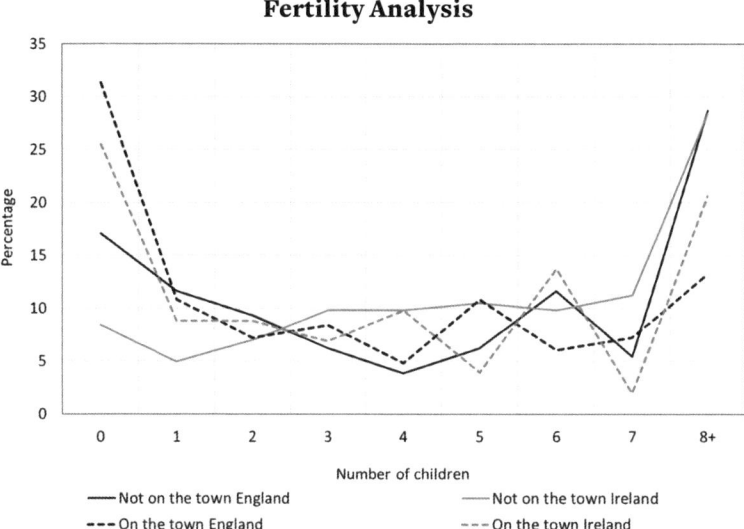

Figure A7 Distribution of number of children (completed fertility), sample of convict women transported to Tasmania aged 20–24 years, 1820–53, who married after transportation and survived to age fifty years, by country of birth and 'on the town' status (n = 599, Founders and Survivors Ships Project)

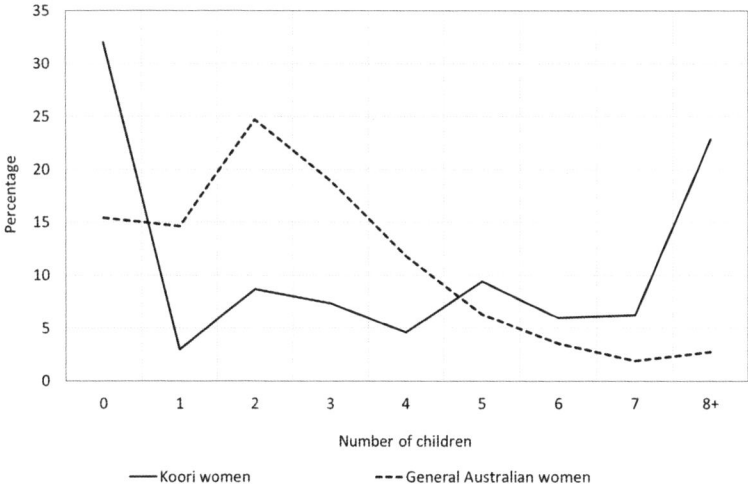

Figure A8 Distribution of number of children (completed fertility), sample of Koori women born 1900–1929 who survived to age 50 years (n = 171), and general Australian women born 1900–1929
Source: Rebecca Kippen calculations using data from the Koori Health Research Database, and 'Women by Age by Children Ever Born', special tabulation of the 1981 Australian Census of Population and Housing, Australian Bureau of Statistics, Canberra, 1999.

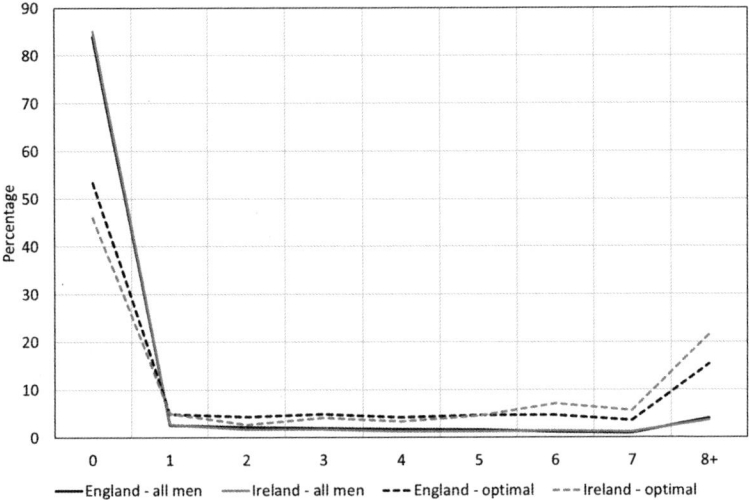

Figure A9 Distribution of number of children born to convict men after transportation, by country of birth, all convict men, and those with an optimal reproductive window (transported age 20–24 years and died after age fifty years)

APPENDIX B

Biographies

HOW TO READ THESE BIOGRAPHIES

The following are schematic biographies, selecting key measures and events from the convict records, births, deaths and marriages, and other sources. Phrases from the indents or other sources that are particularly evocative have been included verbatim. These short biographies will enable you to locate the fuller records collated by the Founders and Survivors (FAS) Ships Project and the Female Convict Research Centre (FCRC), as well as to follow up digitised images of original documents in the public records of Tasmania and Victoria. You will find fuller referencing for newspaper and other sources in these biographies. Note that data like height and literacy are often missing from early records.

At the bottom of each FAS biography, you will find a link under the heading 'recid' (record id). Open that and it will take you either to transcription of the Archives Office of Tasmania (AOT) indent and convict record data or to a record that integrates the AOT data with the researched biography.

The researchers who contributed to the biographies are named in acknowledgement of their work. All biographies have been checked and many have been enlarged or contributed by the author, who accepts full responsibility for any errors.

RESOURCES FOR FURTHER RESEARCH

AOT: the 'name search' will link to all convict department records for that individual, as well as to births, deaths and marriages and inquests.

PROV: online searches for criminal records, children's ward registers, inquests, probate, wills, arrivals and departures by sea, and land records.

FCRC: by registering online you can access their full dataset, which now incorporates all women transported to Van Diemen's Land. This database is constantly updated by the FCRC team, led by Colette McAlpine. New volunteers are always welcome.

FAS: the biographies collated by the volunteers and the research team can be accessed at http://foundersandsurvivors.org. There are a number of Founders and Survivors websites: this one is distinguished by '.org'. Please beware that this is an archived dataset that cannot be updated for lack of continuing financial support and personnel, which means there are mistakes and you should carefully check each entry.

The Prosecution Project: a collaborative research project collecting and analysing historical resources on the history of the criminal trial in Australia, led by Professor Mark Finnane, Griffith University. It can be accessed at https://prosecutionproject.griffith.edu.au/

SOURCES

Convict Biographies

FAS: Founders and Survivors biographies: http://foundersandsurvivors.org/
FCRC: Female Convict Research Centre: https://www.femaleconvicts.org.au/
Digital Panopticon: UK project that combines FAS research with Old Bailey and other criminal archives: https://www.digitalpanopticon.org/

Convict and Criminal Records

AOT: Archives Office of Tasmania: indents, description lists, conduct records, vital registrations, inquests etc.

VPRS: Public Records Office Victoria (PROV): criminal records, children's ward registers, inquests, probates, wills.

NAA: National Archives of Australia: World War I service and repatriation personnel records.
Old Bailey Online.
NSW Police Gazettes.
The Prosecution Project.
TPG: Tasmania Police Gazettes.
VPG: Victorian Police Gazettes.

Digitised Resources

Ancestry UK: Workhouse admission rolls, Newgate Prison registers, censuses.
Ancestry Australia: electoral roles, criminal records, rate books, vital registrations and family trees.
FindMyPast: digitised newspapers and periodicals, vital registrations.
National Archives of Australia.
National Library of Australia: TROVE: digitised newspapers of Australia.

ABBREVIATIONS

ADB: *Australian Dictionary of Biography*, online
AIF: Australian Imperial Force (World War I)
Ass: Assizes
AWL: Absent without leave
CCC: Central Criminal Court (Old Bailey)
Chains: Hard labour in chains
CoE: Church of England, Anglican
CON31: Male conduct record
CON40: Female conduct record
CP: Conditional pardon, free but to remain within the Australian colonies
FAS: Founders and Survivors Ships Project
FC: Free certificate
FCRC: Female Convict Research Centre
f.m.b.s: Family members in indents: (f)ather, (m)other, (b)rother, (s)ister
FS: Free by servitude
HL: Hard labour

Ind: Indent
KIA: Killed in action, World War I
Lashes: Cumulative count of floggings
NP: Native place
Prot: Protestant
QS: Quarter Sessions
RC: Roman Catholic
Sols: Cumulative days in solitary confinement
SSL: Ship's surgeon log
ToL: Ticket-of-leave; that is, parole: required to remain within a prescribed district and report to authorities but free to live in own residence and work for wages or conduct business.
VPG: Victoria Police Gazette

THE BIOGRAPHIES

Anderson, Margaret (*Margaret*, 1843) Born 1825 at Fife, aged 18, on the town 18 months; both parents dead, 4 siblings near Edinburgh; Prot, reads, 61.5". Tried Edinburgh: 7 years for theft of 2 shirts; previous for stealing, vagrancy and drunkenness; SSL: 'quarrelsome and disobedient'; CON41: AWL, drunkenness, absconding; FC 1850. Married 1854 to Edward Box (*Hoogley* to NSW, *Lady Franklin* to VDL) at Launceston. Died in watchhouse, Launceston, 1857: apoplexy, accelerated by excessive drinking. Husband sent letter to *Cornwall Chronicle* 7 Mar 1857 alleging that she was sick and died as a result of police mistreatment. However, he failed to appear at the inquest. [FAS JMcC, FCRC 8016]

Angus, Margaret (*Margaret*, 1843) Born 1816, Dundee, aged 27, married with one child on board; 1 b, 2 s; Prot, reads, 58.5". Tried CCC: 10 years for larceny in a dwelling, 'before convicted'; CON41: repeated drunkenness. Married 1849 to Peter Bushell (*Mount Stewart Elphinstone*, 1845), Hobart; ToL 1850; son on board died at Orphan School aged 2; 2 more sons: Donald b. 1845, Joseph Bushell b. 1851. Margaret Bushell died 1852 from cholera aggravated by excessive drinking. At the Inquest, Dr Officer reported that he found her in a room strewn with faeces and vomit, attended only by her 6-year-old son, Donald. Neighbours reported children crying, male strangers visiting and Donald fetching drink for her. AOT: 1852, Inquest 2670. [FCRC 8017]

BIOGRAPHIES

Appleyard, Peter (*Norfolk,* **1835**) Born 1810, Tadcaster; 25-year-old labourer from Yorkshire transported for 7 years for stealing 4 ducks. He left a wife Ann and 3 children in England. In VDL he was convicted of stealing food and disobeying orders, for which he had his sentence extended and served 10 days in solitary. He gained his ToL in May 1840 and his FC in 1845. In c. 1846 he appears to have married Harriet Ann Wheatley and soon afterwards they crossed to Victoria; 9 children at Alberton. Died 1866/3819 at Alberton of inflammation of the brain. *Lowlands: A Brief History of the Appleyard Family*, by Dianne Appleyard, published by South Gippsland Publishing, Foster, 1986. [FAS JMcC]

Asquith, Christian (*Maria,* **1820**) Born 1800, Holborn, London, aged 20. Tried Middlesex: 7 years for felony; CON31: 75 lashes; some further offences; FC 1837. Married 1828 to Susannah Smith (*Brothers,* 1828), ladies' shoemaker, shepherd and miner. Died 1857/2511 at Upper Hawthorn, Vic., of congestive apoplexy followed by paralysis; 2 of his daughters married Chinese miners. [FAS Stuart Hamilton]

Axford, Mary Ann (*Atwick,* **1838**) Born 1811, Bath, aged 26; 59.5"; 'bad character, convicted before'; 6 months on the town. Tried Bath: 7 years for stealing a hat; CON41: drunk and AWL; FC 1844. Married 1841 to John Dore at Hobart; 4 children, 1 survived. Died Charcoal Gully, Vic. 1868/6185 of congestion of the brain from blows to the head with a jug inflicted by William Douglas while in a drunken spree. [FCRC A103At, Lucy Frost]

Backway, Daniel (*Tortoise,* **1842**) Daniel Backway's lineage in London has been traced to the mid-18th century. Born in 1824, he was christened at St Ann Limehouse in 1830, the son of Daniel Williams Backway, waterman, and Elizabeth, his wife, of Limehouse. Their other 3 children were all christened at the same time, 10 days before their mother died at the age of 33. Daniel's father died on 5 April 1832, probably during the cholera epidemic. Daniel, now only 8, was an orphan and sent to the Limehouse Workhouse. Tried CCC: priors, 'once for deserting my master 3 weeks; similar offence 1 mth'; 7 years for 'stealing a pair of trowsers'; 19 years 'orderly'; 62"; reads and writes; Prot; sweep; b 1, s 1; CON31: 10 days solitary. Married 1853, Mary Ann Moxham at Hobart; 11 children, 5 predeceased him; miner at Maryborough. Died 1882/6017 of pneumonia at home; 3 grandsons in AIF, 2 KIA. [FAS JMcC]

Baldock, Helen/Ellen (*Hector*, **1835**) Born c. 1810, Edinburgh; aged 25, 61.5"; 17 times convicted for disorderly behaviour; 8 years on the town. Tried Edinburgh: 14 years for robbery; SSL: 'well behaved'. Married 1836 to **William Goodall** (*Lady Harewood*, **1829**) in Campbell Town; FS 1848; 7 children, 3 predeceased her. Died 1895 at Allansford, Vic., aged 84 of cardiac disease and paralysis (6 weeks); AIF, 1 KIA Gallipoli. [FAS Steve Rhodes, FCRC 6021].

Banigan/Barrigan/Bannagan, James (*Equestrian*, **1845**) Born 1828, Edinburgh; aged 16, 57"; RC, f Francis, 2 b Matthew, Francis, 1 s Mary, np'; reads and writes; priors for household articles. Tried Edinburgh: 7 years for stealing a gown with 2 others; SSL: 'very well behaved'; CON31: 12 sols; FC 1852. Single. Died 1893/14351, suicide by hanging, aged 65. [FAS Jennifer Kisler]

Banks, Thomas (*John Renwick*, **1843**) Born 1821, Hanley, Staffordshire; aged 20, 66.5", collier, f Thomas, m Anne at Lane End, 1 b John, 4 s Ellen, Ann, Patience, Lizzy; Prot; 10 years: 'breaking into a box in Parsons Vales house during a row. 500 men were present; the colliers turned out because the wages were too low; some got half a crown, some 3/- and some 3/6' [Chartist riots]. After an uneventful time under sentence, FS 1853. Came to Victoria. Became a miner around Daylesford but also became a drunkard. In 1867 was arrested on suspicion of murder but released due to lack of evidence. Minor offences in 1868 and 1869. Died 1876/11604 at Daylesford Hospital from cancer of the intestines and asthenia. Never married. [FAS Geoff Brown]

Bannister, Benjamin (*Aurora*, **1835**) Born 1795, Epping in Essex; aged 41; 64.75", Prot, illiterate; m and 2 b, 2 s at London; wife dead, and 4 children; labourer. Tried Essex QS: 14 years for receiving stolen harness; gaol report: 'bad'; SSL: 'well behaved'; CON31: 17 sols; FS 1844; to Port Phillip 1849. Died 1858/3487 at Melbourne Benevolent Asylum of disease of the heart and pleurisy; 63 years. Did not marry. [FAS Nola Beagley]

Barker, Henry (*Circassian*, **1833**) Born 1816, aged 16; 60"; 2 months for money, flogged. Tried Derby: life for stealing a gown piece; SSL: 'orderly'; CON31: 31 sols, 25 lashes, 6 months in chains; CP 1844. Married 1844 **Lydia Ford** (*Royal Admiral*, **1842**) at Launceston; 5 children; separated; no death found. [FAS JMcC]

BIOGRAPHIES

Beatson, John (*Neptune*, **1838**) Born 1807, Haddington, Scotland, aged 29, mason; 'convicted before and dissipated habits'. Tried Edinburgh: 7 years for 'crime of assault on parents and previous conviction'; SSL: 'Chief Constable on board and behaved exceedingly well. Would think make a good constable on Shore'; CON31: minor offences, HL; CP 1843; common-law relationship with **Catherine Salmon** (*Mellish*, **1830**), 2 children found, born in Victoria. Died 1857/1752 at Boggy Creek, near Kyneton, Vic., aged 54, of pneumonia. [FAS Maureen Mann]

Bellamy, Martha (*Sovereign*, **1827**) Born 1810, Soho, London, aged 17, RC, 58.5"; pock-pitted, 'prostitute', 'stealing a ring and umbrella from a man once in the Watch house for fighting'. Tried Middlesex: life for robbery; SSL: 'has permitted indecent familiarities'; CON40: AWL etc. until 1831. Married 1832 to **William Guise** (*Chapman*, **1824**) at Green Ponds; 8 children, 2 survived her. Died 1888 at 16 Westgarth Street, North Fitzroy, Vic., aged 78, of old age and senile bronchitis. [FAS Steve Rhodes, FCRC 11361]

Bentley, James Francis (*Blundell*, **1844**) Born 1817, Surrey (Scarborough on convict record), aged 27; married; literate; 'right foot crippled walks lame'; 66.5"; 'I was a merchant in Canada'. Tried Manchester: 10 years for forgery, originally sent to Norfolk Island; CP 1851. Married 1852 Catherine Sherwin in Victoria; 7 children. Died 1873/4501 suicide with laudanum at Carlton. See *The Argus* 20 November 1854 for a detailed account of the murder trial: 'Bentley is a full-faced, athletic, stout-built man, of the age of about 45, his wife is a young and handsome woman of about 28. The whole of the prisoners, with the exception of Mrs. Bentley, retained a very cool demeanour throughout the trial. She, however, was observed frequently to cry. A chair was provided for her in the dock.' [FAS Tricia Curry]

Bentley, Mary (*Atwick*, **1838**) Born 1815, Linlithgow, aged 22; 64"; 'of irregular habits and connexions'; 12 months on the town. Tried Edinburgh: 14 years for highway robbery; CON40: disorderly conduct once. Married 1839 to **William Peeler** (*Woodford*, **1828**); 7 children, 4 survived her. Died 1896 at Barker's Creek, Vic., aged 87, of old age and debility. Grandson Walter Peeler VC First AIF, POW on Burma Railway, Second AIF. [FCRC B393At]

Bickley, Sarah (*Asia*, **1847**) Born 1827, Wallsall, Staffordshire, aged 20; reads and writes; 61"; 'on the town one week'. Tried Birmingham: 7 years for stealing monies; SSL: 'good'; CON41: drunk with man in her room; FS 1853. Married (1) 1849 **William Thompson** (*Lord Petre*, **1843**), 1 son; (2) 1879 James Greenwood (*Recovery*, 1837). She murdered Thompson in 1857 at Muckleford, Victoria: 'they lived unhappily under the combined results of intemperance and jealousy', *Ovens & Murray Advertiser*, 15 June 1857. Died 1894/8911 of heart disease at Castlemaine, buried with her son and second husband. [FCRC 1284]

Bidgood, John (*Augusta Jessie*, **1835**) Born 1814, Plymouth, aged 20; 60"; baker. Tried Devon (Plymouth): 7 years 'stg an Umbrella. Once disorderly conduct fined 5/-, punished on board for stealing and flogged'; SSL: 'indifferent'; CON 31: 36 lashes, 21 sols; FS 1841. Married 1843 **Mary Hill** (*Navarino*, **1841**), 7 children, 4 survived him; sugar boiler. Died 1879/4243 at 32 Sackville Street, Collingwood, of cancer of the mouth and asthenia; 2 grandsons in AIF. Left £11 in furniture and tools. [FAS JMcC]

Bird, Frederick (*Waverley*, **1841**), Born 1813, Brussels, Belgium; aged 27; 69.75"; soldier, 84th regt 8 years; f Miles, m, 2 b, 3 s; reads; Ind: 'gentleman's servant'. Tried Dublin: court martial, 14 years for desertion; SSL: 'Strongly recommended, quiet and steady'; CON31: probation extended, sols and chains, CP 1850; apart from discovering the body of his de facto, **Margaret McHague** (*Royal Admiral*, **1841**) in a shaft at Break 'O Day in 1874, there are no other confirmed sightings. He is an interesting case, one of an important subgroup within the male convict population—a deserter. He was tall, born in Europe at the end of the Napoleonic Wars; his family had middle-class names and he knew how to impress his superiors, as he did on the voyage out. However, he was only partially literate, and a drinker—there are possible convictions for drunkenness around Geelong in the 1850s. We found that risk of death increased with height, perhaps indicating the greater propensity to personal violence among former soldiers who were selected for their height.

Blackburn, James (*Isabella*, **1833**) Born 1803, Westham, Essex; 'connexions respectable'; married to Rachel Hems in 1826; civil engineer, architect and surveyor. Tried CCC: 1833 for forgery of cheque for £600; SSL: 'very good. Had charge of the boys prison and gave great satisfaction'; wife and daughter joined him in Hobart; 1839 Department of Public Works created, run by

Blackburn and Cheyne, the colonial architect. Multiple projects and houses in VDL. 1849 family sailed for Port Phillip. Founder of the Immigrants' Home, designing engineer for the Yan Yean water supply. Died 1854/1050 at Brunswick Street, Collingwood, of typhoid fever; 4 children died, 5 survived him. Grandfather of Labor politician and lawyer Maurice Blackburn. See Harley Preston, ADB: 'Although Blackburn's life was predominantly one of unrealized potentialities, he has claims to be considered one of the greatest engineers of his period in Australia and his architectural achievements established him as Tasmania's most advanced and original architect.' [FAS Steve Rhodes]

Blackford, James (*Louisa*, **1845**) Born 1816, Shoreditch, London; aged 17; f&m, 2 b, 2 s at NP. Tried CCC: 8 Sep 1831: transported for life to NSW for theft; 1845 re-transported for 7 years to VDL; CON31 unavailable; shoemaker. Married **Margaret Cosgrave** (*Waverley*, **1846**) in Hobart 1850; 3 children. Last reference in VPRS 515/3590 1869. Death not found. Had AIF descendant. [FAS JMcC]

Bodycott, John (*Marion*, **1844**) Born 1823, Sandby Gate, Leicester; 'for bread 6 weeks; cherries 3 months; 10 years for housebreaking and stealing sugar. Brother transported 4 years ago', f John at NP; 2 b William, Thomas; 4 s Ann, Caroline, Eliza, Maria; stocking weaver, reads and writes, labourer, 66.5". No death found. [FAS JMcC]

Bodycott, Thomas (*Duncan*, **1841**) Born 1819, St Margaret's, Leicester; 'once vagrancy 3 mths; again for same 3 mths; discharged for apples; discharged again for lead'; f John at NP; 2 b William, John; 4 s Ann, Caroline, Eliza, Maria. Reads. Stocking weaver. Scar on forehead. Tattoos, 64". Tried Leicester: 7 years for larceny; returned Leicester; married; 4 children; whole family framework knitters in 1861 Census. Died 1906, aged 87, at Leicester. [FAS JMcC]

Bones, Benjamin (*Henry Porcher*, **1835**) Born 1812, Buxted, Sussex, 22 years, 65.75"; married, 1 child; ploughman. Tried Sussex QS: 7 years for stealing 11 fowls; CON31: minor offences; FC 1843. Married (2) Mary Hawthorn (*Majestic*, 1839) 1845; 4 children discovered. Died Dunolly, Vic., 1886/1210, aged 75, of old age and apoplexy, 2 daughters surviving, 2 sons deceased. At least 2 in AIF. [FAS Geoff Brown]

Bones, Thomas (*Henry Porcher*, **1835**) Born 1805, Kent, 31 years, 66", same offence as brother Benjamin; shepherd, never married. Died 1872/1077, Yarra Bend Lunatic Asylum.

> Stealing in a Dwelling
> Thomas Bones, an old man, pleaded not guilty to an indictment for stealing a pistol and other property belonging to Peter Mortinson, of Frenchman's Gully. Henry Paul Leman, gaol surgeon, deposed that the prisoner appeared perfectly childlike and silly, and incapable of understanding the proceedings and making a proper defence. Prisoner had been so for three months.
> Chas. Forster, governor of the gaol, corroborated the surgeon's evidence. The jury found accordingly, and the prisoner was remanded. Admitted to Yarra Bend Lunatic Asylum the 28th August 1861. (*The Argus*, 26 Oct 1876) [FAS Geoff Brown]

Brentani, Charles (*Aurora*, **1835**) Born 1815, Lake Como, Italy; aged 19; 66.25"; reads and writes Italian; mother at NP, 1 b at Sheffield; 2 s at NP; hawker; RC. Tried York West Riding: 7 years for stealing silver spoons; gaol report: 'general receiving of stolen property connexions very bad'; FC 1841. Married 1844 Ann Campbell, at Launceston, 5 children; jeweller and gold dealer. Died 1853/1001 at Melbourne of delirium tremens. See Douglas Wilkie, 'Frankenstein, Convicts and Wideawake Geniuses: The Life and Death of Charles Brentani', *Victorian Historical Journal*, vol. 87, no. 1, 2016, p. 99. [FAS Douglas Wilkie]

Briant/Bryant, John Moon (*Mangles*, **1835**) Born 1810, Nunney near Frome, Somerset, aged 24, 65.5"; wheelwright; reads & writes; m&f, 6 b, 3 s at NP, one in London; 'industrious Connexions respectable'. Tried Wiltshire QS: 7 years for 'stealing Oak and Elm boards' from master; SSL: 'good'; CON31: mostly punished for working on his own account; flogged but text obscured; FS 1842. Married 1846 Sarah Eliza Rawlings, 9 children, 4 survived him. Died 1891/15163 at Fitzroy, aged 81, 'gentleman' of tuberculosis, cystitis with acute tonsilitis. Probate: no real estate but £11 872 shares in Commercial Bank of Australia. [FAS Steve Rhodes]

Broom, William (*Atlas*, **1833**) Born 1813, Wookey Hole, Somerset, aged 20; 71"; tailor. Tried at Somerset Ass: life for burglary; SSL: 'behaved well'; CON31:

131 lashes; CP 1848. Married **Anne Ward** (*Mexborough*, **1841**), 5 children found, all died as infants; 1864: 5 years for sheep stealing. Died 1887/6919, at Kilmore Hospital, disease of heart and lungs, dropsy. [FAS Jenny Wells]

Burman, Benjamin (*Mangles*, **1835**) Born 1808, South Cave, Yorkshire; aged 27; 65.75"; soldier 34th regiment; reads and writes; wife in America, mother and step-siblings NP. Court Martial at New Brunswick, life for desertion, away 12 hours, commuted to 14 years; SSL: 'behaved very well'; 2 letters in his favour; CON31: nil; CP 1842. Married 1845 Elizabeth Frances Halloran at Brighton, Tasmania; butcher in Victoria; 7 children, 3 deceased. Died 1887/1415 at Daylesford of disease of the heart; 4 grandsons in AIF. [FAS Steve Rhodes]

Burnett, William (*Barossa*, **1844**) Born 1822, Banff, aged 19, 65"; gardener; reads; 1 b John and 2 half-sisters. Tried Aberdeen: 7 years for housebreaking and stealing £17; FS 1847. Married Margaret McFarlane in 1849 at Melbourne; 15 children, 12 survived him. Died 1893/10505. Became miner at Bulldog, now Illabarook; left real estate of £50, personal property £35; AIF. [FAS Lance Dwyer]

Burrell, Jane (*Tory*, **1848**) Born c. 1800 near Lynn, Norfolk; 48 years; 62"; Prot; married, 9 children. Tried Wisbech, Cambridgeshire: 14 years for receiving stolen goods, first conviction; 'very well behaved'. CON41: nil. Died 1879 at New Town Pauper Establishment of morbus cordis. [FCRC 12319]

Burt, Caroline (*Rajah*, **1841**) Born 1826, Poole, Dorset, aged 15, 63.75"; pock-pitted. Tried Dorset QS: 10 years for stealing linen from a hedge with sister Jane, also on board, aged 17 years; CON 41: nil; FS 1850. Married 1842, aged 16, to George Alfred Goodall at Oatlands, 7 children, 6 predeceased her. Died 1862/1736, aged 37, at Inglewood, Vic., of bronchitis. Her husband died the following year of valvular disease of the heart. The only survivor of this family was Thomas, aged 16. Her sister Jane married James Wright in 1848, also at Oatlands; 11 children, 4 predeceased her. Jane died 1911/15039 at the age of 90 in Flynns Creek, near Traralgon. [FAS Steve Rhodes, FCRC 415]

Butler, Edward (*Chapman*, **1827**) Born 1818, Sheffield, aged 17; 62"; tattoos; 'gent servant'; 3 months in Wakefield for 'Stealing Tools in Wakefield House of Correction'. Tried Doncaster: 7 years for picking pockets; CON31: nil. Married 1831 **Ellen Fraser** (*Harmony*, **1829**), 1 daughter. Died 1867/1375 at

197 Victoria Parade, Collingwood, of tumour in the thorax; pawnbroker. [FAS JMcC]

Byrne, Margaret (*John William Dare*, **1852**) Born 1829, Wexford, aged 23; 61"; RC; reads; 1 child John, 3 years old; thrice convicted before, quiet. Tried Wexford: 7 years for stealing shirts; SSL: 'well conducted'; CON41: 6 days cells, 4 months HL for AWL; FS 1857. Married **Thomas Wilkins** (*Forfarshire*, **1843**) at Launceston; 14 children, 5 predeceased her. Died 1885/8242 at Cambridge Street, Collingwood, aged 60, of debility and premature old age; daughter Caroline witnessed her death but did not know the names of her grandparents; 2 grandsons in AIF. [FAS Steve Rhodes, FCRC 6967]

Cavanagh, Henry (*Enchantress*, **1833**) Born 1812, Dublin, aged 23, 64", single. Tried Liverpool: 14 years for 'house robbery', once for burglary, 2 years in Lancaster; FC 1843; 50 stripes. Married **Jane Robertson** (*Rajah*, **1841**) at Longford, 8 children, 7 survived him. Died at Warrnambool, Vic., 1861/1982, suicide by cutting. [FAS JMcC]

Chaplin, William (*Strathfieldsaye*, **1831**) Born Whitchurch, Bristol, aged 20, 63"; waterman; 'connexns &c bad'; SSL: 'orderly'. Tried Bristol: 7 years for 'stealing rope', 'once 2 months for a row'; CON 31: treadwheel 4 days, 12 lashes. Married 1848 at Hobart, **Lydia Leeson** (*Emma Eugenia*, **1844**). Died 1886/12281 at Wellington Street, Collingwood, aged 84, of debility and old age; personal details unknown, 'gentleman'. [FAS Jenny Kisler]

Cherry, Samuel (*Candahar*, **1842**) Born 1822, Mountsorrel, Leicestershire, aged 19, reads and writes, 65.25", shoemaker's labourer; 'joseph kent transported for same offence and my b. James'. Tried Leicester: 7 years for 'stealing hosiery good'; SSL: 'cross ironed for stealing; bad'; CON31: 17 sols; FC 1846; VPRS 515/1208: 1853 horse stealing; 1861 robbery in company with Benjamin Long. No death found. [FAS Lance Dwyer]

Chuter, Thomas (*Woodman*, **1826**) Born 1807, Surrey, aged 18; 63.25"; labourer, sawyer, pitman; 'bad, convicted before'. Tried Surrey Ass: life for burglary; CON31: treadwheel 24 days; 25 lashes; FS 1842. Married Mary Bossom (born Hobart) in 1844, 1 child. Died 1853, probate found. [FAS Colin Tuckerman]

Clements, Adam (*Mount Stewart Elphinstone*, **1845**) Born 1821 near Devizes, aged 24; 61.25", reads a little, farm labourer. Tried Wiltshire Ass: 15 years for highway robbery where 'James Wilson was struck with a stick'; CON31: nil; ToL 1852. Married **Ann McDonald (*Midlothian*, 1853)** 1854 in Hobart; 6 children; grocer. No death found, last mention in Collingwood. Rate books 1891. [FAS Alison Ellett]

Clements, Eliza (*Hindostan*, 1839) alias Eliza White Born 1819 at Bloomsbury, London; aged 20; m Charlotte at NP; 59"; red hair; 3 years on the town; reads; Prot; tattoos. Tried CCC: 4 Mar 1839: 10 years for larceny from the person; priors for being disorderly, felony; CON40: AWL, misconduct, 40 days sol. Married Abraham Powell 1843 in Launceston; in bed with another man 1844; FC 1849; left for Port Phillip 1853; Powell died 'of a decline' in 1854; VPRS 516/540/81/1188 as Eliza White. Last conviction 1868. Death not found. [FAS JMcC, FCRC 6254]

Colreavy/Colreavey, James (*Navarino*, 1843) Born 1795, Co Longford, aged 47; 65.5"; reads and writes; ploughman; married, 9 children, 7 living (1 more born in NSW); priors: for murder 3 months and discharged; for debt 8 months. Tried Longford: 7 years for receiving stolen heifers; 2 children onboard, and application made for wife and other 5 children to come to NSW. Died 1876/10697 at Wellington, NSW, farmer, 84 years, of old age. [FAS Steve Rhodes]

Cooper, Daniel (*Red Rover*, 1831) alias Joseph Brooks Born 1811, Huddersfield, Yorkshire, aged 20; 66.25", farm labourer. Tried York: 14 years for robbery; CON31: 105 lashes, 35 sols; multiple HL in chains, stocks, and sent to Port Arthur. Died 1858/3009 at White Hills, Vic., wound in abdomen inflicted by Lopez in self-defence. [FAS JMcC]

Copping, Mary (*Rajah*, 1841) Born 1822, Windsor; aged 19; 58"; 6 weeks and 1 month in house of correction. Tried Middlesex: 7 years for larceny; CON40: nil. Married 1843 to Joseph Randall (*Susan*, 1837) who died 1870 at New Norfolk; 11 children, 4 survived her. Died 1895/5118 at Robert Street, Collingwood, aged 70, of cancer of the uterus. [FCRC 10550]

Cosgrove, Margaret (*Waverley*, 1847) Born 1828 in Limerick, aged 19, 60.5", illiterate, RC, m Elizabeth, b Dennis, s Johanna, all at NP. Tried King's Co: 10 years burglary, 5th conviction, twice for assault; SSL: quiet; CON40: AWL; FS 1857. Married 1850 at Hobart to **James Blackford (*Louisa*, 1845)**;

3 children, only 1 survived her; VPRS 516/559 as Margaret Blackford. Died 1867/10821, off Little Bourke Street, Melbourne West; phthisis 12 months. [FAS Cecile Trioli, FCRC 12649]

Cray, John (*Isabella*, **1842**) Born 1821, Long Acre, London; aged 20; prior: drunkenness; 65.5", Prot; painter. Tried Westminster: 10 years, 'picking pockets and stealing one pound, a purse and a handkerchief'. Married **Mary Holehouse** (*Tory*, **1845**), Hobart; 12 children; cook. Died 1888/26 at Ballarat Hospital, aged 69, of strangulated hernia; 3 in AIF. [FAS JMcC]

Crisp, Samuel (*Earl St Vincent*, **1826**) Born 1805, Sudbury, Suffolk; 22 years; wife and 2 children; 65", sawyer. Tried at Essex: life for sheep stealing; ToL 1830; brought out wife and 2 sons from Sudbury with permission; she died 1854. Married Elizabeth Farquarson 1857 in Hobart; 11 children (see ADB: Sir Malcolm and Patrick Guy Crisp, and Sir Harold Crisp). Died 1888 at 249 Elizabeth Street, Hobart; cerebral apoplexy; 85 years; timber merchant; 6 in AIF. [FAS JMcC]

Crowson, Samuel (*Georgiana*, **1833**) Born 1805, England, aged 27, 62"; transported before. Tried CCC: life for housebreaking; transported 1824 for picking pockets; SSL: 'orderly on board'; CON31: 75 lashes; 7 sols; CP 1844. Married 1842 Ann Kent (*Navarino*, 1841), FCRC 9723 who disappeared; 1 child. Died 1881/4035, Emma Street, Collingwood. Married Adelaide Britton, 1 child. Died aged 81, bricklayer, of acute diarrhoea and old age. [FAS Maureen Mann]

Cuddihy, Daniel (*Duke of Richmond*, **1844**) Born 1818, Co Tipperary, aged 25, 58.5", quarryman—can blast; reads and writes; mother Peg; no siblings. Married 1854 Bridget Dunne (*Blackfriar*, 1851); 14 years for 'assaulting a habitation'; 3 children found, all born Victoria; AIF descendants. Died 1868 at Stratford, suicide by drowning. [FAS Garry McLoughlin]

Cullen, Margaret (*Lord Auckland*, **1849**) Born 1830, Co Tipperary; aged 18; 58.5", RC, illiterate. Tried Kilkenny: 7 years for stealing wearing apparel; SSL: 'very good'; CON40: nil except for illegitimate child 1851 born at Cascades—died. Married 1851 to **William Starr** (*Marquis of Hastings*, **1842**); ToL 1850. Died 1920/8642, aged 90 at Ballarat Hospital, of senility. [FAS Jackie Wisniowski, FCRC 7682]

Dalton, William (*David Clarke*, **1841**) Born 1822, London, aged 19; m and 1 b, 2 s; shoemaker 15 months; 60.75" (63" by age 38); reads. Tried CCC: 17 Aug 1840, 10 years for housebreaking and stealing some ribbon; married at death but no details; VPRS 515/1892: 10 years on roads for robbery; 'much pock-pitted, tattoo'; wife Margaret Magelburn and 2 children Albert Place, Melbourne. Died 1868/6849 at Melbourne Hospital of 'aneurism of aorta'. [FAS JMcC]

Disney, Elizabeth (*Harmony*, **1829**) Born c. 1790 at City of Cork; 38 years, 62.75"; RC; read only; lost several front teeth, sunken cheeks. Married to William Disney, cabinet-maker of Somers Town, London; 'boy 9, boy 5, boy 4 all with me. I was last living with my husband'; in Newgate before. Tried Middlesex: 7 years for 'stealing a piece of print'; CON40: repeated convictions under sentence for drunkenness. Died October 1849/1783 at Little Scotland (Ashby), Geelong, aged 66; 3 sons all went to Ballarat and did well; grandson Sir James Disney, see ADB. [FAS JMcC, FCRC D92H]

Dowsett, James (*Henry Porcher*, **1836**) Born 1802, Boreham, Essex, aged 34; married with one child, 67.25", 'character and connexions bad, convicted 3 times before'. Tried Colchester: 7 years for stealing wheat; CON31: nil; FC 1842; formed common-law relationship with Mary Cann, who died as Mary Dowsett in 1868; no issue. Died 1864/7902, aged 64, of pneumonia, at Sebastopol Road, Kyneton; equity case on estate: *Argus*, 10 Sep 1875; VPRS index wills etc., 5/163. [FAS Geoff Brown]

Drinkwater, William (*Surrey*, **1833**) Born 1809, Gloucestershire, aged 24; 63.25"; read and write; married, wife and one child at Cam.; 'orderly'. Tried Gloucester: life for horse stealing; 'connexions respectable'; SSL: 'very good'; CON31: conspiracy to perjury; CP 1845. Married Jane Hannon, Hobart; left her in Hobart and had de-facto relationship with **Harriet Shurley** (*Emma Eugenia*, **1844**); married Winifred Ryan in Victoria 1863; 5 children, 2 daughters, wards of the state; son in gaol 1882; 2 babies by last marriage, died in Geelong. Died 1887/10645 at Kew Asylum of chronic disease of the brain; AIF descendants, all descended from his children with Jane Hannon, his Tasmanian wife who was a publican in Hobart until her death in 1866. [FAS JMcC]

Dudgeon, John (*Gilmore*, **1843**) Born 1820, Bermondsey, London, aged 22; 61.5"; reads & writes; Prot; m, 2 b, 1 s; horsehair manufacturer. Tried CCC: 10 years for stealing horse hair (3 cwt) from a shop by breaking into it; SSL: 'ironed for misconduct'; CON31: nil. Married (1) 1860 to Adelaide Abram, at St John's Church, Melbourne, 5 children; (2) Annie Samuel at St Paul's Church (Annie's second marriage was to Agar Wynne), 3 children. Died 1884/1779 at Walpole Street, Kew, aged 61, of cancer of the lung; tobacco manufacturer. [FAS 'visitor']

Duff, Paul (*Isabella Watson*, **1842**) Born 1816, Queen's Co, Ireland, aged 26; 71.75", illiterate, RC, kitchen gardener, single; 2 b: 'Phantom [*sic*] and Frank'. Tried Dublin: for 'assault on Lawrence Holmes [a publican], I hit him with a stick'; CON31: disorderly conduct, begging for tobacco, being drunk and assaulting a woman, 10 sols; ToL 1846; FC Jan 1850; in Victoria: VPRS 515/P1, Paul Duff No. 6888: 2 years on the roads for rape of child 10 years old, 6', 11 st 5 lbs, large scar on upper left arm. Died, unmarried, aged 50 at Ballarat Hospital, 1866, 20 years in Victoria, f&m unknown, single, 'compression of brain from effusion of blood from blow inflicted on him'. Report of the court case: *Argus*, 10 Mar 1866, p. 3. [FAS JMcC]

Dunn, Janet (*Gilbert Henderson*, **1840**) Born c. 1827, Glasgow, aged 12; 47.25", daughter of Janet Dunn, widow, King Street, Glasgow. Trial Glasgow: 7 years for theft of a book; priors: 1 theft and 3 for 'what I do not recollect'; 2 scars side of mouth; CON41: larceny and being in a common brothel (aged 17) (after marriage). Married Archibald Boyle (McKenzie) (*Egyptian*, 1839) in 1845 at Hobart; FC 1847; 2 children; as Janet McKenzie VPRS 516/1323. Died 1881 at Ararat Lunatic Asylum of exhaustion from disease of the brain; admitted to asylum 1871 suffering from mania; inquest VPRS 24: 1881/350. [FAS JMcC, FCRC 5745]

Ellis, Edward (*John Renwick*, **1843**) Born 1819, Hanley, Staffordshire, aged 23; wife Hannah at NP, 2 children; f Thomas, m Sarah, 5 b William, Richard, George, John, Thomas at NP; 2 s Harriet, Mary; illiterate, 62.25"; collier. Tried Stafford: 10 years for 'Demolishing Squire Parker's house at the potteries Staffordshire, at the riots for increase in wages' (Chartist); CON31: nil; CP 1851. Married Anne Tubbridg, Victoria, 1858; 6 more children, 1 predeceased him; gold miner in Ballarat East; moved to Footscray where family settled. Died 1885/5188, aged 64, of disease of the liver, exhaustion; oldest married daughter witnessed death and knew his parents' full names; youngest child was 14; grandson in AIF. [FAS Geoff Brown]

BIOGRAPHIES

Eshitt/Eskitt/Eskett/Escott, Jane (*Garland Grove*, 1841) Born 1825, Hairdy near Glasgow; single, convicted Durham for 'stg money and drapery from my master, never in prison before'; CON41: 49 sols. Married **George Pickering** (*Lord Goderich*, 1841), 1852. Death not found but she was recorded as deceased on Pickering's death certificate, as were 2 of her 3 children by him; an illegitimate son died in the Dynnryne Nursery while she was under sentence. [FAS JMcC, FCRC 5384] She has been confused by researchers with Jane Hescott (*Sea Queen*, 1846), who married William Ward in 1852, and who also settled in Melbourne. Her husband was a night watchman. She died of 'cancer of the womb' aged 38 in 1859 at their home in Lygon Street, then North Melbourne. Her only child was Sophia, aged 7. [FAS JMcC, FCRC 10952]

Evans, Mary (*Royal Admiral*, 1842) Born 1823, St Lukes, London, aged 19; 65"; reads, RC, 'pock-pitted G R & cut on left arm'; f George at Holborn; 2 years on the town. Tried CCC Old Bailey, 29 Nov 1841: simple larceny, 7 years; SSL: 'bad'; CON41: AWL, in common brothel, drunk; VPRS 516/92, 85, 1190: long career of disorderly behaviour, drunkenness and violence. Reported as married in VPRS but no other evidence. Died as Kate Gorman 1878/2565, Melbourne Hospital, of rheumatism, debility, aged 60, 27 years in Victoria, no other details. [FAS Annette Sutton, JMcC, FCRC 10748]

Felton, Ann (*Emma Eugenia*, 1846) Born 1824, Dawley, Shropshire, aged 22; tattoos, 'a prostitute for 9 years'; 60"; read and write. Tried Stafford: 10 years for stealing gold coin from the person; CON40: drunk, AWL, indecent language; FC 1855. Married 1847 William Waters at Hobart; no children; Waters departed for Port Phillip in 1855; in Melbourne by 1858; convicted under name of Ann Wood, VPRS 516/5134. Died 1886/9990 aged 70 at the Melbourne Hospital. [Colette McAlpine, FCRC 4944]

Fennelly, Mary (*Gilbert Henderson*, 1840) Born 1824 at Waterford, Ireland, aged 15, 61", red hair; 'no person came to see me in gaol. I am not married'. Tried Lancaster: 10 years for 'stealing money from Mr John Atkinson my master at Liverpool'; CON41: possession of lace, 12 months' HL; FS 1849. Married (1) 1845 permission to marry James Farrer, 1 son; (2) 1846 married Roger Parkinson (same month and this may be the same man); (3) 1849 Jesse Fairchild at St James Church, Melbourne. Died 1907/6347 at

The Esplanade Hotel, St Kilda, aged 85, of cardiac failure, gangrene and exhaustion. [Colette McAlpine, FCRC 5751]

Fitzgerald, Patrick (*Isabella Watson*, 1842) Born 1830, Kings Co, aged 12; 51"; illiterate; m Bess at Francis Street, 1 b, 1 s; 12 months, 6 months, 3 months for handkerchiefs. Tried Dublin: 7 years for 'stealing a silk handkerchief'; SSL: 'bad, slovenly'; CON31: 88 stripes on the breech; reconvicted; convicted in Victoria: 'VPG 3', Mar 1859, p. 91: Melbourne, convicted of stealing from the person, 17 Nov 1855, 5 years HL; ToL Mar 1859 to Melbourne. Married at St Francis' Church, Melbourne, Anne Bunworth, 7 children; oldest daughter married Joseph Augustus Serong. Died 1894/1351 at 117 Park Street, Collingwood, aged 64, of chronic rheumatic gout and senile phthisis; AIF. [FAS JMcC, Rebecca Kippen]

Fitzgerald, Winifred (*Waverley*, 1842) Born 1825, Carlow, aged 17; m Bess at Dublin, 2 b and 3 s at NP, 2 b transported; 61"; reads; hair reddish brown; tattoos; 2.5 years on the town. Tried Dublin: 7 years for stealing a watch and money; SSL: 'violent and incorrigible'; CON40: gross disorderly conduct, sent to New Norfolk Lunatic Asylum; had child in 1845; FC 1849. Married Joseph Johnson, Melbourne, 1852; VPRS 516/100, 534; number of children unrecorded. Died 1880/299 at Beechworth Lunatic Asylum of pulmonary consumption and disease of the brain, aged 55. [FAS Tricia Curry, FCRC 12532]

Fleming, Catherine (*Rajah*, 1841) Born 1819, Co Clare; aged 22; 59.5"; married; 9 years on the town; reads only; 9 times in prison before. Tried Lancaster: 10 years, stealing from the person; SSL: 'very bad'; CON40: repeated drunkenness, AWL, misconduct and violence towards other prisoners; 42 sols. Married Thomas Bennett 1847 at Hobart; FC 1850, to Port Phillip. Death not confirmed. [FCRC 10566]

Fletcher, Samuel (*Claudine*, 1821) Born 1806, Beeston, near Nottingham; aged 14; 'tried before for stealing half-crown from a Ship, once got 3 months and whipt for stealing stockings once before for a watch acquitted'. Tried Nottingham: 7 years for stealing a shirt; SSL: 'orderly'; CON31: 325 stripes; assaults and theft, new sentence of 7 years; FC 1840. Died Nov 1847/4403, aged 42. [FAS Judy Wells]

Ford, Lydia (*Royal Admiral*, **1842**) Born 1825, the Strand, Westminster; aged 17; lisps; 59.25"; reads and writes. Tried CCC: 7 years for embezzlement and stealing by servants: 'robbing a lodger in my master's house, 3/-'; SSL: 'good'; CON 41: nil; FC 1848. Married 1844 **Henry Barker** (*Circassian*, **1833**); 5 children, 2 survived her. Died 1909/1194 at Ballarat, aged 80, of pneumonia and senility. [FAS Annette Sutton, FCRC 10751]

Forrester, Charles (*Coromandel*, **1838**) Born 1817, Staffordshire, aged 21, 69.75", potter, tattoos; 'very bad habits & character. 8th conviction of Felony connexions bad and numerous'. Tried Stafford QS: 15 years for house breaking; CON31: 25 lashes, most of sentence in chains; de-facto relationship with **Rhoda Wells** (*Royal Admiral*, **1842**); acquitted of her murder on circumstantial evidence. Died 1886/13289 at Upper Macedon, aged 69, of acute pneumonia. [FAS JMcC]

Fowler, Elizabeth (*Navarino*, **1841**) Born 1823, Belfast, aged 17; 58.75"; read and write. Tried CCC: 10 years for larceny by servant in a dwelling house; gaol report: 'passionate and unruly but not devoid of some good feeling'; SSL: 'very good'; CON40: insolence and AWL; 28 sols; FC 1853. Married Richard Howe, 1847, at Launceston; 1 son, 2 daughters (twins); VPRS 516/346. Died 1908/6308, aged 88, Melbourne Benevolent Asylum of fatty degeneration of the heart. [FAS Steve Rhodes, FCRC 9680]

Foy, James (*Surrey*, **1842**) Born 1809, Old Change, London, aged 32; 65"; literate; clerk. Tried CCC: 10 years for embezzlement. Married 1855, Campbell Town, Tas., Anne Gelks; 6 children, 2 survived him. Died 1883/901 at Rokeby Street, Collingwood, of diarrhoea and vomiting, old age; 2 in AIF. [FAS Alison Ellett]

Fraser, Ellen (*Harmony*, **1829**) Born 1809, Wooler, Northumberland, 19 years, 60"; 'reads & writes'; Prot; 'plain cook'; 'relations in Cumberland, f&m dead, I was living last with Grantley Berkeley, Cranfield Bridge under Nurse Maid 3 children', 'I was once in custody for being tipsy'. Tried Middlesex: 14 years for larceny from employer; CON40: illegitimate child who could not be weaned and refusal to disclose the father; FS 1842. Married 1827 **Edward Butler** (*Chapman*, **1827**), 1 daughter Jane Mary who married Rev. James Walter Crisp. Died 1900/8607 at Sydney Road, Coburg, aged 94, of senile decay and cardiac failure (for years). [FAS JMcC, FCRC F56H]

Frith, Charles (*William Jardine*, **1844**) Born 1814, near Doncaster, Yorkshire; aged 30; literate; 65"; shoemaker; married. Tried Sheffield: 10 years for 'stealing a sheep skin and wool'; CON31: 14 sols. Married 1870; leather cutter. Died 1886/12267, at Peel Street, Collingwood, aged 70, of morbis cordis. [FAS Leanne Goss]

Gilligan, Luke (*Marion*, **1844**) Born 1827, Marylebone, London, aged 20; 67.6"; RC, reads and writes; 'for a saw 3 months; fighting 14 days'. Tried CCC: 7 years for stealing a copper can; CON31: 21 sols, 28 months HL in chains; FC 1850; 1853 tried for horse stealing; known as Thomas Turnip/Thomas Bourke/Thomas Smith, VPRS 515/799 and 10638. Died 1890/2773, aged 63, labourer, general debility, want and exposure. [FAS Nola Beagley]

Goodall, William (*Lady Harewood*, **1829**) Born 1809, Broseley, Shropshire; aged 20; 64.5"; miner. Tried Stafford: life for horse stealing; CON31: neglecting to attend church; CP 1841. Married **Ellen Baldock** (*Hector*, **1835**) at Campbell Town; 8 children, 5 survived him; farmer. Died 1885, aged 74, of old age and lingering, at Allansford, Vic.; 6 in AIF. [FAS Steve Rhodes]

Gosling, Benjamin (*Surrey*, **1833**) Born 1812, Sheffield; aged 20, 65"; brass founder. Tried York: 7 years, 'stealing stockings once for setting school on fire acqu. 8 times for vagrancy'; thickly pitted; hulk report: 'bad fellow'; SSL: 'good'. Married 1841 Ann Mary Taylor (*New Grove*, **1835**) [FCRC 9964] at Hobart; VPRS 515/2692, 7210. Died 1876/2396 at Melbourne Hospital, aged 64, of cancer of oesophagus. Ann Mary died at the Melbourne Benevolent Asylum in 1877/8317 of laryngitis, bronchitis. [FAS JMcC]

Gough, Edwin (*Pestongee Bomangee*, **1847**) Born 1821, Westbury, Worcestershire; aged 25; m at NP; 64.75". Tried Denbigh: 9 years for burglary and stealing shawls; CON31: nil; no marriage found in Australia but had 5 children with Elizabeth; labourer. Died 1882/11363, aged 60, at Stafford Street, Collingwood, of softening of the brain, and exhaustion from large and deep-seated abscesses. [FAS Alison Ellett]

Grady, Mary (*Hindostan*, **1839**) (Mary Perry in Victoria, real name Ann Barry) Born 1809, Kerry, aged 30; 58"; RC; child on board. Tried CCC: 7 years for larceny—shoplifting from father of her child in Clerkenwell; SSL: 'extremely insolent to me on several occasions and never satisfied'; CON40: insolence,

AWL; FC 1845; no marriage found; VPRS 616/ 21, 1169. No death found unless died as Ann Barry in Hawthorn in 1889/7768, aged 80. [FAS Jennifer Ellison, FCRC 6345]

Grant, Alexandrina (Jemima McKenzie) (*Tory*, 1845) Born c. 1827 at Inverness, aged 18, 62", reads and writes (claimed she couldn't at her trial), Gaelic speaker; priors: 'once 60 days for theft again for leaving my place 6 months'. Tried Aberdeen: 7 years for 'falsehoods, fraud and wilful imposition'; SSL: 'orderly but precocious'; CON41: AWL, falsehoods, 31 months' HL in solitary cells; 1849 had Roderick, who died. FC 1852. Married William Askew at Melbourne, 1852: 9 more children, of whom 1 male and 2 females predeceased her. Died Jersey Road, Woollahra, NSW 1913/115993. [Arthur Davidson, Perth, Scotland, FAS JMcC, FCRC 12196]

Guise, William (*Chapman*, 1824) Born 1807, Birmingham, aged 17; m at Birmingham; apprenticed to Mr Stevendon, High Street, Birmingham. Tried Birmingham: life for burglary, once before for apparel, served 3 months in same gaol; CON31: absconded from master, 50 lashes; CP 1836. Married **Martha Bellamy (*Sovereign*, 1827)** 1832; 8 children, 5 predeceased him. Died 1878/4459 at Station Street, Carlton, of debility, aged 71; 1 possible AIF. [FAS Steve Rhodes]

Halfpenny, Thomas (*Lady Harewood*, 1829) Born 1808, Hammersmith, London, aged 21, 64.25", groom. Tried Middlesex: 7 years extended by 3 for stealing a handkerchief; CON31: 112 lashes; FS 1831. Married 1839 at St Francis' Church, Melbourne, to Hannah Cogan; married 1844, same church, Anne Sullivan; 14 children. Died 1894/1352 aged 89 at Fairchild Street, Collingwood, of senile debility and cardiac failure; at least 4 in AIF. (FAS JMcC)

Hanley, Ellen/Nellie Roberts (*Greenlaw*, 1844) Born 1826, Limerick, aged 18; m&f and s at Limerick; 2 large scars on forehead, pock-pitted; 62"; reads; prior arrest for stealing: 'got off by my father in the police'. Tried Limerick City: 7 years for stealing frock and petticoat at NP; 1 month on town; SSL: 'unruly but not badly disposed'; CON40: drunk, AWL, indecent language; FC 1850. Married 1850 to **John Roberts (*Frances Charlotte*, 1837)** at Launceston; VPRS 516/4548. Died 1893 in Beechworth Gaol of acute softening of the brain (suffering from paralysis: syphilis) [FAS Cecile Trioli, FCRC 5941]

Harris, Bridget, transported as Biddy Craig (*Waverley*, **1842**) Born 1825, Belfast, aged 17; on the town 18 months; illiterate; 54"; RC; tattoos; aunt at NP. Tried Antrim: 7 years for larceny, 'stealing a tumbler for a cheese discharged, for a shawl 12 months, for a handkerchief discharged'; SSL: 'good'; CON40: many offences, in a brothel, etc., drunkenness; FC 1849. Married 1852 William Mason at Hobart; later had 2 children with George Harris; VPRS 616/76, 607. Died 1872/8823 aged 58 at Campbell's Creek, Vic., of disease of heart and kidneys, sudden death. [FAS Judy Wells, FCRC 12513]

Haynes, George (*Westmoreland*, **1841**) Born 1821, Liverpool, aged 19; f Robert at NP, m Mary, 1 b Robert, 1 s Elizabeth; 'reads and writes on board'; iron founder; 63". Tried Liverpool: 10 years for housebreaking and taking wearing apparel; FC 1851; no trace after mention of siblings being in Victoria. [FAS JMcC]

Hill, Mary (*Navarino*, **1841**) Born 1824, Henley-on-Thames, aged 17; 60". Tried CCC: 10 years for burglary; SSL: 'orderly'; CON40: AWL and insolence once each; FS 1850. Married **John Bidgood** (*Augusta Jessie*, **1835**) 1843 at Hobart; 6 children. Died 1882/9363 at Melbourne Hospital of cerebral haemorrhage. [FAS JMcC, FCRC 9706]

Hinkins, John (*Earl St Vincent*, **1826**) Born 1804, Clerkenwell, London; aged 21; Prot; reads and writes. Tried CCC: 7 years for larceny of two watches; CON 31: 150 lashes; FC 1833. Married (1) 1835 to Jane Theobald in Hobart; (2) 1848 Catherine Weston in Victoria; (3) 1872 Ellen Mary Williams in St Kilda; 2 children from first marriage; teacher, postmaster, deputy registrar of births, deaths and marriages, Essendon. Died 1883 at post office, Mount Alexander Road, Moonee Ponds, aged 78, of syncope, heart and brain disease. [FAS Colin Tuckerman]

Hockey, James (*Sir Charles Forbes*, **1830**) Born 1806, Evercreech, near Shepton Mallet, Somerset; aged 24, married with 2 children; wife in workhouse 1829; 64.75"; butcher. Tried Somerset: 14 years for 'horse stealing once 8 mnths for brass'; CON31: 25 lashes; FC 1847. Married 1839 Ann Barfoot (free), 6 daughters, 1 son. Died 1870/10338 at Elphinstone, Vic., aged 64, of dropsy. [FAS JMcC]

Holehouse, Mary (*Tory*, **1845**) Born 1822, Newport, Wales, nee Morgan, Married husband Wm in 48th Regt, 1 child on board; 3 years on the town;

can read; 63.25"; living Friars Fields, Newport; gaol report: 'Once previously convicted of felony; supposed to have lived in a career of crime about five years; parents and connections disreputable', 'Once for money 3 mos, again for Drunkenness 3 mos', stealing coal 14 days. Tried Monmouth: 7 years for 'stealing £4 from the person'; SSL: 'Quarrelsome Indolent'; CON41: drunk, breaking panes of window. Married **John Cray (*Isabella*, 1842)** in 1849 at Hobart; 1 child before sentence, another under sentence who died; had another 14 children with John Cray, including a last set of twins; at her death, 6 were still living; VPRS 516/P2 2723 as Mary Cray. Died in 1885/7750 at her daughter's house in Broomfield near Creswick of general decay and debility, aged 63. [With the late Terrence Creaney, Liverpool, FAS JMcC, FCRC 12208]

Huxley, Ann (*Edward*, 1834) Born 1792, Holborn, London, aged 46, 56"; married with 8 children, 5 on board, imprisoned before. Tried Surrey QS: 7 years for stealing cotton print; CON41: nil; ToL 1838. Married 1835 John Martin in Tas.; sons Francis and James had criminal careers, as did their sons. Died 1863 at Melbourne, old age and diarrhoea, aged 71; 4 children still living. [FAS JMcC, FCRC 4060]

Ing, Edward (*Augusta Jessie*, 1835) Born 1800, Uxbridge, Middlesex; aged 35; married, 3 children; 59". Tried Middlesex: 7 years for burglary; CON31: almost nil; FS 1841; shepherd. Died 1862/6845, aged 62, injuries from a dray passing over him; both death and inquest are incorrectly indexed under JUG; burial is under ING. [FAS Geoff Brown]

Jones, Ann (*Hindostan*, 1839) Born 1811, St Giles, London, aged 28; 1 s NP, didn't know about parents and brother; on the town 9 years; 64.5"; CON40: drunkenness. Married Robert Warren 1840 at Campbell Town, Tas.; 3 sons, 1 died 1851. Died 1868/8667 at Whitehall Street, Footscray, of disease of the liver and gastritis. [FAS Jennifer Ellison, FCRC 5310]

Keelen/Keelan, Sidney (*Earl Grey*, 1850) Born 1832, Castleblayney, Monaghan, aged 18, 60", Prot, reads, m dead, 'never convicted before good and useful'. Tried Armagh: 7 years for stealing a cow; SSL: 'very good'; CON41: nil; CP 1853, FC 1856. Married (1) 1852 Thomas Jones and John Naden, at Launceston, 2 children by Naden who died in Ballarat 1856; returned to Ireland for lecture tour, 1860; returned to Thomas Jones in Tasmania, who died in 1872, leaving her £1040; (2) married James Maxwell 1874 in Carlton; became property developer. Died mysteriously aged 54 in 1886/1148, decapitated by a train near Ascot Vale Station; left £5360 to her husband. [Colette McAlpine, FCRC 3741]

Kendrick, William (*Persian*, 1830) Born 1811, West Bromwich, Staffordshire; aged 20; groom & carter; 63.5"; 'very bad'. Tried Stafford: 14 years for 'assault with intent to rob'; SSL: 'orderly'; CON31: confined to rural districts, troublesome; FS 1845. Married (1) Jane O'Bryan (*Garland Grove*, 1841); (2) 1843 **Mary Ryan (Ellen Bannon)** (*Garland Grove*, **1843**), 3 children. Died 1869/1629 at Piper's Creek, aged 58, of 'rupture of aneurysm of aorta accelerated by drink'. [FAS Leigh Prideaux]

Keogh/Kehoe Family: chain migration by transportation Martin (*Orator*, 1843); Anne (*Waverley*, 1847); Elizabeth (wife of Martin) (*Kinnear*, 1848); Patrick (*Pestongee Bomangee*, 1849); Margaret (*Midlothian*, 1853). The remaining children were free emigrants: Bridget in 1854, and John and William in 1857. [Xepapas, Kathleen, 'Wexford to Van Diemans Land', unpublished manuscript, Tasmania, 2012, copy in possession of Garry McLoughlin.]

Kimber (Kimmer), James (*Eliza*, 1831) Born 1810, Milton Lilbourne, near Pewsey, Wiltshire; family of agricultural labourers, including his 4 surviving sisters; aged 21; 63"; no priors. Tried Wiltshire: 7 years for machine breaking. Married Rosanna Kenny, Launceston, 1839; 8 children, 4 predeceased him. Died 11 Sep 1895, at Mulberry Cottage, Richmond, aged 85, asthenia after a tram accident. [FAS biography by Annabel Anderson; material from Ancestry.com family tree]

Kimpton, Charlotte (*Lloyds*, 1845) Born 1827 near St Albans, aged 18; 60.75"; reads and writes a little. Tried St Albans QS: 7 years for stealing money 'pd by my mother and aunt'; CON40: nil; FS 1852. Married **Thomas Pearce** (*Asia*, **1840**), 13 children, 7 survived. Died 1890/15401 at Islington Street, Collingwood, aged 60 of chronic rheumatism. [FAS Steve Rhodes, FCRC 7568]

King, Anne (*Angelina*, 1844) transported as Ann Davis (*Angelina*, 1842) aka Ann Lawlor/Thorp/Smith in VPRS 616/8, 451, 2140; born c. 1825, Cheetham Hill, Lancaster; aged 19; 62", tattoos; on the town 4 years. Tried Manchester: 7 years for stealing a chair; previous for larceny and vagrancy; SSL: 'indifferent'; CON40: drunk, in bed with man, in a disorderly house,

AWL; no marriage recorded; FC 1851. No death found, but last conviction in Melbourne, 1873. [FCRC 1507]

Kinnear, Mary (*Margaret*, 1843) Born 1810, Dublin; aged 33; 60.25", reads only; 1 b and 3 s at Dundee; on the town 5 years. Tried Perth: 7 years for housebreaking; SSL: 'inclined to be insolent'; CON40: AWL, disorderly; FC 1849. Died 1852, inflammation of lungs produced by exposure and want (syphilis). [FCRC 8083]

Langham, Samuel (*Claudine*, 1821) Born 1804, Leicester; parents Samuel and Sarah Langham, Belgrave Gate, Leicester, father a stocking weaver. Tried Leicester: 7 years for larceny; second conviction: '1st time stealing cakes, one moth and whipt'. Married at Launceston 1834, Eliza Ware; 6 children. Died 1872/7682 at Yarra Bend Lunatic Asylum, jaundice, aged 60. [FAS Judy Wells]

Leary, Ellen (*Gilbert Henderson*, 1840) Born c. 1827, Dockhead, London; 56", 'front teeth project'. Tried CCC: 7 Aug 1839; 10 years for burglary, 'in prison twice before; stealing £2/10/- from a dwelling house, once for iron 1 week, once 1 Month for candlesticks'; CON40: insolence, disobedience of orders; c. 11 months' solitary; FS 1849. Married Samuel Burgess 1845 at Launceston; went to Port Phillip 1849 and 1850. No death found but a woman named Ellen Burgess was before the courts in Melbourne for drunkenness. [FCRC 5789]

Leaver, Sophia (*Tory*, 1845) Born 1822, Bolton, Lancashire, aged 23; 59.25"; reads and writes; on the town 3 months; 'once before convicted and once imprisoned as a reputed thief'; slight impediment in speech, pock-pitted. Tried Lancaster: 7 years for stealing a shawl and a gown; CON40: AWL and stealing a chemise; FC 1851. Married 1853 William Lydiate at Melbourne; 4 children. Died 1874/5088 at Kyneton Hospital, aged 43, cirrhosis of liver, Bright's disease and ascites; had falsified her age by 10 years to hide her time in VDL. [FAS Nola Beagley, FCRC 12221]

Leeson, Lydia (*Emma Eugenia*, 1844) Born 1799, Nottingham, aged 44; married; 'reads'; 50"; 'a respectable looking woman'; married, 4 children. Tried Nottingham: 14 years for 'stealing two shovels'; CON40: drunk once; CP 1852. Married 1848 Hobart, **William Chaplin (*Strathfieldsaye*, 1831)**. Died 1869/8726, Emerald Street, Collingwood, aged 66, of cirrhosis of the liver; 3 children from first marriage listed; son Henry (b. 1826) was in gaol as a boy at the time of her conviction, later transported to VDL on *Barossa*, 1844. He was convicted in Victoria and nominated his mother and 'father' as being in Collingwood. Failed as a publican in Collingwood and died destitute in Geelong aged 55 in 1881/1536. [FAS Jennifer Kisler, FCRC 4814]

Lewis, Mary/Margaret (*Hindostan*, **1839**) Born 1814, Edinburgh, aged 25, married to James; 64"; RC; reads and writes. Tried CCC: 7 years for obtaining under false pretences; SSL: 'middling'; CON40: drunk, AWL, disturbing the peace; FC 1846. Married 1845 Samuel Sergeant at Hobart; 7 children; 1852 went to Port Phillip alone with 3 of her children and associated with other former convicts around Romeo Lane and Ballarat; VPRS 616/ 75; in 1858, the *Ballarat Star* of 28 Oct described her as 'a well-known Arcadian'. She was an alcoholic. However, it appears that her husband, Samuel Sergeant, rescued her and she died in 1886 at the General Hospital in Hobart, in her 73rd year (Tas Deaths 1886/200) of morbis cordis. [FAS Jennifer Ellison, FCRC 6317]

Light, John (*Eden*, **1836**) Born 1819, Bristol; aged 17; stable boy; 64.5". Tried Oxford Ass: life for 'stealing 3 watches'; CON31: 72 lashes for insolence; ToL 1845. Married Emma Goddard 1851 at Scots' Church, Melbourne; 14 children; miller. Died 1889/8123 at Piper Street, Kyneton, aged 70 of morbis brightis; AIF. [FAS JMcC]

Lloyd, Richard (*Sir Robert Peel*, **1844**) Born 1807, Radnorshire, Wales; aged 36, tried with brother Edward on board; siblings at NP; 69"; reads and writes; farm labourer. Tried Radnor Ass: 10 years for stealing 2 lambs; SSL: 'steady & quiet'; CON31: nil; CP 1852. Married 1843 **Judith Murtagh** (*East London*, **1843**); no issue; carter. Died 1884/9382 at High Street, Kyneton, of bronchitis and catarrhal pneumonia. [FAS 'Organ']

Lochrie, Mary (*Margaret*, **1843**) Born 1826, Glasgow, f&m Neal Thompson and Mary (from death certificate); 59.5"; red hair; RC; reads and writes; 3 years on town. Tried Glasgow: 7 years for 'stealing a Mouseline dress', 5 times before for theft; SSL: 'tidy, clean and quiet'; CON40: AWL once, 6 sols; FC 1852. Married John Harrold (*Henrietta*, 1843) in 1846 at Hobart, 4 children, 2 girls survived; VRPS 516/172 as Mary Ann Harold. Died 1866/59600 at Melbourne Benevolent Asylum of phthisis, aged 38; parents listed but no marriage or children; 1 daughter died 4 years later; the only survivor of her children died in 1919. [FAS Steve Rhodes, FCRC 8088]

BIOGRAPHIES

Long, Benjamin (*Equestrian*, **1845**) Born 1825, Frome, Somerset, aged 22; 64.25"; f&m and 5 sibs at NP; reads and writes; carpenter; 'stealing lead 4 mths; for assault 1 mth'. Tried Bristol: 10 years for house breaking and stealing 2 watches; CON31: absent from work, larceny, 14 sols; carpenter; VPRS 515/8094. Died 1879/11266 at Melbourne Hospital, aged 54 years, of disease of kidneys. [FAS Nola Beagley]

Long, Thomas (*Hyderabad*, **1850**) Born 1824, Galway, aged 26; 68.25"; 'reads a little'; single; parents dead, 5 siblings; labourer. Tried Galway: 7 years for 'stealing barley from a meal cart'; CON31: nil; famine transportee; never married. Died 1879/7432, Easey Street, Collingwood, aged 54, of dropsy and bronchitis. [FAS Lance Dwyer]

Lowry, Catherine (*Rajah*, **1841**) Born c. 1821, Ireland, brought up in Manchester, aged 20; on the town 6 years; illiterate; 63.75"; convicted 5 times before. Tried Salford: 10 years for receiving a watch; leading member of the 'flash mob'. Married, and continued to offend until her death in 1898; children also offended; remained in Tasmania. [FCRC 10607]

Luck, Joseph (*Moffatt*, **1834**) Born 1809, Hertfordshire, aged 24; 68.5"; tattoos. Tried Kent: 14 years 'stealing a shovel, once for a Ring, 3 mos hard labour'; CON31: 6 months HL in chains; FC 1847. Married 1836 Margaret Sutherland (*Westmoreland*, 1836), 1 child, who died 1850. Died 1878/8963, aged 67 years, of phthisis pulmonalis at Kyneton. [FAS Jenny Wells]

Marlow, Samuel (*Sir Godfrey Webster*, **1823**) Born 1799, Isleworth, Surrey, aged 22, 65"; 'working at Borough Market'. Tried Surrey: 14 years for burglary; CON31: 25 lashes; left Tas. 1837. Married Mary Ann Sullivan, Melbourne, 1847; 5 daughters; brewer and cordial maker; architect. Died 1882/2649 aged 83 at Little Bourke Street West, of diarrhoea and haemorrhage; 1 in AIF [FAS Leanne Goss]

Marshall, Gilbert (**per *Recovery* to NSW, 1818, then *Deveron* in 1820 to VDL**) Born c. 1800. Tried Bristol: 1818, 14 years; CON30: no offences after 1831 when found in an indecent position with two women; made constable in VDL. Married Janet Black (*Lady of the Lake*, 1829) in 1834 at New Norfolk, 9 children; carpenter, set up one of the first businesses in Richmond, manufacturing candles in Abinger Street; owned 450 acres on Plenty River that sustained family after his death. Died 1855/5888, accidentally burned to death; AIF descendants. [FAS JMcC]

McAnally, Ellen (*Mexborough*, 1841) Born 1824, Fermanagh, Ireland, aged 17; 52.5"; face much freckled; 12 months on the town; 'theft and 8 or 10 times for vagrancy'. Tried Armagh: 7 years for vagrancy; SSL: 'well behaved'; CON41: 27 sols, absconded, AWL; FC 1849. Married 1848 John Barefoot (*Mary*, 1837) at Launceston; 3 children. Died 1860/8826 aged 36, from asphyxia induced by intoxication at Kyneton. [FAS Alison Ellett, FCRC 9200]

McAuliffe, Thomas (*Egyptian*, 1840) Born 1815, Limerick, Ireland, aged 24; 66"; RC; reads. Tried Clonmel: 7 years for 'attempting to compel to quit' (as part of a house breaking), with brother and others on board; SSL: good; CON31: 4 sols; FS 1847. Married 1850 at Melbourne to Bridget O'Brien, 9 children, 2 deceased; farmer. Died 1873/9832 at Laceby, Vic., aged 49 of cancer; sons were Kelly supporters. [FAS Lance Dwyer]

McCormick, Jeremiah (*John Renwick*, 1843) Born 1818, Manchester, aged 24, weaver, 56.75"; RC, wife Elizabeth, m Sarah, 3 s Eliza, Mary and Ann, all NP; 2 children. Tried Lancaster: 7 years for 'stealing bread from Mrs Daines of Ship Gate in the riots' (Chartist); 'Well behaved, constable in the boys' prison on board'; FS 1852, came to Victoria; hawker and grazier. Married 1856 Catherine Dougherty (*Hope*, 1842) at Beechworth; no further children; conflict with Ned Kelly at Greta led to Kelly's first prison sentence for insulting Mrs McCormick. Died 1889/7689 at Greta of asthma. [FAS Geoff Brown]

McCoy, Judith (*Atwick*, 1838) Born Dublin, 1816; single, 61", 6 months on the town. Tried Liverpool: 7 years, stealing clothes and silver spoons; CON40: numerous offences—drunkenness, AWL, being in a disorderly house (also after marriage). Married Thomas Haydon (*Atlas*, 1833) 1841 in Hobart. Died Bendigo 1853/1867, aged 39. [FAS Tricia Curry, FCRC M335At]

McDonald, Ann (*Midlothian*, 1853) Born 1825, Co Monaghan, aged 28, sister in Scotland; 62.5"; RC; reads. Tried Monaghan: 7 years for fraud for 'obtaining five saddles under false pretences'; SSL: 'fair'; CON40: nil. Married 1854 **Adam Clements (*Mount Stewart Elphinstone*, 1845)** at Hobart; 7 children, all survived her. Died 1878/8221 at Collingwood, aged 52, of remittent fever and exhaustion. [FAS Alison Ellett, FCRC 132257]

BIOGRAPHIES

McHague, Margaret (*Royal Admiral*, **1841**) Born 1820, Dumfries, aged 22; 60"; read and write, CoE; priors: 6 months for stealing from the person. Tried Carlisle QS: 7 years for robbery and stealing money from the person; SSL: 'good'; CON41: drink, AWL; FC 1849. Married 1844 Henry Lees (*Eden*, 1836); midwife. Died 1874/7080 at Break 'O Day, found dead in a shaft. [FAS Glad Wishart, FCRC 10808]

McIver, William (*William Jardine*, **1844**) Born 1826, Glasgow, aged 18, 67.75", can read and write; Prot; cotton dyer; f&m, b 4 and s 1 all in America. Tried Glasgow: 10 years for 'Housebreaking Stealing Wearing Apparel ... 6 times in prison before'. Partnered Sophia Simpson, at Woodend, Vic. (de facto); 6 children. Died Melbourne Hospital, aged 94, in 1910/6243, of senility and heart failure; old age pensioner; only 1 child still alive; AIF. [FAS Leanne Goss]

McLoughlin, Michael (*Duke of Richmond*, **1844**) Born 1821, Queen's Co, aged 22; 66", reads and writes; farm labourer; RC; m Bridget; 2 b William, Tim; 3 s Mary, Peggy, Ellen, all NP. Tried Queen's Co: 10 years for 'stealing a gun' and 'threatening'. Married (1) Julia Keating, 1853, 3 children; (2) Mary Murphy, 1862, 7 children; children named after his mother and siblings. Died 1896/10213, at Kyneton, of liver and kidney disease and exhaustion; AIF. [FAS Garry McLoughlin]

McNeil, Anne (*Tasmania*, **1845**) Born 1815, Roscommon, Ireland, aged 30; 62.5"; illiterate; single, 1 child, RC. Tried Westmeath: 7 years for shirt; CON40: drunk, obscene language; FC 1852. Married 1847 John Spong (*Commodore Hayes*, 1823), 3 children, 1 survived her; midwife. Died 1883/11661 aged 68 at 49 Little Lonsdale Street, of peritonitis. [FAS Steve Rhodes, FCRC 12094]

McQuade, Rose (*East London*, **1843**) Born 1808, Fermanagh, aged 35, 58", reads only; RC; widow, 1 boy Thomas, 9 years. Tried Fermanagh: 10 years for stealing a cow. Married Joseph Hagen (*Marquis of Hastings*, 1839) in 1847 at Hobart; no more children. Died 1859 at Warrnambool, Vic., of acute gastritis, inflammation of the stomach; son was witness, aged 25; AIF. [FAS Colleen Arulappu, FCRC 3941]

Melville/Malvelle/McCallum, Edward/Francis (*Minerva*, **1838**) Born 1823, Inverness, aged 15; 60"; convicted before. Tried Perth: 7 years for housebreaking; CON31: sent to Point Puer, 25 times before the magistrate; sent to Port Arthur; absconded and lived with Aboriginal people for 9 months;

followed by more HL in chains; reached Victoria in October 1851 and turned bushranger. Died 1857 at Melbourne Gaol by strangulation. See Blake, 'Francis Melville (1822–1857)', ADB.

Metcalf, Robert (*Moffatt,* **1834**) Born 1815, Beverley, East Riding, aged 19; 65"; shoemaker. Tried York: 7 years for manslaughter: 'I quarrelled with my master's Son Charles Voss while we were at work, I had a knife in my hand and struck him with it on the left side, he lived 24 hours after it'; SSL: 'behaved well'; CON31: 14 sols; FC 1850. Married 1839 Sarah Ellis (free) at Campbell Town; 6 children; shoemaker. Died 1891/2376 at Kyneton, aged 75, of angina pectoris. [FAS JMcC]

Meyers/Myers, Annette (*Emma Eugenia,* **1851**) Born 1823, Paris, but brought up in Brussels; aged 27; uncle: Sir Francis Meyers; CoE, can read & write, 58.5"; lady's maid. Tried CCC: life for wilful murder, 'I was engaged to marry him, he broke off the match'; SSL: 'indifferent'; CON40: nil; CP 1856. Married 1852, John Desmond (*Samuel Boddington,* 1846), 1 son. Died 1879/9199 at 109 Park Place, Toorak, aged 60, of bronchitis pneumonia. [Colette McAlpine, FCRC 5177]

Miles, Ellen (*Gilbert Henderson,* **1840**) **alias Smith, Jackson** Born 1827, London, aged 12; 54.5"; 'convicted before'; slightly pock-pitted. Tried CCC: 7 years for uttering counterfeit coin; CON40: 57 sols, 61 months HL; FC 1847. Married **Thomas Watkins** (*Runnymeade,* **1840**), 1848; son Thomas born 1847, died; VPRS as Ellen Miles/Watkins/Burns/Grimes/Johnson/Buzzwinker/ Bridget Brady 1858–1912. Died 1916/4380 at Ballarat Benevolent Asylum, aged 89, of old age. [FAS JMcC, FCRC 5812]

Miles, Lydia (*Royal Admiral,* **1842**) Born 1821, Covent Garden, London; f James at NP; 2 b John, Charles; 2 s Mary Ann, Emma; on the town 18 months, illiterate, CoE and RC, 60.5". Tried 29 Nov 1841: 7 years for simple larceny; CON40: nil. Married James Richards (*Surrey,* 1833), 1844, Launceston. Died Creswick Hospital 1868/6168 of carcinoma uteri (3 months), 27 years in Victoria, details of marriage and parents unknown. A James Richards of the right age also died in Victoria in 1868/3473. [FAS Glad Wishart, FCRC 10812)

Miles, Ruth (*Navarino,* **1840**) Sister of Ellen Miles; born Hammersmith, aged 17, 59". Tried CCC: 15 years for uttering and previous conviction; SSL: scrofula;

CON40: 70 sols, 55 months HL or working cells; 2 illegit children, both died; FC 1856. Married Robert Turner 1849; 1860 convicted of drunkenness at Hobart; no further sighting.

> Old Bailey: Royal Offences: coining offences, 12 August 1839
>
> EDWARD BATT. I am the husband of the last witness. I came into the shop in consequence of what I heard, and saw the prisoner go out—I picked up the half-crown—it was the one I saw my wife ring on the steps—I heard her say it was a bad one—I followed the prisoner, and had her taken by a policeman—I delivered the half-crown to him.
>
> Prisoner. He did not give me in charge at all—my father took me to the station-house, and gave me in charge—I received the half-crown from my father, the first day I came out of the House of Correction—he has been trying to transport me ever since my mother died, and my sister as well. [FCRC 9750]

Mills, John (*Andromeda*, **1827**) Born 1810, Yate, Gloucestershire; 'Worst description of cha. His whole family bad. Brothers executed'. Tried Gloucester: 7 years for stealing geese; CON31: nil; FC 1835. Married Hannah Hales 1836; to Port Phillip 1837. Died 1841; brewer; 1 daughter, Emma, married William a'Beckett; 2 in AIF, including Martin Boyd, Melbourne. See Niall, Brenda, *The Boyds*, Melbourne University Press, 2002. [FAS Jenny Wells]

Mooney, Patrick (*John Renwick*, **1845**) Born 1792, Co Meath, Ireland; aged 50; 66"; farm labourer; 28 Regiment 21 years; RC, reads. Married, 1 daughter at Ancoats. Tried Lancaster: 15 years for 'robbing at the riots of 4/6' (Chartist); SSL: 'orderly'; CP 1851; CON31: almost nil. Died 1864/6056, at Kyneton, aged 73 of old age; labourer and Waterloo veteran. [FAS Geoff Brown]

Moran, Francis (*Oriental Queen*, **1853**) Born 1830, Manchester; 24 years; 63.75"; stonemason. Tried Manchester 1850: 7 years for house breaking; CON31: 2 fines; ToL 1853. Married 1854 **Mary Ann Ormisher** (*Emma Eugenia*, **1851**) at Hobart, 9 children; reconvicted VPRS 515/13690. Died 1899/9138 at Cambridge Street, Collingwood, aged 78 of senile debility. [FAS Nola Beagley]

Moriarty, Ellen (*Margaret*, **1843**) Born 1818, Soho, London, aged 25, 61", face pock-pitted, RC; reads; proper name Ellen Vickers, 'Husband Joseph, parted from him 18 months. I last worked with Mr Sampson'; 2 children. Tried CCC:

7 years for larceny; CON40: drunkenness, AWL, illegitimate child; FS 1849. Married John Griffiths 1849 at Ross, 1 child who died aged 3. Died 1867 aged 45 at Longford Racecourse, stabbed to death by Daniel Connors. See *Cornwall Chronicle*, 15 Feb 1868, for 'The Murder at Longford'. [FCRC 8112]

Mosley, Agnes (*Gilbert Henderson*, 1840) Born c. 1826, aged 13; 52.25"; red hair. Tried Glasgow: 7 years for theft, 'lived by thieving'; CON41: AWL, living in a disorderly house; FS 1846. Married Samuel Lewis 1851 in Melbourne; 1856 charged with the manslaughter of her baby but discharged; disappeared to South Australia. [FCRC 5814]

Moxham, Henry (*Layton*, 1839) Born 1822, Salisbury, aged 20; 65"; single; labourer; 'bad, in prison before'. Tried Wiltshire: 15 years for house breaking; CON31: 25 lashes, 8 sols; CP 1847. Married 1851 Catherine Loy in Melbourne; 4 children, 2 deaths. Died 1857/2396 at Perry Street, East Collingwood, aged 35, general dealer, 'bursting of blood vessels'. [FAS Steve Rhodes]

Murfitt/Murfett, James (*Thames*, 1829) Born 1810, Ely; aged 18; 63"; farmer's labourer; tattoos. Tried Cambridge: life for housebreaking; CON31: 25 lashes; CP 1843. Married 1832 to **Ann Ramage (*Mellish*, 1830)**, 11 children, 6 survived him; bricklayer. Died 1894/4607 at Pleasant Street, Ballarat, cancer of oesophageal entrance to the stomach. [FAS Graeme Hickey]

Murray, Catherine (*Emma Eugenia*, 1844) Born 1827, Liverpool, aged 17; 59.5"; RC; reads and writes; 'artful and impudent'. Once convicted 4 times in prison. Tried Lancaster: 7 years for simple larceny, 'stealing clothes from a butcher in a np market'; CON40: numerous offences—violent and abusive conduct aboard the *Anson*, absconding, misconduct. Married 1848 to Thomas Thornton at Launceston; FC 1851. Died 1863/30 at Yarra Bend Asylum of pulmonary consumption. [FCRC 4830]

Murtagh, Judith (*East London*, 1843) Born 1803, Westmeath, Ireland, aged 40; 63.75"; widow with 2 children; RC; illiterate. Tried Westmeath: life for child murder, 'I deny this charge. I am innocent of it'; CON40: nil; CP 1854. Married 1850 **Richard Lloyd (*Sir Robert Peel*, 1844)** at Sorell; no issue. Died 1883 at High Street, Kyneton, aged 76, of dropsy. [FAS 'Organ', FCRC 3948]

Naylor, Bet, transported as Elizabeth Morgan (*America*, 1831) Born 1798, Merthyr Tydfil, 32 years; f&m Paul Hill (seaman) and Jane nee Taylor, born

Glamorganshire, Wales; 3 months for stealing apparel, widow, 3 children, 'Husband died about 3 mos after I was confined'; 1 daughter on board, reads, Prot, 64". Tried Glamorgan: 7 years for housebreaking and stealing a pan, denies being convicted 3 times before; CON40: abusive language, disorderly conduct, gross impropriety; 1845 reconvicted, 3 months for larceny. Married (1) Wales to Reece Morgan, 3 children, all deceased; (2) Tasmania to **William Naylor** (*Surrey*, 1829) 1834, child James adopted, 9 deceased, 1 child registered—Louisa b 1842. Died Ballarat Hospital 1878 #348, old age and diarrhoea, 85 years; witness Louisa Alderton, Ballarat, daughter. (Note: if that record of nine deceased babies is correct, then that would suggest syphilis.)

> Louisa Naylor v Bet Naylor, illegally detaining wearing apparel.
> The plaintiff was daughter to the defendant, the notorious Bet Naylor, of Esmond Street. She stated that she had left her mother's place to live with her sister, at White Horse, and wished to get away her clothes. Her mother, however, vowed that she would burn the things first to compel her to go on the streets again to earn money to get more. The plaintiff further stated she was under twenty-one years of age. On that account the case was dismissed, plaintiff's mother being her natural guardian until she was over that age. (*The Ballarat Star*, 29 Sep 1864, p. 4) [FAS JMcC, FCRC 1407]

Naylor, William (*Surrey*, 1829) Born 1811, 18 years, 62.5". Tried Shoreditch: stealing a jacket; in custody before for stealing clothes. No trace after Bet left Van Diemen's Land; CON31: misconduct and drunkenness.

Neville, Isaac (*Red Rover*, 1831) Born 1806, aged 24, 65.5". Tried Oxford: life for housebreaking; CON31: 36 lashes; CP 1842. Married (1) 1842 Mary Ann Burton (*Navarino*, 1841); (2) de-facto Eleanor Calcut 1846, 3 children; blacksmith. Died 1872/1668 at Kyneton, aged 66, of scirrhus (cancer); AIF. [FAS Maureen Mann]

Oakford, Catherine (*Royal Admiral*, 1842) Born 1822, Christchurch, London; f Sylvester, Blackfriars Road; 1 b Sylvester, 4 sisters—Jane, Nancy, Rachael, Winifred; 12 months on the town, reads & writes, RC, 62.75". Tried CCC 1841: 7 years for larceny, 18 pounds; CON41: absconded 3 times. Married Charles Barrett (*Tortoise*, 1842) 1849, Launceston; no further trace after marriage. [FAS Glad Wishart, FCRC 10824]

O'Brien, Mary (*Blackfriar*, 1851) Born 1822, Co Clare, aged 28, 62.5"; reads; RC; 7 years for a cow; b Pat and s Ann on board. Married 1853 at Morven, Tas., to Patrick Curtis, at the Manse Evandale; 9 children, all born Morven. Died 1904/3301 at Warrnambool, Vic., aged 82, old age pensioner; 7 children surviving; AIF. [FAS Tricia Curry, FCRC 2882] Sister Ann also married in the Presbyterian Church in Evandale, and the family remained there; she died in 1884, aged only 44. [FCRC 2880]

Ogilvie, George (*Barossa*, 1842) Born 1819, Aberdeen, aged 22; reads and writes, ship's blacksmith; 65.5". Tried Aberdeen: 7 years for 'stealing a shirt and a pair of cotton stockings'. Married 1841 Caroline Justin (*Navarino*, 1841); 2 sons. Died 1894, Hobart, of senile decay; grandson Albert George Ogilvie (1890–1939), premier of Tasmania (ADB). [FAS Lance Dwyer]

Ormisher/Omisher, Mary Ann (*Emma Eugenia*, 1851) Born 1832, Liverpool, aged 18; on the town 2 years; priors: '9 times convicted a disorderly prostitute and a thief for the last 5 years'; RC; reads and writes; 63.25". Tried Liverpool: 7 years for stealing money; SSL: 'indifferent'; CON40: 14 days HL; CP 1848. Married 1854 **Francis Moran (*Oriental Queen*, 1853)** at Hobart; 9 children. Died 1902/14617 at Melbourne Hospital, aged 69, of old age. [FAS Geoff Brown, FCRC 5180]

Pearce, Jesse (*Tortoise*, 1842) Born 1821, Bradfield, Berkshire; aged 20; Prot; reads; mother transported to Sydney 2 years before. Tried Berkshire Ass: life for housebreaking and stealing bacon, bread, cheese and money; CON31: nil; CP 1853. Died 1877/11437 aged 56 at Kew Lunatic Asylum, having been admitted demented and bedridden, of pleuro-pneumonia and brain disease; VPRS Inquest 1877/1016. [FAS JMcC]

Pearce, Thomas (*Asia*, 1840) Born 1819, Haymarket London, 'before convicted'. Tried CCC: 10 years, 'stealing a handkerchief, once for ducks'; CON31: 36 lashes, 10 sols; FC 1850. Married **Charlotte Kimpton (*Lloyds*, 1845)** 1848 at Hobart, 13 children, 5 survived; dealer in Collingwood. Died 1901/922. [FAS Steve Rhodes]

Peeler, William (*Woodford*, 1828) Born 1803, Liverpool, aged 25; 64.5"; f&m at Manchester, father shoemaker, Ancoats Lane; 'I worked last for Mr Gray, Pallett Ste at Cotton Card Stripper'. Tried Lancaster: 14 years for housebreaking in New Town; CON31: nil; CP 1838. Married 1839 **Mary Bentley (*Atwick*, 1838)**; 7 children, 3 predeceased him; miner at Barkers Creek. Died 1888/5116 of old age and debility, aged 85; grandson Walter Peeler VC First AIF; POW on Burma Railway, Second AIF. [FAS JMcC]

Perrin, Ann (*Hindostan*, 1839) Born 1790, Aldersgate, London; aged 49; 57"; married, 6 children. Tried CCC: 7 years for larceny, stealing gingham: 'I was in great distress, which made me take it. I had no bed for four nights'; literate; SSL: 'very attentive'; CON40: drunkenness; FS 1846. Married in Tasmania (1) to George Bullis 1847; (2) William Coals 1851; VPRS 616/20. Died 1869/8600 aged 79 at Castlemaine Benevolent Asylum, from old age and a tumour. [FAS Jennifer Ellison, FCRC 6345]

Perry, Hannah (*Rajah*, 1841) Born Tottenham Court Road, London; aged 16; 60.5"; reads; '2 weeks in House of Correction, poor'. Tried CCC: 7 years for stealing pewter pot; SSL: 'very bad worse'; CON40: absconding, larceny, illegitimate child; term extended; FS 1849. Married 1845 William Hollioak (*Aurora*, 1835); 8 children, 6 survived her. Died 1873/6055 aged 49 at Ballarat Hospital of angina pectoris. [FAS Nola Beagley, FCRC 10636]

Perry, Jane (*Margaret*, 1843) Born 1825, near Glasgow, aged 18; 62.25"; reads and writes; house servant; f at NP, 1 b at Hamilton. Tried Glasgow: 7 years for housebreaking; CON41: drunk, misconduct, AWL, 2 illegitimate children, both died; FC 1849. Married 1847 to Edward Spencer (*Mary*, 1830), 6 more children. Died 1858/2605, Specimen Hill, the Loddon, Vic., from consumption, aged 34. [FCRC 8127]

Phillips, Samuel (*Mary 2*, 1830) Born 1804, Weldon, Northamptonshire; 7th of 12 children; ploughman; aged 25 years, 68.5"; illiterate; 'poaching rabbits twice before, 3 mos each'. Tried Northampton: 14 years for 'Going armed, in the night-time, with offensive weapons, with intent to destroy game and rabbits, in the parish of Little Weldon'; he was co-convicted with 2 others so they may have been part of a gang. Married Sarah Patrick in Corby, Mar 1854; CON31: almost nil; FC 1845. He returned to England in 1854 with £1038; died aged 82 in 1886; his farm is still held by his descendants. [FAS Jane Starsmore Duvall, desendant, resident in the United States.]

Pickering, George (*Lord Goderich*, 1841) Born c. 1827, Bethnal Green Road, London; aged 13; f Thomas, wine cooper; m Jane; 2 b Thomas and Geo; 2 s;

illiterate, Prot. Tried CCC: 7 years for stealing a pair of shoes and previous conviction; CON31: fighting; FC 1848. Married **Jane Eskitt** (***Garland Grove*, 1841**) 13 Sep 1852 at Scots' Church, Melbourne; 2 daughters, 1 son; only 1 daughter alive at his death; VPRS 515/P1, 7542, 2749, 1854, 1865, with photos; frequent newspaper reports of offences and court appearances for violence, theft from the person, and drunkenness. Died 1884/9216 at Melbourne Benevolent Asylum, aged 60, of progressive paralysis; he was recorded as a 'fisherman'; his parents were important to him and reported to the MBA clerk; but not his wife and children. [FAS JMcC and Nola Beagley]

> A Violent Vagabond
>
> George Pickering, a notorious oyster-man, was again brought up at the City Court yesterday on the charge of brutally ill using his wife, and also of violently assaulting Detective Elsey in the execution of his duty. It appears that Detective Powell saw the prisoner beating his wife most brutally, and having obtained a warrant for his apprehension, Detective Elsey went to his house, behind the Carlow Hotel, in Little Bourke-street, to arrest him. When the officer stated his business, the prisoner said he never went without having a fight for it, and accompanied his expression with a fierce blow on the officer's chest, whereupon the detective's 'neddy' was called into requisition, and he being thrice armed who had his quarrel just, the vagabond was overcome and taken into custody. The woman appeared in court and showed some severe bruises which had been inflicted on her by blows and kicks from the prisoner. It appears that she has had two children by the prisoner, the leg of one of which he broke a short while ago when in a fit of violent temper. The woman obtained her living by washing, and on the occasion of the assault on her the prisoner threw all her clothes into the street. The fellow's head was cut, and he had evidently received some severe handling from the detective. The Bench sentenced him to three months' hard labour, on his release to be bound over for twelve months in two sureties of £25 each to keep the peace. (*The Argus*, Melbourne, 17 Apr 1856)

Pickering, Thomas (***Moffatt*, 1842**) Brother of George, born 1822, reads and writes (unlike George, who never learned); 'stealing a purse'. Thomas was a bolter under sentence and was twice convicted in Tasmania for burglary—one leading to transfer to Norfolk Island, the second 10 years at Port Arthur. He was finally released in 1864 and disappeared.

Power, Harry/Henry Johnson (*Isabella*, **1842**) Born 1820, Co Waterford, aged 21, illiterate, RC, piecer, 65.25"; m Catherine, 2 b, 2 s; priors: vagrancy and drunkenness. Tried Salford: 7 years for stealing a pair of shoes; flogged 28 lashes on hulk for attempting to escape; CON31: misconduct, larceny, drunk; FC 1848; to Port Phillip 1848; horse dealer then bushranger; mentored Ned Kelly. Died 1891 by drowning in the Murray River. See McLaren, Ian F, 'Henry (Harry) Power (1820–1891)', *ADB* online. [FAS Joan McRae]

Pretty, William (*Surrey*, **1829**) Born 1806, Sudbury, Suffolk; 22 years; 68.5"; silk weaver; married with '2 children with my mother in George St, Bethnal Green'. Tried Kent Ass: life for housebreaking; CON31: nil; CP 1840. Married Elizabeth Crocker, Newgate, London, in 1836; applied for her and their 2 children to come to VDL; another 10 children. Died 1882/9026 aged 76 of chronic nephritis at the Melbourne Benevolent Asylum, Hotham. His son William, born 1828, came to Victoria in 1846 with the Geelong and Portland Bay Immigration Society. A tinsmith, he married Ann Kelly, a *Lady Pemberton* orphan from Ireland; 13 children; died at North Melbourne in 1913. [FAS Colette McAlpine, descendant]

Pryke, Mary Ann (*Sea Queen*, **1846**) Born 1828, Bury St Edmunds, aged 17; f&m William Pryke, builder, and Mary nee Butcher; 61.25"; can read. Tried Bury St Edmunds QS: 7 years for shoplifting (a shawl); SSL: 'indifferent of riotous irritable temper, and controlled by such'; CON40: AWL, fighting; FC 1852. Married 1847 **Humphrey Short** (*Augusta Jessie*, **1838**); 3 sons, 1 daughter; 2 survived her; no criminal records in VPRS as she appears to have been an invalid, but husband and sons offended. Died 1864/1410 at Melbourne Hospital, of syphilis and caries of the skull. [FAS Steve Rhodes, FCRC 11000]

Ramage, Ann (*Mellish*, **1830**) Born 1811, Dalkeith, Edinburgh; aged 19; 60.5". Tried Edinburgh: 14 years housebreaking, 'I was driven to commit this offence thro the illtreatment of my parents'; SSL: 'very good'; CON40: 'being dirty and useless as a servant', insolence, AWL; FS 1843. Married 1832 **James Murfitt** (*Thames*, **1829**); 11 children, 6 survived her. Died 1901/8250 aged 86 at 50 Pleasant Street, Ballarat, of senile decay, organic heart disease. (FAS Steve Rhodes, FCRC 8987]

Reeves, James (*London*, 1844) Born 1822, Paddington, London; aged 21; m, 4 b and 1 s at NP; 62"; reads and writes; Prot; baker; prior: 6 months for a watch. Tried CCC: 7 years for stealing a basket of linen; SSL: 'indifferent'; CON31: insolence, drunk; FC 1851; VPRS 515/483. Died 1878/5613, at Inglewood Hospital, of pneumonia. [FAS Nola Beagley]

Richmond, Margaret, transported as Margaret Richardson (*Hindostan*, 1839) Born 1822, Isle of Wight; f John and 1 b and 1 s at Bloomsbury; 17 years; 57", tattoos including dot on upper lip; reads; 12 months on the town. Tried Middlesex: 7 years, stealing a gown piece in Regent Street; SSL: 'badly disposed'; CON 40: AWL, misconduct 38 sols; FC 1845. Married Thomas Richmond (*Arab*, 1834) 1843; VPRS 515/77 and 917; Inquest 1876/128. Died 1876/6440 of acute diarrhoea, the gaol, Melbourne; known as the 'Bull pup', Anglo-Indian slang for 'known to have fits of bad temper'. [FAS Jennifer Ellison, JMcC, FCRC 6352]

Roberts, John (*Frances Charlotte*, 1837) Born 1820, St Lukes, London, aged 16; 58.5"; labourer; tattoos. Tried CCC: 7 years for larceny from the person; CON31: constant offender, Port Arthur; FC 1845. Married 1850 to **Ellen Hanley (*Greenlaw*, 1844)** at Launceston; VPRS 515/37. Death not found. [FAS JMcC]

Robertson, Jane (*Rajah*, 1841) Born 1824, Hull, aged 17, 59.75", reads, stealing a watch, 5 times in prison, 'giddy but quiet'. Tried Inverness: 7 years for theft. Married **Henry Cavanagh (*Enchantress*, 1833)** 1845 in Longford, 8 children. Died 1902/14892 at Melbourne Immigrants' Home of dysentery and exhaustion; multiple offences in Victoria for drunkenness and disorderly behaviour; discharged from prison to Immigrants' Home, 1902. [FAS Maureen Mann, FCRC 10648]

Robertson, Nancye/Nancey (*Rajah*, 1841) Born 1824, Longtown, Cumberland; aged 17, 56.75"; long scar on left side of mouth; reads; father a licensed hawker who travelled the country with his family. Tried Inverness with cousin Jane Robertson: 7 years for stealing a watch; CON40: drunk, misconduct, AWL. Married Charles Roberts (*Aurora*, 1835) 1843; FC 1847. Died at sea aboard

Shamrock March 1847 from suffocation in a trunk. See *The Australian Journal*, 27 Mar 1847. [FAS Jennifer Ellison, FCRC 10650]

Rogers, Thomas (*Lord Petre,* **1843**) Born 1821, Tenbury, Worcester; aged 22; 63"; f&m, 1 b and 1 s at NP; literate; farm labourer; previous: cutting and maiming, stealing hide. Tried Worcester: 10 years for stealing wine and a pencil case; CON31: 33 lashes. Married 1850 to **Eliza Schofield** (*Asia,* **1847**), 4 children, all deceased. Died 1876/9475, 55 years, Victoria. [FAS Tricia Curry]

Ryan, Mary (real name Ellen Bannon) (*Garland Grove,* **1843**) Born 1813, Liverpool, aged 20; 63.75"; illiterate; RC; tattooed; twice imprisoned; 3 months on the town; f Pat in Liverpool, 1 s Margaret at NP, 1 s Mary transported on *Rajah,* 1841; m Catherine on board with her. Tried Lancaster: 10 years for stealing from the person; SSL: 'not good'; CON40: 2 assaults; FC 1852. Married 1843 **William Kendrick** (*Persian,* **1830**); 3 children found. Died 1855 at Maldon, from domestic violence 'i.e. excessive inflammation of the peritoneum, accelerated by blows'; VPRS Inquest 1855/26; her mother, now married to James Porterfield, was on the diggings with her and gave evidence at the inquest. [FAS Nola Beagley, FCRC 5658]

Salmon, Catherine (*Mellish,* **1830**) Born 1810, Tipperary, aged 20; 62.5"; 3 years on the town; RC, reads. Tried CCC: 7 years for stealing from the person; SSL: 'very good'; CON40: insolence to mistress; FC 1837. Married 1832 to Benjamin Ginn (*Coromandel,* 1820), 2 children; de-facto relationship with **John Beatson** (*Neptune,* **1838**), 2 children found born in Victoria. Died 1876/6119 at Epping Street, Kyneton, aged 70, from valvular disease of the heart. [FAS Graeme Hickey, FCRC 8996]

Scarborough, George (*Caledonian,* **1820**) Born 1802, Kentish Town, London, aged 18, 64", gentleman's servant. Tried Middlesex: 14 years for royal offences: coining. CON31: nil, made constable; FC 1835. Married (1) **Mary Ann Williams** (*Harmony,* **1829**) 1831; (2) Mary Ann Overend, 1859, in Melbourne; 8 children, 3 predeceased him. Died 1880/7116 at Flemington, Vic., of old age and urinary disease; 4 in AIF. [FAS JMcC]

Schofield, Eliza (*Asia,* **1847**) Born 1827, Hull, Yorkshire, aged 20; m Sarah, 5 b and 4 s; CON40: numerous offences. Married **Thomas Rogers** (*Lord Petre,* **1843**) 1850 in Launceston, 4 children, all deceased; FC 1854; VPRS 516 record began 1858, convictions for drunkenness; estranged from husband. Died 1885/8683 at Geelong Gaol of haemoptysis, aged 59. [FCRC 2251]

Sefton, George (*Orator*, **1843**) Born 1819, Co Antrim, aged 23; 70.5"; Prot; reads and writes; f&m and 5 siblings in NP, 1 s in Canada; farm labourer; brother on board for same offence. Tried Antrim: 7 years for stealing a pig; SSL: 'good'. Married at Williamstown, Vic., to Catherine McCormack, 5 children all living. Died 1878/5770 at Kyneton Hospital, aged 60, of chronic Bright's disease, diarrhoea, pleuritis. [FAS Allison Ellett]

Sheriff, Mary (*Atwick*, **1838**) Born 1819, Grassmarket, Edinburgh, aged 18, 61". Tried Edinburgh: 7 years theft, 'theft aggravated by its being committed on a Young Child, and previous conviction'; member of the flash mob. See Frost, Lucy, *Abandoned Women: Scottish Women Transported beyond the Seas*, Allen & Unwin, Crows Nest, 2015. [FCRC S341At]

Short, Humphrey (*Augusta Jessie*, **1838**) Born 1819, Devonshire, aged 19; 66.75"; farm labourer. Tried at Devon Ass: 7 years, 'stealing clothers tried with Brother John once with my brother for bee hives 3 weeks once for a Duck'; SSL: 'willing and well-conducted'; CON31: no lashes but sent to Port Arthur; FC 1848. Married 1847 **Mary Ann Pryke** (*Sea Queen*, **1846**) at Launceston, 4 children, 2 survived; in Victoria, constant offences until 1880; VPRS 515/5537, 7488, 6701, 12203 as Alfred Short, William Weir, Benjamin Short. Died 1882/6069 at Immigrants' Home, of perineal abscess, duration unknown; sons Humphrey and Frederick in VPRS 515/8351 and 5685. [FAS Steve Rhodes]

Shurley/Adlam/Drinkwater, Harriet (*Emma Eugenia*, **1844**) Born 1825, Hurley, Berkshire; aged 20; f&m James Shurry and Martha; sister Elizabeth Shury transported on same ship and died Tasmania; 57.5"; freckled; 'character and connexions bad'; once convicted before. Tried Aylesbury, Bucks: 7 years for shoplifting a shawl; seems to have been running a clothes-stealing racket with her sister for some years; CON41: AWL, 10 sols; FC 1850. Married 1846 Samuel Adlam (*Stratheden*, 1845), 3 sons and 2 daughters, 1 son dying in infancy; moved to Melbourne with Adlam and left him for **William Drinkwater** (*Surrey*, **1833**). Adlam assaulted Drinkwater who retaliated; the sons stayed with their father, who lived off Little Bourke Street and was a dealer in flowers, fish and oranges. In 1861 Adlam was gaoled and the 2 boys, one of whom by the age of 8 was heavily tattooed, were found stealing in a gang and were twice imprisoned; their sisters became wards of the state; the tattooed son continued to offend for the rest of his life. Adlam was distraught at Harriet's desertion of himself and the children. Drinkwater turned against Harriet and she appears to have returned to being looked after by Samuel as she died from consumption in 1862, the death being witnessed by Samuel. She left 4 children aged from 7 to 14. Samuel Adlam moved to Sydney, married again and died there in 1866, aged just 40. [FAS Geoff Brown]

Sidebottom, William (*Medway*, **1825**) Born 1799, Newton, Lancashire, aged 25, 64.25", oastler. Tried Lancaster: life for highway robbery; CON31: 150 lashes, Maria Island; CP 1839. Died Victoria 1849/2677; family history research by Don Sutherland, published by Collingwood Football Club online 6 Jul 2018. [FAS JMcC]

Sinden/Sindon/Lindon, Luke (*Marquis of Hastings*, **1842**) Born 1819, Ringmer, Sussex; aged 22; 4 s; reads and writes; farm labourer; 63.5"; priors: burglary and 'assaulting the Master of the Union'. Tried Sussex: 10 years for burglary. Married Ann Hopkins (free immigrant) 1851, Tas.; son's record: VPRS 515/19770; wife's VPRS 516/2408. May have died 1881/5740 at Richmond, Vic. [FAS JMcC]

Smith, Julia (*Westmoreland*, **1836**) Born 1814, Co Meath, 22 years, 57"; 12 months on the town, widow. Tried CCC: 7 years for 'stealing 40 yards of lace at Marylebone, once for similar offence-3 months'; CON40: 25 sols, 9 months HL; disorderly offences after marriage. Married George Robinson, Richmond, Tas. 1838; went to Port Phillip with her children: 3 daughters including twins, and a son. Ran a brothel in Little Bourke Street. Her twin daughters Julia and Maria both died of complications of syphilis, as did Julia herself at the Melbourne Hospital in 1867/2399. Her daughter Maria appears to have had 18 pregnancies with only 2 children surviving by the time of her own death in 1884. This was therefore two generations of syphilis, with a third generation wiped out with congenital syphilis. See McCalman, J, and Rebecca Kippen, '"A Wise Provision of Nature for the Prevention of Too Many Children": Evidence from the Australian Colonies', in Simon Szreter (ed.), *The Hidden Affliction: Sexually Transmitted Infections and Infertility in History*, University of Rochester Press, New York, 2019, pp. 279–302. [FAS Judy Wells, JMcC, Rebecca Kippen, FCRC 12909]

Smith, Rose Ann (*Margaret*, 1843) Born 1818, Edinburgh, aged 25, 63.25", Prot, can read and write; priors: 3 times drunkenness, breaking windows. Tried Edinburgh: 10 years for receiving an umbrella; FS 1852. Married James Jones (*Jupiter*, 1833) in Hobart 1844; 3 sons, died; partnered with John Giles (*Surrey*, 1833) in Victoria, 3 more sons. Died 1884/3190 at Wangoom, Vic., aged 72, phthisis pulmonalis, haemoptysis; AIF. [FAS JMcC, FCRC 8147]

Stanger, Henry (*Tortoise*, 1842) Born 1816, near Daventry, Northamptonshire, aged 25, 64.75", boatbuilder, Prot, reads and writes, married, 2 b, 6 s; 'once for a gun 6 mths'. Tried Northamptonshire: 14 years for stealing oatmeal; VPG 17 Jul 1876, discharged prisoner, convicted of indecently assaulting a girl under 12 years at Chewton, had been assaulting her for some time; 2 years HL and whipping. Died 1893/13633, aged 77, at Chewton of cerebral haemorrhage; Will; VPRS 1893, 53/489. [FAS Nola Beagley]

Starr, James (*Hyderabad*, 1849) Born 1826, Tipperary, aged 22; 65"; RC, reads a little; m & 2 s at NP; labourer. Tried Tipperary: 7 years for stealing a sheep; CON31: 24 sols, drunk x 2; FC 1854. Never married. Died 1898/12656, aged 76, at Kyneton Hospital, of cirrhosis of liver and exhaustion. [FAS Alison Ellett]

Starr, William (*Marquis of Hastings*, 1842) Born 1820, Norwich, aged 21; 1 b on board; m, 6 b and 1 s at NP; 64"; illiterate; 'several times in prison on suspicion; for lead 6 months'. Tried Norwich QS: 10 years for burglary of 26 gold rings and 11 watches, 12 pairs of spectacles, gold seals and chains, silver medals etc. from a pawnbroker's shop'; SSL: 'good'; CON31: 136 lashes, 31 sols; CP 1852. Married 1851 **Margaret Cullen** (*Lord Auckland*, 1849), 1 child; plasterer. Died Ballarat, 1903/239 aged 83 of aortic regurgitant disease of the heart, cerebral softening and exhaustion. [FAS JMcC]

Studham, Elizabeth (*Mary*, 1831) Baptised 1812 Monkton Isle of Thanet, Kent; aged 21 years, single, illiterate, 62", Prot. Tried: life sentence for arson, setting fire to Poor House building, allegedly at instigation of 5 vagrants; only woman transported for the Swing Riots; rebellious convict; 2 children by different fathers; CP 1846. Married Joseph King 1843 at Launceston, no more children. Died 1874/10443 at 264 Smith Street, Collingwood, widow of bootmaker, from abscess of leg and exhaustion; real estate of house with shop on corner of Sackville Street valued at £350 and estate transferred to master in equity. [FCRC 8717]

Sugden, Samuel (*George III*, 1835) Born 1815, Leeds, aged 20; 68". Tried Leeds: 7 years for 'robbing a man of a watch, tried with Smith and Taylor on board'; SSL: 'excellent. Captain of Boys prison before it was converted into a hospital'; survivor of wreck of *George III*. Married 1851 Eliza Phillips (*Tory*, 1845); no issue. Died 1873/3140 at Plant Street, Ballarat East, of accidental drowning when in a state of intoxication; blacksmith and miner. [FAS Geoff Brown]

Sumner, Hugh (*Ratcliffe*, 1848) Born 1833, Manchester, aged 15; father and siblings at Preston; 65"; pimpled; RC, labourer; reads a little; priors: 'for housebreaking 1 mth and whipped; orchard robbery 6 mths, vagrancy 14 days'. Tried Preston: for highway robbery, stealing a coat and money; CON31: almost nil; FC 1853. Married 1854 Catherine Dunn, at Hobart, 12 children, 7 survived. Died 1917/8147, aged 84, gas stoker, at 8 Hood Street, Collingwood, of senile decay, bronchitis and asphyxia; 4 children still alive. [FAS Steve Rhodes]

Swain, Eliza (*Margaret*, 1843) Born 1819, Manchester, aged 20; illiterate; m Ellen at NP; 57"; 2 years on the town, 9 times in prison. Tried Salford: 10 years for robbery from the person; SSL: 'detected with Richardson frequently since in the forecastle Lazy'; CON40: drunk, AWL, illegitimate child; FC 1852. Married to William McPhie 1848; 1 son, lived 9 days. Died 1856 Commissioner's Gully, Sandhurst, 28 years, paralysis. [FCRC 8151]

Taylor, Lucy, transported as Lucilia De La Constantine (*Emma Eugenia*, 1846) Born 1821, Dublin, aged 25, RC, reads well, 66.75"; ladies maid, needlewoman, nurse; CON41: constant misconduct, drunkenness, larceny, imposition, obscene language, illegitimate child; FC 1856. Married (1) 1849 William Barker, at Ross; (2) William Disley Taylor, at Shooter's Hill Farm, Tas.; VPRS 516/4686. Died 1884 at Melbourne Gaol aged 65 of chronic peritonitis, VPRS Inquest 1844/1275. [Colette McAlpine, FCRC 4929]

Thomas, William (*Surrey*, 1842) Born 1821, Swansea, 64.5"; reads and writes; blacksmith—imperfect; f&m, 1 s and 3 b at NP. Tried CCC: 10 years for burglary; SSL: 'orderly'; FC 1852; VPRS 515/484; name too common to trace to death. [FAS JMcC]

Thompson, William (*Lord Petre*, 1843) Real name James Bryson; born 1818, Paisley; aged 24; 67.5"; dyer; 'intelligent'; reads and writes; Prot; m and b at NP.

Tried Stirling: 10 years for picking a man's pocket of 10/6, twice for similar offence, and housebreaking; SSL: 'cook's mate, very good indeed'; CON 31: nil; CP 1850. Married 1849 to **Sarah Bickley** (*Asia*, 1847) at Spring Bay; 1 son. Died 1857 at Mia Mia, stabbed to death by wife. [FAS Tricia Curry]

Trenwith, William (*Earl St Vincent*, 1826) Born 1804, Penzance, Cornwall, aged 21; 65"; tattoos; 'ladies and gentlemens shoemaker'. Tried Lancaster: life for burglary; CON31: 447 lashes, 30 sols, Port Arthur; CP 1845. Married 1848 Beatrice Davidson (*Emma Eugenia*, 1842), 2 sons; shoemaker. Died 1883 aged 78 at Immigrants' Home, Royal Park, Vic., of general debility. Father of William Arthur Trenwith (1846-1925)—bootmaker, trade unionist and politician, MLA for Richmond 1889-1903, senator 1903-10, see ADB. [FAS Steve Rhodes]

Venville (**Venwell**), **Richard** (*Eliza*, 1831) Born 1808, Great Rissington, Gloucestershire; f&m at Bledington; 21 years, 70"; 'charged with riotously assembling and destroying several threshing [*sic*] at Eastleach' (Swing Riots). Married 1840 at Melbourne, Vic., to Eliza Brown; 12 children, 3 deceased at his death. Died Mount Egerton, Vic., 1896, aged 90, of 'old age and debility, 2 years'. [FAS]

Wagstaff, John Lawrence Mansfield (*Layton*, 1835) Born 1808, Great Gransden, 27 years, 67", tattoos, married; wife at NP; 'Conv before of (Stg) apples. Bad in every respect'. Tried Huntingdon QS: 7 years for stealing timber, prosc. Revd Dr Webb. Married **Elizabeth** (**Bess**) **Ward** (*Waverley*, 1842) at Brighton, Tas., 1847, 10 children found; miner and gardener at Campbell's Creek, arrested but released on suspicion of bushranging, no other offences in Victoria. Died aged 84 years 1892/2176 at Campbell's Creek, Vic., 10 children, 7 living; AIF. [FAS JMcC]

Wagstaffe, Thomas (*John Renwick*, 1843) Born 1817, Hanley, Staffordshire, aged 25, 68.75"; married, reads and writes, potter; 4 days for assault. Tried Stafford: 10 years for 'demolishing a house at longton' (Chartist); CON31: nil; CP 1850. Married 1853 Rebecca Wornes in Victoria; 5 children. Died 1884/10514 aged 67, Bendigo Benevolent Asylum, of haemoptysis phthisis; AIF. [FAS Colin Tuckerman]

Walklate, John Woolf (*Marquis of Hastings*, 1842) Born 1817, the Potteries, Stafford, aged 24, 67", reads and writes, Prot, potter, 'has been gentleman's servant'; married with 1 child; SSL: 'recommended. Very good'; CCC 1841: 14 years for 'robbing my employer Mr Allsop of St Paul's Church of some glass tumblers, milk jug etc.'. Died Launceston 1893. [FAS JMcC]

Ward, Anne (*Mexborough*, **1841**) Born 1825, Newry; aged 17; 62.5"; deeply pock-pitted. Tried Down: 7 years for larceny, 2 priors for 'stealing cloths'; SSL: 'well behaved'; CON40: 12 sols, drunk; FC 1852. Married **William Broom** (*Atlas*, **1833**) at Evandale; 5 children found; rumour that last child had an Aboriginal father; VPRS 516/1405. Died 1873 at Back Creek, 'Tubercular disease of the lungs, accelerated by want out nourishment' (doctor); 'Result of dissipation and drunkenness', added by inquest jury; VPRS Inquest 1873/84. [FAS JMcC]

Ward, Bess (*Waverley*, **1842**) Born 1827, Dundalk, Ireland; aged 15; 60", multiple initials as tattoos; reads, RC; twice in gaol. Tried Dundalk: 7 years for 'stealing blankets for money'; CON40: disturbing the peace, obscene language, living in a state of adultery; FC 1850. Married **John Lawrence Mansfield Wagstaff** (*Layton*, **1835**) at Brighton, Tas., 1847, 10 children. Died 1895/1075, Castlemaine Hospital, aged 63 years, of dilatation of the heart and dropsy. Married, no particulars; VPG: 'Disch Prisoners 5 Feb 1872. Castlemaine, 22 Dec 1871 Larceny, 1 moB Ire, no trade, 1832, 60", nose inclined to R, Mary Gill and wreath on R arm. 4 previous in Victoria. VPG 7 Feb 1876. Discharged from penal establishment Castlemaine. Obscene language—14 days. Native of Belfast, born 1830, 62", brown hair, blue eyes, stout build, bloated appearance'. [FAS JMcC, FCRC 691]

Watkins, Alfred (*Hindostan*, **1841**) Born 1821, Marylebone, London; 61.5"; plasterer; reads and writes; Prot; 5 times in prison for 'petty thefts in the open day'. Tried Middlesex QS: 7 years for 'stealing a piece of pork'; brother on board for same offence; CON31: 20 sols; CP 1846. Married 1848 Margaret Pickering (*Tasmania*, 1844), FCRC 11942—Margaret Pickering as Margaret Watkins/Perkins was convicted for multiple offences as a woman of the town in Victoria; no death found but final newspaper reference was in 1881 for offences in Chewton. Alfred died 1868/6623 at Kyneton Hospital, plasterer, aged 42, of hepatitis. [FAS JMcC]

Watkins, Thomas (*Runnymeade*, **1840**) Born 1823, Deptford, Surrey; aged 16, red hair, 54"; costermonger. Tried CCC: 10 years for stealing from the person;

CON31: 5 sols, 15 stripes on breech. Married **Ellen Miles** (*Gilbert Henderson*, **1840**); no confirmed trace after sentence. [FAS JMcC]

Wells, Rhoda (*Royal Admiral*, **1842**) Born 1822, Stepney, London; aged 20; 56"; reads only; f Customs House officer, f&m at NP; 1 b ,3 s. Tried CCC: 7 years for 'receiving stolen earrings and a Silk Handkf'; CON41: drunk, in bed with a man, AWL; 7 sols; FC 1849. Married 1844 John Jolly at Longford; de-facto relationship with **Charles Forrester** (*Coromandel*, **1838**); no issue. Died 1863/8424, at Mount Macedon, aged 42, from dislocation of neck, murder, VPRS Inquest 1863/259. [FAS Glad Wishart, FCRC 10875]

Westcott, Charles (*Cressy*, **1843**) Born 1823, Bishops Lydeard, Somerset; aged 19, 61.75"; s Betsey at Taunton; f a rope maker; reads and writes; groom; '3 mths for shoes, 4 mths for assault'. Tried Wells: 7 years for 'stealing hatchet & some carpenter's tools'; SSL: 'good'. Married (1) 1856 at Launceston, Charity Jane Medhurst; (2) 1868 in Victoria, Dorothea Isdell; 4 children, 1 survivor. Died 1886/978 aged 65, at Johnston Street, Collingwood, of chronic dysentery and gastro enteritis. Mysterious relationship with second wife: first-born with his first wife was named after her; Dorothea also born Somerset, but parents in Belfast, Ireland; 4 years after their marriage she left him. [FAS Steve Rhodes]

Whitaker, Farewell (*Proteus*, **1831**) Born 1790, Hickling, Norfolk. 40 years, 67.25", 'stout made, arms hairy', farm labourer, reads. Tried: 7 years for machine breaking (Swing Riots). Married, wife Frances and 7 children at NP; 2 b William and Christmas, labourers at NP; 1 s Mary married Richard Watson near Norfolk; 'Honest character and good connexions'. Died 1857/39, Brunswick, Vic., of colonial fever; labourer; 5 years in VDL, 20 in Victoria. [FAS Colin Tuckerman]

White, John (*Ratcliffe*, **1848**) Born 1825, Birmingham, 22 years; 65"; groom, CoE; f&m and b&s at NP; priors: 'for a file 6 mnths'. Tried Birmingham: 7 years for 'stealing 4 handkerchiefs'; FC 1856; CON31: nil. Died 1869/6982 at Kyneton Hospital, aged 44, 'accidentally burnt by conflagration'. [FAS Kathy Dadswell]

Wildman, William (*Clyde*, **1830**) Born 1805, Walworth, aged 25; 65"; 'clerk 2nd class'; 'bad, often in prison before'. Tried Surrey: 7 years for stealing 24 chests of tea; CON31: constant offences initially lightly punished because of his position as a convict clerk, harsher as time passed; FC 1845; to Port Phillip with Geelong and Portland Immigration Society; convicted of forgery in 1856 with Francis Huxley (see Ann Huxley) (*The Argus*, 6 May 1856; VPRS 515/295. Died 1879/9703 at Ballarat Benevolent Asylum of apoplexy, aged 74. [FAS JMcC]

Wilkins, Thomas (*Forfarshire*, **1843**) Born 1808, near Maidstone, Kent; aged 34; agricultural labourer; 65.25"; reads and writes; f and 9 sibs; 'for assault 28 days, for filberts 30 days and acquitted, for rabbits and fowls 6 months. Tried Maidstone: 7 years for 'stealing a ham and 2 pairs of boots'; SSL: 'employed as a cook, very steady'; CON31: 2 sols; FC 1849. Married 1854 **Margaret Byrne** (*John William Dare*, **1852**), 11 children; 6 survived him; farmer in Tas. Died 1886/9997 age 78 at Melbourne Hospital of old age, paralysis of the bladder and exhaustion. [FAS Steve Rhodes]

Williams, Mary Ann (*Harmony*, **1829**) Born 1811, Soho, London, aged 17; 60.25"; Prot, 'f&m at NP Soho London, Jno Williams a Watchman at St Pancras Parish'; 'I lived last with Mr Gold, Gower Place New Road'; on the town 3 months; reads and writes; 'a prostitute'. Tried Middlesex: 7 years for 'Robbing my ready furnished room, stealing Pillow cases'; CON41: nil apart from one absence from Divine Service; FC 1835. Married 1831 **George Scarborough** (*Caledonian*, **1820**) in Launceston; to Port Phillip; 8 children. Died 1856/4562 at Flemington, aged 45, of disease of the womb and exhaustion. [FAS JMcC, FCRC W124H]

Wilson, Mary Ann (*Margaret*, **1843**) Born 1815, Burslem, Staffordshire; aged 28; 62", Wesleyan; reads; married; SSL: 'slovenly'; CON40: AWL, misconduct; 1845 sent to New Norfolk Asylum for 'paralysis'; 'admitted from Gen. Hospital Hobart; received from Brickfields, unfit for labour. Subject to epileptic fits for many years, paralytic and unfit for any description of labour'. Died 1852 at New Norfolk from 'injuries received while intoxicated', aged 37. [FAS JMcC, FCRC 8166]

Wood, Matthew (*Moffatt*, **1842**) Born 1823, Birmingham, aged 18; 65.25"; carpenter 3 years; reads and writes; m, 2 b and 4 s at NP. Tried Warwick: 10 years for housebreaking and stealing shawl and jewellery; CON31: 29 sols; FC 1853. No marriage found with **Ann Felton** (*Emma Eugenia*, **1846**), 1 son. Died 1879/11514, Alfred Hospital, Melbourne, of erysipelas and pneumonia;

VPG 22 May 1876: 'Discharged Prisoner from Pentridge. Tried Melbourne 21 Feb 1876 for assault—3 months. 65.5", grey hair, hazel eyes. Bald on top of head'. [FAS Nola Beagley]

Woodhead, Ashton (*Moffat*, **1838**) Born 1817, Hackleton, near Blackburn; aged 20; 68"; tattoos; dyer. Tried Lancaster: life for 'stealing in a dwelling house value £5'; SSL: 'quiet and orderly'; CON31: 60 lashes, 7 sols. Married 1846 at Hobart Harriet Jones/Steer (free); 10 children; sawyer. Died 1865/6613 aged 51 at Geelong Hospital: 'pneumonia and pyaemia resulting from fracture of the skull inflicted by himself with a hatchet, temporary insanity'; AIF. [FAS JMcC]

Woollen, Joseph (*Lady Nugent*, **1836**) Born 1816, Manchester, aged 20; 68.75". Tried Lincoln QS: 7 years for stealing from the person; boot clicker; hulk report: 'ironed for fighting'; CON31: 20 sols; FC 1844. Married (1) 1844 Emma Mills (*Royal Admiral*, 1842), who left him in 1849; (2) 1865 Caroline O'Neil; 2 children; VPRS 515/4097. Died 1867/10760 at Melbourne Hospital of a diseased liver. [FAS Glad Wishart]

Wright, William 'Tulip' (*Lady Harewood*, **1829**) Born 1793, Waddington, Lincolnshire; 67.5"; married with wife at City of Lincoln with m who 'keeps a School'; tattoos; macadamizing road maker. Tried at Lincoln: 7 years for 'Stg. a Gun and Iron Bars'; SSL: 'orderly'; CON31: nil; CP 1833. Married Mary Ann Underwood, 1837, at Hobart; 7 children. Died 1856/5016 at Bulla from apoplexy (*The Argus*, 10 Dec 1856). [FAS JMcC]

Acknowledgements

There are many people to thank.

First, my academic colleagues who have been on this voyage from the beginning: Rebecca Kippen, who undertook all the demographic analysis; Len Smith, for his constant support; and our wonderful and dedicated Ships Project research staff: Tricia Curry, Nola Beagley, Colette McAlpine of the Female Convicts Research Centre, and the late Cecile Trioli.

Among the volunteers, there is what we came to call the 'hard core' who were there for the long haul and did research on multiple ships or were stalwarts of the Female Convicts Research Centre: Geoff Brown, Steve Rhodes, Colin Tuckerman, Lance Dwyer, Garry McLoughlin, Alison Ellett, Leanne Goss, Glad Wishart, Jan Kerr, Colleen Arulappu, Judy Price, Jenny Elliston, Jenny Kisler, Kathy Dadswell, Maureen Mann, Maureen Austin, Maureen O'Toole, Margaret Inglis, Margaret Nichols, Rob Weldon, Ros Escott, Teddie Oates, Barry and Margaret Parsons, David Noakes, Cheryl Griffin, Stephanie Hume, Dianne Cassidy and the late Jenny Wells.

Others were aboard for a shorter time: Nanette Gottlieb, Glenda Cox, Annette Sutton, Brian Dowse, Bronwyn King, Carolyn Thurtell, Brenda Irwin, Claire Stevenson, Colleen Robinson, Anne Cronin, Darryl Massie, Edward Thomas, Barry Files, Fay Pattison, Fiona McLennan, Peter Fitzpatrick, Lyn Wilkinson, Graeme Hickey, Judith Wood, Keith Oliver, Kevin Pattison, Mary Eckhardt, Rosemary Noble (UK), Stuart Hamilton, Janet Gaff, Sue Wyatt, Sue Walker, Suzanne Smith, Sarah Preston, Vivienne Cash, Wendy Paterson, Christine Hearne, Robert Tuppen, Robyn Harrison and Jacqueline Wisniowski.

None of this could have been achieved without the information technology designed and managed by Sandra Silcot and Claudine Chionh. This was an immense digital humanities project accomplished on a cottage industry budget, and the final architecture of the online workstation and supporting databases was highly innovative and powerful. We are in their debt. We also thank Trudy Cowley for her advice and support.

This project began in 2008 as the Founders & Survivors: Australian Life Courses in Historical Context, led by Hamish Maxwell-Stewart at the University of Tasmania, and I thank the founding research team of Hamish, Rebecca Kippen, Peter Gunn, Ralph Shlomowitz, James Bradley, Alison Venn and Shyamali Dharmage. Special thanks go to Alison Alexander, who supervised the team of transcribers and who has been a fount of Tasmanian historical wisdom, along with Lucy Frost and Dianne Snowden.

Among international academic colleagues, I wish to thank Rick Steckel, who sowed the idea of such a convict project back in Columbus, Ohio, in 2005; Deb Oxley, David Meredith, Simon Szreter, Mark Peel and Claire Anderson in the UK; Cecily Kelleher in Dublin; Lisa Dillon and Kris Inwood in Canada; and Per Axelsson and his colleagues in Umeä, Sweden. Within Australia, I thank Mark Finnane, Andy May and Jim Davidson.

Graeme Davison, David Nichols, Rebecca Kippen, Colette McAlpine, Kylie Gilmartin and Nicola Knight read the manuscript, providing advice and encouragement, and Julian Held restored fading images.

I thank Nathan Hollier and his team at Melbourne University Publishing.

To my colleagues in the Melbourne School of Population & Global Health: you have been dear friends and taught me a great deal.

I thank Mark Backway for leading me to the story of Daniel and as my physiotherapist, for keeping me going over the years.

Lastly, there is my family: Imogen, Julian, Nic and Zia and our little hopes for the future, Katerina and Henry.

As an old ABC Radio Argonaut of the 1950s, can I say to you all: 'Good Rowing'.

Bibliography

Archival and Public Records
AOT: Archives Office of Tasmania: indents, description lists, conduct records, vital registrations, inquests
FCRC: Female Convicts Research Centre Database
NAA: National Archives of Australia: war service records
PROV: Public Records Office Victoria
    VPRS inquests
    VPRS 515: male criminal records
    VPRS 516: female criminal records
    VPRS children's ward registers
    VPRS probates and wills
Births, Deaths and marriages, Victoria
Victorian DC: Victorian Death Certificate
Births, deaths and marriages, New South Wales
City of Collingwood Rate Books (Ancestry.com)
The Proceedings of the Old Bailey, 1674–1913, https://www.oldbaileyonline.org
Royal Women's Hospital: Lying-In Hospital Cohort, 1857–1900 (PROV) and in possession of author
The Prosecution Project, https://prosecutionproject.griffith.edu.au (viewed March 2021).
Digital Panopticon: UK project that combines FAS research with Old Bailey and other criminal archives, https://www.digitalpanopticon.org (viewed March 2021).
Friends of the Orphan Schools, https://www.orphanschool.org.au (viewed March 2021).
HM Criminal Registers, HO27, NA, Correspondence and Warrants, from Letterbook 6–31 December 1851.

Government Reports
Report of the Committee of Inquiry into Female Convict Prison Discipline, Correspondence, Legal Branch CSO 22/1/50 AOT, FCRC transcript.
Victorian Parliamentary Papers (VPP), Legislative Assembly, Select Committee Upon a Bill for the Prevention of Contagious Diseases, vol. 1, 1878.
Victorian Parliamentary Papers (VPP), Parliament of Victoria, Offences Prevention Bill, 1852–53.
Victorian Parliamentary Papers (VPP), *Report from the Select Committee upon the Claims of Henry Fencham as Discoverer of the Bendigo Gold Field. Melbourne*, Legislative Assembly of the Colony of Victoria, VPARLNoD23, 1890.
Victorian Parliamentary Papers (VPP), VPRS 41/PO Unit 44, surveyor O'Brien's letter, 24 September 1862.

Online Genealogy Resources
Ancestry.com
Findmypast.com.au

Newspapers and Periodicals
Bell's Life in Sydney and Sporting Reviewer
Bendigo Advertiser
Bendigo Independent
Berkshire Chronicle
Britannia and Trades Advocate
Colonial Times
Cornwall Chronicle
Geelong Advertiser
Gippsland Guardian
Herald
Hobart Town Courier
Hobarton Guardian
Illustrated Australian News
Kerang Times
Kyneton Observer
Leader
Liverpool Mail
London Evening Standard
Melbourne Argus
McIvor Times and Rodney Advertiser
Mercury and Weekly Courier
Mount Alexander Mail
North Melbourne Courier
Northern Star and Leeds General Advertiser
Port Phillip Gazette
Port Phillip Patriot
Prahran Telegraph
South Bourke Standard
Telegraph (Prahran)
The Aberdeen Journal
The Age
The Argus
The Armagh Guardian
The Australasian
The Bacchus Marsh Express
The Englishwoman's Domestic Magazine
The Newry Telegraph
The People's Advocate
The Record and Emerald Hill and Sandridge Advertiser
The Star (Ballarat)
The Sydney Morning Herald

BIBLIOGRAPHY

The Weekly Times
Warragul Guardian
Warwick and Warwickshire Advertiser
Yorkshire Gazette

Books, Journals, Theses, Articles and Other Sources

Acton, William, *Prostitution, Considered in Its Moral, Social and Sanitary Aspects*, John Churchill and Sons, London, 1857.
Ager, AW, *Crime and Poverty in 19th-century England*, Bloomsbury, London, 2014.
Alexander, Alison, *Tasmania's Convicts: How Felons Built a Free Society*, Allen & Unwin, Sydney, 2010.
Andel, Lucille V, *Clerk of the House: The Reminiscences of Hugh Munro Hull, 1818–1882*, Melbourne, 1984.
Anderson, Clare (ed.), *A Global History of Convicts and Penal Colonies*, Bloomsbury, London, 2020.
Annear, Robyn, *A City Lost and Found: Whelan the Wrecker's Melbourne*, Black Inc, Melbourne, 2014.
Atkinson, Alan, *The Europeans in Australia*, vol. 1, Oxford University Press, Melbourne, 1997.
BALSAC: Quebec Population Database, 1621–1971, https://ehps-net.eu/databases/balsac-quebec-population-database-1621-1971 (viewed March 2021).
Barrett, Bernard, *The Inner Suburbs: The Evolution of an Industrial Area*, Melbourne University Press, Carlton, Vic., 1971.
Bate, Weston, 'Gold: Social Energiser and Definer', *Victorian Historical Journal*, vol. 72, nos 1–2, 2001, pp. 7–26.
——*Lucky City: The First Generation at Ballarat: 1851–1901*, Melbourne University Press, Carlton, Vic., 1983.
——'Why Is Victoria Different?', *Victorian Historical Journal*, vol. 81, no. 1, 2010, pp. 5–17.
Belich, James, *Replenishing the Earth: The Settler Revolution and the Rise of the Anglo World*, Oxford University Press, Oxford, 2009.
Blainey, Geoffrey, 'The Momentous Gold Rushes', *Australian Economic Review*, vol. 50, no. 2, 2010, pp. 209–16.
Blake, LJ, 'Francis Melville (1822–1857)', *Australian Dictionary of Biography*, http://adb.anu.edu.au/biography/melville-francis-4183 (viewed March 2021).
Boucher, Leigh, and Lynette Russell, 'Soliciting Sixpences from Township to Township: Moral Dilemmas in Mid-Nineteenth-Century Melbourne', *Postcolonial Studies*, vol. 15, no. 2, 2012, pp. 149–65.
Boyce, James, *1835: The Founding of Melbourne and the Conquest of Australia*, Black Inc, Melbourne, 2011.
——*Imperial Mud: The Fight for the Fens*, Icon Books, London, 2020.
——*Van Diemen's Land*, Black Inc, Melbourne, 2008.
Boyle, PP, and CO Grada, 'Fertility Trends, Excess Mortality, and the Great Irish Famine', *Demography*, vol. 23, no. 4, 1986, pp. 543–62.
Braithwaite, John, 'Crime in a Convict Republic', *Modern Law Review*, vol. 64, no. 1, January 2001, pp. 11–50.

Breen, Shayne, *Contested Places: Tasmania's Northern Districts from Ancient Times to 1900*, Centre for Tasmanian Studies, Hobart, 2001.
Brodie, Jo, 'Chapter 2: The Voyage of the East London', https://www.femaleconvicts.org.au/index.php/62-the-east-london/204-chapter-2-the-voyage-of-the-east-london (viewed March 2021).
Cahir, Fred, *Black Gold: Aboriginal People on the Goldfields of Victoria, 1850–1870*, ANU Press, Canberra, 2012.
Caldow, Wayne, 'The Early Livestock Trade between Gippsland and Van Diemen's Land', *The La Trobe Journal*, vol. 86, December 2010, pp. 23–36.
Campbell, Malcolm, *Ireland's New Worlds*, University of Wisconsin Press, Madison, WI, 2008.
Cannon, Michael, *Old Melbourne Town*, Loch Haven Books, Main Ridge, Vic., 1991.
——*Vagabond Country: Australian Bush & Town Life in the Victorian Age*, Hyland House, South Yarra, Vic., 1981.
Chambers, Jill, *Wiltshire Machine Breakers* (2 vols), self-published, Stamford, Lincs., 2009.
Christopher, Emma, and Hamish Maxwell-Stewart, 'Convict Transportation in Global Context c. 1700–88', in Alison Bashford and Stuart Macintyre (eds), *The Cambridge History of Australia*, Cambridge University Press, Port Melbourne, 2013, vol. 1.
Clarke, Marcus, 'What Do We Do with Our Boys?' (1870), in LT Hergenhan (ed.), *A Colonial City: High and Low Life—Selected Journalism of Marcus Clarke*, University of Queensland Press, St Lucia, Qld, 1972.
Cleland, J, *A Historical Account of Bills of Mortality, and the Probability of Human Life in Glasgow and Other Large Towns*, Glasgow, 1836.
Collins, Yola, 'The Provision of Hospital Care in Country Victoria, 1840s to 1940s', PhD thesis, University of Melbourne, 1999.
Courtwright, David T, *Violent Land: Single Men and Social Disorder from the Frontier to the City*, Harvard University Press, Cambridge, MA, 1996.
Cowley, Trudy, and Dianne Snowden, *Patchwork Prisoners: The Rajah Quilt and the Women Who Made It*, Research Tasmania, Hobart, 2013.
Crawford, Patricia, '"Civic Fathers" and Children: Continuities from Elizabethan England to the Australian Colonies', *History Australia*, vol. 5, no. 1, 2008.
Crosby, Alfred, *Ecological Imperialism: The Biological Expansion of Europe, 900–1900*, Cambridge University Press, Cambridge, MA, 1986.
Damousi, Joy, *Depraved and Disorderly*, Cambridge University Press, Cambridge, MA, 1997.
Daniels, Kay, 'The Flash Mob: Rebellion, Rough Culture and Sexuality in the Female Factories of Van Diemen's Land', *Australian Feminist Studies*, vol. 18, summer 1993, pp. 133–60.
Davies, Peter, Susan Lawrence and Karen Twigg, 'Grazing Was Not Mining: Managing Victoria's Goldfields Commons', *Geographical Research*, vol. 56, no. 3, 2018, pp. 256–69.
Dawson, SE, 'Ned Kelly's Shooting of George Metcalf, Labourer', *Eras Journal*, vol. 19, no. 1, 2017, pp. 79–93.
Dingle, AE, and DT Merrett, 'Home Owners and Tenants in Melbourne 1891–1911', *Australian Economic History Review*, vol. 12, no. 1, 1972, pp. 21–35.

——'Landlords in Suburban Melbourne, 1891–1911', *Australian Economic History Review*, vol. 17, no. 1, 1977, pp. 1–24.
Dowling, Peter, 'What Charles Sturt Saw in 1839: Syphilis beyond the Colonial Boundaries?', *Health and History*, vol. 19, no. 1, 2017, pp. 44–59.
Edmonds, Penelope, *Urbanizing Frontiers: Indigenous Peoples and Settlers in 19th-century Pacific Rim Cities*, UBC Press, Vancouver, 2010.
Emsley, Clive, *Crime and Society in England, 1750–1900*, 3rd edn, Harlow, England, 2003.
Engelhardt, Sacha C, Patrick Bergeron, Alain Gagnon, Lisa Dillon and Fanie Pelletier, 'Using Geographic Distance as a Potential Proxy for Help in the Assessment of the Grandmother Hypothesis', *Current Biology*, vol. 29, no. 4, 2019, pp. 651–6.
Evans, William (ed.), *Diary of a Welsh Swagman, 1869–1894*, Sun Books, South Melbourne, 1977.
Fahey, Charles, 'Peopling the Victorian Goldfields: From Boom to Bust, 1851–1901', *Australian Economic History Review*, vol. 50, no. 2, 2002, pp. 148–61.
——'The Free Selectors' Landscape: Moulding the Victorian Farming Districts 1870–1915', *Studies in the History of Gardens and Designed Landscapes*, vol. 31, no. 2, 2011, pp. 97–108.
Foxhall, Katherine, 'From Convicts to Colonists: The Health of Prisoners and the Voyage to Australia, 1823–53', *Journal of Imperial and Commonwealth History*, vol. 39, no. 1, 2011, pp. 1–19.
Gammage, Bill, *The Biggest Estate on Earth*, Allen & Unwin, Crows Nest, NSW, 2011.
Gittins, Jean, 'McLachlan, Lachlan (1810–1885)', *Australian Dictionary of Biography*, 1974, http://adb.anu.edu.au/biography/mclachlan-lachlan-4118 (viewed March 2021).
Godfrey, Barry, Kris Inwood and Hamish Maxwell-Stewart, 'Exploring the Life-course and Intergenerational Impact of Convict Transportation', in Veroni I. Eichelsheim and Steve GA van de Weijer (eds), *Intergenerational Continuity of Criminal and Antisocial Behaviour*, Routledge, Oxford, 2018.
Goffman, Erving, *Stigma: Notes on the Management of Spoiled Identity*, Penguin, Harmondsworth, UK, 1998.
Goldfeld, Sharon, Meredith O'Connor, Shiau Chong, Sarah Gray, Elodie O'Connor, Sue Woolfenden, Gerry Redmond, Katrina Williams, Fiona Mensah, Amanda Kvalsvig and Hannah Badland, 'The Impact of Multidimensional Disadvantage of Childhood on Developmental Outcomes in Australia', *International Journal of Epidemiology*, vol. 47, no. 5, 2018, pp. 1485–96.
Goodman, David, 'Gold Fields/Golden Fields: The Language of Agrarianism and the Victorian Gold Rush', *Australian Historical Studies*, vol. 23, 1988, pp. 19–41.
Grimshaw, Patricia, 'Colonising Motherhood: Evangelical Social Reformers and Koorie Women in Victoria, Australia, 1880s to the early 1900s', *Women's History Review*, vol. 8, no. 2, 1999, pp. 329–46.
Gunson, Niel, 'Langham, Frederick (1833–1903)', *Australian Dictionary of Biography*, 1984, http://adb.anu.edu.au/biography/langham-frederick-3987 (viewed March 2021).
Hancock, WK, *Australia*, Ernest Benn, London, 1930.
Hinkins, John T, *Life amongst the Native Race*, WT Quinton, Flemington, Vic., 1884.
Hitchcock, Tim, *Down and Out in Eighteenth Century London*, Hambledon, London, 2004.
Hobsbawm, EJ, and George Rude, *Captain Swing*, Lawrence Wishart, London, 1969.

Holst, Heather, *Making a Home: A History of Castlemaine*, Australian Scholarly Publishing, North Melbourne, 2014.
Howe, Renate, and Shurlee Swain, *All God's Children*, Acorn Press, Canberra, 1989.
Howitt, Richard, *Impressions of Australia Felix*, Longman, Brown, Green and Longmans, London, 1845.
Howitt, William, *Land, Labour and Gold: Two Years in Victoria: With Visits to Sydney and Van Diemen's Land*, Longman, Brown, Green, Longmans, and Roberts, London, 1855.
Human Mortality Database, University of California, Berkeley (USA), and Max Planck Institute for Demographic Research (Germany), http://www.mortality.org (viewed March 2021).
Humphries, Jane, *Childhood and Child Labour in the British Industrial Revolution*, Oxford University Press, Oxford, 2010.
Jackson, RV, 'Building Societies and the Workers in Melbourne in the 1880s', *Labour History*, vol. 47, November 1984, pp. 28–38.
James, John Stanley, *The Vagabond Papers*, ed. Michael Cannon, expanded edn, Monash University Press, Clayton, Vic., 2016.
Jeppesen, Jennie, '"Within the Protection of Law": Debating the Australian Convict-as-Slave Narrative', *History Australia*, vol. 16, no. 3, 2019, pp. 534–48.
Johnson, Paul, and Stephen Nicholas, 'Male and Female Living Standards in England and Wales, 1812–1857', *The Economic History Review*, New Series, vol. 48, no. 3, 1995, pp. 470–81.
Kiddle, Margaret, *Men of Yesterday*, Melbourne University Press, Carlton, Vic., 1961.
Kippen, Rebecca, and Janet McCalman, 'Mortality under and after Sentence of Male Convicts Transported to Van Diemen's Land (Tasmania), 1840–1852', *The History of the Family*, vol. 20, no. 3, 2015, pp. 345–65.
——'Parental Loss in Young Convicts Transported to Van Diemen's Land (Tasmania), 1841–53', *The History of the Family*, vol. 23, no. 4, 2018, pp. 656–78.
Kippin, Natalie R, et al., 'Language Diversity, Language Disorder, and Fetal Alcohol Spectrum Disorder among Youth Sentenced to Detention in Western Australia', *International Journal of Law and Psychiatry*, November–December 2018, pp. 40–9.
Kosten, M, and RJ Mitchell, 'Family Size and Social Class in Nineteenth Century Tasmania, Australia', *Journal of Biosocial Science*, vol. 16, 1984, pp. 55–63.
Kosten, M, J Williams and RJ Mitchell, 'Historical Population Structure of Two Tasmanian Communities Using Surname Analyses', *Journal of Biosocial Science*, vol. 15, 1983, pp. 367–76.
Larson, Ann, *Growing Up in Melbourne: Family Life in the Late Nineteenth Century*, ANU Press, Canberra, 1994.
Lawson, Henry, *Verses Popular and Humorous*, Angus & Robertson, Sydney, 1900.
Leppard-Quinn, Christine, 'Labelling the Transported Prostitute: An Exercise in Textual Archaeology', *Tasmanian Historical Studies*, vol. 18, 2013, pp. 35–59.
Lewis, Brian, *Sunday at Kooyong Road*, Hutchinson, Melbourne, 1976.
Linebaugh, Peter, *The Magna Carta Manifesto: Liberties and Commons for All*, University of California Press, Berkeley, CA, 2008.
Lourandos, Harry, *Continent of Hunter Gatherers*, Cambridge University Press, Cambridge, 1997.

Luddy, Maria, 'An Outcast Community: The "Wrens" of the Curragh', *Women's History Review*, vol. 1, no. 3, 1992, pp. 341–55.
MacFie, P, and N Hargraves, 'The Empire's First Stolen Generation: The First Intake at Point Puer, 1834–39', in 'Exiles of Empire', *Tasmanian Historical Studies*, vol. 6, no. 2, 1999, pp. 29–154.
Malcolm, Elizabeth, '"The House of Strident Shadows": The Asylum, the Family and Emigration in Post-Famine Ireland', in Elizabeth Malcolm and Greta Jones (eds), *Medicine, Disease and the State in Ireland, 1650–1940*, Cork University Press, Cork, 1999, pp. 177–94.
Manifold, JS, *The Penguin Australian Songbook*, Penguin, Ringwood, Vic., 1964, pp. 36–7.
Maxwell-Stewart, Hamish, *Closing Hell's Gates: Death of a Convict Station*, Allen & Unwin, Sydney, 2008.
——'"Those Lads Contrived a Plan": Attempts at Mutiny on Australia-Bound Convict Vessels', *International Review of Social History*, vol. 58, December 2013, pp. 177–96.
Maxwell-Stewart, Hamish, and R Kippen, 'Sickness and Death on Convict Voyages to Australia', in P Baskerville and K Inwood (eds), *Lives in Transition*, McGill-Queen's University Press, Montreal, 2015, pp. 43–70.
Maxwell-Stewart, Hamish, Kris Inwood and Jim Stankovich, 'Prison and the Colonial Family', *The History of the Family*, vol. 20, no. 2, 2015, pp. 231–48.
May, Andrew, *Melbourne Street Life: The Itinerary of Our Days*, Australian Scholarly Publishing, Kew, Vic., 1998.
McCalman, Janet, '"All Just Melted with Heat": Mothers, Babies and "Hot Winds" in Colonial Melbourne', in Tim Sherratt, Tom Griffiths and Libby Robin (eds), *A Change in the Weather: Climate and Culture in Australia*, National Museum of Australia Press, Canberra, 2005, pp. 104–15.
——'To Die without Friends: Solitaries, Drifters and Failures in a New World Society', in Graeme Davison, Pat Jalland and Wilfrid Prest (eds), *Body and Mind: Historical Essays in Honour of F.B. Smith*, Melbourne University Press, Carlton, Vic., 2009, pp. 173–94.
McCalman, Janet, and Len Smith, 'Family and Country: Accounting for Fractured Connections under Colonisation in Victoria, Australia', *Journal of Population Research*, vol. 33, no. 1, 2016, pp. 51–65.
McCalman, Janet, and Rebecca Kippen, 'The Life-course Demography of Convict Transportation to Van Diemen's Land', *The History of the Family*, vol. 25, no. 3, 2020, pp. 432–54.
McCalman, Janet, and Ruth Morley, 'Mother's Health and Babies' Weights: The Biology of Poverty at the Melbourne Lying-In Hospital, 1857–83', *Social History of Medicine*, vol. 16, no. 1, April 2003, pp. 39–56.
McCalman, Janet, Ruth Morley, Len Smith and Ian Anderson, 'Colonial Health Transitions: Aboriginal and "Poor White" Infant Mortality Compared, Victoria 1850–1910', *The History of the Family*, vol. 16, 2011, pp. 62–77.
McCalman, Janet, Len Smith, Ian Anderson, Ruth Morley and Gita Mishra, 'Colonialism and the Health Transition: Aboriginal Australians and Poor Whites Compared, Victoria, 1850–1985', *The History of the Family*, vol. 14, 2009, pp. 253–65.
McCalman, Janet, Rebecca Kippen, Joan McMeeken, John Hopper and Michael Reade, 'Early Results from the "Diggers to Veterans" Longitudinal Study of the Australian

Men Who Served in the First World War: Short- and Long-term Mortality of Early Enlisters', *Historical Life Course Studies*, vol. 8, 2019, pp. 52–72.

McKinley, RA, 'The Ancient Borough: St. Margaret's', in RA McKinley (ed.), *A History of the County of Leicester*, vol. 4, City of Leicester, London, 1958, pp. 350–61.

McLaughlin, Trevor, *Barefoot and Pregnant? Irish Famine Orphans in Australia*, The Genealogical Society of Victoria, Inc., Melbourne, 1991.

McLoughlin, Dympna, 'The Impact of the Great Famine on Subsistent Women', in James Crowley, William J Smyth and Mike Murphy (eds), *Atlas of the Great Irish Famine, 1845–52*, Cork University Press, Cork, 2012.

McMullin, Ross, 'The Impact of Gold on Lawlessness and Crime in Victoria 1851–1854', *Victorian Historical Journal*, vol. 48, no. 2, May 1977, pp. 123–38.

McQuilton, John, *The Kelly Outbreak 1878–1880*, Melbourne University Press, Carlton, Vic., 1979 and 1987.

Megalogenis, George, 'Australasia Rising: Who We Are Becoming', *The Sydney Morning Herald: Good Weekend*, 26 January 2019.

Meredith, David, and Deborah Oxley, 'Contracting Convicts: The Convict Labour Market in Van Diemen's Land 1840–1857', *Australian Economic History Review*, vol. 45, no. 1, 2005, pp. 45–72.

——'The Convict Economy', in Simon Ville and Glenn Withers (eds), *The Cambridge Economic History of Australia*, Cambridge University Press, Port Melbourne, 2015, pp. 97–122.

Mitchell, Colter, John Hobcraft, Sara S McLanahan, Susan Rutherford Siegel, Arthur Berg, Jeanne Brooks-Gunn, Irwin Garfinkel and Daniel Notterman, 'Social Disadvantage, Genetic Sensitivity, and Children's Telomere Length', *PNAS*, vol. 111, no. 16, 2014, pp. 5944–9.

Mokyr, Joel, *Why Ireland Starved: A Quantitative and Analytical History of the Irish Economy, 1800–1850*, Routledge, London, 1983.

Morgan, Patrick, *The Vandemonian Trail: Convicts and Bushrangers in Early Victoria*, Conor Court, Sydney, 2016.

Motion, Andrew, *Wainewright the Poisoner*, Faber and Faber, London, 2000.

Mundy, Godfrey Charles, *Our Antipodes: Or, Residence and Rambles in the Australasian Colonies—With a Glimpse at the Goldfields*, Richard Bentley, London, 1852.

National Trust Tasmania, 'Miss Helen Power Remembers', in *Campbell Town: History and Centenary of Municipal Government*, NTA, Hobart, 1966, pp. 332–3.

Nicholas, Stephen (ed.), *Convict Workers: Reinterpreting Australia's Past*, Cambridge University Press, Melbourne, 1988.

Nicholas, Stephen, and Richard H Steckel, 'Heights and Living Standards of English Workers During the Early Years of Industrializations, 1770–1815', *Journal of Economic History*, vol. 51, no. 4, 1991, pp. 937–57.

Nunn, Cameron, '"Making Them Good and Useful": The Ideology of Juvenile Penal Reformation at Carters' Barracks and Point Puer', *History Australia*, vol. 14, no. 3, 2017, pp. 329–43.

Ouellet-Morin, Isabelle, 'Effect of the MAOA Gene and Levels of Exposure to Violence on Antisocial Outcomes', *The British Journal of Psychiatry*, vol. 208, no. 1, January 2016, pp. 42–8.

Oxley, Deborah, *Convict Maids: The Forced Migration of Women to Australia*, Cambridge University Press, Melbourne, 1996.
Palmer, Darren, 'A New Police in Victoria: Conditions of Crises or Politics of Reform?', *Victorian Historical Journal*, vol. 74, no. 2, 2003, pp. 167–96.
Pascoe, Bruce, *Dark Emu*, Magabala Books, Broome, WA, 2018.
Paterson, AB, *Old Bush Songs*, Angus & Robertson, Sydney, 1905.
Patriquin, Larry, 'Why Was There No "Old Poor Law" in Scotland and Ireland?', *The Journal of Peasant Studies*, vol. 33, no. 2, 2006, pp. 219–47.
Pell, MB, 'On the Rates of Mortality in New South Wales, and on the Construction of Mortality Tables from Census Returns; with a Note on the Formation of Commutation Tables', *Journal of the Institute of Actuaries*, vol. 21, 1879, pp. 257–88.
Perry, Richard (Mrs Frances Perry), *Contributions to an Amateur Magazine in Prose and Verse*, L Booth, London, 1857.
Petrow, Stefan, '"Convict-phobia": Combatting Vandemonian Convicts in 1850s and 1860s Victoria', *Journal of Australian Colonial History*, vol. 14, 2012, pp. 260–71.
Phillips, Watts, *The Wild Tribes of London*, Ward and Lock, London, 1855.
Reeves, Andrew, 'Trade Unionism and the Australian Mining Industry: The Influence of Central Victorian Goldminers, 1870–1920', in Keir Reeves and David Nichols (eds), *Deeper Leads*, Ballarat Heritage Series, Ballarat, 2007, pp. 161–84.
Registrar General, *Fifth Annual Report of the Registrar General of Births, Deaths, and Marriages, in England*, London, 1843.
Reid, Kirsty, *Gender, Crime and Empire: Convicts, Settlers and the State in Early Colonial Australia*, Manchester University Press, Manchester, 2007.
Reynolds, Henry, 'That Hated Stain: The Aftermath of Transportation in Tasmania', *Historical Studies*, vol. 14, no. 53, 1969, pp. 19–31.
Roberts, David, 'Beyond "the Stain": Rethinking the Nature and Impact of the Anti-transportation Movement', discussion forum in *Journal of Australian Colonial Studies*, vol. 14, 2012, pp. 205–79.
——'"More Sinned against than Sinning": George Arnold Wood and the Noble Convict', in D Gare and D Ritter (eds), *Making Australian History: Perspectives on the Past Since 1788*, Thomson, Melbourne, 2007, pp. 122–30.
Robinson, George Augustus, *Journals of GA Robinson, 1840 and 1841*, ed. Gary Presland, Victoria Archaeological Survey, and Aboriginal Affairs Victoria (online), Melbourne, 1977 and 1980, nos 5, 6 and 11.
Robinson, Portia, *The Women of Botany Bay*, Penguin Books, Ringwood, Vic., 1993.
Robson, LL, *The Convict Settlers of Australia*, Melbourne University Press, Carlton, Vic., 1965.
Rosental, Paul-Andre, 'The Novelty of an Old Genre: Louis Henry and the Founding of Historical Demography', *Population* (English edn), 2003, pp. 97–129.
Russell, Lynette, *A Little Bird Told Me: Family Secrets, Necessary Lies*, Allen & Unwin, Crows Nest, NSW, 2002.
Ryan, Henry, 'Diary of the Claudine Convict Ship, 1821', *UK Royal Naval Medical Journals 1817–1856*, available at Ancestry.com
Ryan, Lyndall, 'Colonial Frontier Massacres 1788–1930', https://c21ch.newcastle.edu.au/colonialmassacres/map.php (viewed March 2021).

Sampson, RJ, and John H Laub, 'A Life-course Theory of Cumulative Disadvantage and the Stability of Delinquency', in TP Thornberry (ed.), *Developmental Theories of Crime and Delinquency* (vol. 7), Transactions Publishers, Piscataway, NJ, 1997.
Sante, Luc, *The Other Paris*, Farrar, Strauss and Giroux, New York, 2015.
Scates, Bruce, 'Trenwith, William Arthur (Billy) (1846–1925)', *Australian Dictionary of Biography*, http://adb.anu.edu.au/biography/trenwith-william-arthur-billy-8848 (viewed March 2021).
Schedvin, MB, and CB Schedvin, 'The Nomadic Tribes of Urban Britain: A Prelude to Botany Bay', *Australian Historical Studies*, vol. 18, no. 71, 1978, pp. 254–76.
Scheper-Hughes, Nancy, *Death without Weeping: The Violence of Everyday Life in Brazil*, University of California Press, Berkeley, CA, 1993.
Scott, James C, *Seeing Like a State*, Yale University Press, New York, 1998.
——*The Art of Not Being Governed*, Yale University Press, New Haven, CN, 2009.
Serle, Geoffrey, *The Golden Age*, Melbourne University Press, Carlton, Vic., 1963.
——*The Rush to Be Rich*, Melbourne University Press, Carlton, Vic., 1971.
Shaw, AGL, *Convicts and the Colonies*, Melbourne University Press, Carlton, Vic., 1977.
Shore, Heather, *Artful Dodgers: Youth and Crime in Early 19th-Century London*, Boydell Press, Woodbridge, Suffolk, 2002.
Silberberg, Sue, *A Networked Community: Jewish Melbourne in the Nineteenth Century*, Melbourne University Press, Carlton, Vic., 2020.
Sleight, Simon, *Young People and the Shaping of Public Space in Melbourne*, Ashgate, Farnham, Surrey, 2013.
Smith, FB, 'Curing Alcoholism in Australia, 1880s–1920s', *Journal of Australian Colonial History*, vol. 8, 2008, pp. 137–58.
Smith, Len, Janet McCalman, Ian Anderson, Sandra Smith, Joanne Evans, Gavan McCarthy and Jane Beer, 'Fractional Identities: The Political Arithmetic of Aboriginal Australians', in Per Axelsson and Peter Sköld (eds), *Indigenous Peoples and Demography: The Complex Relationship between People and Statistics*, Berghahn Books, New York and Oxford, 2011, pp. 15–32.
Smith, Richard M, 'Social Security as a Developmental Institution? The Relative Efficacy of Poor Relief Provisions under the English Old Poor Law', in CA Bayly et al., *History, Historians and Development Policy*, Manchester University Press, Manchester, 2011.
Snell, KDM, *Annals of the Labouring Poor: Social Change and Agrarian England, 1660–1900*, Cambridge University Press, Cambridge, 1985.
——*Parish and Belonging: Community, Identity and Welfare in England and Wales, 1700–1950*, Cambridge University Press, Cambridge, 2006.
Snowden, Dianne, *White Rag Burning: Irish Women Committing Arson to Be Transported*, Forty South Publishing, Hobart, 2018.
Summers, Anne, *Damned Whores and God's Police*, Penguin, Ringwood, Vic., 1994.
Sutherland, Alexander, *Victoria and Its Metropolis*, vol. 2, McCarron Bird, Melbourne, 1888.
Swain, Nathaniel R, Patricia A Eadie and Pamela C Snow, 'Speech and Language Therapy for Adolescents in Youth Justice', *International Journal of Language and Communication Disorders*, vol. 55, no. 4, 2020, pp. 458–79.
Swedish Historical Population Statistics, https://snd.gu.se/en/catalogue/study/ext0086 (viewed March 2021).

Szreter, Simon, 'The Capacity to Surprise: The Importance of History for Public Health Policy', *American Journal of Public Health*, vol. 110, no. 3, March 2020, pp. 337–8.

Tanner, Lindsay, 'Labour in Victorian Politics, 1889–1903', *Labour History*, vol. 42, May 1982, pp. 40–53.

Taylor, Angela, *A Forester's Log: The Story of John La Gerche and the Ballarat-Creswick State Forest, 1882–1897*, Melbourne University Press, Melbourne, 1998.

Theobald, Marjorie, *The Accidental Town: Castlemaine, 1851–1861*, Australian Scholarly Publishing, Melbourne, 2020.

Trollope, Anthony, *Australia and New Zealand*, 2 vols, Chapman & Hall, Piccadilly, London, 1873.

Tuffin, Richard, Martin Gibbs, David Roberts, Hamish Maxwell-Stewart, David Roe, Jody Steele, Susan Hood and Barry Godfrey, 'Landscapes of Production and Punishment: Convict Labour in the Australian Context', *Journal of Social Archaeology*, vol. 18, no. 1, 2018, pp. 50–76.

Utah Population Database, https://uofuhealth.utah.edu/huntsman/utah-population-database/data/ (viewed March 2021).

van Raalte, AA, I Sasson and P Martikkainen, 'The Case for Monitoring Life-span Inequality', *Science*, vol. 362, no. 6418, 2018, pp. 1002–4.

Venn, Michael, 'Engineers and Politicians: the Victorian Railways 1854–1904', 2020, https://railstory.org/ (viewed March 2021).

'Walter' (Henry Spencer Ashbee), *My Secret Life* (11 vols), first published in limited edn 1888, London.

Ware, Helen, 'The Recruitment, Regulation and Role of Prostitution in Britain from the Middle of the Nineteenth Century to the Present Day', PhD thesis, Bedford College, University of London, 1969.

Warner, Kate, 'Transportation Revisited: Lessons for Modern Penal Policy?', 31st John West Memorial Lecture, Launceston, Tas., 15 March 2019.

Weaver, John C, *The Great Land Rush and the Making of the Modern World*, University of McGill-Queens Press, Montreal, 2003.

Webb, Stephen, *The Paleopathology of Aboriginal Australians*, Cambridge University Press, Melbourne, 1995.

Wilke, Douglas, 'The Rush that Never Started: Forgotten Origins of the 1851 Gold Discoveries in Victoria', PhD thesis, University of Melbourne, 2014.

Wrigley, EA, and RS Schofield, *English Population History from Family Reconstitution, 1580–1837*, Cambridge University Press, Cambridge, 1997.

Notes

INTRODUCTION
1. *Warragul Guardian*, 9 October 1896, p. 3.
2. Venn.
3. *Liverpool Mail*, 17 September 1839, p. 3.
4. The Proceedings of the Old Bailey, trial of Ruth Miles, 12 August 1839.
5. Christopher and Maxwell-Stewart, pp. 68–90.
6. Hancock, p. 39.
7. Weaver.
8. Belich, pp. 445–6.
9. Snell, *Annals of the Labouring Poor*; *Parish and Belonging*.
10. Boyce, *1835*.
11. Goffman.
12. Scott, *Seeing Like a State*.
13. Atkinson.
14. van Raalte, Sasson and Martikkainen.
15. Rosental; Wrigley and Schofield; Utah Population Database; Swedish Historical Population Statistics; BALSAC.

CHAPTER 1
1. Alexander, pp. 313–50.
2. *The Star* (Ballarat), 14 November 1862, p. 2; 23 February 1864, p. 2; 18 April 1866, p. 3.
3. See Appendix A, Figure A1.
4. Emsley, pp. 36–8.
5. Ibid.
6. Hitchcock, pp. 1–22.
7. Crawford.
8. Szreter; Richard M Smith.
9. Patriquin.
10. Ager.
11. *London Evening Standard*, 8 October 1834, p. 4.
12. Kippen and McCalman, 'Parental Loss in Young Convicts'; Shore, pp. 35–54.
13. McKinley.
14. HM Criminal Registers.
15. Ware, pp. 34–143.
16. 'Walter'.
17. Phillips, pp. 11–12.
18. Emsley, p. 4.
19. *Warwick and Warwickshire Advertiser*, 21 March 1829, p. 1.
20. *Yorkshire Gazette*, 30 August 1834, p. 2.
21. Hobsbawm and Rude.
22. Contributed to the Founders and Survivors Ships Project by Garry McLoughlin, with additional information from his cousins Mary Elizabeth Calwell and Barry Gough.
23. *The Newry Telegraph*, 11 September 1849, p. 3.
24. Snowden.
25. Luddy.
26. Dympna McLoughlin.
27. Mokyr, pp. 278–94.

CHAPTER 2
1. Jeppesen.
2. Maxwell-Stewart, '"Those Lads Contrived a Plan"'.
3. Cowley and Snowden, pp. 9–11.
4. *The Englishwoman's Domestic Magazine*, vol. 1, 1866, pp. 311–17.
5. Maxwell-Stewart and Kippen.
6. Foxhall.
7. Brodie.
8. Henry Ryan.
9. Leppard-Quinn.
10. Maxwell-Stewart, *Closing Hell's Gates*.
11. *Berkshire Chronicle*, 17 October 1829, p. 2.
12. AOT, Margaret Owen (*Gilbert Henderson*, 1840), CON40.
13. Kippen and McCalman, 'Mortality under and after Sentence'.

NOTES

14 Andel, p. 71.
15 Mundy, p. 484.
16 Ibid., p. 483.
17 Motion, p. 280.
18 Mundy, pp. 189–92.
19 Nunn.
20 MacFie and Hargraves.
21 Female Convict Research Centre archives.
22 *Port Phillip Patriot*, 14 September 1846, p. 2.
23 Ibid., 2 December 1847, p. 2.
24 Gunson.
25 Reid.
26 Report of the Committee of Inquiry into Female Convict Prison Discipline, p. 104; Daniels.
27 *Hobarton Guardian*, 12 July 1848, p. 3.

CHAPTER 3
1 AOT, SC195/1/30 Inquest 2728.
2 *Cornwall Chronicle*, 15 February and 15 April 1868.
3 Boyce, *Van Diemen's Land*; 1835.
4 Boyce, *Van Diemen's Land*, pp. 255–7; Linebaugh.
5 Boyce, *Van Diemen's Land*, pp. 45–60.
6 Breen.
7 Boyce, *Van Diemen's Land*, pp. 51–5.
8 See Appendix A, Figure A9.
9 Reid, pp. 94–5.
10 *Colonial Times*, 9 May 1837, p. 4.
11 *Hobart Town Courier*, 30 June 1837, p. 3.
12 *Colonial Times*, 1 March 1842, p. 3.
13 Ibid., 4 March 1845, p. 3.
14 *Britannia and Trades Advocate*, 1 June 1848, p. 2.
15 Charles Wesley, 'Love Divine'.
16 Webb.
17 Lourandos; Gammage; Pascoe.
18 Smith et al.
19 Kiddle, pp. 65–7.
20 Dowling.
21 Crosby.
22 See Lyndall Ryan.
23 GA Robinson, 17–18 January 1840.
24 Ibid., 30 April 1841.
25 Ibid., 8 February 1840.
26 Ibid., 31 January 1841.
27 Ibid., 21 April 1841.
28 Ibid., 15 May 1841.
29 Caldow; Morgan.
30 Kiddle, pp. 102–31.
31 Edmonds.
32 Cannon, *Old Melbourne Town*.
33 *The Argus*, 10 December 1856.
34 Ibid., 28 December 1855, p. 4.
35 *Bendigo Advertiser*, 3 January 1856, p. 3.
36 *The Age*, 13 March 1866, p. 4.
37 *The Argus*, 25 January 1876, p. 2.
38 Ibid., 25 March 1905, p. 4.
39 *Gippsland Guardian*, 9 February 1866.
40 Grimshaw.
41 Hinkins.
42 Ibid.
43 Silberberg.
44 *Melbourne Argus*, 25 September 1846, p. 2.
45 *Port Phillip Gazette*, 12 September 1846, p. 2.
46 *The Argus*, 3 October 1848, p. 2.
47 Ibid., 10 October 1848, p. 2.
48 Ibid., 14 November 1848, p. 2.
49 Ibid., 5 July 1849, p. 2.
50 Roberts, 'Beyond "the Stain"'.
51 Richard Howitt, p. 118.

CHAPTER 4
1 Bate, 'Gold'.
2 Dennis O'Reilly, 'With My Swag All on My Shoulder', in Manifold, pp. 36–7.
3 *The Argus*, 8 October 1851, p. 2.
4 Ibid., 29 September 1851, p. 2.
5 Wilke.
6 *Geelong Advertiser*, 8 August 1851, p. 2.
7 *The Argus*, 23 March 1852, p. 4.
8 Ibid., 8 February 1853, p. 5.
9 Ibid., 11 February 1852, p. 2; 12 July 1856, p. 5; *The Age*, 29 January 1859, p. 6.
10 Megalogenis.
11 Blainey, pp. 209–16.
12 Serle, *The Rush to Be Rich*.

13 Victorian Parliamentary Papers, *Report from the Select Committee*.
14 Serle, *The Golden Age*.
15 Contributed to the Founders and Survivors Ships Project by Jane Starsmore Duvall, United States.
16 Sutherland, p. 692.
17 Chambers, vol. 1, p. 400. Biography contributed to the Founders and Survivors Ships Project by Annabel Anderson.
18 *The People's Advocate*, 24 May 1851, p. 8.
19 *The Argus*, 2 January 1852, p. 2.
20 Blake.
21 *Geelong Advertiser*, 5 February 1852, p. 2.
22 *Bell's Life in Sydney and Sporting Reviewer*, 20 March 1852, p. 2.
23 Ibid.
24 *Cornwall Chronicle*, 10 January 1852, p. 19.
25 *The Sydney Morning Herald*, 29 November 1853, p. 3.
26 Perry, pp. 164–5.
27 Goodman.
28 *The Argus*, 12 February 1852, p. 2.
29 Ibid., 14 February 1852, p. 3.
30 Ibid., p. 2.
31 *Cornwall Chronicle*, 21 January 1852, p. 42.
32 *The Age*, 29 December 1854, p. 4.
33 *Hobart Town Courier*, 1 November 1853, p. 2.
34 *The Argus*, 1 January 1853, p. 3.
35 *The Age*, 29 August 1855, p. 6.
36 Victorian Parliamentary Papers, 1852–53, vol. 2, p. 45.
37 Cowley and Snowden, pp. 184–5.
38 *The Argus*, 2 August 1856, p. 5; Victorian Parliamentary Papers, VPRS 516, vol. 1, no. 516.
39 *The Argus*, 13 July 1852, p. 3.
40 Ibid., 4 January 1854, p. 5.
41 Ibid., 28 September 1854, p. 5.
42 Palmer.
43 McMullin.
44 Calculated roughly and conservatively from a Founders and Survivors analysis of all those who were found to have arrived 'bond' from the *Victorian Police Gazette*, and from a database of female prisoners compiled by Dr Alana Piper for the Prosecution Project led by Professor Mark Finnane of Griffith University. The female offenders were confirmed against the Female Convict Research Centre records. The Vandemonian crime wave peaked before the institution of the *Police Gazette* in 1855, and many early individual records before then for both men and women have disappeared.
45 *The Argus*, 24 January 1853, p. 4.
46 Petrow.
47 *The Argus*, 28 January 1853, p. 4.
48 *Colonial Times*, 13 July 1852, p. 3; *The Argus*, 11 May 1852, p. 4.
49 *The Argus*, 11 May 1854, p. 10.

CHAPTER 5
1 *The Argus*, 28 February 1850, p. 2.
2 *The Age*, 28 October 1854, p. 5.
3 *The Argus*, 19 November 1852, p. 5.
4 May, pp. 142–72.
5 *The Argus*, 1 September 1858, p. 2.
6 *The Argus*, 5 April 1865, p. 5; VPRS 515/7210.
7 *The Argus*, 27 July 1853, p. 5.
8 Ibid., 31 July 1855, p. 5.
9 *The Age*, 5 May 1863, p. 6.
10 Annear.
11 *The Star* (Ballarat), 15 September 1857, p. 3.
12 *The Age*, 6 March 1857, p. 6.
13 Ibid., 7 May 1859, p. 4.
14 Victorian Parliamentary Papers, Legislative Assembly, Select Committee Upon a Bill for the Prevention of Contagious Diseases.
15 *Port Phillip Patriot*, 18 December 1847.
16 *The Age*, 16 March 1868, p. 7.
17 *The Argus*, 10 January 1871, p. 6.
18 Ibid., 21 August 1857, p. 6.
19 Ibid., 31 January 1857, p. 5.
20 *Herald*, 20 January 1876, p. 3.

21 VPRS 24, 1876/128.
22 *The Age*, 7 January 1858, p. 5.
23 *The Argus*, 16 October 1856, p. 4.
24 *Cornwall Chronicle*, 19 July 1856.
25 VPRS 24/PO unit 420, item 1881/350.
26 VPRS 515/37.
27 *The Argus*, 22 November 1851, p. 4; *The Age*, 31 July 1857; *The Argus*, 18 January 1858, p. 5; 21 May 1859, p. 6.
28 *The Age*, 7 May 1859, p. 4.
29 *The Argus*, 19 November 1860, p. 6.
30 Ibid., 17 June 1861, p. 6; *The Age*, 11 June 1862, p. 7.
31 *The Weekly Times*, 14 February 1880, p. 19.
32 *The Argus*, 3 December 1866, p. 6.
33 Victorian Parliamentary Papers, Legislative Assembly, Select Committee Upon a Bill for the Prevention of Contagious Diseases.
34 McCalman and Morley.
35 *The Argus*, 16 January 1857, p. 6.
36 *The Age*, 22 June 1858, p. 6.
37 TAHO CON 1/1/41 file 3119, pp. 70, 105, 137, 140, 147, 153, 160, 209.
38 *Bendigo Advertiser*, 24 December 1856, p. 3.
39 *The Argus*, 20 April 1858, p. 6.
40 Ibid., 16 December 1867, p. 1.
41 Ibid., 20 January 1862, p. 6.
42 Victorian Parliamentary Papers, Legislative Assembly, Select Committee Upon a Bill for the Prevention of Contagious Diseases, Q 386.
43 *London Evening Standard*, 4 March 1839, p. 7.
44 *The Argus*, 30 January 1855, p. 5.
45 *Telegraph* (Prahran), 28 June 1875, p. 3; *North Melbourne Courier*, 9 February 1900, p. 3.
46 *Northern Star and Leeds General Advertiser*, 31 July 1841, p. 16.
47 *London Evening Standard*, 12 November 1841, p. 4.
48 FB Smith.
49 Quoted in Sante, pp. 138–9.

CHAPTER 6
1 Bate, 'Why Is Victoria Different?'
2 Trollope, pp. 105–6.
3 VPRS Inquest 1874/244.
4 Cahir.
5 Boucher and Russell.
6 Smith et al.
7 William Howitt, p. 126.
8 See Theobald, pp. 1–37, for a brilliant account of the alluvial diggings at Mount Alexander.
9 Fahey, 'Peopling the Victorian Goldfields'.
10 Bate, *Lucky City*, p. 91.
11 According to the Founders and Survivors Ships Project dataset (see Appendix A), the deaths at Bendigo, Ballarat and on the goldfields totalled 382 men and 114 women.
12 *Mount Alexander Mail*, 2 November 1855, p. 6.
13 Evans.
14 Bate, *Lucky City*, p. 190; Holst.
15 *The Star* (Ballarat), 26 January 1858, p. 3.
16 Davies, Lawrence and Twigg.
17 Taylor.
18 Collins.
19 Malcolm.
20 Reeves.
21 *The Star* (Ballarat), 29 May 1867, p. 4.
22 McLaughlin, pp. 5–15.
23 *The Argus*, 23 October 1854, p. 5.
24 Ibid., 5 April 1860, p. 5; 19 February 1861, p. 6; *Bendigo Advertiser*, 24 November 1862, p. 3.
25 *The Argus*, 11 October 1867, p. 6; 14 February 1871, p. 4.
26 Ibid., 18 May 1855, p. 6.
27 Ibid., 27 May 1859, p. 4.
28 *The Age*, 12 July 1858, p. 5.
29 *The Star* (Ballarat), 6 February 1858, p. 3.
30 *The Age*, 17 February 1858, p. 5.
31 *The Star* (Ballarat), 7 May 1861, p. 1.
32 Nathan Spielvogel in the *Herald*, 14 January 1939, p. 32.
33 *The Star* (Ballarat), 26 April 1860, p. 2.

34 Ibid., 4 March 1860, p. 1; 26 March 1861, p. 2.
35 Bate, *Lucky City*, pp. 21–2.
36 *The Star* (Ballarat), 19 October 1867, p. 3.
37 Ibid., 2 April 1864, p. 4.
38 Victorian DC: 1878/348, 1883/3988.
39 *The Star* (Ballarat), 30 April 1861, p. 1.
40 Ibid., 7 August 1862, p. 4.
41 *Herald*, 15 February 1866, p. 2.
42 *The Star* (Ballarat), 25 September 1858, p. 2; 8 September 1862, p. 1; research by Colette McAlpine.
43 Victorian DC: 1885/7750, 1888/26.
44 Gittins.
45 *Bendigo Advertiser*, 29 December 1870, p. 2.
46 Ibid., 19 August 1868, p. 2.
47 Ibid., 20 April 1869, p. 2.
48 *The Argus*, 25 March 1873, p. 6.
49 Victorian DC: 1920/8642.

CHAPTER 7
1 See Cannon, *Vagabond Country*, pp. 193–4.
2 VPRS Inquest 1862/774.
3 'Navvies' was a shortening of 'navigators' that referred to labourers.
4 *The Argus*, 6 August 1861, p. 5.
5 VPRS 41/PO Unit 44, surveyor O'Brien's letter, 24 September 1862.
6 Schedvin and Schedvin.
7 Victorian DC: 1869/1435; VPRS.
8 'The Old Bark Hut', in Paterson, pp. 12–16.
9 *Kyneton Observer*, 27 February 1864, p. 2.
10 Ibid., 7 November 1863, p. 2.
11 Ibid., 10 December 1874, p. 2.
12 *Bendigo Advertiser*, 14 February 1868, p. 2.
13 *McIvor Times and Rodney Advertiser*, 4 February 1887, p. 2.
14 Boyce, *Imperial Mud*; Scott, *The Art of Not Being Governed*.
15 Courtwright.
16 *Bendigo Advertiser*, 31 January 1879.
17 *Kyneton Observer*, 22 December 1860, p. 3.
18 Ibid., 25 June 1861, p. 2.
19 Victorian DC: 1883/11536, 1884/3041.

20 *The Age*, 10 June 1857, p. 3.
21 *Kyneton Observer*, 14 September 1878, p. 2.
22 *The Argus*, 29 September 1870, p. 4.
23 *Kyneton Observer*, 12 March 1864, p. 2.
24 *Kerang Times*, 27 April 1888, p. 2.
25 Dawson.
26 VPRS 7591, item 69/823, 1891.
27 Evans.
28 McQuilton, p. 45; see also Fahey, 'The Free Selectors' Landscape'.
29 *Kyneton Observer*, 23 October 1862, p. 2.
30 Campbell, pp. 85–103.
31 Garry McLoughlin, biography of Michael McLoughlin in Founders and Survivors Ships Project.
32 My thanks to Mary Elizabeth Calwell, Garry McLoughlin and Barry Gough for the family history of Michael McLoughlin.
33 *Kyneton Observer*, 18 November 1892, p. 2.

CHAPTER 8
1 Humphries, p. 192.
2 See Appendix A.
3 VPRS Inquest 1861/173.
4 VPRS inquests 1865/843, 1889/1635, 1879/886; LIH Cohort, George born to Harriet Woodhead, 4 October 1879.
5 *The Star* (Ballarat), 30 December 1858, p. 4.
6 Engelhardt et al.
7 VPRS 515/2354.
8 Tanner.
9 Larson, pp. 23–4.
10 Barrett, pp. 55–71.
11 Dingle and Merrett, 'Home Owners and Tenants in Melbourne, 1891–1911'; 'Landlords in Suburban Melbourne, 1891–1911'.
12 *Leader*, 20 June 1863, p. 5.
13 See Appendix A.
14 VPRS 1853/28, item 1/059.
15 VPRS 1857/8, item 2/164; 515/12735 William (Henry); 515/35435 William (Harry) Moxham.
16 VPRS 1881/28, item 21/478.
17 VPRS 1886/7591, item 32/922.

18 *The Age*, 13 February 1879, p. 3; *The Australasian*, 2 August 1884, p. 28; *The Age*, 15 June 1905, p. 6.
19 Collingwood Rate Books: 1864, 1874, 1891.
20 VPRS 1884/7591, item 19/600, 1884.
21 Will of Thomas Pearce, VPRS 1901/28, item 80/304, 1901.
22 VPRS 1882/28, item 24/848, 1882.
23 VPRS 1886/7591, item 33/530, 1886.
24 Jackson.
25 *The Argus*, 28 January 1871, p. 4.
26 McCalman, Morley, Smith and Anderson.
27 Scheper-Hughes.
28 *Bendigo Advertiser*, 24 May 1888, p. 2.
29 VPRS Inquest 1861/486.
30 See Appendix A.
31 *The Argus*, 15 July 1870, p. 5; 12 October 1870, p. 6.
32 VPRS Inquest 1872/222.
33 *The Argus*, 2 January 1861, p. 4; 6 July 1861, p. 6.
34 McCalman, '"All Just Melted with Heat"'.
35 *The Age*, 20 November 1857, p. 6; *The Argus*, 18 March 1903, p. 6.
36 *The Argus*, 17 September 1867, p. 5.
37 Clarke, p. 74; see also Sleight, p. 31.
38 *The Argus*, 23 July 1883, p. 6.
39 *Mercury and Weekly Courier*, 30 August 1879, p. 2.
40 *The Argus*, 29 January 1875, p. 5.

CHAPTER 9
1 *Illustrated Australian News*, 23 November 1867, p. 28.
2 Ibid.
3 *The Australasian*, 21 December 1867, p. 15.
4 *The Bacchus Marsh Express*, 25 January 1868, p. 2.
5 Ibid.
6 *The Aberdeen Journal*, 2 October 1844, p. 4.
7 Ibid.
8 Memorial notice, 'inserted by loving son and daughter': *The Sydney Morning Herald*, 6 July 1914, p. 10.
9 *Prahran Telegraph*, 13 April 1907, p. 5.
10 *Leader*, 30 July 1870, p. 19.
11 Howe and Swain.
12 Victorian DC: 1907/8321.
13 Victorian DC: 1884/1779.
14 *The Armagh Guardian*, 1 June 1860, p. 2.
15 *Mount Alexander Mail*, 17 August 1860, p. 3.
16 *Leader*, 9 October 1886, p. 29; 23 October 1886, p. 30.
17 *The Age*, 30 October 1872, p. 4; *The Argus*, 1 November 1872, p. 5.
18 *The Age*, 22 November 1872, p. 4.
19 *South Bourke Standard*, 18 October 1861, p. 3; *The Record and Emerald Hill and Sandridge Advertiser*, 19 December 1872, p. 2.
20 *Geelong Advertiser*, 16 November 1869, p. 2.
21 Alexander.
22 Kosten, Williams and Mitchell; Kosten and Mitchell.
23 Victorian DC: 1885/1326.
24 See Appendix A.
25 McCalman, 'To Die without Friends'.
26 Braithwaite.
27 Pell.
28 James, pp. 139–67.
29 Scates.
30 *Bendigo Independent*, 14 October 1899, p. 4.
31 *Bendigo Advertiser*, 13 August 1884, p. 2.
32 *The Argus*, 24 August 1864, p. 4.
33 *Leader*, 11 June 1887, p. 36.
34 Readers can consult Professor Mark Finnane's website 'The Prosecution Project' (https://prosecutionproject.griffith.edu.au), hosted by Griffith University, and reconstruct these and other tables for themselves.
35 FB Smith.
36 *The Argus*, 14 November 1870, p. 7.
37 Lewis.
38 *Leader*, 20 December 1902, p. 32.

CHAPTER 10
1 For an excellent discussion of this historiography, see Roberts, '"More

1. Sinned against than Sinning'"; Robson; Shaw.
2. Nicholas and Steckel; Johnson and Nicholas.
3. Nicholas; Oxley; Meredith and Oxley, 'The Convict Economy'.
4. Meredith and Oxley, 'Contracting Convicts'.
5. Anderson.
6. Summers.
7. Portia Robinson.
8. Daniels; Damousi.
9. Maxwell-Stewart, *Closing Hell's Gates*; Tuffin et al.; Maxwell-Stewart, Inwood and Stankovich.
10. See Appendix A, Figure A1.
11. See Appendix A, Figure A2.
12. See Appendix A, Figure A3.
13. See Appendix A, Figure A4; Figure A5.
14. See Appendix A, Figure A6.
15. See Appendix A, Figure A7.
16. A generalised linear model was run separately for males and females, for convicts who arrived when under the age of fifty, and for those who died after fifty (to eliminate premature death that may have limited fertility). The intention was to see whether more children and grandchildren were related to longer life expectancy, controlling for other influencing factors: country of birth, place of birth, year of arrival, age at arrival, time under sentence, solitary confinement, alcohol offences, marriage, and for women, being on the town. The *male* analysis had a highly significant result: controlling for other factors, marriage after transportation was associated with an increased life expectancy of 1.4 years ($p=0.000$), each additional child was linked to an increased life expectancy of 0.25 years ($p=0.000$), and survival to the third generation (that is, grandchildren) was associated with an increased life expectancy of 1.8 years ($p=0.000$). The *female* results were quite different: for women it was survival to the third generation that mattered, and grandchildren were associated with a 2.6-year increase in average life expectancy over age fifty ($p=0.000$). See McCalman and Kippen.
17. McCalman and Kippen.
18. McCalman and Smith.
19. McCalman, Smith, Anderson, Morley and Mishra.
20. See Appendix A, Figure A8.
21. Russell.
22. See Appendix A, Figure A5.
23. Kippin et al.; Sampson and Laub; Ouellet-Morin; Mitchell et al.; Goldfeld et al.
24. Swain, Eadie and Snow.
25. Warner.
26. National Trust Tasmania.
27. Ibid.
28. Ibid.
29. Reynolds.
30. McCalman, Kippen, McMeeken, Hopper and Reade. This is a preliminary publication from the ARC project 'Diggers to Veterans: Risk, Resilience and Recovery in the First AIF'. The AIF descendants of convicts continued to be overrepresented among the very poor in this cohort of war volunteers. These barriers to wealth creation and upward social mobility would not be broken until the postwar era.

Index

à Beckett, William, 84–5
Aboriginal people
  child removal, 245
  colonisation of, 244–6
  impact of gold rush, 138
  massacres and dispossession, 72, 73–7
  population in Victoria, 71–3, 138, 245, 246
  reserves, 82, 83, 138, 245, 246
  secondary infertility, 199, 246
Aboriginal Protection Board, 138
abortion, 199
Aboukir (convict ship), 61
age of consent, 27, 204
agrarian revolution, 17–18
alcohol abuse, 62, 107–8, 132–5, 186–7, 233, 243
alcoholism, 16, 28, 87, 112, 126, 135, 188, 243, 246, 247
Alexander, Alison, 227
America (convict ship), 29
Amherst, 146
Anderson, Clare, 238
Anderson, Margaret (*Margaret*, 1843), 65, 266
Anderson's Creek, 92
Angus, Margaret (*Margaret*, 1843), 65, 266
Anson (convict ship, later hulk), 55, 56
Appleyard, Peter (*Norfolk*, 1835), 30, 82, 267
Ararat, 146
Ararat Lunatic Asylum, 123
Archer, William Henry, 95
artists, 53, 250
Ashby (now Geelong West), 76
Askew, Alexandrina (see Alexandrina Grant), 212–17
aspirationals, 217–24
Asquith, Christian (*Maria*, 1820), 97, 267
Austin, Catherine, 79
Australia Felix, 70–1
Axford, Mary Ann (*Atwick*, 1838), 161, 267

baby farmers, 197
Back Creek, 151
Backway, Daniel (*Tortoise*, 1842)
  background and early life, 22–3, 186, 252
  biography, 267
  deaths of children, 200
  on electoral roll, 144, 147
  family and lineage, 21–2, 112
  fictional backstory, 228
  as gold miner, 21, 112, 141
  transportation to Van Diemen's Land, 21
  travel to Victoria, 21, 109, 112
Baldock, Helen/Ellen (*Hector*, 1835), 62, 69, 268
Ballarat, 92, 140, 141, 146, 147, 153–7, 162
Ballarat Benevolent Asylum, 2, 7, 146, 162, 230, 231, 248
Ballarat Reform League, 143
Ballarat School of Mines, 205
Banigan/Barrigan/Bannagan, James (*Equestrian*, 1845), 170, 268
Banks, Thomas (*John Renwick*, 1843), 32, 268
Bannister, Benjamin (*Aurora*, 1835), 97, 268
Barfoot, Ann, 172–3
Barfoot, John, 172
Barker, Henry (*Circassian*, 1833), 144–5, 268
Barkley, Joseph, 249
Barossa (convict ship), 37
Batman, Henry, 77
Batman, John, 81, 85, 222, 223
Beatson, John (*Neptune*, 1838), 174, 269
Beechworth, 146
Beechworth Lunatic Asylum, 132, 146
Belfast, 27
Bellamy, Martha (*Sovereign*, 1827), 87–8, 269
Bendigo, 146, 147, 157–8
  Charcoal Gully, 158–61
  class divisions, 227–8
  discovery of gold, 92, 96–7
  red-light district, 158

Bendigo Benevolent Asylum, 205, 231
Bendigo School of Mines, 205
benevolent asylums, 146, 162, 230–2
Bennett, Thomas, 109
Bentley (nee Sherran), Catherine, 148–9
Bentley, James Francis (*Blundell*, 1844), 148, 149–50, 269
Bentley, Mary (*Atwick*, 1838), 62, 69, 269
Bentley (nee Ford), Margaret (*Elizabeth and Henry*, 1847), 154
Berry, Graham, 226
Bickley, Sarah (*Asia*, 1847), 161, 269–70
Bidgood, John (*Augusta Jessie*, 1835), 195, 270
bilking, 25, 106, 113, 117, 132
Bird, Frederick (*Waverley*, 1841), 138, 270
Black (later Marshall), Janet (*Lady of the Lake*, 1829), 79, 80–1, 230
Black Act 1723, 29
Black Thursday, 90
Blackburn, James (*Isabella*, 1833), 200–1, 230, 270–1
Blackford (formerly Cosgrove), Margaret (*Waverley*, 1847), 127–9, 275–6
Blackford, James (*Louisa*, 1845), 128, 271
Blackfriar (convict ship), 36
Blackwood, 166, 173
Blackwood Settlement, 173
Blainey, Geoffrey, 96
Blenheim (convict ship), 35
Blue Mountain (Trentham), 166, 182
Bodycott, John (*Marion*, 1844), 24, 271
Bodycott, Thomas (*Duncan*, 1841), 24, 271
Bodycott brothers, 23–4
Bolton, John, 45
Bones, Benjamin (*Henry Porcher*, 1835), 30, 271
Bones, Thomas (*Henry Porcher*, 1835), 30, 272
Boyce, James, 65
Boyd family, 85
Boyle, Archibald (*Egyptian*, 1839), 123
Braithwaite, John, 229
Brentani, Charles (*Aurora*, 1835), 272
brewers, 84–5
Briant/Bryant, John Moon (*Mangles*, 1835), 224–6, 272

Bristol, 26
Brooks, Joseph, 152–3
Brooks, Thomas (*William Miles*, 1828), 48–50
Broom, Mary, 162
Broom, William (*Atlas*, 1833), 162, 272–3
brothels, 69, 117–18, 124–7, 153–7. *See also* prostitution
Bryanton, George, 227
Buninyong, 92
Burman, Alfred, 202
Burman, Arthur, 202
Burman, Benjamin (*Mangles*, 1835), 202, 273
Burnett, William (*Barossa*, 1844), 37–8, 273
burns, 188–90
Burrell, Jane (*Tory*, 1848), 55–7, 273
Burt, Caroline (*Rajah*, 1841), 200, 273
bush fires, 90
bushrangers, 101–3, 232
business women, 67
Butler, Edward (*Chapman*, 1827), 221–2, 273–4
Byles, Jenny, 249–50
Byrne, Margaret (*John William Dare*, 1852), 208, 274

Californian gold rush, 92, 96, 101
Calwell, Arthur Albert, 183
Calwell, Arthur Augustus, 183–4
Cann, Ann, 180, 181
Carlton, 206
Cascades Female Factory, 216
'cashed-up bogans', 105
Castlemaine, 93, 147, 158, 205
Castlemaine Benevolent Asylum, 146, 231
Cavanagh, Henry (*Enchantress*, 1833), 37, 187, 274
Cavanagh, Jane, nee Robertson, (*Rajah*, 1841) 230–1
Cavanagh, Lydia, 187
Cavanagh, Martha, 187
Chaplin, William (*Strathfieldsaye*, 1831), 195, 274
character, 5, 7, 57–8, 82, 142
Charcoal Gully, 157–61
charity, 247
Chartism, 23, 32, 142, 143, 167, 169

INDEX

Cherry, Samuel (*Candahar*, 1842), 173, 274
child abuse and neglect, 27–8, 186, 188, 197–8, 199, 203, 208–9
child mortality, 196, 199–201, 202, 241
child prostitution, 27, 127–9, 204
child rescue, 222
children
　cognitive impairment, 203
　education, 202–3
　play, 202
　sexual exploitation, 204
Chinese farmers, 180
Chuter, Thomas (*Woodman*, 1826), 193, 274
City Mission, 222
Clark, Manning, 237
Clarke, Marcus, 206
Claudine (convict ship), 45, 47, 59
Clements, Adam (*Mount Stewart Elphinstone*, 1845), 194–5, 274–5
Clements, Charlotte, 134–5
Clements, Eliza (*Hindostan*, 1839) alias Eliza White, 122, 134–5, 275
Clunes, 92, 146
cognitive impairment, 230, 247
Cohen, Simon, 225
Coleman, William Edward, 97
collectivism, 142
Collingwood, 192–6, 200, 201–2, 206, 207, 210, 211
Collingwood football team, 211
Colreavy/Colreavey, James (*Navarino*, 1843), 190, 275
commons, 145
convict legacy, rethinking of, 246–52
convict ships
　cohorts, 60–1
　discipline and punishment, 43–5, 61
　naval surgeons, 42, 43–5
　voyage to Van Diemen's land, 41–4
　women's ships, 61
convict transportation
　benefits of, 11
　as chain migration method, 41
　criticism of, 50–1
　from England, 34–5
　impact on making of Australia, 14
　from Ireland, 32–7
　from Scotland, 34–5, 37–8
　to Van Diemen's Land, 3, 40
convict-descended population, 67
convicts
　born bad or made bad? 15–17, 38, 236–44
　cradle-to-grave data on, 239
　family backgrounds, 20–1, 23
　'gentlemen' convicts, 59
　letters home, 48–9
　place of female convicts in Australian narrative, 238–9
　prospects following release, 4–7
　rates of re-offending, 248
　rights as British subjects, 3–4
　voyage to Van Diemen's land, 55–6
　See also Van Diemen's Land penal system; Vandemonians
Convicts' Prevention Act 1852, 112
Cooper, Daniel (*Red Rover*, 1831), 153, 275
Copping, Mary (*Rajah*, 1841), 200, 275
Coranderrk reserve, 82, 83, 138
Cork, 27
Cosgrove (later Blackford), Margaret (*Waverley*, 1847), 127–9, 275–6
Cray, John (*Isabella*, 1842), 116, 155–7, 276
Cray, Mary (daughter of Mary and John), 156, 157
Cray, Mary, (transported as Holehouse), 156, 238
Creswick, 146, 147
crime economy, 25
crime rates, 17, 108, 229, 232–3
Crisp (nee Butler), Jane Mary, 221–2
Crisp, James Walter, 221–2
Crisp, Samuel (*Earl St Vincent*, 1826), 67, 70, 222, 276
Crisp family, 222
Crooke, Dr William, 225–6
Crowson, Samuel (*Georgiana*, 1833), 202, 276
Cuddihy, Daniel (*Duke of Richmond*, 1844), 33, 276
Cullen, Margaret (*Lord Auckland*, 1849), 163, 276
Cummeragunja mission, 246
Curr, Edward, 100

333

Dalton, William (*David Clarke*, 1841), 115, 277
Darwin, Charles, 59, 236–7
Daylesford, 146
death certificates, 174, 222–3, 224, 228–9
death notices, 194
Denison, Sir William, 90
destitution, 64–5, 109
diarrhoea, 200
diphtheria, 200
Disney, Elizabeth (*Harmony*, 1829), 33, 190–1, 277
Doherty, Catherine (*Hope*, 1842), 234
domestic training, 55, 56
domestic violence, 171–3, 174–5, 189
Dowsett, Daniel, 181
Dowsett, James (*Henry Porcher*, 1836), 180–2, 277
Dowsett, Thomas, 181–2
Drinkwater, William (*Surrey*, 1833), 129, 133–4, 277
drunkenness, 62, 107–8, 109, 170, 233, 243
Dublin, 27
Dudgeon, John (*Gilmore*, 1843), 223, 277–8
Duff, Paul (*Isabella Watson*, 1842), 16, 141–2, 278
Duffy, Charles Gavan, 95
Duke of Richmond (convict ship), 33, 34
Duncan (convict ship), 24
Dunn, Janet (*Gilbert Henderson*, 1840), 42, 123, 278
Dunolly, 146
Duvall, Jane Starsmore, 98
dysentery, 200, 241

Earl Grey (convict ship), 35
East London (convict ship), 36, 45
Eastern Market, Melbourne, 117
economic historians, 237–8
economy of makeshifts, 20
Edinburgh, 27
education, 146, 202–3, 204, 205–6
Education Act 1872, 146, 203
Edward (convict ship), 88
Edwards, John, 50
Edwards, Thomas, 114–15
Ellis, Edward (*John Renwick*, 1843), 32, 278

Elmore, Elizabeth, 63
Elphinstone (convict ship), 41
Emerald Hill, 206, 231
employment, character and, 57–8
Enchantress (convict ship), 37
Enclosure Act 1801, 31
England, 4, 17, 18, 19, 20
Eshitt/Eskitt/Eskett/Escott, Jane (later Pickering) (*Garland Grove*, 1841), 109–10, 279
Esmond, James, 92
Esmond Street, Ballarat, 153–7
eugenics, 15
Eureka Hotel, 148, 149
Eureka Rebellion, 143–4, 149
Evans, Mary (later Kate Gorman) (*Royal Admiral*, 1842), 28–9, 132–3, 279

factories, 191–2, 210–11
Factories and Shops Act, 210
Fairchild (formerly Fennelly), Mary (*Gilbert Henderson*, 1840), 219–21, 222–3, 279–80
Fairchild, Jesse, 220–1, 222, 223
families
 backgrounds of convicts, 16, 20–1, 23, 186–7, 243–4
 convict descendants in First AIF, 22, 78, 81, 82, 155, 161, 175, 188, 189, 207, 251
 creating lineages, 67, 185–7, 244
 extended families, 189–91
 intergenerational trauma, 187–9
 marriages of convicts, 62, 67, 70, 82, 85, 163, 174, 244
 and social status, 6
family violence, 189
farm workers, 75
farmers, 178–84
Farrell, John (*Forfarshire*, 1843), 148
Farrer, James, 220, 222
Fawkner, John Pascoe, 79, 226
Felton (later Wood), Ann (*Emma Eugenia*, 1846), 124, 279
Female Convict Research Centre, 263
female factories, 48, 51, 53–4, 62–3, 216
Fennelly (later Fairchild), Mary (*Gilbert Henderson*, 1840), 219–21, 222–3, 279–80

INDEX

Finnane, Catherine, 162
fires, 188–90
First AIF, convict descendants in, 22, 78, 81, 82, 155, 161, 175, 188, 189, 207, 251
Fisher, Elizabeth, 127–8
Fitzgerald, Patrick (*Isabella Watson*, 1842), 200, 280
Fitzgerald, Winifred (*Waverley*, 1842), 131–2, 280
Fitzroy, 192, 206, 225
flashness, 58, 62–3
Fleming, Catherine (*Rajah*, 1841), 109, 280
Fletcher, Samuel (*Claudine*, 1821), 59–60, 280
flogging, 242
foetal alcohol syndrome, 203, 247
forced chain migration, 41
forced labour, 238
Ford, Lydia (*Royal Admiral*, 1842), 144–5, 281
forest conservation, 145
Forrester, Charles (*Coromandel*, 1838), 172, 281
'Founders and Survivors: Convict Life Courses in Historical Context' database, 13
Founders and Survivors Ships Project, 13–14, 242–4, 248, 263
    data, 252–62
Fowler (later Howe), Elizabeth (*Navarino*, 1841), 124–6, 281
Foy, James (*Surrey*, 1842), 207, 281
Framlingham reserve, 82–3, 138, 222
Fraser (later Butler), Ellen (*Harmony*, 1829), 221–2, 281
free immigrants, 86, 87
Frith, Charles (*William Jardine*, 1844), 194, 282
frontier sexual economy, 77
frontier violence, 73–7
Fry, Elizabeth, 48
funeral notices, 194

Game Act 1831, 29
Geelong, ex-convict population, 90
Geelong and Portland Bay Emigration Scheme, 87–8
Gellion, John, 82

'gentlemen' convicts, 59
George III (convict ship), 137
Gilbert Henderson (convict ship), 3, 9, 41, 42–3, 47, 120, 122, 219
Gilligan, Luke (*Marion*, 1844), 170–1, 282
Gippsland, 76, 82
Gisborne, 166
Glasgow, 27
Glover, John, 250
Goddard, Emma, 177
gold rush immigrants, 94–6, 136–7, 139, 192
gold rush in California, 92, 96, 101
gold rush in Victoria
    economic impact, 96, 136–7
    environmental impact, 137–8, 139
    impact on population, 94, 204, 206
    threat to social order, 101–2, 105–6
goldfields in Victoria
    commons, 145
    early finds, 90–1
    Eureka Rebellion, 143–4, 149
    lucky Vandemonian diggers, 96–100, 103–7
    robberies, 101–3, 106–7
    rushes, 150–3
    women on, 151, 152
    work and living conditions, 139–41
Goodall, Thomas, 228
Goodall, William (Jr), 82–3
Goodall, William (*Lady Harewood*, 1829), 62, 70, 77, 82, 147, 179, 222, 228, 282
Goodluck family, 67
Gorman, Kate, (transported as Mary Evans) 132–3
Gosling, Benjamin (*Surrey*, 1833), 115, 282
Gosling, Mary Ann, 115
Gough, Edwin (*Pestongee Bomangee*, 1847), 195, 282
Gould, Ben, 234
Grady, Mary (*Hindostan*, 1839), 282–3
Graham, James, 97
Graham, Thomas, 202
Graham, William, 202
Grant, Alexandrina (*Jemima McKenzie*) (later Alexandrina/Alice Askew) (*Tory*, 1845), 44, 214–17, 283
    skills, 46

Griffiths, Thomas, 79
group forgetting, 227
Guise, William (*Chapman*, 1824), 87, 283

Hale, Hannah, 84
Half-Caste Act 1886, 245
Halfpenny, Philip, 194, 207
Halfpenny, Thomas (*Lady Harewood*, 1829), 84, 194, 207, 283
Hamett, Sir John, 42, 43, 44
Hamilton, James, 165
Hampton, Thomas, 107
Hancock, Keith, 237
Hanley, Ellen/Nellie Roberts (*Greenlaw*, 1844), 123, 283
Harris, Bridget (transported as Biddy Craig, *Waverley*, 1842), 123, 284
Harris, John Danley, 80
Harrold, Emma, 125, 126, 127
Harrold, James, 126
Harrold, John, 126
Harrold, (nee Lochrie) Mary, 125, 126, 127
Hartman, Henry, 107
Hartridge, Maria, 154
Havelock, 152
Hayes, Agnes, 157
Haynes, George (*Westmoreland*, 1841), 190, 284
Henry Porcher (convict ship), 30
Hill, Mary (*Navarino*, 1841), 195, 284
Hindostan, 120, 122
Hinkins, Jane, 83
Hinkins, John (*Earl St Vincent*, 1826), 83-4, 284
Hipper, John (*Asia*, 1840), 193-4
historical demography, 12-13
Hobler, George, 49
Hockey, Elizabeth, 173
Hockey, James (*Sir Charles Forbes*, 1830), 172-3, 284
Holehouse (nee Morgan, later Cray), Mary (*Tory*, 1845), 29, 116, 155-7, 284-5
Holyoake, Margaret, 188
homophobia, 90
Hope, Jonathan, 68
Hopkins, Alfred, 126

Hopkins, Richard, 126
hospitals, 146, 162, 231, 232
housing
  in Collingwood, 191, 192-3, 201-2, 211
  overcrowding, 201-2, 211
Howe (formerly Fowler), Elizabeth (*Navarino*, 1841), 124-6, 281
Howe, Minnie, 125-6
Howe, Richard, 125
Howitt, Richard, 41, 90
Howitt, William, 136, 139-40
Hughes, Lewis, 165-6
hulks, 55, 56, 102-3
Hull, Hugh Munro, 52
Humphries, Jane, 186
Humphries, Louisa, 81
'hut culture', 66
Huxley, Ann (*Edward*, 1834), 88, 285
Huxley, Francis, 88
Hyderabad (convict ship), 61

Immigrants' Home, 230, 231
industrial revolution, 17, 19
infant mortality, 189, 196-8, 241, 245
infectious diseases, 200-1, 241-2
infertility, 199, 244, 246
Ing, Edward (*Augusta Jessie*, 1835), 165-6, 285
Inglewood, 146
intergenerational poverty, 251-2
intergenerational trauma, 187-9
intimate violence, 189
Ireland, 4, 17, 20, 27
Irish convicts, 32-7, 61
Irish famine, 27, 33, 34, 35
Irish farmers, 181, 182
Irish orphans, 149
Isabella Watson (convict ship), 16

Jenkins, Joseph, 142, 179, 231
Jewish convicts, 86
John Renwick (convict ship), 32
Johnson, Joseph, 131
Jones, Ann (*Hindostan*, 1839), 122, 285
Jones, Thomas, 224
juvenile reformatories, 21, 54-5

INDEX

Kangaroo Flat, 158
Keelen/Keelan, Sidney (*Earl Grey*, 1850), 35, 223–4, 285–6
Kelly, Ned, 56, 178, 233–4
Kelly Gang, 178, 229, 233
Kendrick, William (*Persian*, 1830), 171, 286
Keogh/Kehoe family, 35, 286
Kew Lunatic Asylum, 60
Kilmore, 146, 166, 182
Kimber (Kimmer), James (*Eliza*, 1831), 31, 99–100, 179, 286
Kimpton, Charlotte (*Lloyds*, 1845), 195, 286
King, Anne (*Angelina*, 1844), 132, 286–7
Kinnear, Mary (*Margaret*, 1843), 64–5, 287
Kippen, Rebecca, 244
Kirwin, Martin, 33–4
Koroit, 182
Kurnai people, 72, 76
Kyneton, 146, 166
  deaths of Vandemonians, 167–75
  farmers, 178–84
  rebellion by railway workers, 166–7
  tradesmen, 176–8
Kyneton Hospital, 169, 171, 181

La Trobe, Charles, 105, 143
lady swindler, 212–13
Lake Tyers reserve, 82, 138
Lalor, Peter, 143, 144
land, importance of, 4–5
Langford, William, 168
Langham, Frederick, 60
Langham, Samuel (*Claudine*, 1821), 59–60, 66, 287
larrikins, 206–10, 229, 250
Launceston Female Factory, 63
Layton (convict ship), 30
Leary (later Burgess), Ellen (*Gilbert Henderson*, 1840), 42, 122–3, 287
Leaver, Sophia (*Tory*, 1845), 173, 287
Lees, Margaret, 137
Leeson, Lydia (*Emma Eugenia*, 1844), 287–8
Leicester, 23–4
Lewis, Brian, 234
Lewis, Mary/Margaret (*Hindostan*, 1839), 122, 288

Lewis, Samuel, 122
Light, Edwin, 177
Light, John (*Eden*, 1836), 176–7, 288
literacy, 242
Little Bourke Street, 86, 104, 107, 113, 115, 116, 206
Liverpool, 26, 27
living conditions of emancipists, 65–70
Lloyd, Richard (*Sir Robert Peel*, 1844), 174, 288
Lochrie (later Harrold), Mary (*Margaret*, 1843), 65, 110, 126, 128, 288
London
  crime economy, 25–6
  prostitution, 28
London Ladies' Missionary Society, 42–3
Long, Benjamin (*Equestrian*, 1845), 173, 289
Long, Thomas (*Hyderabad*, 1850), 195, 289
Longfoot, Thomas, 28
Lord Goderich (convict ship), 21
Lovett, William, 32, 143
Lowry, Catherine (*Rajah*, 1841), 63, 289
Luck, Joseph (*Moffatt*, 1834), 175, 178, 289
lunatic asylums, 146
Lying-In Hospital, Melbourne, 94, 104, 127, 188, 196

Macquarie Harbour penal station, 48
madness, 129–32
Maldon, 146
Malmsbury, 166
Malmsbury Volunteers, 167
'manliness', 142
manufacturing, 191–2, 204–5
Margaret (convict ship), 37, 64
Marlow, Samuel (*Sir Godfrey Webster*, 1823), 84, 85, 289
marriages of convicts, 62, 67, 70, 82, 85, 163, 174, 242, 244
Marshall, Charles, 80
Marshall, Gilbert (per *Recovery* to NSW, 1818, then *Deveron* to VDL, 1820), 78, 79, 84, 230, 289–90
Mary (convict ship), 29
Maryborough, 21, 141, 144, 145, 152
Masters' and Servants' Act 1856, 66
master–servant relationship, 59, 82

Maund, Dr John, 94, 104
Maxwell, James, 224
McAnally, Ellen (*Mexborough*, 1841), 172, 290
McAuliffe, Thomas (*Egyptian*, 1840), 234, 290
McCombie, Thomas, 106
McCormick, Jeremiah (*John Renwick*, 1843), 32, 234, 290
McCoy, Judith (*Atwick*, 1838), 33, 290
McDonald, Ann (*Midlothian*, 1853), 194, 290
McDonald, William, 214
McHague, Margaret (*Royal Admiral*, 1841), 137, 291
McIver, William (*William Jardine*, 1844), 37, 291
McLachlan, Lachlan, (Bendigo Mac) 157–8, 159, 160–1
McLoughlin, Bridget, 34
McLoughlin, Garry, 33
McLoughlin, Michael (*Duke of Richmond*, 1844), 33–4, 61, 182–3, 190, 228, 291
McLoughlin, Patrick, 34
McLoughlin, William, 183
McMillan, Angus, 75
McMullin, Ross, 111
McNeil, Anne (later Spong) (*Tasmania*, 1845), 199, 291
McQuade, Rose (*East London*, 1843), 36–7, 291
McQuade, William, 36
McQuilton, John, 189
measles, 200, 241
mechanics' institutes, 142
Melbourne, 76
  living conditions, 114
  markets, 117
  physical splendour and economy, 191–2
  police force, 101, 110
  red-light district, 115–16, 118
  theatre district, 113, 116
Melbourne Benevolent Asylum, 22, 115, 126, 134, 195, 225, 226, 230, 231
Melbourne Gaol, 121
Melbourne Hospital, 195, 231
Melville/Malvelle/McCallum, Edward/Francis (*Minerva*, 1838), 102–3, 291–2

mental torment, 242–3
Metcalf, George, 178
Metcalf, Robert (*Moffatt*, 1834), 176, 177–8, 292
Methodism, 58, 69–70, 222
Metropolitan Lunatic Asylum, 133–4
Meyers/Myers, Annette (*Emma Eugenia*, 1851), 218, 292
midwives, 199
Miles, Ellen (*Gilbert Henderson*, 1840), 120, 292
  background and early life, 2–3, 41–2, 252
  as benevolent asylum resident, 230
  as brothel keeper, 153–4
  in Collingwood, 193
  criminal record, 2, 16, 123, 128, 184, 234–5, 248
  death, 2
  imprisonment, 6, 193
  involvement with public institutions, 248
  records of her life, 9–10
  shipmates, 122–3
  siblings, 190
  skills, 6, 42
  solitary confinement, 63
  transportation, 2–3
  violent crime, 16, 132, 193
Miles, Lydia (*Royal Admiral*, 1842), 28–9, 132, 292
Miles, Moses, 2
Miles, Ruth (*Navarino*, 1840), 2–3, 292–3
Mills, Emma, 84–5
Mills, John (*Andromeda*, 1827), 84, 85, 293
miner's right, 32, 144
Mitchell, Sir Thomas, 70
Molesworth Report, 51, 90
Mooney, Patrick (*John Renwick*, 1845), 169–70, 181, 293
moral spectrum, 58–9
Moran, Francis (*Oriental Queen*, 1853), 208, 293
Morgan, Elizabeth (later Bet Naylor) (*America*, 1831), 29, 68, 153, 155
Morgan, Margaret, 68
Moriarty, Ellen (*Margaret*, 1843), 293–4

INDEX

mortality rates, 229
　child mortality, 196, 199–201, 202, 241
　female convicts, 239–40, 241
　infant mortality, 189, 196–8, 241, 245
　male convicts, 239–40, 242
Mosley, Agnes (*Gilbert Henderson*, 1840), 42, 122, 294
Mount Alexander, 92, 97, 103
Mount Macedon, 172
Moxham, Elizabeth, 112
Moxham, Henry (*Layton*, 1839), 193, 294
Moxham, John, 112
Moxham, Mary Ann, 112
Mundy, Godfrey Charles, 53–4
Murfitt/Murfett, James (*Thames*, 1829), 163, 294
Murphy, Mary, 182
Murray (later Thornton), Catherine (*Emma Eugenia*, 1844), 93–4, 294
Murtagh, Judith (*East London*, 1843), 173, 174, 294

Naden, John, 224
Napoleonic Wars, 17, 31
naval surgeons, 42, 43–5
Naylor, Bet (transported as Elizabeth Morgan, *America*, 1831), 68–9, 153, 155, 294–5
Naylor, Louisa, 155
Naylor, William (*Surrey*, 1829), 68, 295
Neville, Isaac (*Red Rover*, 1831), 175, 295
New Norfolk Lunatic Asylum, 131
newspapers, 142–3
Nicholls, Doug, 246
Night Poaching Act 1828, 29
Norfolk (convict ship), 30
North Melbourne, 192, 206, 231
nurses, 163, 199

Oakford, Catherine (*Royal Admiral*, 1842), 28–9, 132, 295
O'Brien, Mary (*Blackfriar*, 1851), 36–7, 296
Ogilvie, George (*Barossa*, 1842), 67, 296
Onus family, 245
Ormisher/Omisher, Mary Ann (*Emma Eugenia*, 1851), 208, 296

Owen, Margaret (*Gilbert Henderson*, 1840), 52
Owens, Eliza, 63
Oxley, Henry, 208
Oxley, Rebecca, 208
oyster bars, 115

Paddy's Market, 117
parish welfare system, 6, 7, 18–20, 23–4, 30–1
Parkinson, Roger, 220
Patrick, Sarah, 30, 98
Pearce, Jesse (*Tortoise*, 1842), 161, 296
Pearce, Thomas (*Asia*, 1840), 296
Peeler, William (*Woodford*, 1828), 62, 296–7
Pellegrini's Espresso Bar, 113
penal colonies, as open prisons, 11
Pentonville Exiles, 89, 90, 101, 111
Perrin, Ann (*Hindostan*, 1839), 122, 297
Perry, Frances, 104–5
Perry, Hannah (later Holyoake) (*Rajah*, 1841), 188, 297
Perry, Jane (*Margaret*, 1843), 65, 297
Perry, Mary, 122
Phillips, Samuel (*Mary 2*, 1830), 29–30, 46, 98–9, 100, 297
Pickering, George (*Lord Goderich*, 1841)
　background and early life, 22, 186
　biography, 297–8
　death, 115, 134
　illiteracy, 23
　in juvenile reformatory, 55
　as oysterman, 115
　siblings, 190
　transportation to Van Diemen's Land, 21
　travel to Victoria, 109–10
Pickering, Jane (mother of George), 22
Pickering, Margaret (*Tasmania*, 1844), 174–5
Pickering, Thomas (brother of George), 22
Pickering, Thomas (father of George), 22
Plymouth, 26
poaching, 29–30
Point Puer juvenile reformatory, Port Arthur, 21, 54–5
Poor Laws, 6, 11, 18–19, 20, 30, 142, 146, 162, 247–8

population
  Aboriginal people in Victoria, 71–3, 138, 245, 246
  convict-descended population, 67
  impact of gold rush, 94, 204, 206
  Victoria, 67, 87, 90, 93, 94, 101, 137, 204
population studies, 239–42
Port Albert, Gippsland, 76
Port Arthur penal station, 48
Port Fairy, 72, 76
Port Phillip, 70
Porter, Fanny, 132, 133
Portland, Victoria, 72, 73, 76
Portsmouth, 26
poverty
  biology of, 196–9
  excess of 'unemployables', 204
  intergenerational poverty, 251–2
  Poor Laws, 6, 11, 18–19, 20, 30, 142, 162
  re-creating the Parish, 145–7
  rural poverty in Britain, 4, 17–18
Power, Agnes, 53, 249
Power, Harry/Henry Johnson (*Isabella*, 1842), 56, 233, 299
Power, Helen, 249
pregnancy outside wedlock, 62
premature death, 196, 245
Pretty, William (*Surrey*, 1829), 87, 299
prisoner rehabilitation, 248
property, speculation and development, 5
prosopography, 10–13
prostitution
  associated offences, 108
  in British seaports, 27–9, 129–30
  brothels, 69, 117–18, 124–7, 153–7
  children, 27, 127–9, 204
  clients, 119
  convicts, 62
  the harlot's progress, 117–21
  madams and mothers, 124–7
  in Melbourne, 77, 118–19
  sisters and mates, 121–3
  theft and, 117
Prout, John Skinner, 250
Pryke (later Short), Mary Ann (*Sea Queen*, 1846), 130–1, 299

public order offences, 108, 110, 111, 163, 230, 233
punishment of convicts
  female factories, 48
  in first two decades of settlement, 48
  flogging, 48, 50, 52, 61, 242
  mental torment, 242–3
  secondary punishment, 48
  sentences, 46
  severe punishment, 61
  silent treatment, 51–2
  solitary confinement, 52, 61
  during voyage to Van Diemen's Land, 43, 45
Pyramid Hill, 176

Queen Victoria Market, 117

railways, 166–7
Rajah (convict ship), 37
Ramage, Ann (*Mellish*, 1830), 163, 299–300
Ramahyuck reserve, 138
Randall, Joseph (*Susan*, 1843), 200
rape, 27, 157, 202, 238
Read, Mary, 126
Red Ribbon Movement, 143
Reeves, James (*London*, 1844), 114–15, 300
Reform Act 1832, 32
respectability, 58–9, 60, 81–2, 84
Reynolds, Henry, 250
Richardson, Ann, 119–20, 122
Richmond, 201, 206
Richmond, Margaret (transported as Margaret Richardson, *Hindostan*, 1839), 90, 119–20, 121–2, 190, 252, 300
Richmond, Thomas (*Arab*, 1845), 120, 121
Roberts, John (*Frances Charlotte*, 1837), 123, 300
Robertson, Jane (later Cavanagh) (*Rajah*, 1841), 37, 88, 187, 230–1, 300
Robertson, Nancye/Nancey (*Rajah*, 1841), 37, 88–9, 300–1
Robinson, George Augustus, 74, 75, 76
Robinson, Julia (*Westmoreland*, 1846), 120–1
Robson, Lloyd, 237

INDEX

Robson, Margaret, 107
Rogers, Richard, 181
Rogers, Thomas (*Lord Petre*, 1843), 158–61, 301
Romeo Lane (bar), 113
Romeo Lane (right-of-way), 113–14, 118, 120, 122, 129, 130, 206
Rosedale, Gippsland, 76
rough culture, 58–9, 239
Rowe, Joseph, 115
Royal Admiral (convict ship), 28
rural poverty, 4, 17–18
Russell, Lynette, 246
Ryan, Mary (real name Ellen Bannon) (*Garland Grove*, 1843), 171–2, 301

Salmon, Catherine (*Mellish*, 1830), 173–4, 301
Salvation Army, 206, 226
Scarborough, George (*Caledonian*, 1820), 78, 79, 80, 81, 179, 301
Scarborough, Mary Ann (*Harmony*, 1829), 78–9
scarlatina, 200
scarlet fever, 200
Schofield (later Rogers), Eliza (*Asia*, 1847), 158–61, 301–2
schools of mines, 146, 205, 206
Scobie, James, 148
Scotland, 4, 17, 20, 27
Scottish convicts, 34–5, 37–8, 214–15, 217
sealers, 72
seaports, 27–8
Second Fleet, 44
secondary infertility, 199, 244, 246
Sefton, Catherine, 176
Sefton, Edward, 176
Sefton, George (*Orator*, 1843), 175–6, 302
self-improvement, 142–3
Serle, Geoffrey, 96, 97
sexual abuse, 247
sexual molestation, 170
Shaw, AGL, 237
Sheeran, Mary, 148–9
shepherds, 75, 87
Sheriff, Mary (*Atwick*, 1838), 63, 302

Ships Project. *See* Founders and Survivors Ships Project
Short (formerly Pryke), Mary Ann (*Sea Queen*, 1846), 130–1, 299
Short, Humphrey (*Augusta Jessie*, 1838), 130, 302
Shurley/Adlam/Drinkwater, Harriet (*Emma Eugenia*, 1844), 129, 130, 302–3
Sidebottom, William (*Medway*, 1825), 85, 303
Sinden/Sindon/Lindon, Luke (*Marquis of Hastings*, 1842), 108, 303
Sindon, Ann, 108
single mothers, 197
Singleton, Dr John, 118
Sir Charles Forbes (convict ship), 97
slavery, 11, 40, 238
sly grog, 116
smallpox, 71–2
Smith, Julia (*Westmoreland*, 1836), 33, 303
Smith, Rose Ann (*Margaret*, 1843), 37, 304
Snodgrass, Peter, 110
social dysphoria, 218
social history
  prosopography, 10–13
  writing of, 8–9
South Melbourne, 231
Southampton, 26
Speenhamland System, 31
Spong, Ann (later McNeil), 199
squatters, 74, 75, 77, 180
St Arnaud, 146
Stanger, Henry (*Tortoise*, 1842), 304
Starr, James (*Hyderabad*, 1849), 170, 304
Starr, William (*Marquis of Hastings*, 1842), 163, 304
Stawell, 146
Stevens, Margaret, 112
Stewart, Mary Ann, 123
Stubber, Robert, 33, 34
Studham, Elizabeth (*Mary*, 1831), 31, 304
Suffolk, Owen, 89–90
Sugden, Samuel (*George III*, 1835), 137, 305
Summers, Anne, 238–9
Sumner, Ada, 210
Sumner, Alice, 210

341

Sumner, Catherine, 209–10
Sumner, Ellen, 210
Sumner, Hugh (*Ratcliffe*, 1848), 209–10, 305
Sumner, Mary Ann, 210
Sutherland, Alexander, 99
Swain, Eliza (*Margaret*, 1843), 305
Swing Rioters, 31, 100
syphilis, 22, 27, 64, 73, 74

Taafe, Jane, 132
Tarraville, Gippsland, 76
Tasmania, impact of convict transportation, 250–1
Taylor, Lucy (transported as Lucilia De La Constantine, *Emma Eugenia*, 1864), 219, 305
The Skeleton Army, 206–7
Theatre Royal, Melbourne, 116
Theobald, Jane, 83
Thomas, William (*Surrey*, 1842), 114–15, 305
Thompson, William (*Lord Petre*, 1843), 161, 305–6
Thornton (formerly Murray), Catherine (*Emma Eugenia*, 1844), 93–4, 294
topsy-turvy, 104
Tortoise (convict ship), 21
Tory (convict ship), 29, 44, 156
toxic stress, 247
Tracy, Dr Richard, 94–6, 104
trade unionism, 147
trades halls, 147
travellers, 167–70
Trentham, 166, 182
Trenwith, William (*Earl St Vincent*, 1826), 230, 306
trustworthiness, 57–8
tuberculosis, 72, 201, 241–2, 245
Tumultuous Risings Act 1831, 61
typhoid, 200, 242

United Kingdom, 17
  enclosure of land, 4, 17–18, 31
  industrial revolution, 19
  Poor Laws, 6, 11, 18–19, 20, 30
  rural poverty, 4, 17–18
unskilled labour, 204

vagrancy, 81, 108
Van Diemen's Land penal system
  administration of, 11–12, 40
  assignment of new convicts, 46
  assignment system, 47–8, 50–1
  compliance by convicts, 52–4
  conduct records, 47–50
  identification of new convicts, 45
  juvenile reformatory, 21, 54–5
  probation system, 51, 56, 61, 66
  punishment of convicts, 48, 50
  resistance by convicts, 52
Vandemonaphobia, 111–12, 152, 232
Vandemonian cast, 100–1
Vandemonian hug, 106, 117
Vandemonians
  aspirationals, 217–24
  assimilation into respectable society, 147, 149–50, 152, 194, 225
  attitude towards authority, 103
  contribution to European settling of Victoria, 7–8, 77–81, 84–5
  crime economy backgrounds, 25–9
  demonisation of, 86–90
  expected place in society, 218
  fading memories about, 229–35
  life spans, 241–4
  lucky diggers, 96–100, 103–7
  nationalities, 24–5
  as social pollutant, 7, 15, 100–1
  taint of 'the old days', 225–9
  urban poor of second generation, 207, 210
venereal diseases, 64, 72–3, 199
Venville/Venwell, Richard (*Eliza*, 1831), 31, 306
Victoria
  before European invasion, 71
  Vandemonian founders, 7–8, 77–81, 84–6
  See also names of towns and suburbs
Victorian Pioneer Index, 228
Victorian Socialist Party, 230
von Mueller, Baron, 95

Wagstaff, Elizabeth, (transported as Bess Ward), 197–8

INDEX

Wagstaff, John Lawrence Mansfield (*Layton*, 1835), 30, 306
Wagstaff, William, 198
Wagstaffe, Thomas (*John Renwick*, 1843), 205, 306
Wainewright, Thomas Griffiths, 53, 249
Walklate, John Woolf (*Marquis of Hastings*, 1842), 70, 306–7
Ward (later Broom), Anne (*Mexborough*, 1841), 161–2, 172, 307
Ward (later Wagstaff) Bess (*Waverley*, 1842), 197–8, 307
Warrnambool, 37, 82, 147, 182, 222
Waters, Sarah (*Harmony*, 1829), 77–9
Watkins (nee Miles), Ellen, 63, 93
Watkins, Alfred (*Hindostan*, 1841), 174–5, 307
Watkins, Thomas (*Runnymeade*, 1840), 6, 63, 93, 193, 307–8
Webb, Harriet, 132–3
Wells, Rhoda (*Royal Admiral*, 1842), 172, 308
Westcott, Charles (*Cressy*, 1843), 200, 308
Western Australian goldfields, 210
Westmoreland (convict ship), 33
whalers, 72, 73
Wheatley, Harriet, 82
Whitaker, Farewell (*Proteus*, 1831), 31–2, 308
White, Eliza, (*see* Clements)
White, John (*Ratcliffe*, 1848), 168, 308
Whitehorse, William, 45
Wildman, William (*Clyde*, 1830), 88, 308–9
Wilkins, Caroline, 208–9
Wilkins, Elizabeth, 209
Wilkins, Thomas (*Forfarshire*, 1843), 208, 309

William Jardine (convict ship), 37
William Miles (convict ship), 48, 50
Williams, Mary Ann (*Harmony*, 1829), 309
wills, 195–6
Wilson, Edward, 90
Wilson, Mary Ann (*Margaret*, 1843), 65, 309
women convicts
   domestic training, 55
   mortality rates, 239–40, 241
   punishment during voyage to Van Diemen's Land, 43
   solitary confinement, 51, 52
   See also female factories
Wood (formerly Felton), Ann (*Emma Eugenia*, 1846), 124, 279
Wood, G Arnold, 237
Wood, Matthew (*Moffatt*, 1842), 124, 309–10
Woodhead, Ashton (*Moffatt*, 1838), 187–8, 310
Woodhead, Ashton (son of Ashton and Harriet), 188
Woodhead, Harriet, 188
Woodhead, Harriet (daughter of Ashton and Harriet), 188
Woollen, Joseph (*Lady Nugent*, 1836), 130, 134, 310
Working Men's College, 205
Wright, William 'Tulip' (*Lady Harewood*, 1829), 77–81, 84, 310

Yan Yean water supply, 201
Yarra Bend Lunatic Asylum, 94
Yarra River, 192
Yorta Yorta people, 71, 246

THE MIEGUNYAH PRESS
This book was designed by Pfisterer + Freeman
and typeset by Cannon Typesetting
The text was set in 11½ pt Freight Text Book
with 16 points of leading
The text is printed on 120 gsm Chen Ming Yun Jing Woodfree
This book was copyedited by Paul Smitz